GERMANY: THE TIDES OF POWER

In *Germany: The Tides of Power*, Michael Balfour sets out to explain the factors that have shaped the German social, political and economic character. Tracing the ebb and flow of power from the Middle Ages onwards, he seeks to lead the reader to an understanding of modern Germany – why it precipitated, and lost, two major wars in this century, how the astonishing growth of wealth over the last half-century was achieved and the significance of its recent reunification.

Professor Balfour considers the way in which German history has been dominated by the failure of her medieval rulers to maintain a strong central government comparable to those of England, France and Spain, and attributes to this early failure Germany's position as an industrial backwater in the early nineteenth century. The difficulty Germany has had in achieving integration is widely discussed, and the author argues that the considerable degree of unity achieved in 1914 and 1940 was largely wasted by its attempts to gain an inordinate amount of world power. By contrast, the astonishing growth of wealth over the last half-century, during which Germany has emerged from her 'power vacuum' to dictate European interest rates, is given particular attention.

As German economic expansion continues into the 1990s, Professor Balfour discusses the events surrounding reunification to consider the power now held by this integrated, technologically advanced nation – and the acceptability of this power to the rest of the world. *Germany: The Tides of Power* will be of great interest to students of history or the social sciences.

Michael Balfour, CBE, taught politics at Oxford University until 1939. During the war he served in the Ministry of Information and became Director of the Branch of the Control Commission supervising the German Information Media in the British zone. From 1966 to 1974 he was Professor of European History at the University of East Anglia. He is now retired.

GERMANY: THE TIDES OF POWER

OF POWER

Leonard Graham

Michael Balfour

London and New York

First published in 1992
by Routledge
11 New Fetter Lane, London EC4P 4EE

Simultaneously published in the USA and Canada
by Routledge
a division of Routledge, Chapman and Hall Inc.
29 West 35th Street, New York, NY 10001

Set in 10/12pt Garamond by J&L Composition Ltd, Filey, North Yorkshire
Printed and bound in Great Britain by Clays Ltd, St Ives plc

British Library Cataloguing-in-Publication Data
Balfour, Michael
Germany: the tides of power
I. Title
943.087

Library of Congress Cataloging-in-Publication Data
Balfour, Michael Leonard Graham
Germany: the tides of power / Michael Balfour.
p.   cm.
Includes bibliographical references and index.
1. Germany – Politics and government – 1945–
2. Germany – Politics and government.
3. Germany (West) – Politics and government.
I. Title.
DD257.B34   1992
320.943 – dc20   91–41075

ISBN 0-415-06787-1
ISBN 0-415-06788-X pbk

CONTENTS

Preface   vi
Map   viii

1 FROM TRIBE TO NATIONAL STATE: THE FIRST
  REICH   1

2 THE SECOND REICH: 1871–1918   13

3 THE FIRST ATTEMPT AT DEMOCRACY: 1918–1933   38

4 THE THIRD REICH: 1933–1945   54

5 THE POST-WAR SETTLEMENT: 1945   81

6 TOWARDS TWO GERMANIES: 1945–1948   92

7 CRISIS AND MIRACLE: 1948–1949   105

8 THE GERMAN REPUBLICS ARE FOUNDED:
  1948–1949   118

9 REARMAMENT AND THE RESTORATION OF
  SOVEREIGNTY: 1949–1955   136

10 ADENAUER'S HIGH NOON: 1955–1961   148

11 THE ERHARD INTERLUDE: 1961–1966   166

12 THE GREAT COALITION: 1966–1969   177

13 THE BRANDT GOVERNMENT: 1969–1974   188

14 THE SCHMIDT GOVERNMENT: 1974–1982   208

15 THE KOHL GOVERNMENT: 1982–1989   221

16 THE IMPOSSIBLE HAPPENS: 1989–1990   231

17 WHAT NOW?   239

Annexe: The current voting system for Federal Elections   247
Statistical appendix   249
Further reading   259
Index   265

PREFACE

In 1966–7 I wrote a book called *West Germany* for the series *Nations of the Modern World*. It described the history of Germany from Roman times to the formation of the Great Coalition in November 1966. By the time that it went out of print at the end of the 1970s, the series had been closed down. I then arranged for a fresh book to be published on its own which carried the story forward to the Federal Election of October 1980; this involved adding some forty pages. It was, however, felt that the utility of the book would gain if the length could be kept much the same. Accordingly the discussion of future problems, with which the earlier book had ended but which the passage of events had made largely otiose, was drastically cut and the treatment of the earlier centuries scaled down. This second book went out of print in the summer of 1990.

I have now repeated the process and added about forty pages; these include a few matters which occurred before 1980 but came to light only after that date, such as the question of a German atom bomb. To avoid increasing the length, I have made compensating cuts, chiefly in the opening pages. I may therefore seem to have conceded the argument to those critics who said that there was no need for a book about today's Germany to start in the Dark Ages. But I remain impenitent in the opinion expressed in my first sentence, even if I have put it more succinctly.

Whereas the two earlier books nominally confined themselves to West Germany, reunification makes it necessary to bring in East Germany as well. But until 1945 the story had been much the same for both parts, while even after that date it was impossible to make events in the West intelligible without referring here and there to the East. I have increased these references but I have not had room to go into the same detail as over the West.

A reviewer of the 1982 book commended me for 'not overtaxing my crystal ball', but even so I committed myself (like many other more distinguished people) to the statement that 'the Soviet Union will deploy all its resources rather than see its satellites pass out of its control'. Today I find it even harder to forecast how the world is going to go and I have cut down my last pages as a result. I have halted my chronicle of events at 2

December 1990 and refrained from trying to keep abreast of all that has been happening during the book's gestation.

As before, I have tried to make Germany's relative position in the world clearer by giving some comparative statistics. Unfortunately there has not yet been time for many reliable figures to emerge from the East.

My chief debt is to my publisher, Andrew Wheatcroft, whom I would like to thank for his patient and practical advice not only about this book but also about earlier ones. Professor Nicholas Kurti advised me about German nuclear research. I much appreciated the action of St Antony's College, Oxford, in making me a member of Common Room. Professor von Marschall and Professor Pietzker of Bonn University were good enough to check the Annexe on the voting system. The Verwaltung of the Deutscher Bundestag, the Germany Embassy in London, the National Institute of Economic and Social Research and the Institut der deutschen Wirtschaft helped me to find figures. The Modern Languages Faculty Library at Oxford and the Goethe Institute in London gave me access to newspaper files. Ann Taylor typed the pages of the new text. I should have found the later chapters of the book much harder to write if I had not been for many years a reader of *Die Zeit* and *The Economist*.

MLGB
Burford
July 1991

5°E

10°

54°N

52°

50°

48°

5°

10°

Copenhagen

D E N M A R K

Flensburg
Schleswig
Kiel
Rostock
SCHLESWIG-
HOLSTEIN
Lübeck
Schwerin
HAMBURG
M E C K L E N
E A S
Heligoland
Emden
Groningen
Oldenburg
BREMEN
LOWER   SAXONY
G E R M
Hanover
(Hannover)
Pots
B R
Brunswick
(Braunschweig)
Magdeburg
(German De
HOLLAND
Osnabrück
Rotterdam
Münster
Bielefeld
Detmold
NORTH RHINE
WESTPHALIA
SAXONY-
ANHALT
Rep
Essen
Dortmund
Göttingen
Halle
Duisburg
W E S T
Leipzig
Düsseldorf
Kassel
Weser
GREATER
Erfurt
Jena
Karl M
Sta
(Chem
BRUSSELS
Cologne
(Köln)
Marburg
Weimar
Liège
Aachen
THURINGIA
S
BELGIUM
Bonn
G E R M A N Y
HESSE
Coblenz
(Koblenz)
Frankfurt-
am-Main
Coburg
Bitburg
Wiesbaden
F r a n c o n i a
Mainz
Bayreuth
RHINELAND-
PALATINE
Darmstadt
Würzburg
Main
(Federal
SAAR
Mannheim
Nuremberg
(Nürnberg)
Metz
Speyer
Heidelberg
Republic   of   Germany)
Karlsruhe
Regensburg
Dan
Nancy
Baden-Baden
Stuttgart
Strasbourg
BADEN-
WÜRTTEMBERG
B A V A R I A
Ulm
Danube
Augsburg
Colmar
MUNICH
(MÜNCHEN)
Freiburg
Berchtesga
Basel
Rhine
Constance
(Konstanz)
Zürich
S W I T Z E R L A N D
FRANCE
LUXEMBOURG
Lorraine
Alsace
Rhine
Rhine
Rhine
Weser
Elbe
Elbe
Main

Germany 1871–1990

1

FROM TRIBE TO NATIONAL STATE: THE FIRST REICH

Two non-events during the Middle Ages combined to have a profound effect on Germany's later history. The first was that the peoples who spoke varieties of the German language (and who must surely have been descended from a single tribe at some point in prehistory) did not develop drastically idiosyncratic versions of it. The second was that various attempts to consolidate them into a single political unit proved in the long run unsuccessful. Many things might have turned out differently either if the Prussians, Saxons, Bavarians and the rest had ceased to be able to understand one another or if a single central government had proved durable. As it was, the Germans retained the ability to feel as a nation but did not acquire the capacity to act as a state.

The reasons why the Frankish, Saxon and Hohenstaufen empires all in due course disintegrated were many: external distractions, premature deaths, dynastic squabbles, incompetent heirs. But the decisive obstacle to unity from 1076 onwards was the hostility of the Papacy and the help thus given to the subordinate princes in their resistance to close Imperial control. Power was dispersed but rested mainly with the seven Electors to the Imperial Crown. The principle was gradually established that their votes should be given to the head of the House of Habsburg, but thereafter he was treated more as an equal than as an overlord.

The Reformation, which at first seemed to offer a new bond uniting Germans against the outside world, in the end carried the process of disintegration further by allowing each ruler to decide the form of religion to be adopted in his territory. Only a minority sided with the old faith but it included the Habsburgs. Lutherans were almost as hostile to Calvinists as to Catholics. Henceforward the only things which Germans possessed in common were a memory and a language (which, however, was given a new focus in Luther's translation of the Bible).

In England, by contrast, the Normans, Plantagenets and Tudors established the King's Justice, the King's English and the King's Highway. These constituted the essence of stable and effective government with all that could flow from it in the shape of peace, security, ease of movement and a reliable, undiscriminating and uniform legal system. These, in turn, are the pre-essentials for the accumulation of capital (with means of transferring it from savers to spenders); its use to put into effect technical invention (which presupposes the accumulation of knowledge and is particularly important in its application to communications) and the growth of population (to provide both personnel for the machines and consumers for the products). The accidents (or, if one prefers, the destiny) of history and geography, and in particular the fact of being insulated by the sea, placed Britain in a peculiarly favourable position for pioneering the technological break-through known as the Industrial Revolution.

Socially, the technology involved an early swelling in the numbers of merchants, well-to-do landed gentry, professional people and craftworkers. This in turn meant that the crucial conflict between a monarchy tending to absolutism and the various elements composing the 'middle classes', who had within them the seeds of a democratic state, was in Britain fought out at a relatively early date and settled in favour of the popular side. This shift of power intensified the awareness of common interest which had been growing under a relatively benevolent royal government since medieval days; the resulting integration (or, to use a simpler term, patriotism) considerably increased the international effectiveness of the state. True, the power of the king was during the eighteenth century replaced by that of an oligarchy, but that oligarchy was never a closed one. It owed much of its resources to commerce and took care to see that commercial interests got free play. Moreover the doctrines which had been evolved to justify the political revolution continued to dominate innovating thought. The result was that when the social repercussions of the Industrial Revolution began to get under way, there were within the ruling classes enough believers in the principles of liberty to provide a focus for the disaffected and to offer them hope that the necessary adjustments could be made without having the social fabric again torn apart by the spiritual and material destruction of revolution.

There has been much discussion recently as to whether Germany took a special path (*Sonderweg*) to modernity. My answer is that, if any country took such a path, it was Britain which obviously enjoyed special conditions enabling her to break ahead first. In Germany most of these conditions were lacking. It was not an accident but the consequence of the absence of this central authority which caused the Wars of Religion to last for thirty years (1618–48), reduced the population by some 35 per cent and left the country divided into 234 territorial units. The endemic fighting made lives and property insecure. Justice was hard to acquire; saving, learning and invention languished. Awareness of common interest and the sense of being master of one's own fate, along with belief in the ability to control one's own environment, were all weak. The new Atlantic routes, which brought so much stimulus to the western coasts of Europe, turned Germany into an economic backwater. While Britain and France were entering on the most eventful period of their histories and expanding in all directions, Germany was at best stagnating. Later generations were to describe these as 'the lost centuries'.

Luther's emphasis on the direct responsibility of the individual to God might have been expected to foster a critical attitude towards the state. But instead his belief in original sin led him to take a pessimistic view of human institutions and a distrust of the masses, which was intensified when in 1525 the excitement of defiance to the existing order spread from the religious to the secular field and burst out in the Peasant's Revolt. By throwing his authority against the rebels, Luther may have lost a chance of making Protestantism a religion of the masses. But in the long run the support of the princes was more important; without it the Reformation might have petered out as earlier movements had done. Yet by taking their side, he put control in their hands. The Lutheran Church became a branch of the state, teaching that God had ordained princes to rule their peoples as fathers rule their families; the business of pastors was to save souls for a heavenly kingdom rather than influence the policies of earthly ones. As all a ruler's subjects had to conform with his religious views, it was natural for his officials to collect from them along with other taxes the dues on which the Church depended. Those who disliked the religion of their ruler could usually find near at hand an alternative more to their taste. All of which goes to explain the virtual absence in Germany of the nonconformist dissenting tradition which in Britain and the United States of America has proved so potent a source of politics which were radical without being irreligious. Even in 1914 there were only 15,000 people in the whole country claiming to belong to 'Free Churches'.

GERMANY'S EASTERN FACE

To say that Germany, being in the centre of Europe, has an eastern as well as a western face may seem a glimpse of the obvious but is all the same a truth of the first importance. For her history has been as much affected by the lands to the one side as by those to the other and, as conditions in the two directions differed, her people have had continually to reconcile dissimilar influences and problems.

When in the second century the Germanic tribes moved west and south, their place on the great northern plain was filled by Slavs. These people remained little affected in religion, society and farming methods by Mediterranean culture. As central Germany developed, the Christian duty of converting the heathen to the east combined with a desire to see the land put to better use.

In Bohemia and Silesia, the operation of conversion and colonization went ahead fairly smoothly but farther north the Prussians, a Slav people akin to the Latvians and Lithuanians, offered the fiercest resistance. A prominent part in subduing them was played by the Teutonic Knights, an order originally formed to free the Holy Land from the infidel which in 1225 moved to north-east Germany and in fifty years of struggle succeeded in imposing on the Prussians German habits even where they could not impose German names. Nor was it only in Prussia that the previous inhabitants became Germanized. A parallel assimilation was achieved widely in the conquered territories, although more among the owners of the lands than among the tillers of them, thus complicating the task of anyone so rash as to try to decide on strictly historical grounds to which state it is that they should now belong.

The process left a lasting mark on the men who conducted it. They came to regard as inferior beings all those – chiefly peasants – who kept any of their original characteristics, until the habitual attitude of the German to the Slav became one of disdain. On numerous occasions in coming centuries German and Slav were to co-operate but this co-operation was never, in German eyes, between equals. Their goal of obtaining and holding the upper hand was almost beyond their resources and they never felt secure against a Slav counter-attack: one in the fifteenth century was not completely reversed for 300 years. In consequence great emphasis was laid on discipline, sacrifice, vigilance and valour. But these are secondary virtues whose value depends on which primary objectives they are invoked to serve.

In the thirteenth century a defence system was established in Brandenburg and peasants from further west were encouraged to settle in swamps surrounding a village called Berlin. Two centuries later the Emperor gave the job of ruling Brandenburg to a friend, Frederick von Hohenzollern, whose family, after originating on a hill top in Swabia, had for generations held an important post in Nuremberg. Early in the seventeenth century the Calvinist Elector of Brandenburg added to his lands by inheritance the Lutheran Dukedom of Prussia. And whereas the German peasants needed to colonize the Slav lands had originally to be allowed exceptional privileges, a variety of forces combined at the end of the Middle Ages to turn them back into serfs bound to the land and dependent on the landlord for justice. The towns decayed in the religious wars, except for a few ports through which the surplus corn, grown by large-scale farming on the noble estates, was shipped to make up for bad harvests farther west. Manufacturing was almost non-existent. From 1400 to 1600 the landowners, or 'Junkers', dominated the country.

They began, however, to lose ground under Frederick William, who was known as 'the Great Elector' and reigned from 1640 to 1688; in 1701 his son Frederick ventured to start calling himself 'King of Prussia'. The Hohenzollern family held the view that a medium-sized state such as theirs could prosper only by exploiting the differences between its bigger neighbours. In view of Prussia's limited resources, the essential minimum of

4

strength which this aim required could be achieved only by the strictest care and control in the use of those resources. But the basic industry to which the fruits of economy were devoted was war, and since mercenaries were expensive, Prussia anticipated revolutionary France by creating a conscript army. On this Frederick II ('the Great', 1712–86) spent two-thirds of his revenue and in it one-sixth of the adult male population was required to serve; by his death it was practically as big as the French. The nobility, in return for granting to the king the right, and the money, to maintain such an army, were given pride of place in the officers' corps. A General Staff was developed to plan and conduct campaigns.

To raise the money and men, however, a civilian service was needed and it was to the bourgeoisie that the kings originally turned for staffing this. In more than one respect it set the pattern for later bureaucracies. As early as 1700 the principle of entry by examination was established and in 1723 it was laid down that applicants for senior grades must have had a university education. By the end of the eighteenth century, officials had acquired security of tenure against arbitrary dismissal. They, like the officers, were expected to serve the king rather than the public and to hold their tongues about work which so often had military implications. Such servants proved their value in enabling the monarchy to assert itself against the aristocracy, but once the struggle was over, nobles too were taken into the service, particularly at the local level. The pillar of Prussian administration became the District Councillor (*Landrat*), who tended to be at one and the same time a local magnate nominated by his peers and a permanent official appointed by the king.

This absolutism was tempered in three ways. First, the Government was among the most up-to-date in Europe, inspired by the ideas of the Enlightenment and tolerating almost any form of religious view; the king encouraged his subjects to reason for themselves, provided only that they obeyed his orders. General education was established in Prussia in 1717, 21 years later than in Scotland but 150 years ahead of England and France. The Prussian Common Law (*Allgemeine Preussische Landrecht*), promulgated in 1794, provided a comprehensive, clear, uniform and impartial code of justice which was not superseded for over a century. First, it exemplified the concept that all public activities should be regulated by legal rules rather than by the changeable views of individuals; this was to become the core of the German approach to politics. Second, the king accepted the same standards as he imposed and regarded himself as the first servant of his people, even if he took his own decisions as to where their interests lay. Finally, Prussia was successful, growing rapidly in size and international reputation. In 1740 she seized Silesia from the Habsburg Empire. In 1772 and 1793 she acquired large areas of Poland. The human tendency to identify with success would by itself be enough to explain why the most autocratic state in Germany was also the only one to evoke among her subjects an effective loyalty as well as a sense of corporate identity.

GERMANY AND THE FRENCH REVOLUTION

Germany as a whole took over a century to recover from the Thirty Years War. The middle classes grew only slowly and were composed more of officials, lawyers, teachers, clergy and merchants than of manufacturers. They it was who provided the protagonists of a slow cultural revival which was at first largely rationalist in character and regarded enlightened individuals as citizens more of the world as a whole than of the principality in which they happened to live.

Gradually, however, signs of a national revival appeared. Language and history, the two great legacies of the medieval Reich to modern Germany, began to be recognized as the essential links uniting the inhabitants of the many political fragments into which the area had been splintered. Looking round the outside world, those inhabitants of the area who had attained the level of self-consciousness needed for effective reflection could not help noticing that elsewhere links of language and culture had become the keystones of the most successful political societies yet evolved. In France and Britain, and to a lesser extent in Holland, Spain and Sweden, national feeling had grown spontaneously as a loyalty to a homogeneous social structure evolved under a settled central government and enjoying the highest level of prosperity yet known to humankind. From this observation it was but a step for Germans to conclude that, since they too had a common language and history, they ought also to have a common government and that lack of such a government might be a major reason for their relative backwardness. The process of political integration, left unfinished in the Middle Ages, should be carried through to completion.

German national spirit was thus a self-conscious growth, based on a deliberate imitation of what had happened spontaneously elsewhere and drawing its essential drive from a sense of deprivation. In Britain and France, the facts preceded and formed the basis for the theory; in Germany the theory was taken over ready-made by the intellectuals in the population and adopted as an ideal to which the facts must be altered to fit.

The execution of this process was notoriously accelerated by the French Revolution. This movement provided the world with an unprecedented demonstration of what could be achieved by a resolute and fanatical government able to fire its people with enthusiasm and thus mobilize the full resources of the nation. In the face of the whirlwind the cosmopolitan rationalism of Goethe's Weimar and the spartan discipline of Frederick's Potsdam alike proved inadequate. The Germans were first inspired and then humiliated. One result was a wave of romantic dissatisfaction with rationalism, another a widespread desire to emulate France in exploiting the national idea for political purposes and in securing support for a war to liberate and unify Germany. The Revolution must be fought with its own weapons.

It was a step towards this end that, in the years following their defeat by

6

Napoleon at Jena (1806), the Prussian authorities put in hand an overhaul of their society – principally accomplished by non-Prussians in the royal service such as Hardenberg, Stein, Scharnhorst and Gneisenau. Outmoded economic restrictions were removed, the towns were given a certain amount of self-government and in the countryside the serfs were emancipated. The professional standing army was reorganized and supplemented by a popular short-service 'Home Guard' (*Landwehr*). The responsibilities of the General Staff were increased. The reformers sought to sacrifice all other values to the re-establishment of Prussia as a major European power. The resulting excitement carried the country into the coalition which overwhelmed Napoleon in 1813 and again two years later.

An atmosphere of this kind favoured the development of that emphasis on the individuality of peoples which distinguished German thought for the following 140 years. Each people was conceived of as a separate entity with distinct characteristics and capacities; the differences were as significant as the similarities. Moreover the state rather than the individual became in the philosophy of Hegel (1770–1831) the embodiment of the national identity and as such the repository of ultimate value. As a result there could be no higher authority than the individual state; the final arbiter in inter-state affairs must therefore be force (although the road to this conclusion was often smoothed by a facile optimism which suggested that, once the national will rather than the ruler's whim was everywhere sovereign, states would share the same views on all questions of mutual interest and thus live in peace with one another). It may be that, because in Western Europe government was on the whole well established over wide areas, political theorists tended to emphasize freedom and individual rights; in Central and Eastern Europe where the effects of division were easy to see, they gave priority to order and the rights of the state.

Hegel was a Professor at the University of Berlin, founded in 1812 by William von Humboldt as an integral part of the Prussian revival. In a country where nationalism began as an intellectual exercise and all professors were appointed and paid by the state, universities have an obvious political role. Berlin in particular deserved its description as the '1st Guards Brigade of Learning'. For this was the intellectual power-house where not only Hegel but also such historians as Ranke and Treitschke generated the distinctive view of the world and of Germany's place in it which the country was to offer as its gospel, a coherent and comprehensive alternative to the rational individualism stemming from the Graeco-Roman tradition.

Yet paradoxically von Humboldt, far from designing the University as a political weapon, made the freedom of the professor to teach and of the student to learn one of the fundamental principles of his system. He also reinforced the tradition that research, the advancement of learning, is not merely the primary function of a university but also an ideal means of stimulating students to independent thought. A school course based upon the principle that no branch of human activity should be alien to the educated person was followed by narrow specialization, with the doctorate as virtually the only degree. Precision and thoroughness thus gained status in public life, perhaps at some cost to a sense of proportion. This trend was reinforced by the requirement that almost all candidates for administrative posts should pass an examination in law, so as to ensure that they understood the principles of the system which they would be called on to apply.

THE FAILURE OF THE LIBERALS

In 1803 Napoleon rationalized Germany, apart from Prussia, by expelling Austria and reducing the remaining units from 300 to 38. Three years later he prevailed on the Habsburg Emperor to abolish the Holy Roman Empire. The statesmen who met in 1814 at the Congress of Vienna found it difficult to put the clock completely back and accordingly confirmed these changes with minor variations, linking the German states (including Austria) in a loose Confederation with a weak Federal Council. At the last moment Prussia was given considerable areas of the Rhineland and Westphalia which she did not welcome (since they meant that her territories were divided into two large blocks with no geographical connection) and in which she was not welcomed (since her dour methods contrasted unfavourably with twenty years of French rule). As a result of this and earlier transactions her predominantly Protestant population of 6 million was increased to 10 million, of whom 5 million, including 1 million Poles, were Catholic.

The problem for German nationalists prior to 1848 was to find a rallying-point. The obvious leader for a united Germany might seem to be the Austrian Emperor, but less than one-third of his dominions was included in the German Confederation and of the 12 million people who were so included almost half were Slav. His predecessors had signally failed to rouse an adequate consolidating loyalty to the central government in the days when this might have been done spontaneously and nobody could rate very highly the chances of holding together a population still retaining cultural badges of membership in so many different groups (such as Czechs, Poles, Magyars, Croats and Italians). An identification of the Habsburg Empire with Germany would be bound to alienate the Emperor's non-German subjects and the interests of the dynasty were for that reason only partially German. The Habsburg Emperors and Prince Metternich, who was their Chief Secretary from 1809 to 1848, were therefore unwilling to risk the loss of their non-German possessions by taking a lead in unifying Germany. At the same time they realized that for Germany to become united would involve the splitting-up of their domains. They were as a result wedded to the existing order because any change must be to their disadvantage.

The nationalists were thus left with two choices. One was to bring about a revolution which would expel all the reigning families and unite in a single state as many as possible of the lands in which Germans lived, even if this meant bringing in some non-Germans as well, owing to the way in which people with different national badges often lived intermingled. The other was to build the new state round Prussia. From 1815 onwards, two-fifths of those Germans who were not Habsburg subjects lived in Prussia so that a united nation-state which left them out would have made nonsense. But the leaders of the national movement, basing themselves on English and French examples, took it for granted that a national state must have a liberal constitution and therefore associated unification with the establishment of representative government. The demand for this also reflected the early stirrings in Germany of the Industrial Revolution and the pressure of groups whose economic position was improving for a corresponding improvement in social status. The Customs Union (*Zollverein*) set up between 1818 and 1844 under Prussian leadership (but excluding Austria) did something in the short term to relieve the pressure for political unification but, by removing economic barriers and thereby hastening technological change, in the long run increased that pressure. Significantly it was Prussia which, in the Ruhr valley and Silesia, possessed two of Europe's chief coalfields.

But although there were considerable numbers of liberals in Prussia, particularly in the western parts, the core provinces east of the Elbe were the last parts of Germany to be affected by industrialization. Here an independent middle class was still small, the ruling class consisting of landowners and officials closely assimilated to them. Liberalism, so far from attracting the Junkers, was anathema to most of them and, rather than pay the price of recasting society, they preferred, like the man asked whether he would rather be a Christian or a gentleman, to remain as they were.

Many of the leading German Liberals had official posts of one kind or another (since teachers and clergymen, as well as many lawyers and doctors, were state servants) which made it unnatural for them to contemplate violent resistance to the government. The respect paid to the rule of law increased their reluctance to break it. When in 1848 an economic recession set off a wave of revolutions in Berlin, Vienna and other cities, the leaders failed to see the need to protect what they had won by organizing a citizen-force which could resist the royal armies. Instead a self-appointed assembly of the educated middle classes met at Frankfurt and drew up a constitution embodying the so called 'small German' solution (i.e. excluding Austria). They then offered the crown of the proposed state to King Frederick William IV of Prussia. When he refused it, the gathering broke up. The King's troops had already restored normality in Berlin and went on to suppress a rising in south-west Germany by craftsmen and peasants who were less inhibited about using force but too weak to do so effectively. When the King tried to set up a German union on his own, Austria threatened war and, by the humiliating Agreement of Olmütz (1850), forced him to abandon the scheme.

Thereafter the liberal cause might have foundered altogether if the economic tide had not been so steadily strengthening its upholders. The groups ranged against them were neither effete nor incompetent nor half hearted. They believed that they had saved Germany from chaos by standing firm in 1848–9 and were ready to do so again if necessary. Moreover as 1848 had shown, the would-be reformers were in two minds about revolution. For the struggle to break the political power of the landowners had been postponed in Germany to an epoch in which working-class consciousness was beginning to stir. Marx, born in Trier in 1818 and educated in Berlin, was doing his best to spread the idea that the proletariat should exploit the bourgeois revolution as a stepping stone to their own dictatorship. Not for the last time, those Germans best able to put their fellow citizens in control of their own destiny shrank from the action needed to do so for fear that, once the impetus was created, its effects might hurtle beyond the goal. And indeed if the bourgeoisie had had the will to fight, the result might well have been a prolonged civil war into which most of the rest of Europe would gradually have been drawn.

Yet a widespread desire for unity persisted. The failure of 1848–50 deepened the sense of frustration which the years after 1815 had aroused and produced a reaction against what were regarded as the unpractical policies responsible for failure. Many of those reaching adulthood between 1850 and 1870 were not only obsessed with the problem of unification but also convinced that only policies of realism (*Realpolitik*) could be expected to overcome the obstacles. Realism involves hard-headed assessment of values and of the power available for applying them, coupled with a readiness to concentrate on those which offer the best 'mix' of desirability and practicability. And whereas in the reforms after 1806 internal liberty had been called for in the name of national unity, it was now denied in the name of national unity. The primacy which these men and women gave to the national cause at the expense, if necessary, of liberties is one of the dominating facts of the next seventy years since this was the generation which was to provide Germany's leaders between 1880 and 1914.

After 1848 all the indications pointed to Prussia as the focus of German unity and to lack of international influence as the price to be paid for remaining disunited. But the Prussian ruling classes still feared that a united Germany would mean the ruin of all the things which they valued, while the other states were too proud of their own identities to accept a merger reducing them to the level of Prussian provinces. Moreover an all-German government, to deserve the name, would have to be responsible for the defence and foreign policy of its territories. Yet these two prerogatives and the control thereby ensured over the kingdom's destinies were precisely what the Prussian leaders felt least inclined to surrender.

10

Although the Liberals probably had a majority among the Prussian voters and although a more liberal ministry was called to power in Prussia in 1858, the history of the next few years, showed how deeply rooted was the opposition to concessions. The crucial clash came on the question of what form the army was to take and where control over it was to rest. Strategic developments had outmoded the Landwehr and made it an obstacle to the organization of an efficient striking force. Accordingly the War Minister von Roon wanted to convert it into the regular army's reserve. The change involved the adaptation of the nation to militarism whereas the reforms of 1806–14 had sought to make the army a reflection of the nation. The Prussian Parliament (*Landtag*) proposed amendments to restore the balance and, when it was disregarded, tried to enforce its will by the power of the purse. The men round King William I took the view that military arrangements were his personal concern as Commander-in-Chief and advised him to stand firm. This he readily did, dissolving Parliament. But even though the constitution divided voters into three classes according to wealth and allowed 3 per cent, 12 per cent and 85 per cent of the total each to elect an equal number of deputies, the opposition came back in greater strength. Still the royal group refused to give way. The King's obstinacy seemed destined to make his name a stock example of the social havoc done by misplaced pertinacity.

From this predicament King William not only was saved but also in the space of eight years raised to the position of Emperor. The man responsible for the transformation was, of course, a highly strung genius with an inordinate appetite and a squeaky voice called Otto von Bismarck. Bismarck once compared the statesman with a traveller in a forest who knows the direction of his route but not the precise point at which he will emerge from the trees. He himself showed supreme skill in keeping in sight during his wanderings as many alternative routes as possible and postponing until the last moment a choice between them. Indeed he often managed to travel by several at the same time and contrive for them to converge at the same point. Men and ideas alike he regarded more as tools than as ends in themselves and, while this goes far to explain his success in solving the problems which faced him, it also explains why he left for those who came after him other problems more intricate still.

Between 1862 and 1866 Bismarck succeeded in defying the Prussian Parliament for four years, relying on the ingenuity of a Jewish banker called Bleichröder to provide the money which it refused to grant. But in addition he had the insight to recognize that German unity in one form or another was inevitable and that the question facing Prussia was not therefore 'whether?' but 'how?' Bent on avoiding the acceptance of other people's terms, he engineered by a series of improvisations what was in effect the conquest of Germany by Prussia. In the war of 1866, with the help of von Moltke's strategic gifts and the remodelled Prussian Army, he overcame

Austrian and Hanoverian opposition to North German unity under Prussian leadership and in the war of 1870 overcame that of France to the incorporation of South Germany within that unity. He further kept these two wars from starting a European conflagration. But in addition he led Prussia to a position in which she could no longer refuse to assume the leadership of Germany and in which neither the other princes nor the Liberals could refuse to accept Prussian predominance. Finally in the 1867 constitution of the North German Confederation, adapted in 1871 to become that of the German Empire, he evolved a compromise which gave all groups enough of what they wanted to be acceptable to most of them.

Yet it is hard to contemplate this epoch-making result without pondering on the turn of chance or fate which provided that, when a man of genius appeared, he did so on the conservative side. If the Liberals had possessed a Bismarck or a Lenin in 1848, how differently the world might have developed! But was the absence of such a man due to accidents of heredity or did the history of Germany prior to 1862 make it impossible for realists to be Liberal?

2

THE SECOND REICH: 1871–1918

INTERNAL AFFAIRS UNDER BISMARCK

In January 1871 the victorious King William of Prussia was proclaimed 'German Emperor' (not 'Emperor of Germany') at Versailles. He thus became the senior rather than the superior of the other German princes. Bismarck indeed maintained that the princes were subordinated to the Empire rather than to the Emperor, and in particular to the Federal Council (*Bundesrat*). To this body, which in name was nothing new, each of the twenty-five member governments sent a delegation proportionate to its importance. Though all the votes of each delegation counted, each voted as a block (on the logical if questionable principle that no government can be of two minds). Of the fifty-eight members, seventeen came from Prussia (which after her victories comprised in area and population about five-eighths of the Federation and completely surrounded twelve of the smaller states), six from Bavaria and four each from Saxony and Württemberg. As no proposal to change the constitution could go forward if fourteen votes were cast against it, Prussia and the South German states acting together were thus in effect given a guarantee against any reforms of which they disapproved. The agreement of the Bundesrat was required before legislation could be submitted to the Imperial Assembly (*Reichstag*) and the Bundesrat was to be consulted on all important questions including declarations of war.

The intention would seem to have been for the Bundesrat to become a sort of Cabinet. But it proved too cumbrous for that purpose and steadily lost influence. Instead power passed progressively into the hands of its chairman, the Imperial Chancellor, who was almost always Minister-President of Prussia and, as such, head of the Prussian delegation. There was no Cabinet in the English sense of the word (the Emperor's 'Cabinet' being composed of his private secretaries) and the 'State Secretaries' for Foreign Affairs, the Interior, Finance, Justice, Posts and (later) the Navy were not Ministers like British Secretaries of State but, more as in the United States, officials responsible to the Chancellor. There was no Federal State Secretary for War, the Prussian Minister of War acting as chairman of the

13

Bundesrat committee on the armed forces and appearing in the Reichstag to speak on military matters. This was because the Prussian Army remained directly responsible to its King, while absorbing the troops of all the smaller states; the armies of Bavaria and Württemberg retained varying degrees of independence in peacetime. The Prussian Parliament remained unaltered, including the three-tier voting for the Landtag.

To this complex and conservative structure, however, Bismarck added a Reichstag elected by secret universal (male) suffrage, as the Frankfurt Assembly of 1848 had proposed. This was something which in 1871 few other states in Europe possessed and its radicalism alarmed the Conservatives. But in practice the Reichstag went far to justify its description by a Socialist as 'the fig-leaf of absolutism'. Apart from the fact that throughout virtually the whole of its existence it provided a majority ready to vote for the existing regime, its powers had three flaws. It could not initiate legislation, it did not appoint the Chancellor and it was soon compelled to curtail drastically its say about defence expenditure. Membership was by law incompatible with membership of the Bundesrat and therefore in practice with the active holding of official posts, although civil servants could and frequently did stand for election as Deputies, being given leave of absence while they sat. (It went without saying that they had to belong to a party supporting the Government. Once when a nobleman who was a National Liberal Deputy and aide-de-camp to the Kaiser voted with the Progressives, he was deprived of the right to wear uniform.)

The Reichstag reflected public opinion and could stop government proposals, including taxation, from becoming law. But it could not enforce its own wishes. The parties were allowed to criticize but given no chance of putting alternative policies into action; they therefore tended to degenerate into irresponsible pressure groups more prone to split up than to coalesce. Deputies were unpaid and seldom promoted so that there was no great attraction in a parliamentary career.

According to the constitution, the Emperor appointed the Chancellor and the other Federal officials. Their tenure of office depended, not on the confidence of a majority in the Reichstag but on the will – one might almost say the whim – of the monarch. What the constitution failed to lay down with clarity was where the powers of the Emperor ended and those of the Chancellor began. It is true there was a clause requiring the Chancellor to countersign and take responsibility for all imperial decrees and orders. But if a Chancellor had ever shown reluctance to perform this function, all the Emperor had to do was to replace him with someone more compliant – there was never any lack of candidates! In theory the Reichstag could have forced on the Emperor a Chancellor of its own choice by refusing to vote for the measures of any holder of the post who did not follow the policies it favoured. But not only had the Prussian Landtag come off worst when it tried to do this in 1863. Most Deputies would have recoiled in horror from

14

the very idea. To decide who should run the country was no more part of a politician's business than it had been in the England of 1760. As a result the country was largely run by a virtually uncontrolled bureaucracy.

Dependence on the Emperor was by no means the only problem facing the man who combined the posts of Imperial Chancellor and Prussian Minister-President. He had to work at the same time with two parliamentary bodies, each chosen on a different basis. How could he hope to do this if the balance of parties in the Reichstag began to differ markedly from that in the Landtag? Moreover, although the Chancellor was largely concerned with foreign policy (since much internal policy remained the preserve of the individual states), he had no right of control over the armed forces which reported direct to the Emperor as King of Prussia.

Such then was the form of the Federation into which most people speaking German had been collected, though there were many left outside, in Switzerland, in Austria and in isolated groups throughout Eastern Europe. Bismarck had squared the constitutional circle by a formula which did not admit of easy revision, but the inhabitants of the new Empire were still far from being an integrated community. Conservatives looked suspiciously at Liberals, aristocrats at the bourgeoisie, industrialists at workers, soldiers at civilians, Protestants at Catholics, north at south, Christians at Jews. In the past, centrifugal forces had often proved too strong. Could they now be held in check? Could the political system be adapted to the consequences of the industrial and social growth which was just beginning to get under way?

A challenge arose almost immediately. The doctrine of papal infallibility, formulated by the Vatican Council in 1870, not only was a slap in the face to liberal opinion but also raised the whole question of the relation of the Catholic Church to the state. In the controversy which followed, laws were passed giving the Imperial and Prussian Governments powers over education and the appointment of bishops, establishing civil marriage and expelling Jesuits and other non-German priests and nuns. The legislation was a logical continuation of the campaign for a unified Germany; the idea of fighting clerical obscurantism was backed with enthusiasm by the Liberals who called it 'the cultural fight' (*Kulturkampf*). Before long, however, Bismarck found that the course which his subordinates supported on grounds of principle raised almost as many political problems as he had expected it to solve and by the end of the 1870s he had had enough of it. The accession of a new Pope led to negotiations which in 1887 finally produced an amicable settlement.

One of his motives for relaxing the Kulturkampf was his view that the gravest threat to the state in future was likely to be social rather than religious. In 1875 the two working-class parties founded by Marx and Lassalle had sunk their differences to form the Social Democratic Workers Party of Germany (SPD). In the 1877 Reichstag Election the votes it obtained rose from 350,000 to 500,000. Continued progress at such a rate would mean serious difficulties. In 1878 Bismarck, taking advantage of two attempts on the Emperor's life, introduced a law to impede Socialist activity without going so far as to ban the Party outright. He did not confine himself to repression. In a series of measures between 1883 and 1889 he inaugurated, for the first time in history, an imaginative system of social insurance and labour arbitration designed to reconcile the workers to their conditions.

Events were to show that few people were in fact more orderly and public-spirited than the average German worker, but their leaders continued for a long time to talk in terms of revolution. Bebel had in 1871 pointed to the Paris Commune as a weak prelude to what would happen before long in Germany. The most intense venom was reserved for anyone who challenged the view that revolution was both necessary and bound to come. Indeed the attitude of the ruling class made it hard to see how the workers could get what they wanted without revolution and it was in fact only after a revolution of sorts that their main demands were met. The owners of property can hardly be blamed for taking the threat of revolt seriously. Germany's lack of any tradition of religious radicalism meant that socialism, as generally on the continent, was materialistic, opposed to religion as the 'opium of the masses'. In the eyes of all respectable citizens, this combination put the Social Democratic Party beyond the pale. Nobody belonging to it could be regarded as loyal; its participation in the conduct of public affairs was unthinkable, it was *regierungsunfähig*. The Party in return organized for its members a self-contained world with its own publications, clubs, banks and shops.

The years immediately after the Franco-Prussian War saw a boom in the German economy but in 1873 this overreached itself and was followed by a period in which growth, though still rapid by pre-industrial standards, was slow enough to arouse widespread concern. Moreover the end of the 1870s saw the arrival in Europe of cheap wheat from the American prairies, thanks to investment in communications and the introduction of iron ships. The landowners of the East-Elbian plains were faced not merely with competition at home but with the loss of the exports which had made the lands round the Baltic into the granary of Europe. Free trade therefore ceased to be to their advantage and their political and social position made it hard to disregard their clamour for protection, whereas their counterparts in Britain had no prospect of prevailing against the middle-class free-traders. Heavy industry (though not commerce) was also anxious to be shielded against competition while in the process of establishing itself. A tariff also suited Bismarck, since he needed money for various projects and the constitution empowered the Federal Government to raise money only by indirect taxation. This led him to a change of policy which has been described as 'the second founding of the Empire'. Whereas his solutions to his problems had hitherto, in accordance with his forecast of 1862, been based on blood

16

and iron, he decided to maintain that settlement by basing it on corn and iron. The alliance between large-scale agriculture and heavy industry was to be the essential foundation of the political system over the next fifty years. Until 1879 it was possible that Germany might make a peaceful transition to modern industrial capitalism; after 1879 that was much less likely.

Bismarck's reorientation split the Liberal Party along the lines of social division which had been visible in 1848. The Progressive left wing refused to vote for the tariff laws and anti-socialist legislation. They continued to demand a constitutional reform which would make the executive responsible to the legislature. Bismarck's need to compensate for the loss of their votes helps to explain his conciliation of Catholics. But unity rather than liberty had been the priority of many among the more prosperous Liberals. When Bismarck demonstrated that it could be achieved without responsible government, they indulged in an uncritical admiration of him and stopped pressing for further reform. The process was justified ideologically by the argument that individual personal liberty and local self-government mattered more than parliamentary and ministerial arrangements. The introduction of laws to secure the former between 1872 and 1883 was claimed to have given Germany her own form of Liberalism; the authoritarian state (*Obrigkeitsstaat*) had been replaced by the state in which law reigned supreme (*Rechtsstaat*), assigning to each citizen his obligations and rights. Various measures relating to currency and commerce helped to adapt the administrative machine to the essential needs of an industrial society. Thus modernization was imposed in Germany from above instead of being extorted by popular pressure from below.

Bismarck might therefore seem to have achieved considerable success in consolidating German society. By the time of his dismissal not only had his Empire proved able to survive for two decades but also Conservatives, Catholics and most Liberals had come to accept it. Moreover the future was to reveal a surprising amount of readiness on the part of the rest of the population to do the same. Dissatisfaction, however, showed itself in two directions.

On the one hand a number of the ruling class succumbed to dreams of aggrandisement and talked of the need for Germany, having established herself as a European Power, to claim her rightful place as a world leader. Like other social groups which gain power by a gradual process rather than a sudden revolution, the German middle classes, on reaching maturity, tended to assimilate themselves to the standards which they found dominant instead of evolving their own. This process was powerfully fostered by many of the institutions of society, notably the student corps in the universities and the much-prized grade of reserve-officer to which the steadily growing appetite of the Army for manpower made the admission of well-to-do bourgeois essential. The Prussian General Staff were pioneers in applying to war and the preparations for it the systematic rationalizing which underlay the Industrial Revolution, but they failed to apply the same yardstick to their own social and political ideas. The moment when Prussia's efforts had been crowned with success might have been appropriate for relaxing her traditional emphasis upon the martial virtues. Instead these were taken over, often by people from other parts of Germany, and exaggerated to the point of distortion. Compassion became taboo; charity and tolerance were too easily condemned along with it. Violence was exalted and little appreciation shown for its effects on other people. Courage turned into contempt for modesty and common sense, self-reliance into disdain for all who did not belong to the warrior caste, discipline into a demand for unquestioning obedience and patriotism into a lust for domination. The law that material resources are useless without the will to use them became a faith that all things were possible to the obstinate. Such a distortion was not merely to prove a menace to Germany's neighbours; it was also seriously to mislead its practitioners about the realities of the world.

Unfortunately that was not all. For besides the people to whom the Empire had brought success and power, there were others to whom it – or strictly speaking the economic and social changes accompanying it – spelt failure and the need to change. Whereas in the pioneer industrial countries, the innovations stretched over several generations, reducing the risk that individuals with particular skills would find themselves obsolete in mid-career, the faster pace which Germany as an imitator was able to achieve proved a mixed blessing. While it certainly accelerated her rise to Great Power status, it did so at the cost of multiplying internal tensions. A number of people found the world turning against them and, instead of adapting to that turn, preferred to decide that it was wrong. Among these people, schoolteachers were prominent.

Their criticisms fastened not simply on the materialism of a world growing rapidly more affluent but on the creeds which had brought this about. They denied the claims of reason, intellect and the critical spirit, preferring instead intuition, imagination, 'history' and faith. They rejected the view that the individual had a right to equal treatment or to freedom, preferring instead that an idealized elite should have the right to give orders which it was the duty of patriots to obey. In short, they wanted their country to break with Western Europe and return to what they regarded as her distinctive national traditions.

The concessions made to Liberalism and democracy in the 1871 settlement disgusted them. The parliamentary system in particular was in their eyes designed to create discord rather than the harmony for which they longed. For they believed that harmony alone would make their country strong enough to take that place in the world struggle for power which the misfortunes of her history had denied to her. But since this harmony was to be a harmony on their own conditions, they rejected the idea of achieving it by discussion and compromise, preferring instead the short cuts of emotion and autocracy. Thus there developed the idea of a national community or *Volk* cemented by a common spirit because it was dominated by attitudes which grew naturally like plants out of the historical background and physical surroundings. Where elements of the Volk refused to fall into line or where other *Völker* got in the way, superficial recollections of Darwin or Nietzsche were invoked to justify an appeal to force. But the general view was that a pure Volk would be a unanimous Volk so that disunity was evidence of an impurity needing to be eradicated. It was in this context that anti-semitism became important.

Jews in Europe, having been long forbidden to own property or ply crafts, had gravitated to the towns. Study of the Talmud fitted them for intellectual occupations such as finance, trade, journalism and the learned professions, especially law – the very skills which were in demand in an industrializing society. As a result they gained a position out of all proportion to their numbers. Although they made up only 1 per cent of the total population of Germany, they amounted to 5 per cent in Berlin, where 25 per cent of the grammar school places were filled by their children. (In Vienna the figures were 8.6 per cent and almost 35 per cent.) They provided 16 per cent of Germany's lawyers and 11 per cent of her doctors. Twelve out of the twenty richest men were Jews. They gained a reputation for being politically radical although this was true only of Jewish Deputies in the Reichstag, not of the Jewish population as a whole. The net result was that they quickly came to symbolize to those who disliked liberal, rational, industrial society all the things which were dislikeable about it. But while the Jews were widely unpopular and many people wanted to see their influence reduced, there were not many who wanted to persecute them physically.

Though the peddlers of these sorts of notions were active enough in the Second Reich, its success and respectability deprived them of serious political influence. Moreover, although their views on several aspects of social policy were to diverge from those of the ruling classes, they saw eye-to-eye on the question of extending Germany's authority abroad, a fact which must have enhanced the attractions of that theme in the rulers' eyes. All the same, their existence hung an extra question mark over the future, especially as many of them earned their living in ways which gave them a hold on youth. Indeed, Germany diverged from much of the rest of Europe in that her middle-class youth, though eager for change, was often looking right rather than left. This was not true of the workers, who were inoculated against Volkism by Marxism – which made all the more remote the prospect of evolving a society into which both groups could fit.

BISMARCK'S FOREIGN POLICY

The only principle on which the Powers of Europe have been able to agree during the past five centuries has been that that continent should not be dominated by one of themselves. Any state which bid for such domination has called into existence a coalition to contain it. But the coalitions have succeeded only because they have obtained invincible support from outside – Britain, Russia, the USA. The new industrial state of 41 million people which came into existence in 1871 was strong enough to bid for such domination if it chose. But Bismarck, whose nightmare was such a coalition, declared Germany to be a satisfied state whose neighbours had nothing to fear. He could not, however, escape from the consequences of the route he had taken to unification.

In 1871 Bismarck imposed on the defeated France a heavy indemnity and annexed Alsace and Lorraine. Nobody thought of asking the inhabitants of those two provinces whether they wanted to become Germans but then nobody had asked them in 1648 whether they wanted to become French; most Alsatians, as well as some Lorrainers, still spoke a German dialect. Bismarck later claimed that it had been his constant endeavour to induce the French to forget their defeat in 1871 as they had forgotten that of 1815 but later kindness could not heal the initial wound; the French leader Gambetta advised his fellow-countrymen to 'think of it always, speak of it never'. Consequently the first aim of German foreign policy needed to be the isolation of France.

This task was complicated by a rather less obvious result of Germany's victories. The successful creation of a new national state gave great encouragement to the other national groups in Eastern Europe which still had no states of their own or (like Serbia and Romania) had numerous members living outside the frontiers of the national state. Many of these lived in the Habsburg Empire, so that any widespread demand for self-government on a national basis was likely in the long run to prove incompatible with the effective functioning and indeed with the very existence of that venerable organization. In 1867 the Magyars had secured self-government for themselves in Hungary, though they amounted to less than half of its population; the Empire, in consequence, became known as 'Austria-Hungary'. The question was how long they and the Germans in Austria could keep the upper hand over the Czechs, Poles, Serbs, Croats, Romanians, Italians and others who made up the rest of Emperor Francis Joseph's multifarious subjects. Moreover the first four of these groups were, as Slavs, susceptible to Russian influence, while Austria-Hungary and Russia had conflicting ambitions in the Balkans. For Germany to choose sides in an Austro-Russian quarrel would incite the country which she did not choose to ally itself with France. Yet if the quarrel developed into war, Germany would have to prevent the weaker side, which was clearly Austria-Hungary, from being beaten, since defeat would probably lead to its break-up and Germany might then be left without any significant ally in the event of a victorious Russia coalescing with France against her.

When in 1875–8 a rising in the Balkan provinces of Turkey almost led to an Austro-Russian war, Bismarck did his utmost to remain the 'honest broker' between the two and in 1878 succeeded in getting a compromise accepted at the Congress of Berlin. But the Tsar's Government resented his impartiality and made what he considered to be threats as to what it might do if on another occasion he were not more co-operative. His reaction was to negotiate a treaty by which Germany and Austria-Hungary promised one another mutual aid if either was attacked by Russia; the existence of the Treaty was known though its exact terms were secret. He then set to work to 'repair the telegraph line to St Petersburg', that is, to give Russia enough assurance about his sympathy for her other aims as to stop her from seeking French help, a task made all the easier by the ideological gulf between the Tsarist autocracy and the Third Republic. In 1881 he persuaded the Russians to join with Germany and Austria in the 'Three Emperors League' in which each country promised to remain neutral if any were attacked by a fourth.

The League lasted until 1887 when its further renewal was made impossible by a fresh Austro-Russian clash over Bulgaria. To complicate matters, France was in a state of nationalist excitement which at one point seemed capable of leading to war with Germany. Thereupon Bismarck secretly concluded the 'Reinsurance Treaty' (*Rückversicherungsvertrag*, meaning literally Treaty providing security for one's back). This Russo-German agreement provided for the two countries to remain neutral if either was involved in a war with a third, except for an Austro-Russian war begun by Russia or a Franco-German war begun by Germany. It was thus made clear to the Russians that they could not afford to attack Austria since, if they did, they would find Germany too against them. On the other hand, Germany would give no help to an attack on Russia by Austria, which would be suicide without such help. In return Bismarck got a promise that Russia would not join in a French attack on Germany, so that the entire German army could be concentrated in the west; France would hardly dare to move single-handed. There remained the danger that, if Russian actions in the Balkans drove the Austrians into war, Germany might feel compelled to rescue Austria from defeat by joining in, despite the promise of neutrality in the Reinsurance Treaty. But, as a safeguard against this contingency, Bismarck had induced Italy and Britain to give undertakings which meant that any Russian move southwards was likely to be opposed by these two countries as well as Austria; Germany might therefore hope to escape being drawn in. As Bismarck considered Germany to be a 'satisfied Power', his ideal was a situation in which all the other Powers except France would need her and be deprived of the inclination to form coalitions against her by their relations with one another. The British Prime Minister Lord Salisbury called this 'employing one's neighbours to pull out each other's teeth'.

By the time the Reinsurance Treaty came up for renewal in 1890, the German scene had changed fundamentally: in 1888 the old Emperor William I died at the age of 90. His son Frederick III had often crossed swords with

Bismarck, was much under the influence of his wife, Queen Victoria's eldest daughter, and sympathized with liberal ideas. But in 1887 he developed cancer and reigned for only ninety days.

Frederick's son, the Kaiser William II, was not quite 30 when he thus unexpectedly came to the throne. He had been born with a damaged left arm, which did not prevent him from making himself a good shot and horseman but put him under constant strain. For the Prussian ideal took much living up to, and a particularly high performance was expected of the ruler. The effort to prevent his disabilities from standing in his way led William to adopt a hearty toughness or an exaggerated air of self-importance which was out of keeping with his real character. Thus he was himself prone to that fault of overemphasizing the Prussian virtues which has already been mentioned. But to complicate matters, he had held out in front of him in the nursery not only the pattern of the Prussian Junker but also that of the Liberal English gentleman. He reacted, like any young man of spirit, against the attempts of his determined and domineering mother to impose her standards on him, yet to his dying day they exercised a fascination which he could never for long resist. The desire to be the Englishman, and to win applause from the British, was alternating all the time with the desire to be the Prussian and to win applause from the Germans. The tension between the two, superimposed on his physical defect and on the tensions inherent in German society, is the ultimate key to his character, which was taut, restless and impetuous, lacking the stability brought by integration. From his mother he also inherited a strong constitution, a quick enquiring mind, a keen intelligence often at odds with his emotions, a preoccupation with himself which left him insensible to the views of others, and an inability to judge character. The creation of a new nation-state of 50 million people in the centre of Europe had caused a fundamental shift in the balance of power and what Germany needed was a balanced and cautious ruler who would hold his people back from adventures and check their inclination to overestimate their power. They could scarcely have got anyone worse qualified for such a task.

Characters such as William and Bismarck were bound to collide and the constitution of the Chancellor's own devising had given the last word to the Emperor. The decisive clash of personality and method came in the spring of 1890 and found expression in no less than six issues at the same time. The most prominent of these was how to handle the Socialists who, in elections to the Reichstag, had succeeded in winning more votes than any other party (though, owing to the out-of-date way in which constituencies were divided, they did not get a proportionate number of seats). The Kaiser was anxious to gain popularity by propitiating them; Bismarck was contemptuous of people whom he described as 'dizzy with humanitarianism' and wanted to stiffen his earlier legislation. He was ready, if necessary, to defy the Reichstag over this, reckoning that the resulting crisis would make him indispensable to the Kaiser. One thing led to another and Bismarck was driven to offer his resignation. He was 75 and, on the various questions at issue, William was as often right as wrong. Indeed posterity might have regarded the removal of the elder statesman as justified if the policies which he had refused to adopt had been consistently followed by his successors. As things were, it probably antedated nature by only a year or two.

Questions of foreign policy hardly figured in the clash. But in the ensuing confusion and before a new State Secretary for Foreign Affairs had been appointed, the decision not to renew the Reinsurance Treaty was taken, rather to the Kaiser's regret. The new men in charge did not properly understand what Bismarck had been aiming at and felt that the intricacies of his policy were beyond them. There was considerable, if superficial, attraction in the argument that Germany needed henceforward to conduct a 'peaceful, clear and loyal' course which would not create the impression of leaving her formal allies in the lurch. Yet within seventeen months of the non-renewal, France and Russia signed a Treaty pledging one another to act together in the event of a threat to peace. The very thing which Bismarck had been most anxious to prevent was thus allowed to come to pass.

GERMANY BECOMES AN INDUSTRIAL LEADER

One of the chief purposes of Chapter 1 was to explain why Germany was late in starting to industrialize. Her development was further delayed by the Napoleonic Wars and by the continuing lack of unity. It was not until the mid-1860s that German output (in terms of real product per person per year) reached the level which Britain had achieved in the 1830s. But German growth, once it began, was all the more rapid and it was naturally stimulated by unification. Britain continued to be the richer of the two countries and the one with a bigger national product both absolutely and per individual (since the German population was one-third higher) but Germany was catching up fast.

When Germany made herself felt on the world's economic stage, the second phase of industrialization was beginning. In the first, the key industries had been textiles, coal-mining, iron-founding, railways and ship-building and most of the vital inventions had been British. But in the second phase, where the key industries were steel, chemicals, electricity, optical goods and the internal combustion engine, many of the inventions were German, as the names Daimler, Benz, Diesel, Zeiss and Siemens testify; of the relatively few British innovations, the Gilchrist, Thomas and Bessemer processes for steel-making and Perkin's discovery of aniline dyes were mainly developed in Germany.

The explanation for the contrast is complex and still partly in dispute. British manufacturers would seem to have lost something of their old enterprise. They could still sell their traditional goods but the markets were changing from relatively developed to underdeveloped countries. Britain's output of trained manpower was inadequate; Germany had four times as many pupils in secondary schools and universities, not to mention technical education. Between 1870 and 1913 Britain devoted 11 per cent of her gross national product to investment whereas the German figure rose from 13.5 to 16. Thirty-nine per cent of the British total went abroad whereas the German proportion was only 11 per cent. Britain was bringing down her costs by providing the 'infrastructure' for obtaining foodstuffs and raw materials from places where they could be produced most cheaply rather than by improving the efficiency of her production methods. In the short term this policy may have made sense; its defect was that it aggravated rather than answered the long-term problem. How was Britain, with a population too big to be fed from home farms, to pay for her essential imports once the countries supplying them had started to make their own shirts and kettles and no longer needed railway engines or coal?

In their anxiety to find foreign markets for their rising output, the Germans showed some interest in colonies in the somewhat ingenuous belief that, since countries with colonies were wealthy, colonies must bring wealth. In 1884–5 Bismarck's Government, for a variety of reasons in which internal politics predominated, did acquire colonies in Africa and the Pacific four times as large as the home country, only to find them expensive and unrewarding. Indeed, if they had been more attractive, other countries would no doubt have acquired them earlier. The disappointment fostered resentment that the parcelling out of the more valuable parts of the overseas world should have been carried out while German attention was still absorbed at home. Undeniably, for reasons already described, Britain's overseas possessions were of great benefit to her. But the pride which she expressed in them prevented both other countries and herself from appreciating the reverse side of the picture. The development of the Empire absorbed a considerable proportion of limited resources and gave a distinctive pattern to her economy. Whether that precise pattern turned out to be to her advantage in the long run is open to argument. But there would have been little advantage to Germany in acquiring colonies (assuming that there had been plenty to be had) unless she had been prepared also to go some way along the British road and accept the repercussions on the rest of her economy. As it was, her banks and merchants saw little prospect of profits in such colonies as she did acquire and invested in them only out of deference to government pressure. Even in the home market German industrialists preferred regulation to competition; cartels and other agreements to fix prices and share out orders were widespread. Entry into many occupations and trades was strictly regulated. Not only were the railways and most of the gas and electricity companies publicly owned but also a certain number of coal-mines and iron-works as well. Thus the balance of social forces in Germany and the tendency towards a managed society meant that the allocation of her economic resources was more the result of deliberate planning than was the case in Britain.

In the end, of course, talk about nations making choices is unhistorical; they take the openings presented to them and seldom have the collective insight to consider whether a better 'mix' may be available. Moreover, if Germany had done less to build up her industrial strength at home, she could not have remained a major military power. As it was, industrialization made her dependent on certain products from overseas and the failure of her political leaders to keep Britain out of the enemy camp meant that in the end this weakness was fatal.

INTERNAL AFFAIRS UNDER THE KAISER

The major internal problem between 1890 and 1918 was the struggle as to how far the German political system should be adapted to the industrial developments just described. The pace of social change accelerated and increasing numbers of people acquired an occupational status and a real income in advance of that enjoyed by their parents. They looked for this to be reflected in a greater say about the running of the country and until this was accorded to them, inclined to support the parties of the left. The seats won by the Social Democrats in particular rose from 35 in 1890 to 81 in 1903 and 110 in 1912.

But though the Socialist threat to the established order might seem to be increasing, other forces were operating in the reverse direction. German workers had always inclined to the petit bourgeois virtues of industry, frugality, loyalty to the community and moral restraint, which do not as a rule turn men into revolutionaries The German educational system made it hard for working-class children to pass through the grammar schools (*Gymnasien*) to the universities but it did help them to acquire technical skills and thus rise up the social ladder, while improved living standards had a similar effect. The various measures of social insurance introduced by Bismarck and extended after his fall were beginning to have a delayed action in reconciling workers to the established order. The leaders of the Social Democrats and still more the functionaries of the trade unions, enjoying a regular salary, had little incentive to put it at risk. They were not only reluctant on general grounds to do anything which might provoke renewed repression but also reluctant to risk the confiscation of the considerable funds which had been built up out of subscriptions. It was from their ranks that Deputies were chosen to represent the Party not only in the Reichstag but still more in the State Parliaments and municipalities (where in some cases there was a Social Democrat majority); the practical experience so gained was as usual a brake on radicalism. Given encouragement from the Government, the success and prosperity achieved by the Second Reich might have induced the workers to follow the example of the Liberals and Catholics by becoming integrated into the existing structure of society.

Government encouragement was not, however, forthcoming. Bismarck's successors at first tried to pursue a moderate course in the hope of securing the widest possible support for the regime. But the policy was blocked by the hostility of the right without achieving enough to reconcile the left and in 1897 it was abandoned in favour of one which sought to rally all those who wanted to keep things as they were. The alliance between corn and iron was given a fresh lease of life. The benevolent intentions towards the workers which the Kaiser had professed in dismissing Bismarck were soon dissipated by the reactionary influence of the court and he took openly to describing Socialists by such abusive terms as 'scoundrels without a Fatherland'. To say who ran the country is hard. The Kaiser certainly established his right to have his way if he wanted but his interventions in policy-making were too slapdash, spasmodic and inconsistent to amount to a programme. His officials could not openly disobey him but had to spend much of their time persuading him to allow them their way or dissuading him from insisting on his own. Compliant though the Reichstag was, a regular majority could no longer be found for a policy of unqualified reaction and during the 1890s there was much talk of a *coup d'état* to abolish universal suffrage. But neither the ruler nor his more responsible advisers ever mustered up the courage to embark on such a course and the reactionaries gradually became inured to living with something which they could not alter. But this made them all the more insistent on maintaining the 1870 distribution of constituencies for the Reichstag (which favoured country districts), the three-tier Prussian suffrage, the open voting which went with it and the tariffs on grain which were its economic counterpart. The Government sought a quiet life by proposing as little legislation as possible.

In face of such immobility, the left wing of the Social Democrats continued to argue that nothing short of a revolution would break down the resistance and give the workers due influence in the state. The right wing called for the Marxist revolutionary programme of the Party to be revised so as to allow for the possibility of securing reform by constitutional means. The leadership, torn between the two extremes, concentrated on holding the Party together; this they succeeded in doing by maintaining the letter of the programme and departing from it in practice whenever occasion arose.

As the Conservatives and National Liberals, from 1898 onwards, made up less than one-third of the Reichstag, the Government became increasingly dependent on the (Catholic) Centre Party. An attempt between 1907 and 1909 to rely instead on the Progressives came quickly to grief because the right refused to make the concessions needed for its success and could not be forced to do so because of their economic and social power. But the Catholics in Germany no longer consisted predominantly of landowners

26

and peasants; Catholicism had always been strong in the Rhineland and Silesia, which had become major industrial districts. Both priesthood and political leadership realized the need to give some evidence of social enlightenment if they were to keep a hold on their followers. Various incidents from 1895 onwards foreshadowed the emergence of an alternative coalition between Centre, Progressives and Social Democrats. The Social Democratic gains in the 1912 Election gave this grouping a majority in the Reichstag while a government on this basis took office in Baden. For the time being, the threat to the corn–iron alliance was not activated but a political crisis clearly loomed ahead.

The main justification offered by German historians for the obstinacy of the ruling classes was that a parliamentary system was too dangerous a thing to introduce into a country surrounded by enemies, since no single party would be strong enough to have an absolute majority and governments would always be unstable coalitions. Popular demands would also threaten the delicate balance between the Reich and state governments and thus create a risk of civil upheaval. Power must stay in the hands of people whose loyalty was unquestioned, while it was unpatriotic to hold discordant opinions and thereby weaken the nation. Germany's internal policy was considered to be dictated by her external position.

But such a view was only half the story. If the attitude of Germany's neighbours towards her was less than friendly, it was mainly because (as will be explained in the next section) they were alarmed about her intentions towards them. And there is evidence to show that the vigorous foreign policy of the Kaiser's Governments was largely adopted in the hope of distracting attention from tensions at home by appealing to national sentiment and calling for unity against threats from outside. External policy was dictated by internal considerations. This was particularly true of the naval expansion from 1897 onwards, not only inaugurated by the Kaiser out of vanity and a desire to emulate Britain but also developed because of its popular appeal. Its chief advocate and executant, Admiral von Tirpitz, gave in 1895 as the main justification for Germany becoming a World Power the prospect that 'such a great new national task and the economic benefits which went with it would provide a good antidote to sophisticated and unsophisticated Social Democrats' (E. Kehr, *Das Primat der Innenpolitik*, p. 165).

This sacrifice of liberal to national values was of doubtful wisdom. Some of the wilder remarks of Socialist leaders may have seemed to justify it but their practice showed them to be just as loyal and considerably more realistic in their appraisal of Germany's position. For the outlook of the ruling classes fostered an overemphasis on power and a disregard of world opinion which led to Germany's capacities being exaggerated. It was a recipe for disaster to risk war by being uncompromising abroad and at the same time, by being uncompromising at home, to alienate people whose support would be essential if war came. The best way to encourage unity was to trust the workers and show consideration for their views. But the half-hearted efforts in this direction of Bethmann Hollweg, Chancellor from 1909 to 1917, won him only hatred and accusations of weakness from the Prussian Conservatives and such bodies as the Pan-German Union, the Navy League and the Defence Union.

The political deadlock made it impossible to do anything effective towards remedying what one of the Kaiser's subjects described as his 'undergraduate impetuosities', leading too often to 'rhetorical derailments' (Baronin von Spitzemberg, *Tagebuch*, p. 416). A particularly bad example of his 'mouth-shooting' occurred in 1908 when he gave to the London *Daily Telegraph* an interview which could not have caused more offence abroad as well as at home if that had been its deliberate intention. Even the Conservatives joined in demanding that something should be done to check William's 'personal rule'. But as long as the Chancellor and his subordinates were chosen by the Emperor and depended for their tenure of office on his pleasure, he could not easily be denied a voice in their policy. Yet if they were not to be appointed by him, what other source was there except the Reichstag? But the existing impotence of that body was shown when in 1914 military high-handedness in Alsace led it to pass what was virtually a vote of no confidence in the Chancellor. The Government made no appreciable change in policy and, when the Social Democrats proposed rather belatedly to enforce one by refusing to grant money, the Centre took the view that Germany's external situation made such a course impossible.

THE ROAD TO WAR

The conclusion of the Franco-Russian Alliance in 1891 (see p. 23) did not cause the alarm in Berlin which might have been expected, in spite of the extent to which Russia thereafter came to depend on French loans. For at this period the chief enemy of both parties to the Treaty was not Germany but Britain who was finding her far-flung dominions involving her in an uncomfortable variety of disputes. In 1898 her traditional antagonism to France reached a head in the Fashoda crisis when the two countries seemed for a moment on the brink of war over the Sudan. Russia's activities in Central Asia were watched with alarm from Whitehall and Delhi for fear that they would spark off a fresh mutiny in India, while Russian ambitions in the Far East were thought capable of starting a scramble to divide up China. The struggle with the Boers in South Africa united almost the whole of Europe against the British, so that the telegram of congratulation which the Kaiser at the prompting of his advisers sent to President Krüger after the Jameson Raid in January 1896 met with general applause on the continent. By contrast Russia's absorption in Asia distracted her attention from the Balkans and until after her defeat by Japan in 1905 her relations with Austria-Hungary were almost cordial.

This situation lulled those responsible for German policy into thinking that the British, and not themselves, were the people in a tight corner. They doubted whether Britain could come to terms with France and were convinced that, if she did, the result would be a breach between France and Russia. British policy was, however, coming into the hands of people who, themselves disliking and fearing German behaviour, considered their attitude to be widely shared in Europe. The result was that when, on two or three occasions between 1898 and 1901, the officious zeal of subordinates led each of the two Governments to think that the other was seeking an alliance, neither felt any need for urgency. Each side distrusted the other and each thought that, by waiting, it could secure better terms later. The approaches had more results than appeared on the surface. When they ended, there was not a single British minister left inclined to start any further attempt at drawing the links closer. With few people in responsible positions prepared to argue the case for friendship, popular animosity had free rein and the Press and public on both sides saw to it that any act capable of arousing suspicion did so. An underlying divergence of will was becoming steadily more obvious and neither nation was prepared to make the compromises which would have been the pre-essential to co-operation. Britain was coming to feel instinctively that German expansion, political, economic and naval, challenged the system which she had built up and on which she depended to keep her people employed and fed.

Britain's first step to relieve the pressure on her was to conclude an alliance with Japan in 1902. The Germans welcomed this as likely to embroil her with Russia and probably with France; in fact, it held the ring while the Japanese, more to Britain's surprise than Germany's, beat the Russians in 1904–5 and precipitated a revolution in St Petersburg. Before this result was evident, the British had responded to a French suggestion that the two countries clear up the points of difference between them. In April 1904 this was done in a series of agreements known collectively as the *Entente Cordiale*. At this, some of the German leaders took fright and decided that, while internal unrest made Russia incapable of action, the opportunity must be secured for showing the French how dangerous it could be to disregard Germany. Morocco, where the British had promised the French a free hand in return for a similar one themselves in Egypt, was chosen as the stage for this demonstration and the Kaiser was sent in April 1905 to show the flag at Tangier. But confusion of purpose and loss of nerve at the crucial moment led to the affair being mishandled; at the Conference of Algeciras in the following year the Germans found themselves virtually alone and emerged almost empty-handed. Instead of disrupting the Entente, they consolidated it and even precipitated military conversations which had the effect of committing Britain morally, though neither legally nor publicly, to come to France's aid in the event of an attack. The coalition against Germany which had been Bismarck's nightmare was steadily taking shape as a reaction to the policy of his successors.

Instead of learning from their mistakes, the Germans repeated them over Russia. An attempt by the Kaiser in 1905 to talk the Tsar into an alliance by personal diplomacy collapsed as soon as the project was referred to their respective Ministers. This should have shown how deeply Russia was committed to the opposite camp, and the commitments increased two years later when Britain copied her procedure with France and made another series of agreements easing her outstanding disputes with Russia. Then in 1908 the Austro-Hungarian Foreign Minister, with little reference to Berlin, outwitted his Russian opposite number in a deal over the Balkans. When the Russians demanded compensation, the Germans tried to be clever and, in the guise of friendly mediators, forced the Russians into a corner, thereby enabling them to attribute to German intimidation the climb-down which they would have had to make in any case. They did not forget their humiliation or forgive the authors of it, while the British and French realized that, to keep Russia's friendship, they must be prepared to offer some support for her interests in the Balkans. Thus the bonds grew tighter on each side and the stock of international willingness to compromise was depleted.

Throughout these years the British were growing slowly but steadily more perturbed about the character and purpose of the German naval programme. In so far as a navy was desired as more than a badge of Great Power status, its expansion was undoubtedly started in order to have an instrument for putting pressure on Britain. But this concept dated from the turn of the century when Britain had many enemies so that a navy considerably smaller than her own could still constitute an inconvenient threat. By 1907 the international situation, as has been described, had completely changed. Yet all suggestions that the Germans should build fewer ships were met by emotional tirades from the Kaiser and his subordinates about constitutional necessities and the right of nations to behave as they wished. The archives make it clear that the German leaders did not believe Britain had the money or the men to sustain a race indefinitely. They refused to recognize the risks involved in challenging the major naval power at sea at the same time as they prepared to impose their will on their neighbours on land. They not only did much to ensure that, when war came, Britain joined in against them, but also spent vast sums of money (and compelled Britain to spend more) on a fleet which in the event proved to be incapable of use in an effective way.

In 1911 the French decided to tighten their hold on Morocco and their Prime Minister, behind the backs not only of the British but also of his colleagues, tried to insure against German objections by offering compensating concessions. But the German State Secretary decided that negotiations would go better if he got his claim staked out before the other side had realized their gains. He therefore persuaded the Kaiser and Chancellor to send a gunboat to the port of Agadir. The British were (with some justice) afraid of a deal being done behind their backs which might even start off a Franco-German reconciliation. Lloyd George, the Chancellor of the Exchequer, therefore gave a warning in a speech at the Mansion House which the Germans interpreted as a threat to themselves and the French used as a justification for resisting German demands. After four months of negotiations France emerged with exactly what she wanted in Morocco and Germany with some small but strategically useful bits of land in Central Africa. The German public, which had been led to expect bigger things, were indignant and put most of the blame on the British, who in exchange acquired the almost certainly unfounded conviction that only their Government's firm action had stopped Germany from attacking France. British arrangements for sending an expeditionary force to France in the event of war were made more formal, though a binding commitment to do this was still withheld. The whole episode, which provides an object-lesson in how diplomacy should not be conducted, left all countries involved less ready to be conciliatory in future.

Yet during the next two years a series of upheavals in the Balkans was prevented from leading to a war between Austria-Hungary and Russia, largely because Germany was prepared to hold back the former while Britain did the same to the latter. In Germany, however, the conviction was growing that, unless the Habsburg Empire was before long enabled to achieve some striking success, it would disintegrate in face of subversion among the subordinate nationalities and in particular the Serbs and Croats, who were receiving aid and encouragement from the independent kingdom of Serbia on the other side of the south-eastern frontier. The Serbs in turn were supported by the Russians who, like the Germans, were encouraging national feeling as an antidote to internal upheaval. The Government in Berlin came to the conclusion that a war with Russia in support of Austria-Hungary was inevitable sooner or later, while the General Staff estimated that the chances of winning would grow worse the longer it was put off. At the next crisis, Austria-Hungary must be made to act against Serbia and Germany must stand firm in support. From this angle, the war would be a defensive one.

The murder of the heir to the Habsburg throne, Archduke Franz Ferdinand, by a Serb in Sarajevo on 28 June 1914 was thought by the German Government to provide Austria-Hungary with an opportunity such as might never recur for disciplining Serbia with the sympathy of the world behind her. Accordingly when the Vienna Government enquired about the German attitude, it was assured that whatever it did would receive full support. The danger of war spreading was realized but the hope was that for a variety of reasons Russia might not choose the occasion for a fight.

The Germans had, however, assumed that the Austrians would strike quickly while the shock caused by the murder was still vivid. Instead they delayed for nearly a month before delivering an ultimatum so stiff that it

31

was obviously intended to be rejected. The Serbian Government disconcertingly agreed to almost all of it within the time-limit of 48 hours so that, when Austria-Hungary none the less broke off relations, declared war and bombarded Belgrade, the sympathies of the world began to change sides. The British Government pressed Germany to join with them in mediating as they had done in the Balkan Wars but Bethmann Hollweg showed great reluctance to act on the suggestion, possibly because he wanted to allow the Austrians a chance to secure a clear prestige success. By the time he had changed his mind, Russia had mobilized and it was too late.

For General von Schlieffen, the Chief of the German General Staff some twenty years earlier, in planning how to fight France and Russia simultaneously, had decided that Germany could not withstand a long war against both Powers and, since a quick victory was unlikely to be forthcoming on the vast plains of the east, the most hopeful strategy would therefore be to throw as many divisions as possible against France and try to knock her out within six weeks, leaving the Austrians to hold up the Russians until this had been done. But one of the factors which made this course attractive was that Germany could mobilize her army faster than Russia. This advantage would, however, be lost unless both mobilizations began simultaneously and therefore the German generals could not afford to wait and give mediation a longer chance. The military timetable took over.

Nor was that all. The German plan of attacking first in the west assumed that either France would declare war on Germany or that it would not matter if Germany were openly the aggressor. To complete the predicament, the General Staff had decided that the Franco-German frontier proper was too short and well-defended to make practicable the quick breakthrough which was so essential. Instead a strong right wing was to make an encircling sweep through Belgium, which was to be invited to give passage to German troops; if she refused (as she did) she was to be overrun, in defiance of a Treaty which Prussia, in common with other European states, had signed in 1839, guaranteeing her neutrality. Although three German Chancellors, including Bethmann Hollweg, had known of this plan, nobody had ever challenged it. The danger of Britain coming to Belgium's help was realized but discounted on the ground that, in a war which was going to last for only six weeks, she would not have time to make herself felt. For Germany had ninety-five divisions to face about sixty French ones; Britain had six to send.

Under the constitution the Chancellor had no control over the military machine. Responsibility for ensuring that the military and civilian sides of the Government were co-ordinated rested with the Emperor. Kaiser William had never realized what the job implied, let alone tried to tackle it. Moreover, by brusquely rebuffing any attempts by civilians to show interest in military matters, he had stacked the cards against their questioning the political implications of the generals' plans. The damage which Germany did to her cause in the eyes of third parties by the way she began the war sprang directly from the whole character of her society.

The attention of the world, and particularly the British, French and American publics, fastened on the fact that it was Germany and Austria-Hungary which had taken the initiative in declaring war and Germany which had on 2 August broken a promise by making an unprovoked attack on Belgium. The German public, however, were encouraged to treat this as a technicality. They were led to believe that it was Russia, France and Britain which were to blame, having allied together out of jealousy to encircle Germany and frustrate her 'legitimate' growth. They were told that she was inspired by no lust for conquest but, for the sake of holding what she had, was seizing her sword with a clean hand and a clear conscience. From this initial discrepancy of view much recrimination was to follow.

THE WAR OF THE THREE GAMBLES

At the end of August it appeared that the first great German gamble was going to succeed and that the campaign of 1914 would be over as quickly as those of 1866 and 1870. But Moltke, nephew of the victor of the earlier wars and now himself German leader, had always been worried about the problem of controlling effectively the much larger numbers of men who would be under his command. Early in September the appearance of a gap between two of his formations on the River Marne led him to lose his nerve and order what he intended to be a purely tactical and temporary retreat. In fact, however, the war of manoeuvre was not to be resumed in the west for over four years and the two opposing armies settled down to dig trenches all the way from the sea to the Swiss frontier. A couple of brilliant victories by Hindenburg and Ludendorff over the Russians could not conceal the fact that the war was going to be a long one and therefore one for which Germany was ill-prepared, as well as one in which sea-power mattered.

But at sea also things went wrong. The Germans had assumed that the British fleet would institute a blockade close to the eastern shores of the North Sea and planned to attack it piecemeal in the hope of whittling down its superiority until a general action could be undertaken on terms not too unfavourable. But a month before war began the British had decided to take advantage of the accidents of geography and set up a 'distant' blockade at the Straits of Dover and between Norway and John o'Groats. Instead of having the British fleet as a convenient target at the mouth of the Elbe, the Germans found that they could get at it only by making a risky journey themselves across the North Sea. To make matters worse, the British disregarded an International Agreement which they had never ratified and, instead of applying their blockade only to munitions, extended it to all kinds of foodstuffs and materials. A time could therefore be foreseen when, unless the blockade was somehow broken, the people and cannon of Germany would be starved into submission. The British fleet never succeeded in winning a clear victory – but it did not need to win one, merely to avoid getting beaten.

What were the Germans to do? A compromise peace based on a return to the pre-war situation would have been regarded by the Allies as tantamount to defeat since it would have been an open admission that their 10 million fighting men were inadequate to bring down the 6 million of the Central Powers, nor had they any intention of winding up one war and thereby giving the Germans a chance to prepare for the next. On the other hand, the whole reputation of the German ruling classes was at stake in the war which, but for their attitudes, might never have come about. They could not hope to keep their privileges if they returned empty-handed and weakened by casualties.

Moreover, that overestimate of their own strength which had done so much to involve the Germans in the war continued to delude them while they fought it. The majority of people, even in responsible positions, had little idea of the real situation; the public were never told the truth about the opening battles. The belief was general that the country would gain by her struggle which was to bring her the 'breakthrough to world power'. Although she was represented as fighting only in self-defence there was widespread agreement that, as a compensation for having to do so once as well as a security against having to do so twice, she was entitled to 'guarantees'. German war-aims varied from time to time in accordance with the strategic position, but until late in 1918, control over most or all of Belgium, France's Longwy–Briey basin with its valuable ores, Poland, the Baltic states, extensive indemnities and colonial concessions were constant themes. Behind these demands loomed the wider dream of bringing under German control the whole of 'Middle Europe' from Antwerp to Odessa. Such greed not only removed any inclination to offer terms which the Allies might have considered but also prevented Germany from getting neutral opinion on her side by a show of moderation. Yet for long the only people inside Germany to challenge this megalomania were the despised Social Democrats.

If a compromise peace was thus ruled out, the alternative was to resume the original strategy of securing an overwhelming victory on one front so that all available resources could then be concentrated in the hope of doing the same on the other. To this the first three years of fighting were in effect devoted and, in spite of a certain dispersion of effort being caused by differences of view as to which front offered the best chances of a knock-out blow, success came in 1917 with the collapse of Tsarist Russia. Kerensky's liberal regime which gained power in February of that year was in half a mind to keep on fighting. To get them replaced by more compliant people, the German Government gave the Bolsheviks £250,000 and enabled Lenin to return from exile in Switzerland. But before this opportunity of supping with the devil had presented itself, the effects of the blockade had brought Germany close to desperation while Austria-Hungary was in an even worse condition. Something had to be done to escape from Britain's stranglehold and the only course which offered any prospect of doing this was to starve Britain herself out by indiscriminate submarine warfare. Indeed this could have been tried earlier if Germany had formed her navy with light craft and submarines rather than battleships she dared not use.

But by the time enough U-boats had been built to give them a chance of being effective, it had become clear that, if ships were sunk without first making sure that they belonged to the enemy, a number of the victims would be American and that this would bring the USA into the war on the Allies' side. A dreadful and much resented choice presented itself between risking the loss of the war by failure to press home a submarine blockade of Britain and making such a blockade effective and thus losing the war as a result of American intervention. An attempt to avoid the choice by getting the Americans to act as mediators failed because the Germans refused to say exactly what terms they would accept. The soldiers and sailors, who underestimated the implications of an American entry and the speed with which this would take effect, claimed that they could force Britain to give in before a single American soldier could land in Europe and early in 1917 they got permission to try their luck. This second gamble met the same fate as the first. Britain, though hard-pressed for a time, found means of defence against the submarines, the United States declared war in April and their first troops reached France in July.

The same month brought a political upheaval inside Germany. At the start of the war the Social Democrats had given the lie to the accusations of the right by voting unanimously for the war credits. But their left wing had never taken kindly to this policy and the example of Russia's revolution now led to their breakaway as Independents. The party leadership, afraid of losing control, felt obliged to adopt as the official policy the demand being made by the Petrograd Council of Workers and Soldiers for 'a peace without annexations or reparations'. Bethmann Hollweg had sought to retain the loyalty of the masses by inducing the Kaiser to make an indefinite promise about reforming the Prussian voting system. To the great indignation of the right, the Socialists pressed for prompt action and Erzberger, the Centre leader, supported them with a speech which, for the first time, gave the German public some idea of the true war situation. The coalition of Centre, Progressives and Social Democrats again asserted itself to pass through the Reichstag a resolution which, after recalling the 1914 claim that 'Germany had no lust for conquest', demanded a negotiated peace.

The next steps threw a revealing light on German conditions. Hindenburg and Ludendorff, who since 1916 had held the High Command, declared that Bethmann Hollweg had lost their confidence and that they could no longer work with him. The leaders of the right-wing parties agreed, while those of the new majority wanted him replaced by someone more flexible and open-minded. He therefore decided to resign. But the Reichstag majority still could not bring itself to insist on a Chancellor of its own choosing and indeed would have precipitated a crisis had it done so since the High Command would undoubtedly have refused to accept the kind of man who would have been appointed. After a frantic search for a Chancellor who would be acceptable to both the soldiers and the parties, a nonentity was installed. He made common cause with the High Command and the Reichstag's 'Peace Resolution' was watered down by 'interpretations'. The truth was that the reactionary and nationalist groups in Germany, embodied in Hindenburg and Ludendorff, had taken the management of civilian as well as military affairs into their own hands and nothing short of force was going to get them to relinquish it. Unfortunately for the country, the force had to be applied by their enemies.

For the moment, however, all energies were bent on taking advantage of the Russian decision, after the Communist October Revolution, to stop fighting, and on concentrating all available forces for a final effort in the west before the Americans could fully make themselves felt. Yet to win decisively the Germans had not only to conquer in the field but also to break the blockade and for this they had to get all they could in the way of food and raw materials from Russia. Nor could they resist the temptation of exploiting the fact that they appeared to have Slavs at their mercy. In the Peace of Brest-Litovsk they imposed terms so harsh as seriously to impair Germany's title to merciful treatment herself later, and in the process of failing to extract the wheat, oil and ores which they wanted, tied up 1 million soldiers whom they were to need badly in the west. For although the offensive in March 1918 began by making quick progress and nearly broke the Franco-British line, it gradually ground to a halt without actually achieving this. Later attempts to renew it met the same fate and when in July the Allies counter-attacked with a growing superiority of arms (including tanks) behind them, the fighting morale of the German troops at long last broke. At the end of September the High Command, in a moment of panic, told the Kaiser that they saw no alternative to asking for an armistice on the basis of the 'Fourteen Points' which the American President Wilson had proposed as a basis for peace in January 1918. Germany had lost her third gamble.

One of these 'Points' however was 'the destruction of every arbitrary power that can separately, secretly and of its single choice disturb the peace of the world', and the Allies made clear that they included in that description the political system which had hitherto directed the destinies of the German people. On the day on which the Kaiser ordered an armistice to be sought, he announced that 'men who possessed the public confidence' were to take a larger part in the government. The Chancellor was to be made responsible to the Reichstag. Deputies were to be allowed to become Ministers without having to resign their seats and authority over the armed forces was transferred from the Emperor to a Minister of War.

Surprisingly enough the first democratic Chancellor, Max, was a Prince even though Baden from which he came was the most liberal of the German states. But before he took over, consternation had been caused among the party leaders when a spokesman of the High Command revealed the true situation to them. For four long years the German people had held out with remarkable tenacity against unfavourable odds; a great part of the credit was due to the fidelity and competence of their officials, but it was the hope of making their country greater which had kept them going. Once the knowledge spread, with little advance warning, that success was not to be had, they naturally asked why they should go on enduring the hardships of war. The number of people who wanted a radical recasting of society was small. But as long as the only group which offered to bring peace quickly was the extreme left wing, others who did not share their social views would listen to them. Prince Max's Cabinet seemed too implicated in the past and failed to get on quickly enough with the job of liquidating it. At the end of October, Austria-Hungary stopped fighting. Sailors in Kiel mutinied when ordered to sea to fight a last hopeless battle. A Workers' Republic was proclaimed in Munich. On 9 November the Berlin workers went on strike and the garrison fraternized with them. Prince Max handed over power to a government of Social Democrats and Progressives under Friedrich Ebert who had once been a saddler and, in a moment of excitement tinged with panic, one of its members proclaimed a Republic. At his headquarters in Belgium, the Kaiser was with some difficulty persuaded to abdicate and next day sought refuge in Holland. The other German princes followed his example, when the King of Saxony was advised to abdicate by a delegation in top hats and frock coats, he replied in his broad accent, 'Eh well, mayke yer mook yerselves' and added, 'Luvly repooblicans you be'!

On 11 November a delegation led by Erzberger signed an armistice whose severe terms were designed to put out of question any attempt at renewing the conflict. But that was the last thing which the majority of the German people wanted at that moment to do. The achieving of this result had however cost the lives of at least 13 million people of whom 2.7 million were German.

3

THE FIRST ATTEMPT AT
DEMOCRACY: 1918–1933

THE REVOLUTION WHICH LOST ITS WAY

On the night of the Kaiser's flight Ebert sat at the Chancellor's desk in
Berlin and contemplated his problems. Germany seemed to be heading for
chaos; the system which had been held together for so long by such great
efforts threatened to collapse as soon as the motive for making the efforts
disappeared. External failure threatened to reverse the internal integration
which had been achieved since 1871. There was a danger that separatist
movements in the different states would undo Bismarck's work of unification. All over the country the soldiers and workers were forming themselves
into Councils (which in Russia were called Soviets) and hoisting red flags.
Those in the capital were talking in wild terms and it was natural, if
incorrect, to suppose that the same held good everywhere. The Spartakists,
as the left-wing Socialists called themselves, clearly intended to follow the
Russian example and, by seizing the leadership of the Councils, precipitate
a social revolution. But Ebert had no intention of being the German
Kerensky. He and his immediate colleagues were Democrats before they
were Socialists. Long years spent trying to establish parliamentary government in Germany had accustomed them to think in terms of order and
fairness; their first instinct was to let the German people as a whole decide
on the future by a free vote. But their chances of putting through their ideas
depended on the force at their command. What attitude was the Army going
to take?

There lay in front of Ebert a telephone giving direct access to General
Headquarters. Suddenly its bell rang. Ebert lifted the receiver and heard the
voice of Hindenburg's deputy, Groener. The armistice terms which he had
just received were such that a strong government would be needed to carry
them out. For one thing, they required the German army to withdraw to
the east bank of the Rhine within a month. To do this so fast was a major
administrative task. Would the Government back the generals or would it
seek to undermine their authority? The men at the two ends of the line
needed one another and out of their conversation a working alliance was born.

The effect of that alliance, however, was to put the fate of the Republic into the hands of the military and the term 'military' increasingly meant men who were imbued with the autocratic traditions of the Second Reich and unsympathetic to the idea of government by the people. For the temporary soldiers who had left peacetime jobs in order to fight hurried back to them, leaving the regular troops behind. Some of these, when their units were disbanded in compliance with Allied requirements, were formed into special groups called *Freikorps* and largely used to protect the eastern frontier. What was true of them went for much of the administrative hierarchy, the Civil Service, the judicial system, the universities and the Churches. The people staffing these institutions found themselves compelled to serve under a changed set of masters but this did not make them change their views. The landlords and industrialists were left with their property intact.

True to their Marxist training, the left-wing Socialists, some of whom in December 1918 founded the German Communist Party (KDP), argued that in these circumstances the political revolution would not endure unless it was followed up by measures which deprived the old ruling classes of the economic and social bases of their power and put into all the key positions new men committed to the new system. The majority of the Social Democrats, however, though aware of the need to safeguard the constitutional changes which had been achieved, were afraid that extending them outside politics would precipitate violent resistance and that dispensing with the services of trained administrators in the very difficult conditions of the time would lead to starvation and chaos. They were further afraid that, if civil war did break out, they would either be unable to win it or could do so only at the cost of themselves setting up a dictatorship. For the forces of reaction in Germany were more numerous and better organized than they had been in Russia and there were no land-hungry peasants to back up the workers.

The theory that Germany had to choose between reaction and revolution has in recent years been challenged. It has been argued that the danger from the left and the strength of the right were both overestimated. The revolutionaries certainly composed only a small proportion of the Councils and Ebert might well have steered control of these into moderate hands instead of holding them, as he did, at arm's length. As it was, a Congress of them held in December agreed that a National Assembly should be convened and decisions about the future left to it. There was no need for interference with property rights. The vital need was to put convinced Democrats into key posts instead of relying on experts whose claim to be 'non-political' was only temporarily valid. Regular soldiers, even officers, with democratic convictions were to be found who could have been the nucleus of a citizen force; Groener's nervousness suggests a lack of confidence in the army's ability to prevail.

The die was cast, however, in January 1919 when the Army and Freikorps were allowed by Ebert's Government to suppress a Spartakist rising in Berlin and murder the leaders Karl Liebknecht and Rosa Luxemburg. Left-wing writers have called this 'German democracy's Battle of the Marne'. The bitter feelings which resulted made it all the harder for the left to present a united front to the right. Gradually, however, the authority of the Government was established although extremists held power in Munich with scarcely a break till May.

The National Assembly elected on 19 January met at Weimar, to mark a breach with Prussian traditions and to escape the influence of events in Berlin. Between February and June it drew up a constitution. A proposal to abolish Prussia was defeated and Germany was divided into seventeen units on traditional lines, which were called 'Lands' rather than 'States'. The black, red and gold flag (the colours of 1848) was adopted in place of the Imperial black, red and white (to the distress of monarchists). The abolition of Prussia's three-tier franchise turned the area from a stronghold of reaction into one of Social Democracy. The powers of the Reich Government were strengthened, particularly in finance and military affairs. The Bundesrat was replaced as Second Chamber by a Reichsrat with limited delaying powers. The Head of State was to be a President, chosen by popular vote for seven years; he was to sign treaties, command the Armed Forces and appoint the Chancellor and other Ministers who had to have the support of (but not necessarily belong to) the Reichstag. The President could also dissolve the Reichstag before its time was up. An article later to become notorious gave him power to take emergency action when public security and order were seriously disrupted or threatened. This, however, could be cancelled in retrospect if the Reichstag so demanded. Ebert became the first President.

The new Reichstag was to be elected every four years by universal suffrage (including votes for women) and proportional representation, so that each party was to obtain one seat for every 60,000 votes that it received. This system meant that people voted for a party rather than an individual. It resulted in a very accurate representation of opinion but encouraged the multiplication of separate parties. Much of the blame for the political situation which subsequently developed in the Republic tended to be placed on it. But in fact all it did was to exaggerate rather than counteract a position which was bound to cause trouble and which had been foreshadowed by the election to the National Assembly itself. The Communists boycotted that event and the Independent Socialists won only 22 seats. But the Social Democrats themselves obtained only 163 out of 421. Thus they were unable to get a majority without the support of the Centre (89 seats) or the Democratic Party (as the Progressives, with 74 seats, renamed themselves). Further to the right came the People's Party (the former National Liberals, 42 seats) and the Nationalist Party (the former Conservatives, 22 seats). Thus the group which had formed the opposition under the Empire came to power under the Republic but the formation of each Cabinet was going to involve negotiations between two or three parties before it could be sure of support, while the middle- and working-class representatives who habitually engaged in such negotiations were flanked to the left and right by groups whose loyalty to the regime was questionable. The Republic's chances of success depended on the possibility of strengthening the centre at the expense of the extremes. It would be doomed if affairs so developed as to encourage the reverse process. In 1920 and again in 1922 the Social Democrats went out of office rather than work with the People's Party. This was hardly a good omen.

Moreover the former ruling classes went through an unnerving experience. At the outset and at short notice, they had the bottom knocked out of their view of life and expectation of the future. Then for months they lived in conditions which reminded them (though as it proved, wrongly) of the beginnings of the French and Russian revolutions. A community which traditionally set great store by order and discipline persuaded itself that the foundations of these qualities were being undermined. They refused to accept that Germany could have been beaten in battle but maintained that the army had been betrayed by the civilians. They regarded the new regime as something alien to German traditions and unsuited to German conditions which was being imposed at the behest of their enemies. Much of Germany, as the poet Rilke was later to say, 'wanted to persist and not to alter' (R.M. Rilke, *Letters to a Young Woman*, 2 February 1923).

PEACE WITHOUT HONOUR

Most Germans considered that they had agreed to make peace on the basis of President Wilson's Fourteen Points. But four of those points did not directly concern Germany at all and five more stated broad principles on such matters as open diplomacy, the freedom of the seas and the removal of economic barriers. Another called for 'a free, open-minded and absolutely impartial adjustment' of all colonial claims. The remaining four required the evacuation of all Russian, French and Belgian territory, the restoration of damage in France and Belgium, the return of Alsace and Lorraine to France and finally the creation of 'an independent Polish state which should include territories inhabited by indisputably Polish populations and be assured a free and secure access to the sea'.

The Treaty presented to a German delegation at Versailles on 7 May 1919 had been arrived at by inter-Allied bargaining behind closed doors and was handed over for comment rather than negotiation. But it cannot be said in its treatment of Germany to have clearly violated any of the actual 'Points'. The refusal to allow the Germans in the new Republic of Austria to join the Reich was inconsistent with the hopes which Wilson had held out about satisfying national aspirations but the matter had not featured in the 'Points'. For all of Germany's colonies to have been taken away from her was hardly an impartial adjustment of her claims and the Germans found much to dispute about the character of the population in many of the territories which were to be handed over to Poland. But these were partly adjusted by plebiscites and in any case details of this kind were only marginally responsible for the storm of indignation which broke out in Germany when the terms became known. Most Germans had in fact failed to read (or at any rate to remember) the small print of the various Allied pre-surrender statements and had based their expectations not so much on the 'Points' as on the spirit in which they thought Wilson would persuade the other countries to approach the peace. The hope had also been that, by adopting a democratic form of government, they would get a milder peace. Germany, however, was required to hand over about 27,000 square miles in Europe and 6 million people, to allow the East Prussian homeland to be cut off from the rest of the country (since otherwise Poland could not be given her free and secure access to the sea) and to pay considerable sums in reparations (in security against which the whole country west of the Rhine was to be occupied for fifteen years). Both reparations and occupation were only extensions of the terms imposed on France in 1871 and in fact represented modifications of what had been originally proposed by the advocates of a 'hard' peace. But this was not remembered by uninformed German observers, and their leaders did not choose to remind them of it.

On the ground that a legal justification was needed for the imposing of reparations, Article 231 of the Treaty required Germany, along with her Allies, to accept 'responsibility' for 'causing all the loss and damage to which her opponents had been subjected as a consequence of the war imposed on them by German aggression'. This was promptly labelled by the Germans 'the war-guilt clause', in spite of the fact that the word 'guilt' did not occur in it and imparted an element of moral judgement lacking in the original. It had indeed been Germany which had declared war on France and Russia and had invaded Belgium, thus indisputably committing aggression according to the rules of international law. Subsequent research (as summarized on pp. 28–33) has tended to the conclusion that Germany did much deliberately to precipitate the war. But a very different picture had been painted for the German people, who as a result bitterly resented the charge of 'war-guilt' and embarked on a campaign to disprove it. Moreover they knew that the Allies had during the war made a great impact on neutral opinion by denouncing them for exalting might above right – but considered that this was precisely what was now being done to them.

For the time being, however, the nation was helpless. Groener reported that armed resistance was out of the question (though not all his subordinates agreed with him). Bitter protests and elaborate arguments secured only marginal changes in the terms, coupled with an ultimatum to sign or take the consequences (which would have included the occupation of the Ruhr and a renewal of the blockade, hitherto only partially lifted). The Social

Democrats and Centre reluctantly decided to advocate compliance and obtained a majority in the National Assembly against the votes of all the Parties to the right of them, with the result that the Treaty was signed at Versailles on 28 June 1919 (exactly five years after Sarajevo). Prompting signature was the fear that the Allied penalties for refusal would lead to social breakdown and the dissolution of the Reich. On the other hand it might have been preferable to what inevitably became signature in bad faith, with a widespread if undeclared intention to escape as quickly and as fully as possible from fulfilment of the terms. Defiance might have brought the Allies more quickly up against the permanent realities and, by showing them the limits of their power, have served the world's interests better in the long run. But belief to the contrary did not imply treachery to the nation; the men who took the thankless decision did not merit the attacks which they suffered later and which amounted in the case of Erzberger and the Jewish Foreign Minister Rathenau to assassination. The most serious practical defect of the Treaty was that the superiority of force needed to make it possible did not remain to uphold it. The British and French could never have won a clear victory without US help but in November 1919 the Senate refused to ratify the Treaty and the country relapsed into isolation. The French reacted by demanding that the Treaty be enforced more strictly, the British by favouring its revision.

Large numbers of the German people had been so schooled to believe in their country's superiority as to be unable to reconcile themselves to the fact of its defeat. Some dreamt of repeating the national rising against Napoleon; others set themselves to 'organize sympathy' abroad. The tendency to reject the outcome of the fighting received powerful encouragement when Hindenburg misinterpreted a British newspaper article as endorsing the view that the German armed forces had been 'stabbed in the back' by the inability of the home front to hold out. He also put much of the blame on Allied propaganda, implying that that had been deceptive when it had in reality concentrated on publicizing Wilson's speeches and the facts of the military situation.

With the example of Prussia's resistance to Napoleon in mind, the Allies had insisted on the German Army (henceforward known as the *Reichswehr*) being cut down to a long-service force of 100,000 personnel, on the General Staff being suppressed and on the possession of tanks, aircraft and certain other weapons being prohibited. They required all troops in excess of this figure to be demobilized and the effort to comply brought the Government into collision with the Freikorps. In March 1920 an Allied order demanding the dissolution of these bands led some of them to advance on Berlin and endeavour to set up a right-wing government under a Pan-German farm inspector called Kapp. General von Seeckt, the officer responsible for organizing the Reichswehr, had not been unaware of what was in train but took no steps to prevent it and allowed his troops to intervene only when the action of the trade unions in calling a general strike made it clear that the rising (*Putsch*) was going to fail.

Afterwards the unions presented the Cabinet with a number of demands for a new and more democratic Minister of Defence, for a greater say in policy and for closer democratic control over the Reichswehr. These demands were first watered down by Ministers and then, after the emergency was over, forgotten. Had they been successfully enforced, the subsequent history of the Republic might have been considerably altered. But enforcing them might have precipitated a head-on collision with the Reichswehr, who for their part insisted on the resignation of the Minister of Defence because 'no member of the Government which had supported the general strike could ever regain the confidence of the armed forces'. The effect of the civilian victory was to turn these forces to the right and increase the tension between them and the Social Democrats.

Suspecting that the Reichswehr was trying to get round disarmament and worried by a treaty of friendship which the Republican Government signed with the Soviet Union at Rapallo in Italy in April 1922, the Allies gave that government little latitude. Disregarding both the basic principles of economics and Germany's internal problems, they treated requests for postponing the payment of reparations as attempts at evasion (which in part they were). Mounting disagreement on this score led the French and Belgians in January 1923 to occupy the Ruhr and redouble their efforts to get separatist governments set up in the Rhineland. This step, from which the British dissociated themselves and to which the Germans replied by passive resistance, cost its authors more than they gained by it and gave a final blow to the German economy.

Instead of paying for the war by higher taxes, the Imperial Government had met the cost by loans which it intended to make its enemies repay after their defeat. When instead those enemies won (and required Germany to pay for the debts which they themselves had incurred to one another), the result was fundamentally to alter the relationship between money and goods, so that by 1919 the Mark was only worth one-third of its pre-war value. Government expenditure rose whereas revenues fell. Although industrial activity recovered a little, reparations upset the balance of payments and by June 1922 the Mark's value had dropped to 1 per cent of its 1914 value. The French suspected the Germans of deliberately facilitating this inflation in the hope of proving that reparations were impossible. The Ruhr occupation naturally made things worse; the currency became practically valueless and output fell to almost half the 1913 level.

At this point reason slowly began to prevail. To secure support for abandoning passive resistance, a 'Great Coalition' Cabinet from Social Democrats to People's Party was formed under Gustav Stresemann, who before the war had been a chauvinistic National Liberal. It was confronted with threats from left and right. In Saxony, always a radical stronghold, the local Socialists defied their leaders by insisting that Communists must be brought into the Cabinet. Much the same happened in Thuringia. In Prussia and Bavaria Nationalists were considering risings to overthrow the Republic and prevent a surrender being made to the French. The Bavarian conspiracy included Ludendorff, now a nationalist crank, and a 34-year-old Austrian agitator called Adolf Hitler whose National Socialist German Workers Party (NSDAP) was beginning to find its feet. Some government officials and the local commander of the Reichswehr were also implicated. Stresemann, on 26 September, proclaimed a state of emergency and gave to the War Minister and Seeckt many of the arbitrary powers which the latter had been thinking of seizing. The Reichswehr commander in Saxony was authorized to proclaim a state of siege, depose the Cabinet and install a Reich Commissioner. Thanks to Social Democrat support, Stresemann was able to get Reichstag endorsement for his actions. These included the discarding not only of passive resistance but also of the old currency. A new one was substituted based upon the total value of German real property. This change favoured people who had owned material things rather than money or government stocks. The new *Rentenmark* worked because the Germans were ready to believe in it, but the reduction in monetary values dealt a lasting psychological blow at thrift and confidence.

The conspirators in Munich vacillated and Hitler thought he could force their hands. But when on 8 November he proclaimed a revolution in a beer cellar, Ludendorff made him march his followers into the centre of the city, where they were shot down by the police. He turned his subsequent trial into an occasion for propaganda and devoted his six-months' imprisonment to writing *Mein Kampf*. The kid gloves with which the Reich Government handled the Bavarian situation contrasted so remarkably with their vigorous action in Saxony that the Social Democrats withdrew their support from Stresemann, who resigned the Chancellorship at the end of November but remained Foreign Minister in a series of subsequent Cabinets more to the right.

The Republic thus survived the emergency of 1923, though for some time its continuance and the continued unity of Germany had been a matter of touch-and-go. The next contribution to consolidation was to come from the Allies. Before Stresemann resigned, he had already secured their consent to an examination of the reparations problem by a group of technicians and thus completed the essential steps towards a long-term settlement.

PRECARIOUS FULFILMENT

The Dawes Plan (named after the American Chairman of the Committee which drew it up) proposed an apparently realistic programme for paying reparations, provided for sufficient international control of Germany to ensure that this programme could be maintained and backed up the

45

arrangement by an international loan. The Plan was linked with a gradual French withdrawal from the Ruhr. Even so, its acceptance was bitterly opposed by the German Nationalists.

In February 1925, President Ebert died, having been to the last the target of bitter and undeserved vituperation. At the first election for his successor, no candidate got the necessary votes and just before the second, the Nationalist Party talked Hindenburg into standing. The Communists insisted on splitting the left-of-centre vote by putting up their own candidate and as a result the old Field Marshal of 78 won by a short head. For the next seven years he treated his oath to the constitution seriously and listened to his Ministers even when they were Social Democrats.

Stresemann as Foreign Minister maintained that the only practicable policy for Germany was to recover the confidence of the world by scrupulously fulfilling her commitments, in the hope of getting the restrictions imposed on her gradually relaxed. By the autumn of 1925 he had succeeded well enough for a group of treaties to be signed at Locarno in Switzerland. In these France, Belgium and Germany accepted the existing frontiers between them (including a demilitarized zone along the Rhine) and agreed to settle all disputes by arbitration; Britain and Italy promised to come to the help of the victim if this agreement was ever violated. In the east, Germany, Poland and Czechoslovakia promised never to seek to alter their common frontiers by force but the German Government did not dare to defy public opinion to the extent of formally renouncing the areas taken away at Versailles and no guarantees of third-party help against aggression were given. The other countries promised to support German entry into the League of Nations (which followed after tiresome hitches in 1926) and to begin winding up the occupation of the Rhineland. The instruments embodying these Allied concessions were criticized as 'instruments of shame' by the Nationalists but the Reichstag approved them by a five to three majority.

Stresemann's aims were not confined to the west and in 1925 he also concluded a Trade Treaty with the Soviet Union, followed six months later by a Treaty in which each signatory promised to remain neutral if the other were attacked. An even closer liaison with the Russians was being built up by Seeckt, who as early as 1920 said that 'only in firm co-operation with Russia will Germany have a chance of regaining her position as a World Power' and two years later recorded that 'Poland's existence is intolerable – incompatible with the survival of Germany' (F.L. Carsten, *The Reichswehr and Politics*, pp. 68 and 140). Seeckt evaded the disarmament provisions of the Versailles Treaty by building up a force sufficiently highly trained (and free of Socialists) to act as a cadre for a subsequent rapid expansion, and by getting secret facilities in Russia for trying out prototypes of forbidden weapons. This was known to Stresemann and other Ministers but their somewhat half-hearted attempts at interference were brushed aside.

In the second half of the 1920s the Republic seemed to be on the verge of establishing itself. The Nationalists lost ground and the National Socialists dwindled to insignificance. The Social Democrats, after being out of office at national level since 1923 (though controlling a number of *Länder* notably Prussia) gained strength in the 1928 elections and joined a 'Great Coalition' Cabinet. But there were still disturbing aspects. Much of the prosperity was based on loans from abroad and indeed Germany's ability to pay reparations depended on the fact that she was being lent a sum three times as great by the USA. Fourteen parties were represented in the 1928 Reichstag. There were five governments in as many years and the bargaining needed to produce a new Cabinet sometimes lasted a week.

But above all there were the incessant attacks of the right wing on the policy of fulfilment, on the very existence of the Republic and on the characters of the people who were trying to make it successful. The old agrarian–industrial combination was still active and awaiting its chance, although it is an oversimplification to say with the Communists that Nazism was instigated and paid for by big business. Various republican measures were blamed for the lack of profits, and hence of investment, which was seen as a major cause of Germany's economic difficulties. The defeat, the peace terms, the Allied occupation, reparations and the inflation had swollen the ranks of those who regarded the entire course of German history since 1870 as a mistake. Such people now longed for a German revolution which would bring into being a new, third, Reich, based upon the application of traditional German principles to the modern situation. On the practical consequences of this application there were considerable differences of view. While many nationally minded conservatives continued to regard Communism (with which they virtually equated Social Democracy) as the main enemy, others had picked up from the left hostility to hereditary privilege, just as they had often picked up from Liberals scepticism about Christian beliefs. Without being against private property as such, they insisted that it must be used for the benefit of the community. The one point on which all were agreed was hostility to Jews.

Paradoxically the Social Democratic gains at the 1928 elections made matters worse rather than better because they resulted in the leadership of the Nationalists passing into the hands of Hugenberg, an industrialist with large newspaper and film interests; he made it his aim not to join in governing the Republic but to make republican government impossible. In 1929, on American initiative, a new 'Young' Plan for reparations was drawn up, scaling down the amount which Germany was to pay. Although German industrialists and bankers (led by the head of the *Reichsbank* Dr Schacht) had sat on the drafting committee, Hugenberg and his associates demanded that all the concessions made in it by the Allies should be accepted but all further reparations payments refused. In association with Hitler the Nationalists organized a plebiscite against the Plan but they got only 14 per cent of the votes and the Plan was confirmed by the Reichstag in March 1930. Dr Schacht, however, resigned in protest; possibly his acute nose scented a change in the wind.

THE WILD MEN GET THEIR CHANCE

The 'Great Crash' on the New York Stock Exchange on 29 October 1929 led to the undoing of many things, including the Weimar Republic. Injudicious speculators went bankrupt; loans were called in and cancelled in a chain reaction all over the world. International trade and demand for raw materials shrank; prices fell and the total process was thus intensified.

This was the situation which gave an opening to one of the more remarkable characters in history. Adolf Hitler was born in 1889 in Upper Austria. He came to Germany only in 1913 and became a citizen of the Republic only in 1932. His mind was framed, largely by self-education, in Linz and Vienna during the last days of Habsburg rule at a time when the Germans in Austria were losing out in the political struggle. Those who did not relapse into resignation or escape into cultural activities compensated for the failure by adopting extreme attitudes of racial nationalism and in particular a vicious disdain for the apparent authors of their humiliation – democrats, Slavs, Jews. Hitler reproduced their situation in a microcosm, compensating for an initial lack of success by belief in his mission, coupled with hatred of those who failed to recognize it. To him history was the record of national struggles for living space and world domination. Any nation in which the values of western civilization were prevalent was thereby weakened in that struggle. The essential domestic task of the politician should therefore be to deprive of influence and even eliminate those who propagated such values. Outstanding in this process were the Communists and Jews.

The primitive character of this fundamental faith was to Hitler an advantage since in his view most people were capable of absorbing only simple ideas. In pursuing power he was aided by an unusually developed ability to divine intuitively the mental processes of others. He succeeded as a speaker because what he said was what he knew that the audience wanted to hear. He succeeded as a politician because he could foresee what his antagonists were going to think or do and choose the arguments and actions best calculated to make them do as he wanted or to frustrate them. The same faculties made him a wily tactician, exploiting each individual's weakness, playing off one group of supporters against another, postponing as long as possible commitments which might deprive him of support but never losing sight of his ultimate objectives.

Above all, he was lucky in his epoch. The advance of technology had enabled the orator for the first time in history to speak directly to a mass audience which was not physically present. But at the same time and particularly in Germany, it had cut numbers of people adrift from their inherited environment, leaving them resentful and apprehensive, unable to understand what lay behind their plight or how it could be remedied. A complex economic web had come into existence which often put the livelihood of the individual outside his own control and at the mercy of forces or people whom he could not precisely identify. Hitler's main audience was at the outset one of people living in a small way who in the professions, trade, industry and agriculture alike found themselves pushed to the wall in favour of larger units and a continent-wide division of labour. They were bewildered in an unfamiliar situation which nobody seemed able to master and for which their self-respect made them unwilling to take the blame. The slump, coming on top of the years 1918–24, eroded the social integration achieved in Germany prior to 1914 and the only remaining banner round which there seemed a chance of rallying was that of the nation. Fear of Communism and dislike for Jews were the negative forms of this loyalty.

The potential supporters of a 'German revolution' embraced a wide spectrum of outlooks. Hitler succeeded because he 'mobilized disaffection' by promising, with a complete lack of scruple, all things to all men. On the one hand the events of 1920 and 1923 had shown that no right-wing movement had a chance of success if the masses stood out solidly against it. Yet a mass movement was anathema to those who thought that national revival should bring to power an elite leadership, while the possessing classes, whose subscriptions were essential for victory, were not to be had for anything which smacked of socialism. The National Socialists, like the National Liberals and the Social Democrats (and perhaps today the Christian Democrats) were faced with the problem of keeping a balance between the two elements in their title. If Hitler was to be believed, Germany's troubles had not been due to an exaggerated idea of the position to which she was entitled in the world but to those decadent and alien elements in her population which had sapped her people's belief in their destiny and thus enabled her external enemies to overcome her. If she could eliminate such elements and recapture faith, she could regain material and psychological prosperity. It was almost the exact reverse of the truth but in the circumstances it carried conviction.

Even before the American crash, the growth of unemployment in Germany had upset the financing of the relatively new system of unemployment pay and strained relations inside the Great Coalition Government between the Socialists, speaking for the workers, and the People's Party for the employers. The fresh developments brought increased unemployment (to reach 5 million in the winter of 1930–1 and 6 million a year later); government expenditure went up, revenues fell. In the spring of 1930 the tensions inside the Cabinet paralysed its capacity for action and on 27 March its Socialist Chancellor resigned. Some historians regard that date as marking the end of the Republic.

For the President, partly on Reichswehr advice, entrusted the forming of a new government to a Centre Deputy called Heinrich Brüning. He was a devout Catholic, a brave ex-officer, an upright man and an expert in economics. He considered that the only way to solve the problems lay in savagely deflating the economy and cutting expenditure and wages till the Budget was balanced and by slow degrees the cheapness of money revived investment round the world. Even if this had not been at the time the generally accepted orthodoxy, Brüning himself doubted whether a reflationary policy of deficit financing would be feasible in a single country, especially when recent experience had made that country acutely nervous of inflation. Yet a deflationary policy meant a return to the hard living conditions from which Germany had escaped only after 1925 and involved a degree of disillusionment and sacrifice which might well destroy (particularly in the middle classes) the last vestiges of support for a democratic system. Indeed the problem of settling exactly how the sacrifices were to be distributed was clearly beyond the capacity of the parties and the Reichstag. Accordingly there was a tacit understanding between Brüning and those anti-democratic conservatives who helped him to power that, as soon as he encountered difficulty, he would resort to rule by an exploitation of the Article in the Constitution about emergency decrees (see p. 40). This meant in effect a return towards the system of the Second Reich where the Chancellor had been responsible, not to the Reichstag, but to the Head of State; as soon as Hindenburg refused his signature to an emergency decree, Brüning's position would become untenable.

Not that the Government ruled in defiance of the Reichstag. The only occasion when a majority of Deputies voted against it occurred in July 1930 and Brüning thereupon called a general election. Its results showed the difficulty of the situation; the Social Democrats and the middle-class parties (including the Nationalists) lost ground whereas the National Socialists leapt from 12 seats to become the second strongest party with 107 and the Communists rose from 54 to 77. Henceforward the Reichstag was convened only at intervals to pass a few trivial laws; it then agreed to a long adjournment during which the Government ruled by decree.

In the spring of 1931, hoping to offset internal misery by external success, the German and Austrian Governments announced their intention of setting up a common Customs Union. France was determined to prevent this evasion of the post-war ban on a political union between the two countries and caused the collapse of a major Austrian bank by withholding promised loans. Germany came to Austria's rescue but two months later two of the four major German banks had to be given state support. Britain came to Germany's rescue but an immediate crisis led to the resignation of the Labour Government and soon afterwards its successor, the National Government, had to devalue the pound by taking it off the gold standard. These dramatic developments did no good to Germany's public finances or to the confidence of her people. A moratorium on all reparations and war-debt payments reluctantly recognized that American inability to go on making loans left everyone else unable to meet their obligations. But the effect of this concession was weakened by being limited in the first instance to twelve months. During the winter of 1931–2 Brüning sought to have it made permanent but negotiations were not finished quickly enough to help him. A proposal to modify the disarmament clauses of the Treaty of Versailles, made with a view to strengthening his internal position, similarly failed in its effect because it was delayed by French objections. It is, however, doubtful whether, if action had been quicker, much would have been gained. What the German people wanted was work and prosperity; mere diplomatic successes made little impression.

By the spring of 1932 the sands were beginning to run out. There was no sign of economic improvement. The Nazis were growing in strength and boldness; they were winning support outside the classes and areas to which they had originally appealed, and particularly in North Germany. Some senior Reichswehr officers and more junior ones sympathized with Nazi objectives, while all hoped to gain influence and promotion under a right-wing government. Industrialists, with whom Hugenberg had close connections, expected such a government to cut social benefits and make profits easier to earn. There was considerable, though carefully fostered, nervousness about the Communist gain in votes (which never exceeded 17 per cent of the total). There was widespread demand for 'strong men' who would take 'strong measures' to regain prosperity. There was a belief that, if the Nazis were allowed a subordinate place in such a government, the enthusiasm behind them could be mobilized and their sting drawn. The decision lay with a monarchist aged 85 whose faculties were beginning to weaken.

In April 1932 Hindenburg's seven-year term of office expired and the election of a new President became inescapable. The straits to which the Republic had come were illustrated by the fact that no truly democratic candidate could be found who would have had any chance of election against a rival who got the backing of the right, though this was partly due to the insistence of the Communists on putting up a candidate of their own. In the end the Field-Marshal was helped back into office, against the competing candidatures of Hitler, a Nationalist and a Communist, by the votes of the groups which had opposed his original election! But he bore a grudge against the people who had forced on him this separation from his natural soul-mates and who now brought him under violent criticism by insisting that he agree to ban the paramilitary gangs whom the Nazis called 'storm-troopers'. Intensive and unscrupulous intrigues developed behind the scenes, in which Hindenburg's son Oscar and General von Schleicher, the *éminence grise* of the Reichswehr, played a large part. At the end of May they finally deterred the President from signing any more decree-laws for Brüning, whose Cabinet thereupon resigned. He has been reproached for not showing more fight. But without Reichswehr support, which was highly uncertain, a fight would have been hard to win. All the same, democracy might have survived if as much vigour and confidence had been shown in defending as in attacking it.

Brüning's successor, von Papen, was a Catholic aristocrat and ex-cavalry officer of considerable charm but somewhat dubious reputation, little political experience and less judgement. Schleicher joined him as Defence Minister, with five nobles and two commoners in what became known as the 'Cabinet of the Barons'. Papen had sat in the Prussian Landtag for the Centre but that party refused him its support and he was soon defeated in the Reichstag; a fresh election doubled the strength of the Nazis, slightly increased the Communists and decimated the middle-class parties but failed to solve the problem of where Papen was to find a majority. The stage had been reached at which the only possible alternative to admitting the Nazis to office would have been an attempt to rally against them all the non-Nationalist groups, but the Communist attitude made this impossible. An attempt to run Germany on right-wing lines while excluding the Party with the overwhelming majority of Nationalist votes made no sense and could not last; the Nazis, however, refused the terms which Papen offered. In a further election in November they for the first time lost ground. Schleicher took over as Chancellor in the belief that he could persuade a wing of the Party led by Gregor Strasser, who were inclined to take the 'Socialist' part of their title seriously, to break with Hitler and join the Centre and trade unions in supporting the Government. But Strasser lost his nerve and left the country and Hitler reunited the Party while Schleicher's attempt to develop a social programme lost him the support of the industrialists without gaining that of the unions. If this was how Hitler was to be kept out, Brüning should never have been discarded.

By now it was not a question of whether Hitler should come to power but on what terms. The upper-class Nationalists were divided into those who did not trust him and those who trusted in their own capacity to control him. He reassured the first by promising to use only constitutional methods and thwarted the second by insistence on obtaining the post of Chancellor, even though his votes and his funds showed serious signs of dropping. The initiative in the final negotiations was taken by Papen who felt he had been double-crossed by von Schleicher and wanted revenge. He induced a group of Rhineland businessmen to replenish the Nazi exchequer. On 30 January 1933 the Field-Marshal was finally talked into giving the post of Chancellor to the man whom he described as 'the Bohemian Lance-Corporal' (under the mistaken impression that that was where Hitler had been born). Papen was made Vice-Chancellor to watch him, Hugenberg became Minister of Economics and there were six other Nationalists in a Cabinet of twelve. The plotters failed to realize that with Frick as Nazi

Minister of the Interior, with Göring doubling the newly created post of Air Minister and that of Prime Minister of Prussia and with the Reichswehr under the charge of the crypto-Nazi General von Blomberg, the Nazis effectively controlled the police and the troops.

There has been much subsequent discussion as to who was to blame for letting the Nazis into power. Relatively few people were wholeheartedly in favour of the move, which explains why so many felt able afterwards to deny ever having been Nazis. But a number of groups had for various reasons come to believe (often as the result of adroit propaganda) that such a development could be turned to their advantage. On the other hand there was not really anybody left by 1933 who had both the will and the resources needed to resist. The workers would not do it, as had been shown in July 1932 when Papen turned the Social Democratic Government out of power in Prussia; the view was taken that men demoralized by lack of work and food could not be expected to make a general strike in protest succeed. The Allies would not do it, for they neither accelerated concessions to help Brüning nor denied them to his successors. The Communists had been schooled to believe that a Nazi government would precipitate their own accession to power; they talked of the Social Democrats as 'the moderate wing of Fascism'. The Reichstag was so divided as to be impotent. Army, President and civil service were at best fair-weather friends. Once again Germany had sacrificed liberal values to national ones and once again the result was to be an arrogant misjudgement of national strength which led to disaster. But any reasonable observer is bound to admit that the environment in which Germany had made an attempt at democracy was exceptionally unfavourable.

4

THE THIRD REICH: 1933–1945

THE TOTALITARIAN STATE

Part of the Nazi technique lay in never allowing their competitors a let-up or the German people a dull moment. No sooner was Hitler installed as Chancellor than another election was announced – the third in eight months. The propaganda machine, which now had full access to the radio system, was turned on in full strength (subject only to the discovery that Hitler was a poor speaker in the studio). The Storm-Troopers, 40,000 of whom were taken on as auxiliaries by the Prussian police, were let loose in the streets. We are unlikely ever to know for certain how the Reichstag building was set on fire on the night of 27 February; it is perfectly possible that the half-witted Dutchman found inside really did the job on his own. What is beyond dispute is the energy with which the Nazis exploited the supposed Communist conspiracy. On the following day, Hindenburg was induced to sign an emergency decree suspending many of the vital personal liberties, authorizing the Reich Government to interfere in the Länder and making death the penalty for a number of crimes.

But when the election came on 5 March, the result was far from being the triumph which was represented: 13 million out of 32 million voted for democratic parties and the Communists lost no more than nineteen seats; the Nazis won only 43.7 per cent of the poll and were left relying on the Nationalists for a majority in the Reichstag. When it met, the Deputies were presented with an Enabling Bill which would for five years authorize the Chancellor, without reference to the President and irrespective of what might be said in the Constitution, to issue laws on any subject he chose. Only one Deputy (a Social Democrat) spoke against it and only Social Democrats voted against it (the Communists having already been proscribed). Hitler thus made himself dictator by legal methods while the Reichstag abdicated its functions and henceforward met only at intervals to be harangued.

'Co-ordination' (*Gleichschaltung*) now became the catch-phrase of the day and, as its visual symbol, the Swastika flag waved everywhere. (The black, white and red colours recovered their place from the black, red and gold.) The Nazis worked on the principle that all institutions and activities inside the state must be made to serve the purposes of the dominant group; many middle-class professional organizations had been infiltrated already. Germany, long inclined to authoritarian rule, now became totalitarian: sleep was said to be the only thing left private. The Party professed its intention of taking over the state. Reich Commissioners had been put into a number of Länder after the Reichstag fire but on 7 April they were replaced by Reich Governors; the man chosen for this post was usually the Party leader for the area (*Gau*) corresponding most closely to the Land in question. Papen found himself replaced by Göring in Prussia. Germany thus became for the first time a thoroughly centralized state; totalitarianism could not tolerate local freedom.

So it was in almost all aspects of life. On 11 March Goebbels, one of the most talented but unscrupulous publicists who ever lived, was added to the Cabinet as Minister for Public Enlightenment and Propaganda. He proceeded to organize a 'Reich Chamber of Culture' with subsidiaries covering all forms of publicity and the arts. Persons who were not accepted as members were forbidden to engage in any activity within its field. Editors were told what to say, even where to print the news. A number of papers were left in apparent independence, to conciliate people whose opposition might be dangerous and to impress the outside world but in due course they were nearly all acquired secretly by one of several Nazi holding companies. The press as a result acquired a dull uniformity and wits adapted a current slogan to run 'One Reich, one Führer, one Paper!'

The unions were dissolved and replaced by the German Labour Front. Farmers were organized in the Reich Food Estate, schoolmasters in the Teachers League, women in the *Frauenschaft*, youth in the *Hitler Jugend*, sport under the *Reichssportleiter*. University senates were no longer allowed to choose their own Rectors but had to accept the Minister's nominee, while for the first time Germany acquired a single Minister of Education responsible for the whole country. (Of 7,758 university teachers in 1932, 1,145 had been dismissed by 1934.) The police force was also unified by being subordinated to the SS. The German people were thus left with the choice of falling into line by joining the organization appropriate to their work or endangering their livelihood. But those who had the choice were in one sense fortunate, for it was not open to Communists or other known opponents of the regime, while the supposed superiority of the Aryan race led to all Jews being deprived of public positions and severely limited in their private activities. The ordinary prisons were inadequate to hold the numbers detained for political reasons and 'concentration camps' were established to accommodate them; these, though not yet slaughterhouses, soon earned an ugly reputation.

A number of Nazi leaders were put into official posts, as the simplest way of giving legal authority to their actions, but a system which relied as much as the German one did on the letter of the law could be run only by people trained for the purpose. There were many other positions needing skills which too few Party members possessed. The result was a two-way process of absorption. The abler Nazis were taken into the official machine but at the same time many officials joined the Party – often being required to do so as a condition of holding their jobs. If the Party took over the state and particularly the Police, the state went a long way to taking over the Party. But this meant that the regime was served, as the Republic had been, by a number of people who were only fair-weather friends.

The principle of leadership (*Führerprinzip*) laid down that decisions should come downwards from the top, but the Third Reich was no exception to the rule of all bureaucracies that problems for decision are put up from below. Hitler, however, disliked the desk-work involved in studying issues. Unless he had strong views of his own, he preferred to stand aside until it became clear which point of view would come out on top whereupon he endorsed it. In the end, he had about forty-two executive bodies reporting directly to him (though some had little to do). Everyone had a rival against whom he sought to get the Leader's support. Thus although Goebbels was supposed to be in charge of propaganda, Dietrich, Ammann and Rosenberg had independent responsibilities in various parts of the field. The Foreign Office was till 1938 duplicated by the Ribbentrop Bureau. The Ministry of Economics had after 1936 to compete with Göring as Commissioner for the Four-Year Plan, which itself went far to supersede the Army Economic Office. Frick, as Minister of the Interior, struggled with Himmler for control of the police. The Army's exclusive authority was increasingly challenged by the SS Black Guards. The Cabinet never met after February 1938; its secretary once suggested inviting its members to gather for a drink but the idea was forbidden as too dangerous. The net result has been described as 'calculated chaos'. As time went on, decisions were taken more and more haphazardly, with the help of whoever happened to be around; often they were left to one of Hitler's four secretariats. At first this did not matter too much, since the Nazis never embarked on a serious programme of administrative reform at home and things were much more orderly in the military sphere, but the lack of system proved more of a handicap during the war when the home front came under strain. It is curious that a country which can organize so well lower down should twice over have organized so badly at the top!

In industry the principles of leadership were applied to establish a planned economy much on Communist lines, though mainly managed by capitalists. Each concern was told what to produce at what price and issued with the necessary raw materials. Instead of decisions about output being taken in relation to consumer demand as expressed in prices, the demand which was effective was that backed by government order. 'Small businesses were bullied into *Gleichschaltung*, big business was bribed' (D. Schoenbaum, *Hitler's Social Revolution*, p. 130).

The result was that, after some early months of enthusiasm, few people were wholly content. Old-established but incompetent Party members found themselves with little to do. Instead of small businesses having the economic system reorganized for their benefit, the trends to large-scale industry were reinforced, partly to conciliate the tycoons, partly in preparation for war. All those concerned with institutions and spheres which were being co-ordinated resented the pressure put on them and the loss of autonomy. The great and good disliked the flattery lavished on the small man (to distract his attention from what was not happening) and the need to deal on an equal footing with men of humble origins. The lawyers and all who had been brought up to revere the principles of the Rechtsstaat watched with growing concern the tendency of Nazi tribunals and judges to make their own law. The technicians and administrators were increasingly disturbed by the confusion and corruption which Nazi methods encouraged but feared that, if they refused their collaboration, things would only get worse. Those who had looked for an improvement in the Republic's rather libertarian standards of public life were fobbed off with the excuse that they were being unreasonable in expecting this to happen while a revolution was in progress. At the outset many, remembering what had gone before and swayed by insidious arguments dinned into their ears, were anxious to give the regime a fair trial. Later they hesitated to turn against leaders who had had so much success in economic and foreign policy. Time was needed for members of a legalistically minded society to realize that resistance to the legal order might be justifiable on moral grounds. Thus the Nazi leaders succeeded not only in giving Germany once again the unity needed for effective action but also in maintaining this for ten years on what was seldom more than a provisional basis.

In any case an individual who was shocked by the cruelty, the violence and the denial of human rights (as were too few) could not find much positive action to take beyond circulating information discreetly and giving surreptitious aid to victims. Reliable knowledge was hard to come by (though rumours abounded), all organizations were being drawn into the Nazi net, the police were ubiquitous, informers frequent and all channels of communication liable to be watched. Germans did not have to know exactly what went on in concentration camps in order to fight shy of being sent to one. The most that developed was a distinctive type of activity better described by the German word *Widerstand* than as 'Opposition' or 'Resistance'. To any person not directly attacked, the temptation to go along with the regime on account of its redeeming features was strong. Even when it became apparent that Germany had got into the hands of megalomaniac gangsters who would stop at nothing, there seemed tragically little that any ordinary decent person could do about it. Many of Germany's best and most gifted citizens, including Albert Einstein and Thomas Mann, saw no tolerable course other than emigration. Of the scientists who did so, nineteen were to win Nobel prizes.

The problem was well illustrated by the Churches. The Party expected to 'co-ordinate' both Catholics and Protestants with no more difficulty than had been experienced in the professions and universities. The Evangelical (Protestant) Churches had always been conservatively inclined and susceptible to both nationalism and anti-semitism. There was a widespread desire to unite the twenty-eight Land churches into a single nation-wide institution. Some theologians had flirted with the idea of a 'German Christianity' which would eliminate what were considered to be Semitic elements introduced into Christian beliefs by 'the Rabbi Paul' and others! Consequently elections to a Synod for a new National Church resulted in a majority favouring its foundation. But when the practical implications became evident in the shape of personalities and doctrines, many pastors were driven in revulsion to band together under Martin Niemöller in a defensive 'Confessing Church'.

The struggle between this Church and the regime lasted throughout the Third Reich. Numbers of pastors, including Niemöller, went to prison or concentration camps; not a few were executed. Both sides became increasingly convinced of the impossibility of serving two ultimate masters. The Party abandoned little by little its effort to use the Churches for its own purposes and started instead to drive them to the wall by financial and legal measures. By 1939 these methods had achieved considerable success. Thereafter a tacit truce was observed. The Party judged it inopportune to alienate the many believers among the armed forces by open persecution but used the emergencies of war to justify such steps as the requisitioning of Church property and the Church leaders were anxious not to lose sympathy by appearing unpatriotic.

The story with the Catholics was not radically different. The Papal Secretary of State (from 1939 Pope as Pius XII) had been Nuncio in Germany from 1917 to 1929 and there acquired a profound fear of Communism. The traditions of the Church inclined it to sympathize with an authoritarian rather than a liberal regime. Papen soon tempted the Vatican with the offer of a Concordat on a Reich basis, something which had been long desired but hitherto ruled out by Socialist opposition. The price paid for its signature in July 1933 was the abandonment of the Centre Party and withdrawal of the Church from all political activities. The terms, had they been kept, would have assured the Church freedom for worship, education and social activity, as well as the safeguarding of its personnel against molestation. But the Nazis regarded promises as tools to be discarded as soon as their purpose had been served, and a stream of Church protests, culminating in March 1937 in the encyclical *Mit brennender Sorge* (which had to be smuggled into the pulpits) resulted only in tactics of gradual erosion being substituted for more direct methods. The existence of a Concordat made official resistance more difficult for fear of giving the Government a pretext for denouncing it and made unofficial resistance more difficult out of respect for the hierarchy. After 1941 the Catholic dilemma became acute and could have been resolved only by a compromise peace since either a Communist or a Nazi victory seemed bound to be won at the Church's expense.

There was, however, one institution in Germany which did succeed for a long time in retaining its independence. That was the Reichswehr, still Prussian dominated; enrolment in it was once described as 'the aristocratic form of emigration' (G. Behn, Letter of 12 August 1949). For the only hope of security against the Nazis lay in superior and organized force. The Navy, which had always been more nationalist, and the Air Force, which owed its existence to the new regime, proved more susceptible to influence. Envious eyes were indeed cast on the soldiers' independence and not least by the Storm-Troopers under their leader Röhm. By 1934 these rowdies had largely lost their function. As soon as everything had been co-ordinated, there was little left to bully or break up. But the brown-shirts hankered for something to do, they hankered for a second Socialist revolution, they hankered to turn the aristocrats out of the officer corps and convert the Reichswehr into a people's army. They pressed the Führer to agree to their plans.

They were not Hitler's only difficulty. There was widespread dissatisfaction among his Nationalist allies over the way he had treated them as tools. As early as June 1933 Hugenberg had allowed himself to be provoked into resignation. The Nationalist private army, the *Stahlhelm*, was manoeuvred into impotence about the same time. Even the vestiges of the Freikorps were showered with plaudits but seen off the stage. Papen found himself increasingly on the outside. In a speech at Marburg in June 1934, with the encouragement of Hindenburg, he allowed words to be put into his mouth which criticized the Party's excesses and called for a restoration of the monarchy. When Goebbels suppressed the speech, Papen took the matter to Hindenburg. Hitler got there before him, only to be received by von Blomberg whose demeanour was for once too firm to merit his usual nickname of 'rubber lion'.

What made the situation acute was that Hindenburg's life was running out. The conservatives planned to use his death as the occasion for bringing in one of the Kaiser's grandsons as Emperor. Hitler had no intention of being edged out in this way and planned to succeed the President himself. With the encouragement of Göring and Himmler (who was emerging as the man behind the SS Black Guards), he did a deal by which Reichswehr support for such an arrangement was traded for the virtual liquidation of the Storm-Troops. Hitler's side of the bargain was fulfilled on 30 June in 'The Night of the Long Knives' when Röhm and over 100 people were summarily done away with on charges of immorality and plotting. The opportunity was taken to settle old scores and remove men with inconvenient knowledge such as von Schleicher; one innocent music critic was shot by thugs who mistook him for somebody else of the same name. Papen was allowed to escape with his life and go as ambassador to Austria. Hitler told the Reichstag that for an hour of crisis he had become Chief Justice for the German People, thereby shocking all those who expected men to be executed only after having been found guilty by due process of law. But the pay-off came five weeks later when Hindenburg died and all the armed forces obeyed the order to take an oath of personal allegiance to Hitler as Führer and Chancellor (the title of President being allowed to lapse).

The full consequences of this change were only gradually revealed. The generals were progressively disabused of the idea that their independence had been safeguarded. It was true that they were rid of Röhm and the Storm-Troopers, who soon ceased to have any practical purpose at all. But they found that the beneficiaries of this elimination were Himmler and the SS, who constituted much more formidable rivals. To go on with, they had bound themselves (and oaths meant much in German military tradition) to someone who was going to insist on being his own strategist. This connection was drawn closer in February 1938 when von Blomberg inadvertently married a barmaid of dubious reputation. Göring and Himmler, and possibly Hitler, knew of the lady's antecedents before they attended the ceremony, and encouraged Blomberg to dig his own grave in the hope of benefiting themselves, Göring by becoming Minister of Defence. After Blomberg had been forced to resign, the secret police trumped up a charge of homosexuality against his obvious successor General von Fritsch (by persuading a man who had been blackmailing a Major von Frisch that he had got the name wrong). The way was thus clear for Hitler (and not Göring) to annex to himself the job of Commander-in-Chief of the three defence forces, or *Wehrmacht* as they came to be called collectively.

An expansionist solution to Germany's economic ills had been ruled out under the Republic for fear of the effect it would have on public confidence in the Mark and on the balance of payments. But Hitler cared nothing for economic orthodoxy and called back Dr Schacht to provide expert ingenuity, making him Minister of Economics on Hugenberg's resignation. Gleichschaltung was then extended to the monetary system. All payments to and from foreign countries were put under control and a network of clearing agreements negotiated with individual countries. Germany's creditors and those who wanted to sell non-essential goods to her were given the choice between taking most or all of their payment in kind, or in blocked (i.e. unconvertible) Marks, or going without. So keen were foreign producers to find markets that most of them put up with this treatment.

At home the abandonment of deflation enabled the Government to spend or stimulate capital investment on rearmament, industrial expansion and public works, of which the motorways (*Autobahnen*) are the most notable monument. The benefits of this expenditure were felt throughout the economy at a time when natural forces were anyhow coming into play to reverse the depression. By 1937 GNP per head had risen 10 per cent over

1929. Moreover Hitler not only kept more men in a variety of uniforms but also created in the Labour Service (*Reichsarbeitsdienst*) (which like the Autobahnen was an idea started on a small scale in the Republic) a system by which all young men between 18 and 25 were required to work for six months on projects of general benefit to the community such as afforestation or land drainage. These various measures explain why unemployment fell to 3.8 million by the end of 1933 and went lower thereafter. Its reduction was a considerable feather in the Nazi cap.

There has been considerable argument as to how much German recovery owed to rearmament. No doubt the 1935 increase in the size of the Reichswehr to 350,000, the manufacture of equipment for thirty-six divisions, the creation of an air force and the building of plants for making synthetic rubber and oil (to reduce Germany's vulnerability to blockade) all played a part. Göring once told the public that they must choose between guns and butter. But that was largely ulterior decoration. Hitler was then and for long afterwards frightened of alienating the masses by asking them for too heavy sacrifices; in practice they got both guns and butter. The Four-Year Plan for Industry, issued in August 1936, was intended to ensure that, in the conflict for priorities, guns did not lose out. The result was to exacerbate that conflict. At the end of 1937 Schacht resigned on the grounds that the demands being made on the economy exceeded its resources. By 1939 supplies of foreign currencies were virtually exhausted. Germany went to war with her stocks of raw materials so low that the British Ministry of Economic Warfare could not believe the figures which they had obtained and doubled them. One of the reasons for Hitler's aggressive activities in 1938–9 may have been the need to extricate himself from an awkward corner.

THE BLUFFS THAT SUCCEEDED

Hitler had absorbed the ideas of the geopoliticians according to which great states need to command large areas as sources of supply and markets. He intended to find these primarily in the east. But on coming to power he and his colleagues were well aware of Germany's weaknesses. His problem was how to head off other states from intervening to overthrow him while those weaknesses were being remedied. This dilemma was handled with great skill. Human inertia, fear of war, desire for fairness, fear of Communism, international jealousies and personal vanities were exploited at appropriate moments. Coups were staged when public attention was otherwise occupied and notably on Saturday mornings. Much was made of the wrongs done to Germany; solemn professions of peaceful intentions alternated with unilateral acts of defiance. The very secrecy surrounding German rearmament was exaggerated to convey the impression that she was already more dangerous than the facts warranted.

For a fair judgement on the reaction of other countries, certain considerations must be remembered. It had long been a principle of international affairs that a country's internal politics were its own concern with which outside states should not meddle. People were widely afraid of another war, expecting aerial bombardment in particular to be even more devastating than it proved. The course of events since 1918 had disillusioned them about the advantage of winning a war. There was a widespread desire to learn from history and avoid repeating what were taken to have been the mistakes of 1914, 1919 and 1923. Those who most loathed National Socialism were also the people most likely to admit that it was to some extent the product of other countries' actions. Materialist interpretations of history were in vogue and people hoped, by adopting more generous policies, to bring Hitler to a more reasonable frame of mind or, if that was not possible, to induce better Germans to overthrow him. Where they went wrong, of course, was in failing to understand that only superior force could deflect a man so bent on world power, that internal resistance was unlikely to occur except in conjunction with external resistance (if then) and that promises did not mean the same to Nazis as to most of us. People of good will were gradually driven to the realization that there was no satisfactory alternative to the use of force. But by the time that happened, the amount of force needed was considerable and the experience underlying the realization had generated a cold exasperation which boded ill for Germany.

There is little to be gained by lingering over most of the steps on the road. A conciliatory speech by Hitler on 13 May 1933 was followed in October by Germany's withdrawal from the Geneva Disarmament Conference and the League of Nations, which went unpunished. In January 1934 the Poles, whose apprehension had been considerable, were pleasantly surprised by the offer of a non-aggression pact. Not only did they fall for this but also they allowed the new intimacy for a time to put into the background their older links with France. Later that year, however, Hitler made his first mistake. In between the Night of the Long Knives and the death of Hindenburg, the Austrian Nazis were allowed to attempt a rising in Vienna. The job was bungled and the attempt failed. Mussolini massed troops on the Austro-Italian frontier and gave every sign of being prepared to cross it if the Germans moved. Hitler's quick repudiation of any such intention showed that this was language which he understood but he for his part learnt a lesson in the importance of thorough preparation.

In March 1935 Hitler officially admitted that Germany possessed the air force forbidden to her by the Versailles Treaty. When the world showed little excitement over something which it had come to take for granted, he went on to announce plans for an enlarged conscript army. This left open the question of the fleet, which had been forbidden to possess ships of more than 10,000 tons or more than 25,000 men. Britain with considerable distaste began to prepare for a return to naval competition. Her relief can be imagined when she was offered a promise to limit new German building to 35 per cent of her own level and an agreement authorizing the Nazis to break the Peace Treaty up to this level was quickly concluded. The price was estrangement from France and Italy (who on Nazi insistence had been left unconsulted) and the gift to Hitler of a propaganda success as great as that involved in the Concordat; of course the document was valueless since, once the Germans felt capable of building beyond its limits, they would have found a pretext for denouncing it (as they did in 1939). All the same, the German Navy was not in a position by the time war came to wage it effectively against Britain.

The winter of 1935/6 was occupied by Mussolini's Abyssinian campaign and his dispute with the League of Nations. This suited Hitler excellently for, if Mussolini came out on top, the chances of the League being invoked against Germany later would be reduced, while if the League won, Mussolini would no longer be able to protect Austria; the actual outcome combined both results. The failure to get sanctions made effective led to recriminations inside France and Britain as well as between the two countries. Germany was thus given the opportunity in March 1936 to send her troops into the demilitarized zone along the Rhine. As long as such a zone existed, she could not undertake any action in the east without being vulnerable in the west. The moment was therefore the last at which Britain and France could have intervened to overthrow Nazism with relative ease. Had they marched, the Germans would have withdrawn. But they were taken by surprise and obsessed with uncomfortable memories of the passive resistance which had greeted the French in the Ruhr in 1923. Hitler's bluff, which had caused his generals much anxiety, met with nothing more serious than protests. In the circumstances, it would not have been surprising if, in the plebiscite which he organized, the 99 per cent of the German voters who were said to have expressed approval actually did so.

The Führer had all along recognized that allies would be an asset in the process of achieving predominance. The ally he would have liked was Britain; he considered the Kaiser's biggest mistake to have been challenging Britain and Russia at the same time. But such an alliance would suit him only if Britain were prepared to let Germany become supreme in Europe, and much as Britain shrank from paying the price of preventing such supremacy, the cost of not preventing it would be finding herself at the mercy of a regime which she profoundly mistrusted. She took time over making up her mind and Hitler had to be content instead with exploiting Italy's isolation and the apparent similarity of the two political systems. Mussolini was gratified and in November 1936 described the relationship between the two countries as 'not a diaphragm but an axis'. During the Spanish Civil War of 1936–9 the two dictators, in common with Stalin, treated their signature of non-intervention agreements as scraps of paper. While most of the troops sent were Italian, the Germans used the peninsular as a testing-ground for their new weapons: they must have found the performance of their dive-bombers in devastating the town of Guernica in April 1937 encouraging. But the closer Mussolini drew to Hitler, the harder did it become for him to stand up for his interests in Austria and the Balkans.

On 5 November 1937 Hitler expounded to his Chiefs of Staff and Foreign Minister his plans for the future. The size and density of Germany's population gave her in his view the right to a greater living-space than she possessed. Self-sufficiency was impossible, dependence on imported supplies too dangerous. Her future was therefore conditional on obtaining more space in Europe. The history of all ages proved that expansion could be carried out only by breaking down resistance and taking risks. Two hate-filled enemies, Britain and France, stood in the way. Neither was invincible but must be considered, along with Russia, as 'power factors in our calculations'. Provided he lived long enough, it was his unshakeable determination to solve Germany's space problem by 1943–5 at the latest. In certain circumstances he might move as early as 1938. The process of rearmament was already approaching completion so that soon the position would begin to deteriorate. The first target must be the overthrow of Austria and Czechoslovakia, to prevent an attack from the rear in the event of trouble in the west. Neither Britain nor France would intervene.

The Führer's audience was horrified, not so much at the thought of war as at the thought that the war might be one which Germany could not win. But when they told Hitler this, his reaction was to remove them from their posts; this was the reason behind the fall of Blomberg and Fritsch (see p. 60). The French Ambassador described the occasion as 'a dry thirtieth of June'. Within a week of taking over as Commander-in-Chief, Hitler summoned Dr Schuschnigg, the Chancellor of Austria, and browbeat him into taking two Nazis into his Cabinet. Schuschnigg was in a weak position. His predecessor had crushed the Austrian Social Democrats instead of making allies of them. The police and army were so riddled with Nazis as to be unreliable. Mussolini had written Austria off. The British and French publics, unenlightened as to strategic considerations, saw no reason why the Germans in Austria should be prevented from joining their fellow-nationals if they wanted to, and were certainly not prepared to adopt the only course by which this might have been prevented, namely war.

Schuschnigg, however, declared that he would hold a plebiscite to decide whether the Austrians wanted to give up their independence. The Nazis were not prepared to risk a negative answer; their own answer was to send their troops across the frontier. When the plebiscite was held a month later, 99.7 per cent of the population were said to have voted to join the Reich. Meanwhile the Vienna Nazis expended their prejudices on the city's 180,000 Jews.

It was now the turn of Czechoslovakia. Although the capture of Austria put the head of that country into the tiger's jaws that head was protected all round by fortified mountain barriers and by a well-equipped, well-trained army of thirty-five divisions. But Czechoslovakia had inherited from Habsburg days – and indeed even earlier – a weakness which was to prove fatal. In the 'Sudetenland', it contained over 3 million people speaking German, most of whom lived close to the German frontier. These people had not been badly treated since they lost their old predominance to the Czechs in 1919, but they resented being ruled by those on whom they had previously looked down. Hitler had for long been fanning their dissatisfaction and by 1935 the Sudeten German Party, which voiced their claims, had become the strongest in the country. He now set out to exploit their supposed grievances, not with the object of getting those grievances alleviated but of making the world, and particularly the British and French publics, think that the Czechs were in the wrong. In May 1938 he decided to 'smash Czechoslovakia' by military action before October. When he conveyed this decision to the generals, they were once again horrified. Not only did they seriously doubt whether the thirty-six divisions which they had available could break through the Czech fortifications but also they could obtain the troops which they did propose to use only by reducing to thirteen divisions those left in the west for keeping out some fifty-six French ones. If the French moved (and they were bound by treaty to come to the help of the Czechs) they could not possibly be held up. General Beck, the Army Chief-of-Staff, was so disturbed that he resigned his post in mid-August: his successor Halder then worked out plans to seize Hitler as soon as the order to attack Czechoslovakia was finally given. Information about these plans was conveyed to the British Government which was implored to stand firm.

Hitler welcomed Beck's departure though he did not think fit to make it public. He was convinced that he could bluff the Western Powers out of acting, and by a chain of events culminating in the Munich Conference on 29 September, this was precisely what he achieved. He was deprived for the time being, to his annoyance, of the pleasure of actually marching into Prague but he secured without war the handing-over to Germany of all the Sudeten German areas, with which went the Czech ability to put up a successful fight later. The British Government under Chamberlain was sceptical about the Czech ability to resist and about the will of the German generals to rebel. It had only two divisions ready to send to the Continent. It suspected that the French would not have their hearts in a war and knew that the rest of the Commonwealth would not. It vastly exaggerated the likelihood of German air raids and the damage which they could do; crucial improvements in the defences against them were due to become available in the next twelve months. Being unsure itself, it could give no clear lead to the public, which was deeply divided. A promise by Hitler that this would be his 'last territorial demand' inclined it to give him the benefit of the doubt. The French agreed with relief and Mussolini provided a way out of a last-minute impasse. The Czechs were compelled by their allies to accept a surrender worked out over their heads.

THE BLUFF THAT WAS CALLED

For the first time since the Middle Ages, virtually all the German-speaking people in Central Europe (except for Switzerland) were now united in a state of 80 million people. But what Hitler failed to realize in his self-satisfaction was that, as far as the British people were concerned, he had exhausted his credit and their patience. Events in the following months did nothing to make them better disposed towards Germany. In November the murder of a German diplomat in Paris by a Jew with a grievance was used as an excuse for an attack on Jews throughout Germany, in which some were killed, many arrested and much property destroyed. In the past, anti-Jewish violence had mostly been perpetrated unofficially while police looked the other way; the 'Crystal Night' (so-called because of the broken shop-windows) was the first large-scale operation to be officially engineered and its execution whetted appetites.

The rump of Czechoslovakia had been divided, at Nazi instigation, into three provinces. When in March 1939 two of these tried to break away from the third, Dr Hacha, who had become President after Munich, dismissed their governments and proclaimed martial law. For this, he was ordered to Berlin and there compelled to advise his people not to resist the occupation of their country by German troops. This 'Rape of Czechoslovakia' so shocked the world that the seizure of Memel from Lithuania five days later went almost unnoticed. But Hitler had taken a more momentous step than he realized, for his action could no longer be justified on the principle of 'national self-determination' while it showed that his remark about having no more 'territorial demands' had been a lie. He thus demonstrated that there was no knowing where he would stop, since nothing he said could be trusted. Britain could not risk letting such a man dominate the Continent, no matter what the cost of stopping him might be.

The British Government's response was to promise all possible support to Poland should that country's independence be threatened. France was already pledged to such a course by treaty. The British promise, of course, made strategic nonsense. The Polish Army was bigger than the Czech but less well-equipped and the Polish frontiers were harder to defend. There was no easy way of getting British or French troops to Poland. The only effective method of protecting Poland against Germany would have been to secure for the Poles the help of the Russians, but the Russian price was permission to annex the Baltic states of Estonia, Latvia and Lithuania, while the Poles refused to let the Russians into their country for fear of having it turned Communist.

The British change of policy did not deter Hitler; even if she were on this occasion to live up to her warnings and fight (a contingency about which his expectations fluctuated), she would not have time to make her power felt. On 3 April he ordered his generals to be ready by 1 September to seize Danzig and destroy Polish military strength. On 28 April he made a speech in which he ridiculed President Roosevelt's proposals for preventing war and tore up the Polish-German Treaty of 1934 as well as the Anglo-German Naval Treaty of 1935. In May a formal military Alliance – the 'Pact of Steel' – was signed with Italy. But the Führer had few illusions about the quality of the metal, realizing that Italy's pro-German policy was mainly due to Mussolini, who was most unwilling to go to war. Hitler had a much larger fish on the line and finally landed it on 23 August when the conclusion of a non-aggression Pact between Germany and Russia caused a sensation. How could a party which had always proclaimed Bolshevism to be one of its greatest enemies, which along with Italy and Japan was a signatory to an anti-Comintern Pact, bring itself to make terms with the leader of world Communism? Had the Russians lost their senses for them to join hands with people pledged to destroy them?

Hitler of course never intended the Pact to be lasting. But for the time being it secured him against Russian interference while he dealt with Poland. Stalin was unlikely to have been under any delusions about Hitler's good faith. But the Pact contained a secret clause dividing Eastern Europe into spheres of influence and assigning to Russia Finland, Estonia, Latvia, Eastern Poland and Bessarabia. If Russian influence could be established in these countries, the Germans, should they break their word, would have all the more hostile territory to cross before they reached Russia proper. Stalin may also have hoped that the attack on Poland would embroil Hitler with Britain and France, that the resulting war would weaken both sides to Russia's benefit, and that a Nazi attack on the Soviet Union would thus be postponed, perhaps for ever. The Pact cost the Kremlin nothing except the loyalty of a few (but by no means all) European Communists.

With Russia's neutrality in his pocket, Hitler might have been expected to hesitate no longer. Indeed he told his generals on 22 August that his only fear was an attempt to mediate by some *Schweinhund*. Yet the reasoning which made Stalin want Britain to fight made Hitler want her to be neutral and he held up the attack on Poland for a week in the hope of finding her an excuse for remaining so. But the minimum British condition was the abandonment of the attack and they would not even put pressure on the Poles to accept specious proposals of Hitler's about coming to Berlin to negotiate. The date-line of 1 September fixed in the military timetable arrived without anything having been settled and only when the troops were already moving did the Nazis produce a reasonable set of terms which they declared would have been offered to the Poles supposing that negotiations had ever begun. Once the Polish frontier had been violated, the British refused to consider any proposal for mediation unless Germany agreed to withdraw again. This Hitler would not dream of doing and so on 3 September Britain reluctantly declared war, leaving an even more reluctant France with no honourable alternative but to follow suit.

EUROPE AT HIS FEET

Thanks to the unprecedented way in which the Wehrmacht exploited the internal combustion engine, the campaign in Poland was over before the French had had time to move (supposing that they had wished to do so) and almost before the Russians had had time to seize their share of the spoils. The German Air Force had never in fact had any plans for bombing Britain and little active fighting took place in the west. On 6 October Hitler, in a victorious speech to the Reichstag, proposed to Britain and France that they should make peace on the basis of the new frontiers. But before they had had time to consider the proposal (which they rejected) he had ordered his generals to make plans for an attack on France through Luxembourg, Belgium and Holland. When told to be ready by mid-November, the Army leaders were so alarmed as once again to consider removing him. Neither party carried out its intentions. The starting date for the operation was postponed fourteen times and the winter was chiefly remarkable for a naval action which led to a German 'Pocket Battleship' (i.e. one designed to fall under the limit of 10,000 tons) scuttling itself in South America and a bitter northern war which led the Russians to think that they had ensured the subservience of the Finns.

The coming of spring brought a dramatic end to the 'phoney' war. On 8 April the British Navy violated Norwegian neutrality by laying mines in channels which the Germans were using for ships bringing iron ore from Sweden. Next day the German Navy violated Norwegian neutrality by landing troops without warning at six of the country's ports. Denmark was also invaded. Five of the ports were taken without difficulty but at Oslo plans miscarried. The King and Cabinet managed to get away and refused all suggestions that they should surrender. For the last ten days of April small British and French forces endeavoured to help in resistance but the Germans had gained too big a start. At the end of the month the effort was abandoned as hopeless, the King and Ministers were evacuated to Britain and Norway left to the traitor Quisling and a German commissar. Only at Narvik, inside the Arctic Circle, did fighting go on for another month until events elsewhere made withdrawal inevitable. The loss not only impaired the British blockade but also facilitated German naval operations.

Then on 10 May the assault on the West was launched. Belgium, Luxembourg and the Netherlands were entered without notice. In addition to the techniques which had overwhelmed Poland, parachutists, gliders and airborne troops were used to create confusion and leap over obstacles like rivers and forts. An air raid on Rotterdam killed some 900 civilians while negotiations for surrender were already under way. Concern for their own neutrality had kept the Belgian and Dutch Governments from having more than the most superficial contacts with the French and British and though the armies of the latter now raced forwards to their aid, the effort was partly responsible for the disaster which followed.

For the Germans had calculated that the enemy would expect them to repeat their 1914 strategy by which the main weight of the attack was concentrated on the right wing and used in a wide encircling movement through the Low Countries. This had indeed been their original intention and plans for such an operation had come into Allied hands in January. But later on Hitler had adopted a new and daring scheme proposed by General von Manstein. Four days after the original invasion, when the British had had time to rush to their left flank, a concentrated force of armoured divisions, supported by motorized infantry, fell upon the French centre, although the hilly nature of the country was supposed to make it unsuited to tanks. The Allies in fact had more tanks but were not able to deploy them or prevent the Germans from reaching the sea on 20 May. Though the Dutch had to stop fighting on 15 May, the Belgian, British and French forces managed to halt the German right wing east of Brussels but this achievement was rendered futile when they were taken in the rear. The German spearhead moved rapidly north along the coast, took Boulogne, surrounded Calais and by 24 May stood poised outside Dunkirk for the final kill.

At that point it was halted by Hitler, with the approval of its commander, General von Rundstedt, for what appear to have been a variety of reasons. One was to keep the tanks intact for later use against the main French Army further south. The second was Göring's desire to secure for his air force (*Luftwaffe*) the credit for the final act. The third was the belief that anything left after the air force had finished could be 'mopped up' by ordinary infantry. But finally Hitler was reluctant to bring Britain to her knees. All he wanted from her was an acknowledgement (presumably by a government more friendly than that just formed by Churchill) of Germany's position on the Continent. To destroy the British Empire would in his view benefit 'not Germany but only Japan, the United States and others'. His air force, however, in face of bad weather and British fighters, fell down on its assignment and, to the surprise of the High Command accustomed to think in terms of land warfare, the British succeeded in evacuating nearly the whole of their troops, the essential trained nucleus on which a new army was to be built, as well as many of the French. The Germans had to be content with the capture of 40,000 French, quantities of equipment and the surrender on 28 May of the Belgians, on the orders of King Leopold against the advice of his Cabinet.

On 5 June, the morning after the last British troops had left Dunkirk, the Germans launched the final phase of the campaign by attacking the remaining French forces further south. These were demoralized and outclassed and were soon in full retreat. Paris fell on 14 June and three days later Marshal Pétain, the new Prime Minister, asked for an armistice. It was given to his delegates on 20 June on the same spot, and indeed in the same restaurant-car, as the Allied terms had been handed to Erzberger in November 1918. The German terms were now no more merciful. Not only were Alsace and Lorraine taken back but also the whole of the north and west of France was to be occupied. Her fleet was to be disarmed to keep it out of British hands. All prisoners were to remain in German custody till the war ended (which proved a more serious stipulation than anyone imagined at the time) and all anti-Nazi refugees were to be handed over. Nothing was said about reparations – the Germans proceeded to take what they wanted. Mussolini, who had waited to declare war until 11 June, had managed to get hold of only a small strip of frontier territory and that was all he was allowed to keep.

Hitler had thus succeeded in less than six weeks in an even greater achievement than the one which had eluded the Hohenzollerns. The whole of Western Europe from the North Cape to the Spanish frontier, from Memel to Trieste, lay at his feet and the lands to the south-west and south-east looked likely to do his bidding. Only Britain stood out and nobody in Europe thought Britain could resist much longer – few even of the British saw how they could ever reverse his success. This he had brought about with the help of German enthusiasm, German efficiency and German resources – but very largely by his own intuition and against expert advice. Even those of his countrymen who still disapproved of him felt unable to withhold respect, while an American who saw him at the French surrender described his face as being 'afire with scorn, anger, hate, revenge and triumph' (W. Shirer, *The Rise and Fall of the Third Reich*, p. 97).

THE LONG ROAD BACK

Hitler and his generals never seem to have considered that they might have to invade Britain and had made few plans or preparations for doing so. For an invasion to succeed, the attacker had to command two out of the three elements. The Germans were supreme on land and if their troops could be got across the Channel, would have made quick work of the British Army. But the British were supreme at sea, particularly as the Germans had suffered heavy losses in the Norwegian campaign. Britain's warships were, however, vulnerable to air-attack, while airborne forces could be used as advance troops provided that they could be quickly reinforced by sea-borne ones. But to use aircraft for either of these purposes would be risky as long as the British had fighters available with which to attack them. Everything therefore turned on the air and here Göring set out to show the Luftwaffe's superiority; although his losses were all along heavier than those of the Royal Air Force, he might have succeeded had he concentrated his attacks on the British fighter aircraft, control centres and radar stations. But not only did the Germans fail to appreciate the extent to which radar and 'Ultra' (intelligence obtained by breaking the codes of intercepted signals) were combining to give the enemy advance knowledge of their movements; at the crucial moment their attention was diverted. One night a dozen German planes lost their way and dropped their bombs blindly on what was in fact the centre of London; the British thought that this bombing was deliberate and retaliated by making two raids on Berlin, in which a certain number of planes found the target. Little physical damage was done but the psychological effect was considerable for, if the German victories were as complete as was being made out, the German capital should have been invulnerable. Hitler called for retaliation and London was heavily bombed by night for a week. Then on 15 September a massive daylight attack was ordered; the RAF had used the interval to recover and shot down 52 planes (some accounts say 60) for the loss of 26. The barges and other boats which the Wehrmacht had collected in Channel ports for use in the invasion had already suffered severely from British bombing; the autumn had arrived and the weather was expected to get worse. On 17 September the operation was postponed indefinitely and on 12 October called off until 1941. Night bombing of Britain throughout the winter (the 'Blitz') had little military effect.

One cannot help wondering what would have happened if Hitler had returned in the following year with all the resources of Europe behind him. But Britain had never been his main objective and when her defeat eluded him, he decided not to let failure hold up his timetable. He had frequently spoken of the Germans as 'a people without living space' (*Volk ohne Raum*). He had said in *Mein Kampf*, 'If we speak of soil in Europe today, we can primarily have in mind only Russia and her vassal border states.' And the Germans had been observing with displeasure the way in which during the western campaigns Stalin had been strengthening his hold on those same border states. When Molotov, the Russian Foreign Minister, visited Berlin in November 1940, he was awkward and uncompromising; Russia's requirements were too big for Hitler to concede. He persuaded himself that what was preventing Britain from making peace was her hope of Russian (rather than American) help and at the beginning of December he ordered the Wehrmacht to put itself in a position to attack the Soviet Union at any date from 15 May 1941 onwards.

Russia was not the only direction in which things were going wrong. The hopes which Britain set on the United States of America were justified when in December 1940 Roosevelt proposed his scheme for lending or leasing to her all the war material she wanted, and thus ruled out the danger of her having to stop fighting for lack of money to buy munitions. General Franco refused to bring Spain into the war and so deprive Britain of Gibraltar. Mussolini, although well on the way to being driven out of North Africa by the British, launched in October an unsuccessful invasion of Greece. German troops had to be dispatched to stiffen up both areas and it was decided that the Balkans must be cleared before the Russian operation began. Despite the complications of a popular revolt in Yugoslavia, the whole area including Crete was conquered ahead of schedule. During the episode Rudolf Hess, the crank who was Hitler's deputy, sought to put himself back in the limelight by flying on his own to Scotland in the hope of inducing the British opposition (a figment of his imagination) to turn Churchill out and make peace before they and their Empire were annihilated; he certainly succeeded in creating a nine-days' wonder, not least among the German leaders, but one that was soon obliterated by other events.

The attack on Russia was not started till 22 June but the lateness of the date did not worry its instigators; they were confident of being able to complete another lightning campaign within six weeks. At first their hopes seemed well founded. The Russians had had notice of the impending attack from over eighty different sources but may have decided that the warnings were a capitalist plot intended to embroil them with Germany. Their troops were taken by surprise and the Germans got two-thirds of the way to Moscow in three weeks. The remaining third took longer but on 9 October Otto Dietrich was authorized to tell the world that the campaign in the east was decided. But the Russians had more troops than the Germans expected; their heavy tanks were superior and they fought with great stubbornness. The autumn rains set in earlier than usual; the Wehrmacht got bogged down before it reached the capital and was caught unprepared and in the open by the Russian winter. The Germans might have done better if they had set out to win the support of anti-Communists in Russia by promising them self-government. But not merely did Hitler scorn the idea of such a grant; it would have been inconsistent with his general views on race to have made such a promise. When news spread of the inhuman way in which captured Russians were being treated, it did not encourage the rank and file of the Red Army to give in.

On 6 December General Zhukov counter-attacked with troops trained and equipped to fight at sub-zero temperatures. The Germans began to give ground; their Führer, adding the job of Army Commander-in-Chief to his other functions and superseding demoralized generals in quantity, forbade them to do so. Thereby, he possibly prevented a headlong retreat but could not prevent operations from coming to a virtual halt for the next four months. Meanwhile Japan's attack at Pearl Harbor on 7 December (which came as a surprise to the Germans) brought the United States into the war. At the stage when Hitler had been confident of beating Russia, he had sought to distract American attention from Europe by inciting Japan to attack Britain in the Pacific. The idea of a Pacific war, but one against the USA as well as Britain, was received so favourably in Tokyo that later, when

Hitler would have welcomed Japanese help against Russia, they could not be persuaded to change targets. Their obstinacy proved disastrous. Sorge, the Soviet secret agent in Tokyo, just had time before being caught to advise Moscow of the Japanese decision to strike south (rather than west) and it was therefore with confidence that the Soviet command could take troops away from East Siberia to turn the tide against the Germans. But Hitler aggravated the situation gratuitously by taking the initiative of himself declaring war on the United States, thereby helping Roosevelt to win acceptance for his strategy of giving the European war priority over the Pacific one.

As their Führer realized, the Germans now faced a different kind of war from the one which they had got used to winning. For, like his predecessors in 1914, Hitler had gambled on his campaigns being short; unlike them, his gambles had come off. The equipment and munitions needed for such speedy operations could be produced at relative leisure beforehand and the losses made good at equal leisure afterwards. Many of the reserve soldiers, called up from the factory benches, got back to them again before civilians had noticed much interruption in normal supplies. Germany had therefore had no need for industrial mobilization on the scale achieved by Britain after 1940. The failure to knock out Russia in a single summer, along with the entry of the USA, brought this happy state of affairs to an end. The Germans and their allies were now outnumbered on the scale of 2 to 9, while the biggest productive machine yet known in history was set to work at full stretch against them, so that progressively they were to be the side which found itself at a logistic disadvantage. Their tactical methods had lost the advantage of surprise; the rest of the world was hard at work coping and copying. Belief in the invincibility of the Wehrmacht had been shattered in front of Moscow and there had been over 1 million casualties in Russia.

In such circumstances Hitler's readiness to take risks, which had been a major reason for his success, turned into a liability. Strain and unhealthy seclusion in his headquarters were beginning to tell on him; the remedial drugs which his doctors prescribed did more harm than good. Göring was growing lazy and incompetent; Himmler gained more power than was desirable. Yet the challenge of the new conditions was met with considerable success. Between February 1942 and July 1944 the output of German armaments rose threefold, that of tanks sixfold. By 1943 the proportion of GNP devoted to military expenditure roughly equalled the British figure. Although the American contribution made it out of the question for Germany to match her enemies in quantity, the shortfall was until 1944 partly made good by superior design. The credit for this was due to Fritz Todt and then, after his death in February 1942, to Hitler's favourite architect Albert Speer, who between them turned the organization originally created to construct the Autobahnen into a new central body which set overriding priorities for all production.

Another reason why the German people escaped serious privation till a late stage in the war was that the produce and possessions of occupied Europe were mercilessly requisitioned to ease the life of the master race. It has been estimated that 15 per cent of Denmark's GNP was taken to Germany without payment – and Denmark was better treated than most. France was made to pay reparations at more than four times the rate against which Germany had protested so vigorously under the Dawes and Young Plans (see pp. 45 and 47). In addition the Germans removed 9 million tons of cereals, three-quarters of the total steel production and large quantities of textiles. Numbers of special machines were carted out of the country for use in Germany. By the end of September 1944 some 7.5 million civilians from other countries of Europe were working in Germany as slave labourers under miserable living conditions. The persons concerned had often been chosen by hazard; one of the customs of the SS was to round people up as they came out of church or the cinema! In addition 40 per cent of prisoners-of-war were employed on making munitions or other war work, in contravention of international law. Some 3 million Russian prisoners – over half the total number – were so badly treated that they died. It is small wonder that Germany's difficulties on the battlefields were accompanied by growing difficulties in securing co-operation from the occupied populations.

German brutality was not confined to exploiting subjects and captives. Slavs and Jews were murdered on a mass scale for the simple crime of having belonged to what were regarded as inferior races. By 1940 over 1 million Poles had been uprooted from their homes in the provinces nearest to Germany (where they were replaced by Germans expelled from Russia or the Baltic states) and driven eastwards across the Vistula where they were left to maintain their existence on starvation rations. In all some 6 million Poles are believed to have died violently during the war (though some of these were killed by the Russians). In 1939 there are thought to have been 10 million Jews living in the lands which came under Hitler's control. When the war ended, between 4.5 million and 6 million had been exterminated, some by firing squads, others (because firing squads were too slow) in the gas chambers of concentration camps. Paradoxically the scale of extermination grew as defeat came closer since the Nazi leaders were determined to satisfy their hate while they still had power.

This is not the place to make a full catalogue of the crimes against humanity which were committed by Germans on the orders of Germans during the five-and-a-half years of war. But there are two reasons why the Holocaust should not be glossed over, like a bad dream. One is that the memory inevitably infected the attitude of other peoples towards Germany and Germans after 1945 – and especially that of the nations which received the worst treatment. The second consists in the need to remember the Nazi record when considering the claim that the German nation, in battling against Communism, was performing a heroic role in the cause of civilization and that the Atlantic Powers, in allowing it to be defeated, were guilty of a fatal miscalculation. To be sure, Nazism had no monopoly of cruelty and crudity, but to have allowed it to take the place of Communism would hardly have contributed to the greater happiness of humankind.

Although from the beginning of 1942 onwards the balance of material resources was heavily against Germany, time was needed for the superiority of her opponents to be deployed and the events of the first nine months of that year, with striking Japanese victories in the Pacific, were such as to conceal the real state of affairs. In the summer German armies swept over the frontiers of Egypt and up to the summits of the Caucasus. But in order to have the troops needed to get there, Hitler had to fill the centre of his Russian front with Hungarian, Romanian and Italian divisions; even so, his generals were held before they could cross the Volga or reach either the Nile or the oilfields of Baku. Indeed the advances which he did make proved the high water-mark of his success. For in the autumn Montgomery defeated the *Afrika Korps* at Alamein, Eisenhower landed with an Anglo-American force at the other end of North Africa and the Russians, breaking through the second-rate satellite divisions, surrounded the Sixth German Army of 285,000 men at Stalingrad. Hitler refused to consider withdrawing them, ordering them to die rather than give in. Their desperate position was for long concealed from the German people while attempts were made to supply them from the air. These failed and at the end of January 1943 the 91,000 still alive surrendered; German morale received a blow from which it never fully recovered. The turning-point of the war had arrived; henceforward it was not a question of whether Germany could win but of whether she could avoid defeat.

A week before the Stalingrad surrender, at a conference at Casablanca, Roosevelt, backed by Churchill, had announced that 'peace can come to the world only by the total elimination of German, Japanese and Italian war power ... [which] means the unconditional surrender of Germany, Italy and Japan'. Churchill a year later pointed out to Parliament that the Allies would not in consequence be bound to the German people after their surrender by any Pact or obligation.

> No such arguments will be admitted by us as were used by Germany after the last war, saying that they had surrendered in consequence of President Wilson's 'Fourteen Points' [p. 36]. If we are bound, we are bound by our consciences to civilisation. We are not bound ... as the result of a bargain struck.
>
> (W.S. Churchill in House of Commons, 22 February 1944)

This attempt to learn from history has been criticized on the ground that it prolonged the war, since the prospect of a relatively mild peace might have induced the German generals and administrators, who were becoming increasingly critical of Hitler and concerned about his consequences for the country, to overthrow him and negotiate conditions of surrender.

Roosevelt and Churchill, however, headed a strong school of thought in Britain and the USA which held that the aim of the war was not just to overthrow Hitler and the Nazis but to eliminate from German life the authoritarian nationalist influences (labelled loosely by Churchill as 'Prussian militarism') which were held to be responsible for the five wars started by Germany during the previous eighty years. What was needed to this end was a clear demonstration that militarism did not pay, in the shape of complete defeat in the field (making impossible another 'stab-in-the-back' legend), the occupation of the whole country (so as to ensure a thorough-going reconstruction of society such as the Germans had failed to carry through for themselves after 1918) and the disbandment (rather than mere reduction) of the German armed forces. But such a drastic settlement would mean the elimination of Germany as a power factor in Europe for at least a generation and this was the very thing which the generals, by training and temperament, were chiefly anxious to avoid. Consequently any attempt to negotiate conditions of surrender would quickly have reached deadlock.

For the British and Americans by themselves to have imposed on Germany the terms which their leaders thought necessary would have been a costly and perhaps impossible task. Nor did those leaders have any intention of attempting it. Another of their main concerns was to keep Russia in the war until complete victory had been won. In this, 'unconditional surrender' had a part to play since it reduced the risk of inter-allied disagreement about terms leading Russia to make a separate peace and provided the Russians with some reassurance against the fear that the British and US Governments were themselves prepared to make a separate peace with a non-Nazi but conservative German regime.

But this is the aspect of 'unconditional surrender' which has most led to post-war criticism of the doctrine. For by eliminating German power in Central Europe and helping Russia to advance to the Elbe, it brought the dividing-line between the free and Communist worlds several hundred miles further west than might otherwise have been the case. One of the major reasons underlying the desire of the German generals to keep their power intact was precisely their belief in the need for a strong barrier to keep the Russians out. Moreover it can be argued that the German state which the Western Allies brought about did not in the end differ much from the one which the generals might have established (except that it only covered two-thirds of the area) so that nothing was gained and a good deal lost by refusing to compromise. Yet speculation on what might have been is a pursuit of questionable value. For not only were the forces opposed to a compromise peace in a majority in Britain and the USA, but also Roosevelt, and to a lesser extent Churchill, would have had to be different men before they could have taken a totally different line. And if they had been different men, the whole course of history would have been altered in many other incalculable ways and not simply in this momentous but particular respect.

The problem might have been avoided if a democratic non-militarist movement had developed in Germany to overthrow the Nazis and seize the Government. But this was never an available option, not so much because of the lack of suitable people as because of the impossibility of organizing resistance privately. As long as such resistance remained unobtrusive, its effects were limited and as soon as they began to become serious, they would also have become obtrusive enough to get sternly suppressed. The Army was the only body with the security needed to plan and with the formations of armed men needed to overcome rulers who were in no mood to relinquish power voluntarily. Indeed it is not certain that the Army would have prevailed against the SS: an attempted coup might have precipitated civil war, which was another reason why generals hesitated about attempting one. The military would no doubt have called in civilians to form a government, presumably from much the same circles as had held office during the Weimar Republic. But the dependence of that Republic on the military was widely regarded in the West as an object-lesson which must not be repeated.

If the first nine months of 1942 had been dismal for the Atlantic Powers, the same months in 1943 brought a series of disasters to the Axis. In May North Africa was lost, with the surrender of over 100,000 German and Italian troops, and in July Eisenhower's forces landed in Sicily. Mussolini was overthrown in favour of a government under Marshal Badoglio which began secret negotiations for surrender. An armistice was proclaimed in September at the same time as Anglo-American forces landed south of Naples, but the Germans managed to withdraw their troops intact and establish a front south of Rome. Mussolini was rescued and put back on his pedestal but his image had been permanently dented and the dent did not go unnoticed in Germany. If Fascism could fall so easily, how secure was Nazism? The offensive at Kursk which was designed to rescue the situation for the Germans in Russia was not ready for launching until July and then proved a failure; the enemy, by a counter-attack, turned it into a steady retreat towards the frontiers of Poland and Romania. In the Atlantic the British cracked the codes which the German submarines were using so that the losses of food and munitions on their way from North America were drastically reduced.

By this time the British bombing attacks, which had been growing steadily in weight since 1940, were making life very uncomfortable for the inhabitants of most German cities; a series of raids on Hamburg from 24 July to 3 August caused particular damage and loss of life. As bombing by day had led to unacceptable losses and as precision bombing at night had proved impossible, the attacks had to be directed at central urban areas rather than strictly military targets. This strategy has been criticized in that its weight fell on civilians but had relatively little effect on the German war effort, as the figures for arms production (see p. 73) show. When initiated it of course represented one of the few ways in which Britain could strike back at

Germany and the spirit which prevented surrender from being seriously considered was also the spirit which insisted on using whatever weapons were available. The RAF's existence as an independent force had always been justified on the theory that future wars would be won by air power and that, since 'the bomber would always get through', the only satisfactory defence was retaliatory attack. Too many material and psychological resources had been invested in putting this doctrine into practice for an admission that it was mistaken to be easily made, especially as long as 'the fog of war' complicated the collection of evidence and led to its military effects being considerably overestimated. Moreover, until the autumn of 1943 its advocates would have argued that it had not been used on a large enough scale for its results to be fairly judged. In the spring of that year Goebbels and other leaders of the German home front had been seriously afraid of civilian morale collapsing. All in all, it is easy to see in retrospect why the strategy should have been adhered to for so long.

By the autumn of 1943 chances of victory had become faint although until the summer of 1944 there were reasonable grounds for Germans to hope that they could avoid total defeat. The chances of doing so would have been improved if Hitler had been got rid of. But no general in command of troops was prepared to start a revolt. Consequently the conspirators at the next lower level of the Army began to see in assassination the only hope of forcing their superiors to move. The Führer was, however, so closely guarded as to render an attempt on his life extremely difficult; those who had access to him were not prepared to act while those ready to act had no access. An attempt in March 1943 which might have changed the course of history failed because a bomb smuggled on to his aircraft failed to detonate. From October 1943 onwards the chief organizer of the conspiracy was Colonel Claus Count von Stauffenberg, a staff officer of the Reserve Army Headquarters in Berlin. In the following June he took up a new post which required him to report periodically to Hitler in East Prussia and on 20 July he managed to plant a bomb which, after his departure, exploded at Hitler's feet. The coup failed, however, partly because Hitler was not killed but partly also because nobody but Stauffenberg was in a position to give the necessary orders from Berlin and by the time he got back there to do so, the news that Hitler was still alive prevented them from being obeyed. As a result of the summary trials which followed, a Field Marshal, 22 generals and 142 other eminent Germans were hanged. Thereafter nobody dared any further attempts. If the opposition had never attempted a rising but left the task of removing the Nazis to the Allies, many valuable lives would have been saved to help in building up a new society after defeat. But a lasting blot would have been left on the German record if no risks had ever been run to get rid of the gangster regime. That the attempt should be made mattered more than that it should succeed.

It was indeed hastened forward because the June invasion of Normandy by British and US armies under Eisenhower was threatening to bring the war in the west to a speedy end. Hitler's much-advertised V-weapons gave south-east England an inkling of what future conflicts might be like but came too late to affect the course of the present one. In fact the Allied advance ran out of steam in September along Germany's western frontier and an attempt to get round the flank by seizing a bridgehead over the Rhine at Arnhem failed. But it was clear, especially after the repulse of a German winter offensive in the Ardennes, that Allied progress would be resumed irresistibly in the spring. In August the Russians had reached Warsaw but halted there for two months while the Germans annihilated the non-Communist Polish insurgents who had risen in the hope of helping the Allied cause. Stalin felt strong enough to dispense with the assistance of people who were not committed to Communism, thus condemning 200,000 to death, and the British and Americans were too far away to help.

The Russians resumed their offensive in mid-winter. By now they were reaching districts like East Prussia and Silesia which had long been German and the civilian population faced a choice between flight through the snows and the hazards of capture. Goebbels increased his efforts to arouse in his audience strength through fear:

> If the German people were to lay down their arms . . . the Soviets would occupy the whole of Eastern and South-eastern Europe, plus the largest piece of the Reich. In front of these territories . . . an iron curtain would come down behind which the mass slaughter of the people would take place.

> (J. Goebbels in *Das Reich*, 25 February 1945)

But the material prerequisites for resistance were vanishing. For one thing, the Wehrmacht, weakened by all the casualties it had suffered and fighting on two fronts, was outnumbered. Second, Western air superiority had become such that precision bombing by day was at last practicable and was directed with particular effect at oil installations. As a result the Luftwaffe was all but grounded for lack of spirit while Speer's production efforts led to more tanks being turned out than could be fuelled. The shortage was aggravated by a Russian thrust into Romania so that the Germans lost the use of its oil wells. Germany's ultimate defeat was due above all to lack of men and lack of oil.

Realizing that all was lost, Hitler tried to increase rather than lessen the damage to the country. On 19 March he gave orders for the German earth to be 'scorched' in face of the invader. When Speer protested against denying the nation the possibility of future reconstruction, the Führer burst out:

> If the war is lost, the nation also will perish. This fate is inevitable. There is no necessity to take into consideration the basis on which the people will need to continue a most primitive existence. On the

contrary it will be better to destroy these things ourselves because this nation will have proved to be the weaker one and the future will belong solely to the stronger eastern nation.

(A. Speer, *Inside the Third Reich*, p. 588)

Fortunately Speer had not lost his ability to disobey and, with his staff and Wehrmacht support, showed almost as much ingenuity in frustrating his master's wishes as he had previously done in facilitating them.

By now it was merely a question of whose troops would reach Berlin first. The German commanders would have gladly helped the Anglo-Americans to do so by surrendering to them, while continuing to resist in the east. But fear of provoking the Russians was still strong enough in the west for the proposition to be firmly rejected and for the Anglo-American armies, which were anyhow outrunning their supply lines, to be halted. Hitler, by this time a nervous wreck, retreated into his underground shelter (*Bunker*) in the centre of Berlin and it was there on 30 April at the age of 56 that he died; the most plausible interpretation of the evidence suggests that he was shot at his own request by his long-time mistress and recent bride Eva Braun, who then took poison herself. (For a discussion of Hitler's death, see R.G.L. Waite, *Hitler: The Psychopathic God*, p. 415.) Five days previously, American and Russian forces had met near Leipzig. Seven days later Jodl, the Chief of the Wehrmacht Directing Staff, signed at Eisenhower's headquarters a document of unconditional surrender for all such troops as were still fighting. This time, unlike 1918, the generals were not allowed to evade responsibility for the outcome of the appeal to arms.

The war in Europe was over and the Third Reich at an end. To say how many people's lives they had cost is difficult since many extermination agencies kept no records. But the figure now given in the leading German encyclopaedia is 55 million. About 8 million of those were German.

5

THE POST-WAR SETTLEMENT: 1945

PLANS PRIOR TO SURRENDER

For over two years before the Germans surrendered unconditionally, the Allies had been trying to settle what was to happen afterwards. Some things had been agreed without too much difficulty. Americans, British and Russians all took, for example, the view that the whole country must be occupied. An Allied Control Council in Berlin was, for the time being, to replace a German government and each of the three Powers was to be responsible for maintaining order and for seeing that the Council's decisions were carried out in a 'Zone' approximating to one-third of the country. Berlin was to constitute a special area, occupied and administered by all three Allies, each of whom would be assigned a 'Sector' of the city. Then at the Yalta Conference in February 1945 Stalin was persuaded to allow the French a seat on the Control Council, a Zone of occupation and a Sector in Berlin.

For any decision of the Control Council to be valid, all four members had to consent to it. This put a premium on inter-governmental agreement. No great difficulty was found in deciding that National Socialism must be eliminated, its representatives removed from positions of influence and its laws annulled. Nor did any of the victors object to the disbandment of the German armed forces and the destruction of all military material. There was even unanimity that the future Germany must be 'democratic', though events were to prove that East and West attached different meanings to that elastic word. Where agreement ceased was over frontiers and reparations.

From the outset, the Russians had insisted on hanging on to virtually all those parts of Poland which they had annexed in 1939. The country would be 180,000 sq. km smaller and would lose 11.6 million people (many of them admittedly more Russian than Polish). Consequently there was general agreement that Poland must be compensated by annexations in the north and west at the expense of Germany; these were to go 'up to the line of the Oder', a river which, after flowing south from the Baltic, turns south-east through Silesia. It thus involved transferring half of that province to Poland.

But at Yalta the Russians proposed that, where the Oder turns, the frontier should continue south along the (western) Neisse river to the Czech border, thus giving Poland the *whole* of Silesia.

This alteration was resisted by the Americans and British, Churchill in particular protesting against 'stuffing the Polish goose so full of German food that it gets indigestion'. The conference agreed that 'the final delimitation of the western frontier of Poland should await the Peace Conference'. This procrastination did not, however, stop the Russians from handing over to the Poles the whole area up to the Neisse soon after they had wrested it from the Germans. By such largesse (which even then amounted to only four-sevenths of what they were taking from the Poles) the Russians not only increased the distance which any future German army would have to march over non-German land before reaching Moscow but also ensured for the Poles the enmity of many Germans and thus reckoned to safeguard themselves against any later risk of a Polish–German deal at their expense. (What the German nationalists were likely to resent even more was the loss of East Prussia with all its memories. This the Russians and Poles divided between them, without any attempt being made by either the Americans or British to object.)

A question which had produced uncertainty rather than disagreement was the disposal of the rest of Germany. At Yalta dismemberment was agreed on in principle and a committee set up to work out the details. By the time this committee met, all three governments were for various reasons beginning to have second thoughts. No plan of division was prepared and on 9 May Stalin publicly denied that the Soviet Union intended to dismantle or destroy Germany. However, the idea of putting the Ruhr under some sort of international control was taken for granted.

But what was the post-war Ruhr to be like? Western governments were divided between those who believed that the only way to stop Germany from aggression was by depriving her of the tools essential for war and others who argued that, since the prosperity of Europe was bound up with that of Germany and since she must therefore be left with some industries capable of being adapted to use in war, the aim must be to see that the country got into the hands of people who were not aggressive. The leader of the 'hawks' was Henry Morgenthau, the Secretary of the US Treasury, who for a few weeks in the late summer of 1944 managed to get the support of Roosevelt and Churchill for his ideas. These were based on the ease with which modern industry can beat ploughshares into swords and so proposed to deprive Germany of almost all her heavy industry.

The Russian approach was different since, to their Marxist eyes, Germany's aggressive tendencies were the inevitable result of her capitalist structure. The appropriate remedy therefore was not to worry about the control of the political government but about ownership of the means of production. Their less ideological interests included getting from the Germans as much compensation as possible for the damage which had been inflicted on them. Taught by the experience of reparations after 1919, they proposed to exact this in kind rather than money. Factories and equipment were to be removed from Germany and taken to the victor countries; factories left in Germany were used to produce goods for the Allies while prisoners of war and Nazis captured on defeat were to be kept for ten years to work on reconstruction. What is not clear is whether they realized how much more difficult such treatment would make it to win Germany for Communism. There were already many reasons for Germans and Russians to dislike one another. If a harsh peace were added, the chances of Germany adopting Communism voluntarily would be minimal. Yet if the Russians were not prepared to meet the wishes of the Anglo-Americans and preferred to run the risk of a quarrel, they would find themselves wanting to win the friendship of the Germans against the West.

At Yalta the Soviet Government proposed that the total value of reparations should be set at $20 billion, of which their own share would be half. Neither the British nor the Americans opposed the idea in principle and the conference's communiqué, while not mentioning any specific sum, said that Germany was to be obliged to 'make compensation in kind to the greatest extent possible'. How much that would be was left for decision by a Reparations Commission.

The postponement of the question was not adroit enough to prevent the Russians from starting exactions immediately they got into Germany. Over and above the official removal of things as various as railway lines and atomic scientists, individual soldiers were for some time allowed great licence to do as they chose with people and property. Germany was full of stories of the excesses of Soviet troops, many of whom came from Central Asia rather than Russia.

A SUMMER OF MAKE-DO AND MEND

Thus Germany in May 1945 fell into the hands of four governments which had not yet reached either agreement or final disagreement about certain vital points concerning the way she was to be treated. Further discussion of these questions at top level was accordingly urgent. A variety of reasons, however, prevented it from taking place for two months and in the 'deadly hiatus' the proposed Control Commission was unable to start work; the commanders of the four armies, meeting in Berlin on 5 June, could do no more than proclaim its establishment, the division of Germany into Zones and the assumption of supreme authority with respect to the country by their four governments. The precise basis of their power, along with the question of what happened to German sovereignty after unconditional surrender, was for some time regarded as a merely academic question.

The policies followed in the American and British Zones had been largely worked out by the joint Anglo-American staff at Eisenhower's Headquarters before they were dissolved in July. Accordingly they bore some relation to one another, though the Americans (who were bending their energies to the defeat of the Japanese) were in more of a hurry than the British to get on with decentralization, denazification and democratization. The French and Russians had their own ideas of how to go about things; these were followed with rather more ruthlessness and a good deal less attention to fairness and uniformity. (A German said later: 'The British like us but don't always notice that we're there; the Americans like us but treat us like badly-behaved children; the French hate us on equal terms.')

To have ruled Germany on a uniform basis during those months would anyhow have been difficult, for the havoc played with the transport system during the final stages of the fighting, along with the inertia accompanying defeat, had removed the previous German drive to keep wheels turning. The territory was fragmented into small districts and the established channels of supply and exchange could no longer function. The Nazi Government had financed the second war much as the Imperial Government had financed the first. Taxes were raised to a smaller extent than in Britain or the USA and over two-thirds of the war's cost was met by borrowing; the volume of money in circulation increased about five times. The inflation which would naturally have resulted was held in check by rigid controls over prices and wages. Defeat then destroyed the confidence of the public in the currency.

Not that Germany was as seriously harmed by the war as her outward appearance suggested. The bombing and fighting had done great social damage, particularly to private houses and public buildings, but underneath the rubble of factories, much of the machinery was intact or capable of fairly easy repair. The amount of irretrievable damage to plant was estimated at 15–20 per cent, while thanks to wartime expansion Germany's productive capacity in 1944 was 20 per cent higher than it had been in 1936. The obstacle to recovery lay more in dislocation than in destruction.

The dislocation involved supplies, accommodation, transport, finance and ideas. But above all in the early days it involved people. Travel was unusually difficult but an unusually large number of people were nevertheless travelling. Some 7 million members of the German armed forces surrendered to the British and Americans; they had to be rounded up, disarmed and either held for trial or dispersed to their homes. A number of Allied prisoners-of-war and just over half the 6 million foreign workers had to be repatriated. For the remainder, mainly Poles, Balts and Ukrainians, homes which were under Communist rule had lost their attraction. Nevertheless an agreement with the Russians for the mutual exchange of one another's citizens led to those who were or had become Soviet citizens being sent back, often against their will, often to a cruel fate which was often undeserved.

Some 10 million Germans who had evacuated the bombed cities sought to return, if only to discover what had happened to their relatives and property. A considerable number more had fled westwards in face of the Russian advance. And no sooner had the Poles, Czechs and Magyars thrown off German control than, remembering the way in which the Nazis had exploited the German colonies in their midst, they began to expel the members of those colonies and send them back to Germany proper. The most notable of these groups were the 3 million Sudeten Germans who now had to take the consequences of having in 1938 put loyalty to Germany above loyalty to the state in which they lived; the refusal of the restored Czech Government to risk the same thing happening again may have been drastic but was certainly intelligible. What was more, the Poles administering the parts of Germany east of the Oder–Neisse line started turning out the inhabitants (8.8 million in 1939) since they needed the land to provide fresh homes for their own people who were being expelled by the Russians in the east. There was every prospect of the population of Germany being swollen by over 10 million extra people. How in these circumstances the country could be deprived of most of its industry was a question which began increasingly to be asked.

The immediate task was seen, in the West at any rate, as consisting in getting everyone provided with a sufficient minimum of shelter and food to prevent revolution, starvation and disease. To do this, communications had to be patched up and essential transport made possible; above all, the harvest had to be got in. But the German administrative system was in collapse. The Nazi leaders had made themselves scarce and, although a remarkable number of officials remembered having sufficient doubts about the Third Reich to justify an assurance that they had never been Nazis, it was a tricky question as to what reliance should be placed on them. If a literal interpretation were given to all that the Allied leaders had said about rooting out Nazism, practically nobody who held a public post during the previous twelve years (including lawyers and teachers) could be allowed to keep it – though how the country would then be run was obscure. In these early days, however, the question of whom to use had to be settled off-the-cuff, locally, by men with a jaundiced view of German history and a rudimentary command of the German language. For the time being, there were narrow limits to the amount which Germans on their own could do. The Allies might proclaim that their aim was to control rather than to govern, but they alone possessed the organization, the authority and above all the power to dispose of internal resources and gain access to external ones. For anything to happen, the officials of the military governments had to have a large hand in it.

The number of practical tasks pressing to be done and the obscurity about the form to be taken by the new state provided the British with a welcome excuse for giving politics a rest, whereas the Americans set up a government in Bavaria as early as May. Things were different in the Russian Zone, where a trained group of ten German Communists led by Walther Ulbricht was brought from Moscow at the beginning of May and set to work. To the surprise of everybody, including some of themselves, they did not immediately establish a Communist regime but made great play with 'anti-Fascist' committees in which anyone who could claim to have opposed the Nazis was encouraged to join. When it came to choosing the new local officials, account was taken of the character of each district as well as of technical considerations; only the first deputy mayor, the personnel officer and the education officer had to be Communists. 'The result must look democratic but the reins must really be in our own hands' (W. Leonhard, *Child of the Revolution*, p. 303). In keeping with this policy, the registration of the Communist Party on 25 June was quickly followed by those of the Social Democrats, Christian Democrats and Liberal Democrats.

Although the division of Germany into Zones of occupation was announced on 5 June, it did not come fully into effect for another month. Until that time, the troops of the three main Allies remained where they had been when fighting stopped. The western boundary of the Russian area thus ran along the Elbe instead of at a distance varying (except in the extreme north) between 50 and 150 miles west of that river, while on the other hand the whole of Berlin was under Soviet control. Churchill, who had regretted the halting of the Western armies before they reached Berlin, was reluctant to give up the extra territory until it became clear how much attention the Russians were going to pay to Anglo-American wishes on frontiers, reparations, the supply of foodstuffs from East to West Germany and various other matters at issue in Austria, Poland and the Balkans. But the Americans considered, and before long were able to quote the Russian commander Marshal Zhukov in confirmation, that the Russians would insist on previous agreements about zonal boundaries being honoured before they would allow the West access to Berlin, or Vienna, let the Control Council start working or indeed come to the conference table at all. Moreover both Russian help and American troops from Europe were wanted to polish off the war against Japan and neither would be available if a show-down was precipitated at that juncture. Accordingly on 12 June President Truman agreed to withdraw his forces and Churchill reluctantly concurred.

As an integral part of the bargain, American and British troops moved to take over the Sectors allotted to them in Berlin, where the royal suburb of Potsdam was to be the scene of a Summit meeting between the Americans, Britains and Russians on 16 July. The whole idea of a jointly occupied city two-thirds of the way across the Russian Zone was unprecedented. Its adoption reflected not only the wartime assumption of the Americans that co-operation with the Russians would be as easy as with the British but also the belief that, in a Germany which was to be treated as a unity, boundaries between Zones would be significant only for the stationing of troops and not for government. The task of fixing the limits was therefore left for the military commanders to perform when the time came, though nothing was done to brief those commanders in advance.

When they met on 29 June, Zhukov, the Russian commander, refused to grant his Western colleagues two out of the three railways, one out of the two highways and one out of the three airfields for which they asked. Moreover he made clear that what they did receive would come as a privilege rather than a right, while he passed over in silence their request that all traffic be free from customs control and military (but not police) search. Faced with the need for an immediate decision and reluctant to hold up the Allied arrival in Berlin, not to mention the Summit Conference, by haggling, the British and American generals contented themselves with what they could get, merely reserving the right to reopen the matter in the Control Council (unaware that in it the Russians would have a veto). Partly to save time, partly to leave elbow-room for future discussions, they did not even obtain written confirmation of what had been agreed. They imagined that they had only to consider the rights and interests of their own troops. Only when they met again ten days later to settle how the city should be ruled were they faced with a Russian demand that supplies of food and coal for the Western Sectors must be obtained and brought from the Western Zones; only later still did the question arise of how far and under what conditions German persons and goods possessed rights of movement between the city and the West.

THE POTSDAM CONFERENCE

The meeting which took place at Potsdam between 17 July and 2 August 1945 was not a peace conference and was in no position to dictate a Treaty to the leading enemy state, since there was no German government to sign such a document. Instead the conclusions were given to the world in a 'Protocol of Proceedings' drawn up somewhat hastily in the closing hours; it was not considered to need ratification by either Congress or Parliament. Thirteen of its twenty-one sections, amounting to about two-fifths of its total space, did not concern Germany.

The Political Principles, based upon an American draft, were agreed to without much argument. Germany was to be completely disarmed and kept indefinitely in that condition. The Nationalist Socialist Party and everything connected with it was to be dissolved: all Nazi laws which provided the basis of the regime or established discrimination on grounds of race, creed or political opinion (though not necessarily other legislation passed since 1933) were to be cancelled. All members of the Party who had been 'more than nominal participants in its activities' were to be removed from office, while leaders and high officials were to be interned and war crimininals were to be brought to judgement. A significant clause laid down that 'so far as practicable' the German population throughout the country was to be

treated uniformly. Preparations were to be made for the eventual reconstruction of German political life on a democratic basis, particularly by the
encouragement of democratic political parties and the introduction of self-
government from local councils upwards. Freedom of speech, press and
religion were (subject to considerations of security) to be permitted.
Although no central government was to be established for the time being,
five or more central administrative departments were to be set up, which
were intended to issue to lower levels the orders needed to get the policy
of the Control Council put into execution. One of the objects of the
Occupation was declared to be the convincing of the German people that
they had suffered a total military defeat and could not escape responsibility
for the inevitable distress and chaos which they had brought on themselves.

The Economic Principles, again based on an American draft, were more
contentious but principally in relation to reparations. Of Morgenthau's ideas
little was left beyond an injunction to restrict to Germany's peacetime needs
the production of metals, chemicals and other items essential to a war
economy, whereas 'primary emphasis' was to be given to the development
of agriculture and peaceful domestic industries. The economy was to be
decentralized but Germany was to be treated as a single economic unit,
common economic policies were to be established and essential commodities
equitably distributed between the Zones so as to produce a balanced
economy and reduce the need for imports. To the fullest extent practicable,
Germans were to be made to administer their own controls.

Productive capacity, even if for peaceful purposes, could be removed as
reparations. But a separate clause laid down that sufficient goods and
services were to be produced and maintained as, after meeting the needs of
the occupying forces and (non-German) 'displaced persons', 'were essential
to maintain in Germany average living standards not exceeding the average
of ... European countries'. Much subsequent discussion started from the
assumption that Germany was here promised a floor rather than a ceiling
and it is hard to see what other effect the words 'essential to maintain' could
have been intended to have. But the inclusion of the words 'not exceeding'
is out of line with this interpretation and virtually deprives the statement of
any meaning at all. To complicate matters, yet another clause laid down that
payment of reparations was to leave enough resources for the German
people to be able to subsist without external aid, that is, to be able to pay
with exports for essential imports.

Here lay the seeds of future arguments. There was general agreement that
reparations were to be obtained by 'removals', presumably of plant. No
reference was made in the Protocol to the requisitioning of future production (which had been envisaged at Yalta) and the Americans took the view
that Potsdam superseded Yalta. If, however, it did not, the question would
arise of the relative priority of reparations and exports. For production taken
away as reparations clearly could not be sold as exports and if exports failed

to reach a level high enough to pay for all essential imports, then the bill for those imports would have to be paid from some other source, which could hardly be anything other than the governments of the Powers occupying the Zones in question. The Russian answer was that imports which could not be paid for, no matter how essential, were not to be made. The Western Powers wanted in the long run to have a prosperous Germany because they believed it to be necessary for a prosperous Europe and they wanted Europe to be prosperous so that it could make its due contribution to a prosperous international trade. The Russians did not mind if Europe became destitute because they calculated that it was then all the more likely to turn Communist.

The crucial issues were the size of reparations and the amount of plant which might be removed. Stalin and Molotov fought hard to secure acceptance of the $20 billion which they had proposed at Yalta. But the Americans and British made clear that they would break off negotiations rather than name any figure at all. Instead they proposed that the Control Council be left to work out how much productive capacity Germany could spare in the light of the other economic terms. The Russian action in taking equipment out of their Zone without waiting for Four-Power approval then led to an American proposal that each occupying Power should draw reparations from its own Zone. But the Russians had been promised half the total whereas it was estimated that only 40 per cent of German productive capacity came from their Zone. Accordingly, to honour the pledge, they were offered in supplement one-sixth of the amount agreed to be surplus in the Western Zones.

This solution was then traded against a virtual Western climb-down over frontiers. As has been said, the Poles were occupying the whole area up to the Oder–Neisse line. When the West complained about being confronted with an accomplished fact and about the way in which the German inhabitants had been driven out, they were met by a half-true assurance that the Germans had all fled of their own accord, so that the areas would remain an uncultivated desert unless the Poles were allowed to settle in it. Possession proved nine-tenths of the law but the West's face was saved by a proviso that a final decision on the frontier should not be taken till the Peace Conference (then expected to occur quite soon). The meeting thus ended in a compromise, with each side imposing its will where it had the power.

Even so, the agreement proved to have several flaws. First, the French were not a party to it nor was their acceptance of its terms made a pre-condition of their admission to the Control Council. This put them in a position to veto any aspects they disliked; these included the establishment of political parties and trade unions on a nation-wide basis and the creation of the central administrative departments. Their obstruction, which the Americans for reasons not altogether clear refused to override, meant that there was no German channel by which the decisions of the Control Council could be transmitted to such lower-level German administrations as did exist or were formed. The gap had to be filled by the Military Governors who took to dealing directly with hand-picked Land Governments set up in the various Zones and even to establishing Advisory Councils for each Zone as a whole. Consequently the Zone boundaries acquired a political significance which they were not originally intended to have. On the other hand the failure to create a central German administration may have saved the Western Powers from having to cope with one which was Communist-dominated.

Second, a number of the terms used in the Protocol, such as 'democratic basis', 'so far as practicable', 'essential to maintain' and 'removals' were inadequately defined and their interpretation left to the Control Council. But where the Council could not agree, and action was nevertheless urgent, individual Zone commanders were free to go their own way; further scope for diversity of interpretation was given by a clause allowing account to be taken 'where appropriate, of varying local conditions'. In such matters as denazification and education, the most that the Council ever succeeded in doing was to bless and throw an appearance of harmony over measures already being taken in the various Zones. The only denazification action of any importance carried through on a quadripartite basis resulted from US insistence that the chief available Nazis should be dealt with by judicial process rather than disposed of in a summary way or left for judgement to the Germans. This led to the trial by an International Military Tribunal in Nuremberg of Göring and twenty-two other members of the Nazi hierarchy who had fallen into Allied hands. After ten months of hearings in which much highly illuminating evidence was brought to light, eleven were condemned to death, seven imprisoned and three acquitted.

Early in the morning of the day on which the Potsdam Conference was due to open, a flash of blinding intensity lit up the desert of New Mexico. Any effect on the Conference is hard to detect; the Americans did not become noticeably more uncompromising nor the Russians more conciliatory. Undoubtedly, however, the event made itself felt during the following months. The Russians neither asked nor were invited to share in the secret and a proposal to vest control of all atomic development in the United Nations came to nothing. But the task of rebuilding Russia must have looked more formidable than ever to her leaders when they realized that to remain a Great Power, she must forthwith set aside the extensive resources needed to give her a bomb of her own.

For Germany also the explosion had implications which were more profound than appreciated. Even if quadripartite control were to prove temporary, the loss of territory and wealth imposed at Potsdam must have seemed to render the manufacture of a German bomb out of the question for a long time and thus put a further bar in the way of breaking through to become a World Power. But the bomb decisively underlined the effect of modern weapons in making war so lethal as to cause all participants more loss than gain and thus to become unthinkable except as an act of desperation. But with war ruled out, any attempt to reverse the Potsdam settlement, except by mutual consent, had also to be ruled out. Yet paradoxically the fear of such an attempt being made by a Germany in control of nuclear arms was to complicate subsequent efforts at relaxing European tension.

Why did Germany's scientists fail to produce an atom bomb? By 1938 they knew just as well as the British and Americans that the atom could be split and that it might be possible to develop an exceptionally high explosive as a result. What neither side at that stage knew was how to put laboratory research into large-scale practice. The Germans made two mistakes, both the result of over-confidence. The first was to suppose that anything the enemy could do, they could do faster. The second was to believe that Germany could win the war at a relatively early date without the bomb. Accordingly they judged there to be no particular urgency over developing a weapon which they expected, correctly, to be a time-consuming process requiring far more resources than they were ever likely to procure in wartime. They were primarily interested in developing the civilian uses of nuclear power, which they assumed they could do at relative leisure after victory. They saw no need to force the pace. The British and Americans, by contrast, haunted by the fear that the Germans might be ahead of them, gave top priority to the work and were given first call on the USA's resources, so vast that the Germans could hardly have matched them, even if they had tried. By the time Germany realized that defeat was a possibility, it was too late to get work on the bomb speeded up, especially as progress was being continually dislocated at one point or another by Allied bombing and sabotage. It is not clear how close the Germans got to achieving a chain reaction. The theory that they procrastinated in order to keep such a terrible weapon out of the hands of a man as unscrupulous as Hitler is a myth developed after they had seen the results of Hiroshima. Until then, they were patriotic men who wanted to help their country to win (M. Walker, *German National Socialism and the Quest for Nuclear Power*).

6

TOWARDS TWO GERMANIES:
1945–1948

THE ECONOMIC TANGLE

Throughout the winter of 1945/6 the Economic Directorate of the Control Council, putting the horse after the cart, laboured to spell out what the broad conclusions of the Potsdam Conference would mean in concrete terms. By the end of March they had managed to agree on the shape which German industry should henceforward assume. Fourteen of its branches were to be prohibited altogether, twelve more to be limited to a percentage of pre-war output varying from eleven to eighty. The steel industry was to be allowed an output only slightly larger than pre-war Germany had needed for miscellaneous uses in light industry. Such plant in these branches as was surplus to requirements was to be made available for reparations or dismantled. In all, 1,636 factories were to be closed down in the UK and US Zones. In spite of the confiscation as reparations of Germany's merchant marine and overseas assets, and so of the cessation of the invisible income flowing from them, the balance of trade was to show a surplus by 1949. But this assumed that the money earned before the war from the exports of heavy industry would be replaced by sales of coal and consumer goods, although the total output of these was still expected to be below the 1938 level. No allowance was made for the loss of output caused by the shift of resources, by the amputation of territory in the east or the need to sustain a population swollen by refugees. The German standard of living was to be reduced to 74 per cent of the pre-war average, which happened to be the figure reached in 1932, the slump year paving Hitler's way to power.

The publication of this plan served to bring home forcibly to the British and American publics the implications of the policy to which their leaders had committed them and the reactions were not surprisingly emphatic. Growing difficulties in the Balkans, Iran and elsewhere made the Americans ask whether they were not sacrificing too much for Russian co-operation and getting too little in return. The Russians for their part were finding that the system of removing equipment for use at home left a lot to be desired and were turning more and more to keeping factories in Germany and removing the output instead. The West argued that, as the Potsdam Protocol had made no provision for the use of output as reparations, all such output as was not indispensable inside Germany must be used for exports. None of the foodstuffs which had been wont to flow from the East (and particularly from East Prussia and the areas occupied by the Poles) were reaching the Western Zones; in the chaos of the time there was little surplus to come though there might have been more if the Russian authorities, to undermine the economic position of the landowners, had not increased the confusion by introducing in August 1945 a programme of land redistribution. Consequently the populations of the US and UK Zones, far from self-sufficient at the best of times, were being kept alive on a subsistence diet by 1.5 million tons of food imports paid for by the British and American taxpayers. British Ministers as well as people began to ask indignantly why they should sacrifice scarce foreign exchange and forego increases in their own rations in order to help out the people who had caused all the trouble. What they were in reality doing, of course, was indirectly helping out the Russian people who had done so much to win the war, but this was neither appreciated nor explained. The situation would have been eased if the Americans had made the loan which up to the summer of 1945 they had encouraged the Russians to expect from them but for various reasons the negotiation of this was postponed until a period at which the terms insisted on by Washington were such as Moscow was unprepared to accept. Instead the subsidies which the USA had been paying during the war (Lend-Lease) were cut off abruptly when Japan surrendered without any substitute having been arranged.

In point of fact, reparations from the Western Zones reached only 5 per cent of industrial capacity, fell chiefly on industries which in terms of 1938 requirements (though not, as it proved, 1958 ones) were over-equipped and cleared the ground for the later installation (with government subsidy) of fresh and more modern equipment. As the plants taken away were not often of any use to the new owners, the policy was productive of neither serious damage nor benefit. But considerable faith in human incompetence would have been required to foresee this and during the time when the precise effect of the policy was in doubt (and this was much prolonged by the endeavours of the administrators to be methodical and fair all round) great alarm and acrimony were caused. Nobody was going to put much effort into stepping up the output of a factory as long as there was still a possibility that it might be picked on for dismantling.

Yet for more factories to have been functioning would have aggravated rather than eased the situation. Germany had during the war been drawing her supplies from occupied Europe with little regard for local needs. These needs, however, recovered top priority the moment that German power was withdrawn. Consequently there was little available for Germany to import. The only countries with resources to spare lay overseas, mostly in the

Americas, but purchases from them had to be paid for in dollars. Germany's own currency was virtually worthless and she had little to export. Before she could earn more by exporting, she needed the materials with which to make the goods. About the turn of 1945–6 the economic chief in the US Zone went on record as considering that 'we must have $100 million to finance essential imports, other than food, if we are to succeed' (L.D. Clay, *Decision in Germany*, p. 196).

Coal vividly illustrated the difficulties. All Europe was short and Britain, a traditional source of supply, had none to spare. The countries which Germany had occupied, and particularly France, insistently demanded that her output should be used to alleviate their needs. As coal exports would earn valuable exchange, there was good reason in Germany's own interest for making them and some were in fact made – though at cut prices. But as German production was down to about a quarter of the pre-war level, these exports left little for German industry, transport and public utilities, and virtually nothing for domestic use. Owing to lack of coal, the steel industry could not achieve even the output allowed under the Allied Plan and without steel other industries, including coal, found it hard to raise their production, while crop yields were held down by lack of basic slag as fertilizer. The occupation authorities, particularly in the British Zone where most of the collieries were situated, were taken to task by the liberated countries on the one hand for not exporting more coal and on the other hand by the Germans for exporting too much. The Germans further complained that if the coal had been kept in their country and used by their industries to make goods, these would earn much more as exports than coal by itself. But this would have meant restoring employment in Germany rather than among her victims and was therefore out of the question.

GERMAN ATTITUDES

The people of Germany were too much obsessed with their own plight to absorb information about conditions outside their frontiers. This did not mean that their outlook remained unchanged by defeat. During the closing stages of the war (and probably over a longer period) the proportion of 'hard core' Nazis and active anti-Nazis would seem to have been roughly balanced at about 10 per cent, with the former slightly preponderating; 25 per cent had been 'believers with reservations', 40 per cent unpolitical opportunists and 15 per cent passive opponents. The hard core was now in internment or concealment, aware for the most part that their only hope was to lie low and trust to time bringing a reaction. The reservations of the erstwhile believers had swollen to preclude admissions about what they had once approved and some indeed may have become genuinely convinced that ideas which could lead to such disaster must have been mistaken. In common with the opportunists, they were ready to go along with the new order even if they were more inclined to criticize its shortcomings than to appreciate the reasons for them. They showed great reluctance to absorb the version of the past and the picture of the present which the British and Americans pressed upon them as if out of a subconscious fear of having to admit that, as the Potsdam Protocol put it, 'the German people cannot escape responsibility for what they have brought upon themselves'. Between November 1945 and January 1948, those who said in opinion polls that they considered Nazism to have been 'a good thing badly carried out' were never less than 42 per cent.

The anti-Nazis, both active and passive, were in a more difficult position. The perpetual fear of arrest and the self-control needed to avoid trouble had in many cases been replaced by profound searchings of heart about the validity of German values, an obsession with the problem of guilt and a conflict between remorse and patriotism. To admit to mistakes and make recompense might be regarded as surrendering the national case and justifying Allied policy, while nobody could be sure that in a few years 'collaboration' with the victors might not prove as much a cause for reproach as it had just become in liberated Europe. Many of the most positive minds emerged scarred by their experience in the Third Reich. To their resentment of the Allied wartime refusal to make resistance easier by modifying the demand for unconditional surrender, there was now added disappointment that so much responsibility was kept in Allied hands, so little preference shown to those who had proved by their record that they were worthy of confidence. In the long run this Allied caution, born largely of uncertainty, paid dividends, since it postponed the danger of a reaction and saved many valuable democrats from damaging their usefulness by an over-eager association with the victors. In any case those who wanted to assume responsibility were for the first few months in a minority. Most Germans wanted nothing better than to collect their thoughts and their belongings – indeed, much of their time was absorbed in securing the essentials of life. Once again, the integrating processes in Germany had been put into reverse by failure.

Such circumstances hardly encouraged a revival of political life. But parties had been given leave to organize themselves in the Western Zones by September 1945 though they did so at first under close supervision and on a local basis. The most notable innovation was the foundation, as in several other Western countries, of a party designed to rally all the forces which were both anti-Communist and anti-Nazi under the positive slogans of religion and democracy. The Christian Democratic Union (which in Bavaria called itself the Christian Social Union – CSU) combined Protestants with Catholics (thereby differing markedly from the old Centre) and heirs of the National Liberal tradition with a pronounced radical wing. The Liberal or Free Democratic Party sought to inherit the anti-clerical *laissez-faire* tradition of the middle classes; it also accommodated a number of persons compromised by their association with Nazism. The Social Democrats and Communists both based themselves on organizations which had maintained a precarious underground existence during the Third Reich. The Lower Saxony Land Party, originally founded to reactivate Hanover's past independence, gradually extended the range of what it sought to resurrect.

Two arguments were prevalent in favour of the left-wing parties working together. One was that if such a front had existed in 1933, National Socialism might have been kept from power. The other lay in the general agreement that the essential step towards eradicating the aggressive authoritarian influences in German society lay in bringing the means of production and main sources of wealth under communal control. The chance which had been allowed to slip in 1919 must this time be seized; land reform and nationalization of the basic industries must not be confined to the Soviet Zone. One of the main reasons why the Social Democrats were impatient with the Anglo-American refusal to put power immediately into German hands was that the accomplishment of this process was thereby delayed. But to the Americans nationalization was a dirty word and, although the British Labour Government was engaged in just such a programme at home and did take under government control the coal and steel industries in its Zone, in the end the precarious state of the UK economy made it too dependent on American help for it to be able to go its own way in Germany. The British had to agree to the whole issue being shelved until the Germans were in a position to decide for themselves, while a parallel shelving of a nationalization clause in the Germans' own constitution for Land Hesse made clear that the decision was to be taken above Land level.

This compromise solution may appear to be justified by subsequent events, since, when the West Germans did come to decide, their verdict was unmistakably adverse. It would therefore seem that, as in 1919, a thoroughgoing programme of socialization could not have been carried out and maintained without political dictatorship. What is more, the US administration would have had much greater difficulty in getting Congressional approval for help to Germany if that country could have been represented as being well on the road to socialism. On the other hand there is no doubt that the political climate of Germany immediately after 1945 was more radical than it subsequently became. An early election would almost certainly have produced a majority favouring socialization. What must, however, be doubted is whether co-operation between Social Democrats and Communists would have lasted long, for soon the animosities which had weakened the German left all through its history began to reassert themselves.

The policy of the Russian Government towards Germany and the behaviour of the Soviet troops in that country were proving a serious obstacle to the popularity of the Communist Party and in all Zones the workers looked increasingly towards the Social Democrats. Ulbricht and the other Communist leaders in the Russian Zone sought to turn this awkward development to their advantage by launching the idea of a single anti-capitalist party and in February 1946 induced the executive of the Berlin SPD, led by Otto Grotewohl, to vote for the fusion of their party with the Communists in a new Socialist Unity Party (SED). Two days later, however, a mass meeting of Berlin SPD refused to confirm the executive's decision and at the end of March Social Democrats in the three Western Sectors of the city were encouraged by SPD leaders from West Germany to poll a vote of 82 per cent against the merger (though not against more limited co-operation). What the Social Democrats in the Russian Sector may have thought remains uncertain since the authorities there refused to let opinion be tested and forced the fusion through. When, six months later, elections were held throughout Berlin under quadripartite supervision, the SPD led in all twenty of the city's boroughs, whereas the SED got less than half as many votes, trailing behind the CDU.

Thus began a process in which the SED received steady favouritism in the areas under Russian control, where increasing difficulties were put in the way of the SPD and to a lesser extent of the other middle-class parties as well. Since the SED won little support in the Western Sectors of the city and did not exist in the Western Zones, the development created a major distinction between the two parts of Germany. The division between radical and moderate which had existed between the Marxist and Lassallean wings when the Social Democratic Workers' Party was founded in 1875, had given rise to the gap between revolutionary theory and revisionist practice before 1914, had led to the breakaway of the Independent Social Democrats in 1917, and had produced the rivalry between the Social Democrats and Communists throughout the Weimar Republic. It now took on a geographical form. One part of Germany, under Russian direction, was made to put socialism before democracy; the other, under Western influence, reversed the priorities.

Western Germany was also witnessing the gradual evolution of a federal structure as a means of achieving the aim of decentralizaton which had replaced that of dismemberment. The Americans as early as the summer of 1945 confirmed the right of Bavaria to remain a distinct political unit and brought into being a new Land of Greater Hesse. The need to provide the French with a Zone, combined with American communications requirements, led to the northern parts of Baden and Württemberg being divided from the south, although, whereas the French kept their pieces distinct, the Americans combined theirs to form a composite Land. The enclave of Bremen formed a fourth Land. Elections for Land Parliaments (*Landtäge*) were held in June 1946. In Bavaria they led to a majority for the CSU, in Hesse and Bremen to ones for the Socialists and in Württemberg-Baden to an indecisive result.

In the British Zone four Länder were set up. Hamburg and Schleswig-Holstein formed natural units and Lower Saxony a convenient combination of what had been several smaller ones. In July 1946 two Prussian provinces were merged to form the Land of North Rhine-Westphalia, with a population as large as the Netherlands. North Rhine-Westphalia was the only Land in the British zone in which the Socialists did not emerge as the strongest party when elections were held in April 1947, though even there the CDU came a good deal short of an absolute majority.

The French Zone consisted of South Baden, South Württemberg-Hohenzollern, the Rhineland-Palatinate and the Saar; its occupiers dreamt of incorporating the latter, which provided much of their coal, into France proper (see p. 138). Elections throughout the Zone in May 1947 showed a CDU majority in all four Länder. Meanwhile the Soviet Zone was divided into five Länder (though this was to prove a temporary arrangement). As a net result Germany (including Berlin) became organized into eighteen units which, while still varying in population from the 11.8 million of North Rhine-Westphalia to the 226,000 of Bremen, were on the whole better balanced than ever before. The vast preponderance of Prussia (see p. 13) had been eliminated even before the Control Council in February 1947 passed a law bringing that state's existence formally to an end. The responsibilities assigned to the Land Governments and subordinate authorities did much to determine the way in which powers were to be divided between the federal and Land Governments under the Federal Republic.

BIZONIA

By the time that Land Governments had been elected, however, a considerable change had come over the whole administrative structure of the Western Zones. For the problem of repriming the German economic pump could not be indefinitely deferred, yet could not be solved within the boundaries of a single Zone. Apart from the difficulty of treating as a separate unit something never designed for that purpose, the Americans, who alone were in a position to provide the wherewithal, were prepared to risk their money only in a unit which had a prospect of proving viable. The British, themselves dependent on American support, could not for much longer afford to go on spending $80 million a year in support of an area with a population half their own total. Consequently in July 1946 the American Secretary of State, James F. Byrnes, offered to merge the US Zone for economic purposes with that of any other Power willing to join and before the end of the month the British had accepted. The Russians and French tried to make conditions and found themselves left in the cold. Machinery was set up to make sure that all available goods were exported, that the proceeds were used to buy imports and that the necessary imports were made available. As Byrnes said at Stuttgart on 6 September, 'Germany is part of Europe and recovery in Europe, and particularly in the states adjoining Germany, will be slow indeed if Germany with her great resources of iron and coal is turned into a poorhouse.'

It had been fundamental to Morgenthau's arguments that Germany was *not* necessary to Europe and to Russian arguments that reparations must have priority over the German standard of living. The Byrnes speech was a landmark because it explicitly rejected both points of view. Whereas hitherto an early American withdrawal from Europe had been taken for granted, Byrnes announced his country's intention to remain as long as the Occupation lasted. Thanks to their insistence on taking reparations from current production, the Russians found themselves denied any influence over developments in West Germany while, if the American policy succeeded, the prospects of German Communists gaining control there would vanish away. But through Soviet spectacles, this change was seen as the result of international capitalism rehabilitating the economic system which had produced Nazism and recreating the danger of another German onslaught on the Communist world. A feeling of betrayal and alarm combined with an awareness of weakness to make them hold more firmly than ever onto what they had and refuse concessions. A meeting of Foreign Ministers in Moscow in March 1947 coincided with Truman's announcement that the USA would give active support to all free people resisting subjugation by armed minorities or outside aggression. Molotov combined a renewed bid for $10 billion reparations with a demand that the fusion of the Zones be cancelled. As he offered little in return, he convinced Byrne's successor General Marshall that the Russians were stalling in the hope that time would be on their side and that all Western Europe would soon go Communist.

The attempt to carry over into peace the wartime alliance with Russia had cost a year's delay in the reconstruction of Europe. The effects of the delay became painfully prominent when the winter of 1946/7 proved exceptionally cold. The waterways which play so large a part in German transport froze over; the roads and railways were still in too precarious a state to carry the displaced traffic. Supplies had for so long been short that everything was distributed as soon as it arrived; when it failed to arrive there were no stocks to fall back on. Rations could not be honoured, power stations ran out of coal, factories closed. But the crisis was not peculiar to Germany. All over Western Europe countries were running out of not only supplies but also of the foreign exchange needed to buy them. In France, the Low Countries and Italy production, which by a great effort had been brought within sight of pre-war levels, stopped expanding. In August 1947 the British attempt to make the pound convertible in accordance with the terms of a laboriously negotiated US loan had to be abandoned after seven-tenths of the $5 billion loan had been exhausted. Also in August the French Government suspended all dollar imports except coal, cereals and other essentials; in September the Italian Government stopped purchases even of coal and oil.

Such was the impending prospect when General Marshall made his Harvard speech on 5 June announcing that if the countries of Europe could agree on a combined plan for recovery, the US Government would finance it. The task of reconstruction had proved much bigger than anyone had foreseen; now at least there was a prospect of it being tackled on an adequate scale. Bevin for Britain grasped at the offer, and Bidault for France followed suit. But at a conference in Paris at the end of the month, Molotov insisted that the money must be given to individual countries to dispose of as they thought fit. To this the Americans were not disposed to agree and it was clear that, to win their agreement, any joint schemes must be aimed at the restoration of free trading conditions incompatible with the operation of a centrally controlled economy. The Russians accordingly walked out of the discussions and compelled Poland and Czechoslovakia to do the same. Sixteen Western countries then proceeded to draft a four-year programme which was accepted by Congress during the winter and began to operate in mid-1948. In this programme the provision of aid to the Western Zones of Germany formed an integral part, whereas the Soviet Zone was excluded by the Russian reaction. It was therefore an important further step towards the division of the country.

But before the Western Zones could be fully set on the path of recovery, two further steps were needed and for neither was Russian agreement likely to be forthcoming. First of all the totally artificial position of the currency had to be altered. The occupation authorities had kept in existence the controls which the Nazis had adopted (see p. 84) but did little towards reducing the volume of currency beyond imposing drastic nominal taxation and thereby discouraging initiative. Money ceased to be of any importance and the legal channels of trade were less and less used; goods were exchanged either in barter or at exorbitant sums on the black market. Cigarettes in particular proved a form of payment which was both convenient and utilitarian. Evasion of regulations became respectable while bribery and other demoralizing practices flourished. The widespread realization that a reform must come increased the reluctance to hold currency and much of what was manufactured got hidden away until the reform should be announced. The volume of money available had to be brought into line with the volume of goods available, either by raising the prices of the goods or by reducing the value of the money. But the Russians insisted on being issued with some of the plates for the new notes and being left to do their own printing; the other Allies would not agree. The introduction of the reform was virtually impracticable without a central bank of issue and there was little prospect of such a bank being able to function on a quadripartite basis when one of the participants held economic views diametrically opposed to those of the others. Moreover Communist and free enterprise ideas of who should be the main sufferers in a monetary reform were inevitably at variance. Discussions in the Control Council got nowhere. An ugly choice grew inevitable between jeopardizing the success of the other recovery measures and deepening the breach between the two parts of Germany.

Though there could be only one answer to this question, the giving of it was eased by developments in another direction. For some time, and particularly since the 'Great Freeze' of 1947, it had been growing apparent that, if the Germans were to make anything of their country, they must be allowed more say in its control. They had recovered much of their interest in life since 'Hour 0' (*Stunde Null*) in 1945 and lost much of their deference towards their masters, to whose misjudgments, rather than to the complexities of the world situation, they attributed the fact that conditions seemed to be getting worse instead of better. But political responsibility meant setting up a central government and when the Council of Foreign Ministers met in London in December 1947, it became clearer than ever that the minimum Russian price for such a step would be a free hand over reparations and the cancellation of the measures so far taken to unite the Western Zones. After the Council had adjourned indefinitely, the American and British decided to shut another of the doors hitherto left open and give to the economic machinery of 'Bizonia' the political character which they had so far carefully withheld from it. The French had been led by their opposition to a central German government to turn down the original fusion offer but they were induced to think again by the warning that, if they insisted on running their Zone independently, it would receive no Marshall Aid. They accordingly came to a London conference in the spring of 1948 and there somewhat reluctantly agreed to merge their Zone with the other two, bring the Western Zones as a unit into the Organization for European Economic Co-operation (OEEC, the body set up to run the Marshall Plan) and allow the Germans to begin drafting a constitution. The Russians were not long in replying. On 10 March Marshal Sokolovsky walked out of the Control Council in Berlin and from 1 April increasing restrictions began to be placed on personal travel between the Western and the Soviet Zones. The episode of Four-Power control was in effect at an end, though its formal winding-up was to take a further fourteen months.

A BALANCE-SHEET OF OCCUPATION

Many mistakes were undoubtedly made by the Western Powers during the Occupation of Germany, since the period was one in which the world situation made satisfactory solutions of common problems even more difficult to attain than usual. The positive achievements of the episode are too often lost to sight. Amid conditions which could easily have led to civil war or epidemic disease, both were avoided, and when all the world was hungry, the number of Germans whose deaths could be directly attributed to starvation was insignificant (though weakness due to lack of food certainly increased susceptibility to other diseases). This result was not due to luck but to hard work and generosity. The Americans had given $11,300 million to Europe before the Marshall Plan so much as came into operation, while US relief agencies spent $29 million from private sources between 1946 and 1948. Owing to the need to divert food to Europe, rations were as short in Great Britain in 1947 as at any time during the war. The Germans were wont to say that the demand for total surrender carried with it the assumption of total responsibility; the principle is open to argument but it is one on which the Anglo-American record can stand up to examination.

But what of the attempt to change Germany and provide the world with some guarantee against renewed aggression? Did not this depend on the Anglo-Americans and Russians being able to agree on the ways in which Germany was to be changed? Once the West began to quarrel with the East, could it afford to quarrel with the Germans by insisting on changes which the Germans did not want? And even assuming that East and West had agreed on what will to impose, is not the very attempt to impose outlooks and change minds misconceived? Not only does the overt attempt provoke a natural resistance but also ideas and institutions are so clearly interconnected and so largely influenced by the total character of a culture as to make isolated changes inadequate and wholesale ones impossible. It is tempting to condemn as a waste of effort the whole policy labelled 're-education' (a term likely to arouse prejudice against it) and to condemn with it the entire process of 'denazification'.

Any such judgement would however be unhistorical and excessive. Unhistorical because it is absurd to suppose that after a war such as that of 1939–45, when success had been won after great effort and sacrifice, the victor peoples would have given power to leaders who said, 'There is nothing we can do to prevent this happening again.' To have argued in the middle of the war that Nazism and German nationalism could not be 'rooted out' would have played straight into the hands of those demanding a vindictive peace. The idea of inducing Germans to change themselves deserves to be judged as an attempt at providing an alternative to a purely penal solution. In view of the inadequacy and impermanence of the attempts to change after 1919, the process could not be left entirely to the Germans; there were certainly a number who wished to change but it could not be safely assumed that they would be numerous and determined enough to get their way without aid. Moreover, once it had been decided to insist on 'Unconditional Surrender', the Allies were bound to march into Germany and, once there, almost bound to stay until the elements of order had been restored. If the Nazi downfall had led to civil war inside Germany, the Allies would in all likelihood have been drawn in, no matter whether they intended to occupy the whole country or not. This inevitably made the views of the conquerors influential, even decisive, in settling what was to replace the Third Reich.

If ever a country was crying out for a clean slate and a fresh start, it was Germany in 1945. Of course no slate can ever be completely clean and no start completely fresh. But complete and undeniable defeat did make conscientious and intelligent Germans (of whom the veteran historian Meinecke is an outstanding example) reconsider, as nothing else would have done, the role and values of their country – here is perhaps the final justification for insisting on unconditional surrender. And in the vacuum thus created, it was healthy that Western alternatives should be presented to them and that they should have been given active help in rebuilding their links with Western culture after twelve years of isolation. For this was how 're-education' was most effectively practised – a parallel process to the re-establishment in the economic field of channels of trade destroyed by twelve years of autarchy.

Certainly people's minds cannot be changed to order and the possibility of leading the Germans to a new view of the world depended for any chance of success on securing the co-operation of Germans who could not be accused of lacking patriotism. But there were numbers who welcomed the opportunity of access to new ideas. There were also many who were as worried as their enemies by the excesses of their nation and, without necessarily accepting an outsider's diagnosis, were concerned to find a remedy.

The opposite process of trying to drive out of public life all who had participated 'except nominally' in the fallen regime may also have been carried too far and conducted too slowly, but to conclude that nothing of the sort should ever have been attempted is again unhistorical. To have expected that at the end of a war which was professedly directed 'against the evil things', a war which ended by the uncovering of the extermination camps, public opinion would have allowed bygones to be bygones is to ignore human nature. To have concentrated exclusively on crimes done by individuals to individuals (as some have advocated) would have meant letting many of the accused off lightly, since their influence had often been indirect. Among the people who would have been most critical if the Allies had made no attempt at punishment would have been the very Germans whose opinions were most important for the future.

If more imagination and zeal had been used in working out the practical implications of pledges made indignantly during the war, the scale of the operation would have been reduced; the Nazi Party had some 8 million members, with another 4 million in associated organizations, and to drive out of public life one-fifth of the population is not a practicable proposition. There would have been great advantages in a procedure which gave those moderately compromised a quick chance to work their passage back by payment in money, kind or labour to a fund for reconstruction and compensation rather than by detention, but a major difficulty was the need for the Anglo-Americans to be seen to be acting with some attempt at justice, since this called for the collection of evidence and the application of judicial procedures, all of which take time. (The Allies are often said to have adopted and acted on the view that the German people were collectively guilty. Undoubtedly such a view was on occasion expressed, especially after the concentration camps came into Allied hands in the closing weeks of the war. But most of those who were responsible for settling policy towards Germany in Britain and the USA saw the objections to 'drawing up an indictment against a whole people' and preferred to stress the collective 'responsibility' of Germans in the sense that they had been unable to prevent what had happened from happening so that, even when this failure had not been due to a lack of will but to a lack of power, they must collectively bear the consequences in the shape of defeat's aftermath. Individuals could not disassociate themselves from the nation's fate.)

Even supposing that the Russians had not become a menace, the Control Council could not have gone on governing Germany for much longer than it did. There are narrow limits to the possibility of ruling a developed industrial country as though it were a colony, especially in an epoch when colonies all over the world were demanding and being granted the right to self-determination. Once the Germans had recovered the will to control their own destinies, the only alternative to letting them do so and avoiding a wave of sabotage and recrimination would have been a descent into iron repression. Indeed the only reason why more unrest and resistance did not develop in the Western Zones may have been the stimulus to co-operation which both rulers and ruled found in the Russians. The Occupation was bound to be an interlude and might have been better used if this had been recognized from the outset.

Above all, the interval of external control afforded the Germans time to sort themselves out. The Weimar Republic had been handicapped from birth by the conditions under which it had to start work. A new German regime after 1945 could not wholly avoid the association with failure which had been one of the chronic handicaps of the democracy in Germany. But, by postponing the assumption of responsibility for four years so that the first post-war West German Government took over when things were beginning to improve and when the alternative to it was a matter of experience rather than conjecture, the chances of it fairly soon achieving a reasonably creditable record were much increased. The cards were stacked so heavily against the Occupation being successful that the new system needed only moderate success in order to seem an improvement on its predecessor!

7

CRISIS AND MIRACLE:
1948–1949

CURRENCY REFORM AND ITS CONSEQUENCES

The withdrawal of the Russians from quadripartite discussions and the decision of the French to conform removed the obstacles to a reform of the currency. On 20 June 1948, according to a plan worked out by the Americans with German advice, the old *Reichsmark* was made valueless in the three Western Zones and replaced by the *Deutschmark*. Everyone was immediately allowed to exchange forty of the old Marks for forty of the new ones but before they could get any more, they had to disclose how much money they had in cash or at the bank. The original intention had been to issue them with only one-tenth of this amount in the new currency but experience showed that this would not reduce the volume of money sufficiently and the rate was therefore lowered to 100:6.5. All debts, however, had to be paid off at the 10:1 rate so that creditors came out well. Existing securities of the government, municipalities and public corporations were replaced on a much smaller scale by new government bonds with the object of bringing the assets of the banks nearer to their (greatly diminished) liabilities. Thus Germans once again saw their intangible assets reduced in value to almost nothing. Banks were also given new, but scaled down, reserves in the form of deposits with a new central bank of issue, the *Bank Deutscher Länder* (which in 1957 became the *Bundesbank*). The note circulation was fixed at DM 10 billion, a ceiling which the Occupation authorities pledged themselves to observe in order to give the population faith in the new currency. The degree of devaluation gave Germany a level of costs which was relatively low by comparison with other industrial countries and therefore favoured German exports.

As in 1923 the reform bore harshly on those who held their savings in money rather than in goods, though to some extent this was made up for by the relatively light taxation with which they had been let off during the war. The original intention had been to make a 'levelling of burdens' (*Lastenausgleich*) an integral part of the reform so that those who came off best would be forced to help those less lucky. But the Americans insisted that the devising of such a readjustment must be left to the Germans and four years of argument were needed before a final measure could be agreed on (see p. 151). But whatever the social effects may have been, economically the reform came at exactly the right time and, after several nervous moments, proved highly successful. A sufficient volume of goods was beginning to emerge from the factories for there to be something to buy and the capacity to produce more was available. The initial issue of the new currency was small enough to leave everyone short of money and therefore reversed the previous situation by making cash more sought after than material objects. As a result, goods which had been hoarded were unloaded, the shops filled up and the black market disappeared overnight. For some time the German people had been ready to exert their habitual industry but had lacked any incentive to do so; they now set to work with a will.

The Western Allies had not intended to extend the Currency Reform to their Sectors of Berlin and on 18 June wrote to the Russians expressing the hope that a single currency could be agreed for the city as a whole. Their only condition was that it must be handled as a completely quadripartite measure. But the Russians, who had just dealt another blow to co-operation by walking out of the quadripartite *Kommandatura* governing the city, turned the offer down. Marshal Sokolovsky announced that banknotes issued in the Western Zones would not be allowed to circulate in the Soviet Zone nor in Berlin which, in contradiction to the 1944 agreements (see p. 81), he described as being 'part of the Soviet Occupation Zone'. The Western move had obviously caught the Russians unprepared since they had no new currency notes ready. But they could not tolerate for long a situation in which a unit was nominally worth ten times more on the east side of the zonal boundary than it was on the west side. Consequently, on 22 June they improvised a somewhat less drastic measure of their own, sticking stamps on to the old notes to show the new values. These they then made valid throughout Berlin. But the Western authorities feared that if the currency in their Sectors was to be the same as in the Eastern yet different from that in West Germany, the trend of trade would soon go in a Communist direction. Accordingly on 25 June they declared that both Eastern and Western Marks would be valid in the Western Sectors. The ratio between the two established itself in free exchange as one to two but quickly altered to one to four.

There were cogent reasons why a reform of the currency could not be postponed much longer but its introduction on a tripartite basis provided the Russians with too clear a challenge for them to let pass. Declaring the Western action was illegal, the Soviet authorities on 24 June extended to freight movements between Berlin and the Western Zones the restrictions which had already been applied to movements of people (see p. 87). They reckoned correctly this step would catch the West at its most vulnerable point. The circumstances of the American and British entry into Berlin had left them without any written definition or even confirmation of their rights of access. This precarious position had been aggravated by the acceptance in July 1945 of the Russian demand that the supplies of food and coal for the Western Sectors must come from the Western Zones (though it is arguable that the Russians would have been in a stronger position in the long run if they had made the Western Sectors depend on the East for both supplies and markets). Although the possibility of communications being interrupted by the Russians had been at intervals the subject of speculation, no attempt at preparing for the contingency had been thought worthwhile; stocks in the city were limited and in some public services such as electricity the Western Sectors still depended on the Eastern. The Russians therefore had some justification for thinking that they had the Western Allies in a corner, facing a choice between four courses, all unpleasant. One was to withdraw immediately, a second to stay until starved out and a third was to negotiate an agreement for continued access, in exchange for abandoning their plans to rebuild West Germany. Any of these courses would have suggested to the world that the West could not or would not get its way and protect its friends. There was of course the fourth option, to force a way in, despite the Russian superiority in conventional forces, and this the American Commander General Clay wanted to do. A column of troops would have been more likely to be met by demolitions rather than by arms and might have ended up by having to garrison the entire route so as to keep it open, but the matter was never put to the test because the three governments preferred to explore a fifth solution.

In the twentieth century land and water were no longer the only ways into the city; there was also the air. Three air corridors to the city were authorized in a quadripartite document and the Russians could close them only by being the first to use force. Nobody imagined at the outset that a city of 2.25 million people could be kept supplied indefinitely by air but no other expedient was available and even if surrender to the Russians could be postponed for a few weeks, the delay might give time for a settlement to be worked out. But the Russians thought that they held winning cards and in negotiations during the early autumn of 1948 showed themselves intransigent. By then the 'Air Lift' was getting under way and functioning well enough to suggest that, provided enough planes could be made available, it would afford the West a means of escape from the corner in which they found themselves. The question was whether the necessary rate of one plane every two minutes could be kept going through the winter.

The credit for answering that question successfully belongs not only to Western technology but also to the population of West Berlin, under their Mayor Ernst Reuter, who showed themselves ready to bear considerable privations, notably in the lack of heating, light and work, so as to avoid falling under Communist rule. Fortunately the weather was relatively mild; had it been such as to make flying impossible for many days on end, things might have become desperate. In three ways also the Russians refrained from pushing their advantages home. After one of their fighters had at the outset caused the crash of a British airliner, they did not persevere in harassing Western planes, whereas by slowing down the timetable they could have materially reduced the amount brought in. They never withdrew their representative in the quadripartite Air Control Centre regulating traffic to and from the city, and although one of the radio beacons used in guiding aircraft was situated in the Soviet Sector, it was allowed to go on functioning unimpaired. What may well have prompted this caution was the knowledge that, although they had atom bombs in the making, the first one would not be exploded till August 1949, four months after the blockade ended. They had probably felt compelled to make their attempt to force the Western hand earlier than they would ideally have chosen.

By the spring of 1949 the attempt had clearly failed and a counter-blockade instituted by the West on the movement of goods to the Soviet Zone was starting to pinch. Feelers were secretly put out through the Russian representative at the United Nations and on 4 May 1949 the world learnt with some surprise that the blockade was to be lifted. Eleven days later the four Foreign Ministers met in Paris to find a permanent settlement for Berlin, but after arguing without result for nearly a month decided to leave the future legal position of the city as ill-defined as it had been before the blockade began.

Certain vital changes had however taken place, some of which were irrevocable. In August and September 1948 the Communists organized spontaneous demonstrations in front of Berlin's Town Hall in the Soviet Sector, and councillors from the Western Sectors were thereby prevented from reaching meetings; when a meeting did finally take place, it was invaded by the crowd and forced to stop. As the police for the area refused to intervene, the majority of the City Council decided to transfer meetings to the British Sector. In accordance with the constitution of the city (which had received quadripartite blessing), they called new elections for December. In the Western Sectors, where the SED was forbidden by its own leaders to take part, these resulted in almost a two-thirds majority for the SPD. In the Soviet Sector, however, the Communists declared the former mayor and executive committee deposed, replaced them with their own people and saw to it that the elections resulted in an SED victory. The divided city thus obtained two governments, neither of which recognized the other.

But the consequences of the blockade were not confined to Berlin. In July 1948 the Labour Government agreed to make British airfields available for squadrons of American B29 bombers, along with the atomic bombs which these machines carried. The West thereby acquired the capacity to deliver nuclear weapons behind the Iron Curtain, whereas the Russians, lacking corresponding advantages on the western side of the Atlantic, were unable to reach the USA. By November ninety such aircraft were stationed in

Britain and after the blockade ended, they were not withdrawn. For Russian policy had led the West to take a fresh look at its arrangements for mutual defence, with the result that a Canadian suggestion made in April 1948 was a year later realized and the North Atlantic Treaty Organization created. By the NATO Treaty the US Government, with the approval of Congress, joined the Alliance which Britain, France and Benelux had concluded in 1948. The Truman doctrine of that year was expanded into the first American commitment ever made in peacetime for taking military action in the event of an attack on any part of Western Europe; the size of US resources, and the immense superiority in nuclear ones, meant that the accession transformed the Alliance, even though it may only have formalized a situation which already existed in practice. The Russians could no longer have any excuse for not realizing that Western Europe was under the American nuclear shield. Germany, it is true, was still outside the Alliance but the feeling of common fate which had been engendered during the blockade between the people of West Germany and their nominal masters created a psychological situation which was bound before long to be given formal expression. The Russians had achieved the opposite of their intentions and had brought into being a bloc which was once described, with a backward look at the war, as 'The Allies and their Associated Enemies'.

ECONOMIC RECONSTRUCTION

On the Sunday on which the Currency Reform was introduced, the German Director of the Economic Administration Office for Bizonia went to the microphone and promised to the West German people the removal of all but a bare minimum of the multifarious controls existing on prices, wages and supplies. The name of the man responsible for this bold step was Ludwig Erhard. He was not being quite as rash as might appear, for the sectors kept under control included such things as bread, meat, milk, rents, electricity, oil, coal and steel which influenced much of the rest of the economy, while wage control was retained until the autumn. But to cut in this manner through the complex of restrictions which the Occupying Powers had inherited from the Nazis was enough to unnerve many of the Control staff, and great strength of mind was needed to push the change through. But the Americans had a soft spot for anyone who, not content with arguing in favour of free enterprise, was actually prepared to practise it, while the idea commended itself to the Germans because it would reduce the opportunities for Allied interference. It also, of course, increased the differences between the two parts of Germany.

In the second half of 1948 industrial production rose by 50 per cent and in the following year by a further 25 per cent. By 1953 average living standards were higher than in 1938, while in the fourteen years following

1950 the Gross National Product trebled. In 1958 West Germany passed Britain to become the world's second largest exporter and by 1961 was the third largest industrial producer. What is perhaps more surprising is that Germany's net balance of foreign trade on current account showed from 1951 to 1961 (and again from 1966 to 1978) an uninterrupted surplus, occasionally of high proportions. No wonder that people talked of an 'economic miracle' and that the prestige of Dr Erhard rose to great heights. In reality, however, the phenomenon was due to the happy coincidence of a large number of factors, not all of them likely to last. In the euphoria of the hour, this fact tended to be overlooked and the assumption was too easily made that, because the policy of a 'Social Market Economy' had proved brilliantly successful in a particular situation, it would continue to bring equally good results indefinitely. For this reason an analysis of the main features in the West German economy after 1948 is important for an understanding of subsequent developments:

1　The European Recovery Programme (to give 'Marshall Aid' its official title) came into full operation within a month of the Currency Reform and in the course of the next four crucial years West Germany was the fourth largest beneficiary, receiving in all $1,389 million (about one-tenth of the total). Without these dollars to draw on for vital purchases, the German balance of payments over the period 1948–51 would have caused even more anxiety than it did. Moreover Marshall Aid meant that West Germany was recovering in the middle of a half-continent doing the same; each stimulated the other.

2　As has been said (see pp. 84 and 93), German industrial equipment was less seriously affected by the war and the reparations programme than was popularly supposed, while both processes literally cleared the ground for re-equipment, often with the help of a government subsidy which in other circumstances would have been considered illicit. Some firms which might not otherwise have modernized their plant and products were forced to do so.

3　The loss of the lands beyond the Oder–Neisse as a source of food has often been considered a great disadvantage for Germany. But in fact these areas were relatively uneconomic producers by comparison with extra-European sources and had been saved from drastic readjustment only by tariffs. As soon as West Germany could find the exports to pay for substitute imports, she stood to gain by the switch (though the position was later complicated by the expensive Common Agricultural Policy of the EEC).

4　In the years following 1945 many people had been unable to see how West Germany could ever support the vast addition to her population caused by the influx of refugees from the East. And indeed, as soon as many nominal jobs were made uneconomic by the Currency Reform, unemployment rose to 2 million and did not fall below half a million till 1955, while the provision of houses for the newcomers (coming on top of the need to replace the destroyed and damaged homes of the pre-war population) did prove a major burden on the economy. On the other hand the presence of a plentiful supply of labour (and one which was being continually replenished) removed what was to prove a major hindrance to growth in other, more stable countries. Moreover the additional labour, having left its roots behind, could easily be moved to where it was needed (though in practice many new firms established themselves in country districts where refugees happened to have congregated). One estimate has put the value of this labour to West Germany at ten times the benefit derived from Marshall Aid (W. Abelshauser in *Historische Konjunktur Forschung*, ed. Schröder and Spreel, p. 106).

5   West Germany is often considered to have gained because her economy was not burdened until the mid-1950s by any defence expenditure of her own but only by the costs of her occupiers (which until 1952 were fixed without reference to her). These did not include any expenditure falling outside the country but for some time they took up a proportion of her resources comparable to the defence outlays of many other countries; in 1950 they amounted to 37.5 per cent of her budget and 4.6 per cent of her GNP, while in 1951 the figures rose to 42.6 per cent and 6.4 per cent respectively. It was only after the expansion of the economy got under way that they fell, to 27 per cent and 3.5 per cent in 1953. This burden was, however, counterbalanced by the considerable amount of military expenditure made directly or indirectly in West Germany by foreign governments which was *not* charged to the Occupation costs. Between 1955 and 1964 the country's net balance on government invisibles (mostly military) was favourable to the extent of £2,600 million.

6   The German people as a whole are industrious and methodical by tradition and training. Their standard of education has long been high so that they make an admirable labour force for an industrial country. Supplies of skilled management talent were ample, not least from highly trained General Staff officers forced to seek fresh jobs as a result of disarmament.

7   Patriotism, extensive unemployment, lack of funds (as a result of the Currency Reform) and the fact that in Germany membership had never been anything like complete all combined to keep the trade unions from making exorbitant demands. Union structure had been reorganized after the war (partly at British prompting) by the concentration of all workers into twelve unions, with the result that inter-union rivalry and demarcation disputes were much reduced, while German labour has never been able to establish the principle of the closed shop

111

(which would now be illegal under the Basic Law). In 1947, on German initiative, tolerated by the British, workers had received a considerable say in the management of the coal and steel industries ('Co-determination' or *Mitbestimmung*); the extension of this principle to the rest of industry was under discussion and might have been prejudiced if the unions had made themselves awkward. For all these reasons, demands for wage increases remained moderate, while production was not disrupted by strikes. The failure of a 24-hour general strike in November 1948 reinforced this trend which was one of the most important elements in the whole situation. (Letter from W. Harris-Burland in *The Times*, 27 January 1977.)

8　Nearly everyone in Germany had suffered some material loss or come down in the world. Consequently almost everybody was prepared to work hard and anxious to make money in order to rebuild their capital and provide themselves with fresh security. Hard work was also a way of diverting minds from worrying about who was to blame for the past. West German society, like West Germany itself, was starting again from zero and could use all its resources to build up instead of facing the British problem of how to make greatly reduced resources stretch to maintain an established position. Sacred cows were comparatively rare and vested interests on the defensive.

9　Thanks to the restraint of the unions, wages remained at a relatively low level and salaries did the same, amounting (1950–60) to only 47 per cent of GNP as compared with 58 per cent in Britain. Although both showed a steady rise over the years, the rates were, for a long time, slower than the growth in output. Thanks to the general desire to rebuild personal positions, the propensity to consume was the lowest in Western Europe. The rate of saving was high while the profits of firms were ploughed back in fresh investment instead of being distributed in wages and dividends. Private consumption accounted for only 59 per cent of GNP as against 65 per cent in Britain (1950–60). The demand for consumer goods, being to begin with limited, could be largely met by home production and by the hoarded stocks which Currency Reform brought on to the market. Imports of such things remained relatively restricted.

10　The Government exempted overtime from tax and gave considerable premiums to savers. Taxes on the higher income brackets were relatively unprogressive. Considerable inequalities in income were thus tolerated and even encouraged, while the ability of the successful to save was increased. Firms were allowed to write off investments against tax unusually quickly.

11　As will be seen in Chapters 8 and 9, the new political system quickly established itself on a firm basis and the growing prosperity combined with the relative stability of prices to create confidence in the future in spite of the Communist threat on the very boundary of the country. The general mood was to encourage investment.

12 The role of German banks in providing capital for industrial investment became even more pronounced after 1949 owing to the high demand for capital. Two particular aspects deserve mention. First, the banks and other credit institutions were borrowing short and lending long, thereby approximately quadrupling the amount of medium- and long-term loans available. This practice is often regarded as a recipe for disaster but the truth seems to be that, while it is apt to intensify depressions, it enhances booms. Second, a far smaller proportion of household savings than in the UK or US was being reloaned to households in the form of house mortgages or hire-purchase loans. As a result about eight times the UK–US proportion was available for lending to industry.

13 Thanks to all the factors mentioned, the rate of investment was high. Gross domestic capital formation rose between 1950 and 1960 by 157 per cent in real terms, as compared with 46 per cent in Britain. Total fixed investment at home during the same period absorbed 21.9 per cent of GNP as compared with a British figure of 16.6 per cent. Marshall Aid funds were used to remove particular bottlenecks identified as holding back expansion. But as saving was also high, this rate of investment did not lead to serious inflation or price rises.

14 A frequent result of high investment is an increase in demand for imports so that the national trade figures are thrown into deficit as Britain knows to her cost. Why did this not occur in West Germany? One answer is that in the early years it did. Until March 1951 Germany was in serious deficit, especially in the European Payments Union (the financial side of Marshall Aid) where she exhausted her credit quota by December 1950 and had to be granted a further $120 million of which she used three-quarters in the next two months. The situation was aggravated by the rapid rise in world prices resulting from the Korean War and the action of German importers in buying unusually large quantities in order to avoid having to pay higher prices later. It was also aggravated by the cuts in import quotas ('liberalization') which all members of the Organization for European Economic Co-operation had agreed to make. The West German position led for a time to considerable criticism in OEEC, where it was argued that the West Germans were making other people pay their way for them in order to avoid damaging their long-term interests. Great pressure was put on Erhard to reimpose import quotas and tighten credit. His view was that such measures would merely hold back production just as it was getting under way and invite retaliation against German exports. He also argued that at a time of rising prices it was better to hold goods than money. At the end of February 1951 he was driven to suspend

liberalization and tighten credit but just at that moment West Germany's balance of payments took a turn for the better. By the end of May she had repaid all her special credit and some of her previous debts. From that time forward she moved steadily into a stronger credit position and Erhard's reputation soared higher than ever. The explanation seems to have been threefold.

First, heavy purchases of raw materials at the start of the Korean boom led to stocks being built up, after which imports could be reduced. Moreover, once the peak of the boom was passed, prices fell as quickly as they had risen so that the bill for subsequent imports was lowered. West Germany's buying policy, though initially expensive, in the long run paid off.

Second, in spite of the large amount of replacement needed inside Germany, factors already described kept consumer demand within limits and consequently also limited the imports to which such demand gave rise. The extensive efforts made by the Nazis during the 1930s to render Germany self-sufficient seem to have had some permanent effect in reducing the need for imports.

Third, the rearmament programme set going throughout the Western world by the Korean War called above all for finished manufactures, and particularly for modern types of machinery. As these were just the types of machinery which West Germany's reconstructed industry was well equipped to supply, external demand for its goods soared. Even apart from Korea, the world's needs for goods to replace those which would normally have been disposed of between 1939 and 1945 was still unsatisfied, while the steady liberalization of trade, the pursuit by governments of policies of full employment and the requirements of backward areas for equipment for development all combined to keep demand for manufactures high. The resources which Germany had devoted before 1914, as well as between 1933 and 1945, to armaments now went to producing engineering goods for export.

In an economy such as West Germany's, where foreign trade absorbs a relatively high proportion of output, buoyant exports are of particular importance since it is their course which principally gives manufacturers confidence about the long-term prospects of demand. But the view taken about the future course of demand is the chief factor in influencing the readiness of manufacturers to invest and an economy's growth rate depends above all on investment in productive equipment. With output expanding rapidly, productivity is also likely to rise, thanks to economies of scale and generally improved organization, thereby reducing costs and increasing still further competitiveness on foreign markets. In addition the return obtainable on investment is likely to rise, making it more attractive in comparison with other uses of money and hence stimulating it.

The essence of the German 'miracle' was that at a time when world demand was high, German industry found itself with spare capacity, the right products and relatively low costs, so that exporting was easy and profitable, and hence popular. Once this export-led expansion got under way, the prospect of making profits attracted investment into export industries whose growing earnings made it easy to pay for all the imports which increasing manufacturing for export involved. The pool of unemployed, continually refilled until 1961 by migrants from East Germany, for a long time prevented shortage of labour from constricting output. Thanks to the high rate of investment, production grew at a rate which allowed for ample increases in prices and wages without inflation. The exchange rate remained favourable (in spite of being devalued less than most other European currencies in 1949 and being up-valued in 1961 and 1969) and the costs of West Germany's competitors mostly rose faster than hers did (to say nothing of the fact that she sold on quality and servicing as much as on price) so that she could afford increases without pricing herself out of the market. All in all, she was in the exceptional and fortunate position of a 'virtuous spiral' (such as Britain enjoyed between 1750 and 1850).

15   Neither the old Reichsmark nor the new Deutschmark was a 'reserve currency' and West Germany was not under any obligation to provide other countries with capital. Indeed the authorities put up interest rates to check home demand with the result that, in spite of a big export surplus, money flowed *into* rather than *out* of the country. Owing to the lack of institutions needed to make foreign investment easy, not to mention the caution engendered by having had her holdings abroad twice confiscated for reparations, West Germany was to be slow in burdening her balance of payments with heavy capital movements abroad. Even in 1966 her total overseas investments, at DM 8.5 billion, were about one-twentieth the size of Britain's – and her income from them of course proportionately lower. A relatively generous agreement made by her creditors in 1953, before the full extent of her prosperity became evident, enabled her to pay off by moderate instalments the debts inherited from the Weimar Republic and those incurred since 1945.

16   In times of slump, governments are blamed for much that is not their fault; in times of prosperity, the reverse occurs. For this reason the part played by official policy in producing West Germany's success story has been left to the end so as to emphasise the number of other factors involved. But undoubtedly government action contributed in many ways to the total result. Some have already been mentioned, such as the provision of subsidies to help replace bombed or dismantled equipment and the exemption of overtime earnings from tax. Between 1950 and 1955 exports were stimulated, in defiance of international agreements,

by certain taxes being refunded in respect of them. (There was for long a widespread belief among British industrialists that the success of their German competitors was due to 'improper' and secret government aid. Not only did extensive enquiries in 1966 fail to reveal anything beyond the aids mentioned here, and other schemes parallel to those available in Britain, but also they showed that German industry for long believed exactly the same thing about 'secret aid' to British industry!). Measures taken to stimulate internal competition may have contributed to improvements in product design. The abolition of import quotas was originally imposed on West Germany by OEEC but in the mid-1950s the Government went further and deliberately made unilateral cuts in a number of tariffs with the double object of encouraging exports and depriving inefficient domestic manufacturers of a sheltered life in the home market.

These, however, are not the government actions commonly given credit for the West German achievement. Many, particularly in circles where official interference with industry is disliked, have attributed this achievement first and foremost to Erhard's courage in removing controls and using state power to enforce free competition. Though the extent of the freedom has been exaggerated, it did serve a useful purpose. Thanks to cartels and other restrictive agreements, as well as the chronic itch of an authoritarian government to regulate, Germany even before 1933 had never known an economy in which market forces were really allowed free play, and by 1948 the controlled economy had got into a strait-jacket which distorted its natural shape. Initiative was being held back and resources used unprofitably. Their more rational allocation was unlikely ever to have been achieved by central government direction. Nobody knew in which way the horse would naturally choose to go and, in order to discover the answer, it had for a time to be given its head, particularly as regards consumption. But without the incentives to save and invest which have been described, the results of freedom might have been very different.

The second government policy for which much credit has been claimed is the deflationary policy of the Finance Ministry and *Bank Deutscher Länder* in restricting credit and holding down the monetary supply in a world where desire for full employment was producing a steady trend to inflation. Undoubtedly these policies did help to check home demand and encourage exports. A tendency for consumer prices to rise in the early months was also nipped in the bud. But when so many other powerful factors were working in the same direction, a contribution from monetary policy was probably superfluous. During the earlier years, however, the West German leaders may well be excused for lacking confidence that non-monetary forces by themselves would do the trick; the importance of the country earning its way in the world was great enough to justify their wanting to make assurance doubly sure.

116

Previous versions of this book ended this chapter by asking whether the West German authorities were wise to go on depressing demand for as long as they did.

Once a country has paid for all the imports it needs, the only virtue in continuing to expand exports lies in the hope of living more easily later or in having sufficient reserves to draw on if things go wrong. But there is a limit to the extent to which monetary reserves can be built up without causing grave trouble to the other countries from which the money is drawn. Hence a country which wishes to be a persistent creditor must in the long run be prepared to be a persistent investor abroad as well. This in due course West Germany did but various obstacles had accumulated to make the development a slow one. There would therefore seem to have been all the less reason why the West German people should not have been allowed to become prosperous faster than they did, even at the cost of some inflation.

What this analysis failed to foresee, however, was reunification. The day was coming when Germany would need all the resources she could command.

8

THE GERMAN REPUBLICS ARE FOUNDED: 1948–1949

THE WESTERN PARTIES JOCKEY FOR POSITION

The first time that Kurt Schumacher, the Social Democrat, ever encountered Konrad Adenauer, the Christian Democrat, was at a meeting of the German Advisory Council for the British Zone in March 1946. The one is believed to have said to the other, 'Every objective observer will admit that the SPD is the largest party with the greatest future and will remain so.' At the time the prognostication was made, most people in West Germany (though not Adenauer) would have agreed with it. Yet within four years Adenauer was to enter on a tenure of the Chancellorship lasting fourteen years, whereas Schumacher's party was destined to wait seventeen years before taking office and do so only after he himself had been dead for fourteen.

The outstanding reason why expectations were thus falsified is of course the quarrel between the Atlantic Powers and the Soviet Union. This cut Germany in two and completed the process by which the north-east and centre of the country, including nearly all the lands which Prussia had held before 1815, was lost by the West. At the end of 1937, Germany had covered 470,000 sq km. Of this, 118,000 sq km had been taken in 1945 by the Russians and Poles and 104,000 sq km constituted the Soviet Zone. The area lost not only was predominantly Protestant but also under the Weimar Republic had included many Socialist strongholds. Although the remaining 248,000 sq km (about the same area as Great Britain and Northern Ireland) still contained as many Protestants as Catholics, it was almost bound to find its centre of gravity in the Rhineland and south where Catholicism predominated and social antagonisms were on the whole less keen.

The division of the country was of course not merely geographical but ideological as well, and the increasing imposition of a Communist system in the east produced in the west a reaction to the disadvantage of the left wing generally. Many Americans regarded 'pinks' as no more than a sub-species of 'reds' and although the Socialists had the sympathy of Britain's Labour Government, Britain's difficulties at home limited her ability to push her views abroad. In proportion as order and prosperity returned to

West Germany, the more conservatively minded of her citizens, recovering their nerve, advanced the line of the last ditch in which they were prepared to die and proposals for which they would have been glad to settle in 1945 became out of the question four years later. All these influences caused the Socialist tide to ebb in the west before power had been put back into German hands.

Personal factors also affected the result. Kurt Schumacher was a Prussian from the eastern borderlands who had dedicated his life to the Socialist cause without ever occupying a position which gave him practical experience in government. Having lost an arm in the First World War, he had disdained in 1933 to seek safety in exile and had as a result spent ten years in concentration camps. Though the iron certainly entered into his soul, he was never one to sit on the fence. Such was his faith in his creed that as a subordinate he was inevitably a rebel and as a leader inevitably an autocrat. Before political parties had been authorized to operate above local levels, he managed to convene a meeting of Socialist leaders in Hanover and assert his authority. He was the moving spirit in preventing the Berlin SPD from accepting Ulbricht's proposals for fusion, thereby saving the Party in the Western Zones from Communist infiltration, but wrecking the chances of left-wing unity. By a great effort of will-power he overcame the physical damage which had been done to his body but what he could not remedy was the rigidity which had been imposed on his mind. He tried to apply to the Germany of 1950 the outlook which he had acquired in the Germany of 1930. He persisted in believing that a proletarian revolution was imminent and showed great bitterness towards the Americans (though circumstances made him work most of it off on the British) for preventing it from taking place (as he considered, out of capitalist prejudice). Believing that the Socialists' reputation for lack of patriotism had damaged them in the Weimar Republic, he set out to voice German claims to the US and British Occupation authorities regardless of what they were already doing and of the reasons why they found it hard to do more. This lack of support and understanding from one whom they expected in his own interests to take their side reduced their willingness to help the objectives which he had at heart. He regarded the CDU as a refuge for anti-democratic reactionaries and refused to consider co-operation except on his own terms. In particular he demanded neutrality in politics from the clergy and once described the Vatican as 'the fifth occupying power'. Thus he ended by alienating all the people whose aid he needed and damaging a cause for which there was more to be said than he allowed to appear.

Prominent among his mistakes was the underestimation of his CDU antagonist. Konrad Adenauer was a 70-year-old veteran of the Centre who during the Weimar period had distinguished himself as Lord Mayor of his birthplace, Cologne, had become a member of the Prussian State Council and had once been considered for the post of Chancellor. So downright a personality and so convinced a Catholic was incapable of getting on with the Nazis; he was dismissed from his post and retired to cultivate his roses and his taste for wine. In 1945 he emerged and was reinstated by the Americans as Lord Mayor, only to be dismissed by the British six months later and forbidden to take part in politics. The nominal reason was alleged dilatoriness in reconstruction; the real cause is likely to have been obstinacy in dealing with the military authorities, coming on top of agitation against his 'reactionary' views by Socialist *émigrés*. Although there was some truth in the latter charge, it could have been made equally against a number of other people who were being admitted to posts of responsibility. If, in addition to ex-Nazis and Communists, 'reactionaries' were to be barred from office, there would not have been enough people left to run the country.

The long-term effects of the dismissal were considerable, not so much because it prejudiced Adenauer against the British (the episode left on the whole lack of enthusiasm rather than ill-will) but because it removed him from the ranks of Allied-appointed administrators at a crucial moment and, as the ban on his political activity was soon lifted, enabled him to devote his time to precisely such activity. Before little more than a month was up, CDU executives from all parts of the British Zone were called in January 1946 to a meeting to decide who should represent the Party on the Zonal Advisory Council. While the rest of those present were hesitating how to begin, Adenauer characteristically sat down and said, 'As I am the senior person present, you will no doubt wish me to take the chair.' (He also arranged for the meeting to be held in a monastery where the food was, for those days, unusually good, so that everyone was feeling benevolent!) Nobody saw fit to challenge this assumption of authority, which he promptly used to rule that, as the meeting had been called to choose representatives for the British Zone, only those officially invited to attend in that capacity (many of them picked by Adenauer himself) could participate in the discussion. Hermes from Berlin was forced to leave the room while the other main aspirant to the chair was a refugee from Pomerania who lacked supporters in north-west Germany. Adenauer thus had no difficulty in getting himself confirmed as chairman – a position which he lost no time in exploiting. The various Land parties in the Zone were forbidden to correspond with outside bodies except through his Zonal Party Headquarters. His main rivals were the groups in Berlin (which he seldom or never visited) and south Germany. To hold them off until he was ready, he procrastinated over the formation of a federal party organization and in fact no such organization came into existence until over a year after he became Chancellor. The Russians played into his hands by denying authority in the areas under their control first to Hermes and then, at the end of 1947, to Kaiser and Lemmer, the Berlin CDU leaders, thus making it less and less possible to claim that the Party must be centred on the old capital. The southerners were kept at arm's length until the moment was ripe for a deal. But most remarkable was the way in which the wily old man contrived to neutralize Karl Arnold, who throughout this period was CDU Minister-President of North Rhine-Westphalia, the Land in which Adenauer lived.

There was more to these manoeuvrings than a personal struggle for power. The same climate of thought which encouraged the expectation of Social Democratic predominance had encouraged the more socialist wing of the CDU with which Kaiser, Lemmer and Arnold were particularly associated. The community of the future was generally assumed to involve widespread socialization, and to favour the small man. A planned economy was expected to remain essential if Europe was to make the best use of her scanty resources. The 'Ahlen Programme' of the Party, adopted in February 1947, centred round the idea of a 'semi-public economy'. 'The new structure of the German economy must start from the realization that the period of uncurtailed rule by private capitalism is over. The mere replacement of private capitalism must, however, also be avoided.'

Adenauer had agreed to the Ahlen programme (which at the time of its formulation possessed considerable electoral appeal) but had no love for it. He was biding his time until a good word for private enterprise might become fashionable again. Kaiser in December 1946 supported Bevin's scheme for bringing the coal and steel industries of the Ruhr into public ownership (see pp. 96, 112), but Adenauer insisted that a decision on this must be postponed until the German economy was free. Here he saw eye to eye with Clay, who in October 1947 wrote that, if only the Americans could succeed in deferring the issue of socializing industry until free enterprise had had time to bring economic improvement, it might cease to be a live political issue. When in the summer of 1948 the Landtag for North Rhine-Westphalia passed, against the advice of Adenauer and the votes of the CDU, a bill nationalizing the coal-mines, it was American pressure which made the British Military Government insist that the issue be held over until it could be considered at national level.

In this situation the Bizonal Economic Administration acquired key significance. In June 1947 this institution (see p. 98) was reorganized and an Economic Council set up to control it. On this Council both the CDU and the SPD possessed an equal number of representatives; thus neither party could dominate it in isolation. The CDU would at first have been ready to work with the SPD but Schumacher, who controlled the SPD delegation without belonging to it, refused to co-operate except as a dominant partner. He not only insisted on the directorship of the economic branch being given to a Social Democrat but also refused into the bargain to 'buy' this appointment by relinquishing to the CDU three of the eight Economic Ministries which his Party monopolized in the Länder of the British and American Zones. The result was that the CDU joined forces with the Free Democrats and the German Party (as the Lower Saxon Land Party had rechristened itself) and so excluded Social Democrats from the administrative board altogether. Moreover in March 1948 the man originally appointed as the Director of Economics resigned and was replaced after long discussions by a professor whom the Social Democrats and the Americans had eighteen months earlier sacked from the job of Bavarian Minister of Economics. Although Ludwig Erhard as yet belonged to no particular party, his appointment and the success of the policy to which he committed himself were of critical importance for the more conservative wing of the CDU (see p. 109).

Like Schumacher, Adenauer kept clear of the Economic Council but many of the CDU delegates to it were his friends. He could be just as pertinacious as Schumacher but was far more adroit. Possessing some of Bismarck's flair for distinguishing the possible from the desirable and anticipating how people would react, he would never have overplayed his hand in the way Schumacher did. For an old man, he could be remarkably quick-witted and these gifts combined with a not inconsiderable intelligence to make him more than a match for his rivals and opponents. As a Catholic Rhinelander he had grown up under a Prussian administration in the full flush of enthusiasm for a Germany at last unified. As a result his loyalties were tempered by awareness of the advantages of belonging to a large centralized state, while his genuine national patriotism was widened by recognizing a European tradition. Nationalism in its more radical form repelled him as brash, unintelligent and uncivilized, but he could understand its appeal to people concerned for the welfare of their country. By temperament and training an autocrat who preferred 'yes-men' to colleagues with ideas of their own, he knew that effective leadership depends upon men being managed rather than intimidated. An unrepentant individualist, he had a lively sense of responsibility for the welfare of others while submission to an authoritarian Church had taught him that individual ends must be sought in and through social organization. This mix of qualities explains why he became a rallying-point for post-war Germany. Aided considerably by luck he gave West Germany seventeen years of prosperity and order in which, for the first time in the country's history, democracy became associated with success.

THE DRAFTING OF THE BASIC LAW

The Anglo-American-French Conference in London in the spring of 1948 (see p. 101) finally agreed on four documents. The first called for the convening of a

Constituent Assembly [to] draw up a democratic constitution which will establish for the participating states a governmental structure of federal type which is best adapted to the eventual re-establishment of German unity at present disrupted and which will protect the rights of participating states, provide adequate central authority and contain guarantees of individual rights and freedom.

The second called for a re-examination of Land boundaries. The third set out in general terms the powers which the Allies proposed to reserve for themselves after the creation of a German government. The fourth (withheld from the Germans for the time being) set out the criteria by which the Military Governors were to decide whether the constitution produced by the Assembly was acceptable.

The body to which these documents were directed was not the Economic Council but the Ministers-President of the eleven Länder in the Western Zones. They consisted at this time of five Social Democrats, five Christian Democrats (one being Arnold) and one Free Democrat. But when they met at Koblenz 8–10 July 1948, a fortnight after the beginning of the Berlin blockade, they rejected the idea of calling a Constituent Assembly to draft a constitution as prejudicial to the chance of re-establishing German unity. This attitude owed much to the influence of Schumacher who, in his anxiety to secure the reunification so important for his Party, still hoped to persuade the Communists to co-operate on his own terms. The Military Governors were highly surprised to find their gift horse looked in the mouth; Clay described the attitude as a 'catastrophic disregard of the total European situation'. In the end, however, a more constructive outlook prevailed and the Ministers-President consented to convene a 'Parliamentary Council' to draft a 'Basic Law' (*Grundgesetz*); the Allied proposal to confirm this law by a referendum was dropped in favour of ratification by Landtäge.

The party leaders had not been consulted over this decision but it was from the Parties rather than from the Länder Cabinets or the Bizonal Administration that were drawn the members of the Parliamentary Council which met at Bonn on 1 September. Each Landtag elected one representative for every 750,000 of population, an arrangement which gave the CDU/CSU and SPD twenty-seven members each, the FDP five and the German Party, Centre and Communists two each. As the votes of the last three were seldom all cast on the same side, the FDP often found itself able to exert decisive influence. Schumacher was laid up with serious illness from March 1948 to April 1949 and could direct the SPD delegation only from his sick-bed, whereas Adenauer was chosen as President of the Council and set promptly to work at reducing the influence of the Ministers-President over its proceedings; they were not invited to take any part and not much attention was paid to a draft constitution which they had prepared. A first draft of the Council's own document was ready by the year-end and, after further discussion, was presented to the Military Governors on 13 February 1949. On 2 March they replied, objecting to certain compromises laboriously achieved by the Germans as regards centralization, and the whole matter went back into the melting pot.

Early in April the three Foreign Ministers authorized the Military Governors to make concessions but on American insistence the knowledge of this was held back from the Germans. Schumacher refused to consider the modifications for which the Governors were calling whereas the Christian Democrats were reluctantly reconciling themselves to giving way. At that juncture the Foreign Ministers' message was published; a final compromise was reached; the text of the Basic Law was agreed by the Parliamentary Council against a minority of eight on 8 May (simultaneously with the lifting of the Berlin blockade), approved by the Allies four days later and brought into force on 23 May 1949. Only the Bavarian Landtag refused to accept the Law, arguing that it gave too much power to the central government but, as they agreed to accept it as valid if the other Länder did so, they were considered to have shouted 'No' but whispered 'Yes'. An election was held on 14 August and the Federal Parliament first met on 7 September.

During the various discussions there were three main questions at issue. The first and biggest concerned the respective powers to be allotted to the Federal and Land governments, especially in matters of finance. American pressure, the first document provided by the Allies and the reluctance of the Länder to lose influence made considerable decentralization inevitable, but the SPD and FDP were in favour of making the centre as strong as possible, while the Bavarians, the Ministers-President and the Military Governors wanted it to be weak. The CDU/CSU was split, with its left wing inclining to the Social Democratic position, and Adenauer had to fight for a compromise; he bitterly resented the fact that the SPD got the credit for standing up to the Occupying Powers and attributed this to backstairs influence with the British Labour Government.

The second and related issue concerned the Second Chamber. The SPD and the CDU in the British Zone (including Adenauer) favoured a Senate elected by the Landtäge in relation to party strength and proportional to Land population: the southern CDU/CSU, the Centre and German Party fought vigorously for a Federal Council (Bundesrat) made up, as in the past, of delegates from the Land Governments. At the crucial moment a bargain was struck by which the SPD withdrew their opposition to the Council form in return for a reduction in the powers which it was to have over legislation, only to find at a later date that a provision giving the Bundesrat power to vote on any legislation which affected the Länder made it much stronger than anyone had allowed for. Today nearly half the laws that are proposed fall into this category.

Voting procedure in Federal elections was not laid down in the Basic Law but in a separate document prepared by the Parliamentary Council. The widespread belief that proportional representation had been to blame for the Weimar Republic's failure led many to favour a British system of election by simple majority in single-member constituencies. Objection had, however, been raised against this on the ground that, in the conditions of Germany, it would lead to one party sweeping the board most of the time. As a result a compromise was evolved which the Parliamentary Council adopted. The 402 seats (now 662) in the lower Chamber were to be divided into two parts and each elector given two votes. The first votes would be used to elect 201 candidates in single-member constituencies; the second votes would be collected Land by Land and each party allocated as many seats as it was entitled to by its proportion of the votes as counted by a special procedure. The total number of seats to which a party was entitled was to be decided by the second method; those of its candidates who had been elected by the first method would be counted first and the total number made up by drawing names off a list compiled by the party before the election. Thus the constituency voting was to some extent window-dressing, though it did connect each constituency with an individual; the strength of each party was decided by proportional representation as in Weimar.

The Military Governors were worried by this scheme and tried to insist on modifications, but succeeded in securing only two. By the first, the proportion of seats to be directly elected was raised to 60 per cent – which did not really affect the issue and lasted only till 1953. By the second, seats were to be denied altogether to any party which could neither win three constituencies nor obtain at least 5 per cent of the votes cast in any one Land; this has materially helped to produce that absence of small splinter parties which distinguishes Bonn from Weimar. The Law as thus amended was then promulgated by the Governors.

The Parliamentary Council had included representatives of West Berlin and the Council's intention was to make West Berlin into a twelfth Land of the new Republic. The news of this intention produced a protest from the Russians; the Western Powers, anxious to do nothing which might give the East a pretext for further assaults on the city's freedom, insisted on the proposal in its original form being dropped. Instead representatives of West Berlin were allowed to sit, but not to vote, in the Federal Parliament. In 1950 it was agreed that West Berlin should have a constitution of its own, with a House of Deputies and Senate, but the House of Deputies was allowed to adopt such laws of the Republic as it thought fit, subject always to reserved powers of control by the Allied Commandants in the city. Most West German laws were adopted for Berlin but there were some exceptions, notably for laws imposing conscription. In June 1990 Berlin was put on the same footing as the other Länder.

THE BASIC LAW

The Basic Law (*Grundgesetz*) for the Federal Republic of Germany (*Bundesrepublik Deutschland* – BRD) opens with a preamble saying that it has been decided on by the German people in eleven named Länder (i.e. excluding the East and Berlin), inspired by the wish to preserve their unity as a nation and a state and to serve the peace of the world as a fully qualified member of a united Europe, in virtue of their power to make a constitution with the object of giving their political life a fresh form for a transitional period. Nothing is said about either the Occupying Powers or the Land Governments authorizing the German people to take this step which is thus tacitly claimed to rest upon an inalienable right inherent in the people. Such a claim corresponds to Adenauer's thesis that the Allies were wrong by international law in interpreting unconditional surrender to mean a complete transfer of government authority into their hands. The preamble goes on to state that the inhabitants of the Länder concerned were acting for all those Germans who were prevented from taking part. There was still incumbent on the entire German people the task of completing the unity and freedom of Germany in free self-determination. It was at one time argued that these sentences made it necessary for the Basic Law to be amended before any Federal government could reach agreement with another government ruling over Germans in any other part of Germany but in July 1973 the Constitutional Court decided that this was not so, provided that the agreement did nothing to make reunification impossible.

The first chapter of the Law consists of nineteen articles defining fundamental rights. The opening article proclaims the dignity of people to be unassailable and says that in consequence the German people recognize certain inviolable and inalienable human rights as the foundations of every human community, as well as of peace and justice in the world. This wording neatly evades the question whether these rights exist prior to the state or, as the classic German view maintained, are derived from it, so that an individual is precluded from claiming rights against it. There follows, however, an article which says that personal freedom may be encroached on only pursuant to a law, while Article 19 provides that laws restricting basic rights must apply generally, must name the right encroached on and the article of the Basic Law protecting it and must refrain from infringing the 'essential content' of the right. These limitations bar the police and courts from interfering with rights by virtue of a supposed power given them by nature or customary law to maintain public order or security. This police power was used even under the Weimar Republic to justify considerable interference with private freedom, especially where 'public morals' were supposed to be involved.

The third article provides for equality between the sexes, a radical departure for many Germans. The Parliamentary Council gave a chilly reception to the idea when it was proposed by the Social Democrats but yielded reluctantly to a storm of letters from fervent women. Discrimination on account of sex, descent, race, language, nationality, origin, belief or political views is also forbidden. Other articles provide for freedom of expression (though such freedom is not to justify disloyalty to the free democratic order), of research, teaching, assembly, organization, communication and movement. Articles protecting marriage and the right of parents to decide on the religious education of their children were put in to meet the wishes of the Christian Democrats, although education is strictly a Land rather than a Federal responsibility.

The Social Democrats wished to include a right to strike but dropped the proposal when its opponents pointed out serious difficulties of interpretation; the Free Democrats did not press a proposal to forbid the 'closed shop'. But Article 12 says that all Germans have the right to a free choice of profession, place of work and place of education and a requirement that individuals must join a union before being able to work in a place where they have obtained a job would probably be held to infringe this. An attempt has also been made to use it to prevent universities from excluding on the ground of lack of room applicants who were otherwise qualified, but the Constitutional Court decided not to uphold this. Property is guaranteed but land, natural resources and means of production can be taken into public ownership by law, provided that compensation is paid.

The next chapter of eighteen articles deals with the relationship between the Federation and the Länder. At all lower levels of government there are to be representative bodies based on general, direct, free, equal and secret voting. Black, red and gold are again the republican colours. Article 23 lists the eleven Länder in which the Law was valid at the time of its enactment. It was to be brought into force in other parts of Germany after they acceded. An important article not only provides that the internal organization of political parties must conform to democratic principles but also condemns as unconstitutional parties which by their aims or the behaviour of their members set out to influence (*beeinträchtigen*) or set aside the free democratic order. (The idea that party organization is something which needs a special law to regulate it is typical of the way in which the German approach to public affairs differs from the British.) Another article authorizes the Federal Government to part with sovereign rights in so far as this may be involved by membership of a system which seeks to preserve peace by mutual collective security or to secure peaceful and permanent order in Europe. (In 1992 this article was held by some to preclude the Government from sending a contingent to the Gulf War as it was outside Europe.) Actions were declared unconstitu tional which threatened to disturb the peace of nations or lead to aggressive war. Federal Law takes precedence over Land Law. Foreign relations are declared a Federal matter. If a Land fails to carry out duties imposed on it by the Basic Law or other Federal Laws, the Federal Government can with the approval of the Federal Council (i.e. of other Länder Governments) step in. Provision is made for boundary changes between the Länder; the only use so far made of this has been the amalgamation of the three original

Länder of Baden, Baden-Württemberg and Württemberg-Hohenzollern (see p. 97) into a single Land.

The third chapter (twelve articles) deals with the Federal Assembly (Bundestag). Originally only those over 21 were allowed to vote but this was lowered to 18 in 1971. The Bundestag is chosen for four years and there are provisions to ensure that it is both called together and (ultimately) dissolved. Ministers do not need to belong to it (and do not all do so) but have the right to attend all sessions (including committees, of which one for foreign affairs and one for defence are statutory) and must do so if summoned. Deputies enjoy the usual immunities and are paid £40,000 a year plus an expense allowance of £22,000 (1990). Officials who wish to stand as candidates are not required to resign their posts beforehand, but, in accordance with previous German and much European practice, are entitled to go on leave during elections and, if successful, during their period of office.

The Federal Council (Bundesrat) is disposed of in four articles. Consisting, as already mentioned (see p. 24), of representatives chosen by the Länder Governments, it provides the forum in which Federal and Länder officials can work out (largely in committee) problems affecting their respective spheres of responsibility. It has in consequence been described as a Parliament of Under-Secretaries (*Oberregierungsräte*) though, when it comes to plenary sessions, votes are valid only if cast by Ministers. The Bundesrat now contains sixty-eight members, six each from Länder with populations of over 6 million, four each from Länder with populations between 2 million and 6 million and three each from those with under 2 million. This basis of allocation originally represented a compromise between the Social Democrats, who wanted all Länder to be equal (which would have given them initially eighteen seats to a CDU fifteen), and the other parties, who wanted representation to be exactly proportionate to population (which would have given the CDU twenty-five seats to an SPD nineteen). In accordance with previous practice (see p. 13), the votes for each Land have to be cast as a block.

The approval of the Bundesrat is required for a wide range of legislation on the ground that in one way or another it affects the affairs of the Länder. Where such approval is not required, the Bundesrat is still entitled to vote against such legislation. If it does so by an ordinary majority, the vote can be overridden by a similar vote in the Bundestag. Where the Council's adverse vote is carried by a two-thirds majority, the Assembly must in turn produce a two-thirds majority to give the law validity. Government proposals for legislation are normally submitted to the Bundesrat before they go to the Bundestag. Differences between the two Chambers are ironed out by a joint Mediation Committee.

The fifth chapter of eight articles deals with the Federal President who is elected by a Federal Convention consisting of the members of the Bundestag and an equal number of Land representatives chosen by the Land

Assemblies on the basis of proportional representation. This arrangement represents a reaction against the Weimar Constitution where the President was elected by direct popular vote. It is one of several points in the Basic Law where the framers showed their distrust of the masses. This is further displayed in the requirement (taken over from the Constitution of 1871) that, with four exceptions, every act of the President requires the counter-signature of the Chancellor or responsible Minister in order to be valid. President von Weizsäcker has recently provoked argument as to whether speeches by the President, which go beyond mere commonplaces, require such countersignature. The President holds office for five years and can be re-elected only once; of the six holders of the office thus far, three have had a second term.

Perhaps the most important chapter (of eight articles) concerns the Federal Government which consists of the Chancellor and Ministers. The Ministers, for whom no number is prescribed, are appointed by the President on the nomination of the Chancellor. The Chancellor is elected by the Bundestag without debate on the proposal of the President (here acting on his own authority). If the person proposed does not obtain a majority of votes, the Bundestag can within a fortnight propose its own candidate who, if he or she obtains the votes of over half the Deputies, must be appointed by the President. If this does not happen, a fresh vote has to be taken immediately the fortnight is over. If anyone then receives the votes of more than half the Deputies, the President must appoint that person; if nobody fulfils this requirement, the President has to choose between appointing the person who gets most votes and dissolving the Bundestag (acting again on his own authority). In practice the President has always waited until soundings among the Deputies have disclosed an individual whom a majority are prepared to vote for as Chancellor and only then proceeded to nominate that person. But this course might not be practicable, if, as the authors of the Basic Law were anticipating, there were a number of small parties.

To deprive a Chancellor of office, the Bundestag must not merely vote by a majority against him but must, at least forty-eight hours previously, nominate a successor, whom the President is then bound to appoint. This 'constructive vote of no-confidence' was taken over from the constitution of Baden-Württemberg where it was suggested by an American professor; it is intended to obviate the situation where two extremes unite to eject a Chancellor, without being able to agree on a successor. If a Chancellor asks the Bundestag for a vote of confidence, and fails to win a majority, the Chancellor can (Article 68) demand within three weeks from the President a dissolution of the Assembly and fresh elections. The Chancellor's right to do this lapses, however, if the Assembly can, before the dissolution takes place, agree on an alternative Chancellor. Experience showed in 1972 (see p. 196) and 1983 (see p. 219) that this procedure does not provide adequately for the situation in which a fresh election becomes desirable in the middle of a parliamentary term so as to give legitimacy to a new government which, in one way or another, differs from its predecessor. If the Chancellor does not want a dissolution, the President can, given the approval of the Bundesrat, declare a law passed as a matter of emergency even against the votes of the Bundestag. This procedure can be repeated for six months but cannot thereafter be resorted to again as long as the Chancellor concerned holds office. Laws which amend or otherwise affect the Basic Law cannot be passed in this way. Inside the Cabinet, the Chancellor is responsible for deciding the general principles of policy to be followed, while individual Ministers are left to apply those principles within their own departments. Clashes between Ministers are decided by the Cabinet. This arrangement represents a compromise between a Presidential Cabinet of the American type and the collective responsibility of Ministers on the British pattern. How it works in practice depends on the personalities of the Chancellor and the remaining Ministers; Adenauer frequently interfered with his subordinates, Schmidt and Kohl are said to have kept them under firm control, whereas Erhard, Kiesinger and Brandt in varying degrees found difficulty in establishing their authority.

For a long time there were no Junior Ministers. This considerably reduced the patronage available to and thus the influence of the Government. Moreover it laid a heavy burden on the single Minister in each department, although, in accordance with German tradition (see p. 13), the State Secretary (or senior civil servant in the Department) undertook many responsibilities such as answering parliamentary questions which in Britain would be considered political. In 1967, however, the Coalition Government decided to appoint seven Deputies as 'Parliamentary State Secretaries' with a view to improving contact between the political and administrative worlds. Some commentators made heavy weather over this innovation on the ground that it would restrict undesirably the functions of the existing State Secretaries. However, it would seem to have proved its worth as there are now thirty-three Parliamentary State Secretaries. But Ministers are still regarded as broad-minded if they leave in position the official State Secretary whom they find there on taking up office, and do not insist on installing people who share their own political views.

The remaining five chapters and seventy-seven articles of the Law deal in considerable detail with the passing of legislation, with its execution and with administration, justice and finance. There are three broad types of legislation.

1   Exclusive, where the Länder can legislate only if a Federal law gives them express authority to do so. In this field come nationality, freedom of movement, currency, weights and measures, customs and trade treaties, railways, air travel, posts and telecommunications, rights of Federal

officials, commercial law, criminal police. Foreign affairs were added in 1952, Defence in 1954.

2 Concurrent, where the Länder can legislate in so far as the Federal Government makes no use of the powers given to it in fields where legislation, to be effective and avoid clashes, must extend to more than one Land. The Basic Law lists twenty-three subjects for such legislation, most of which relate to law and economics though matters like environmental protection and infectious diseases and rules for road and sea transport are also included. Subsidies to educational institutes and hospitals were added in 1969.

3 Other, where Länder are free to legislate as they choose, subject to the Basic Law.

In 1971 the Federation was authorized to pass laws laying down the outlines (*Rahmenvorschriften*) regarding the legal position of officials at all levels of administration, higher education, the preservation of nature, town planning and water supply.

The position is further complicated by the fact that, in accordance with German tradition, much Federal legislation is in fact administered by the Länder. The Federal Government supervises this process and has power to issue general regulations as to how it shall be done which, provided that they obtain the approval of the Bundesrat, are binding on the Länder. Other matters, however, such as Finance, Railways and Posts, are administered by federal authorities scattered throughout the country. The Ministers-President in 1948–9 allowed for only 3,225 established posts in the headquarters offices; although this number has since multiplied, the proportion of civil service posts at the centre remains comparatively small.

In the financial field the Americans horrified the German administrators by proposing that both Federal and Länder Governments should be free to levy the same kinds of taxation. Instead, an elaborate division was made, on lines traditional in Germany, by which the proceeds of certain taxes (mainly indirect) were to go to the Federation and others (including property taxes, driving licences and the beer tax) to the Länder, while revenue from income and corporation tax was to be divided between the two on a stated percentage, the adjustment of which has proved a standing bone of contention. A further elaborate compensation arrangement, requiring the approval of the Bundesrat, evens out the burden between the relatively rich and the relatively poor Länder. The net effect of the whole arrangement is to make German financial affairs complex and inelastic since the Federal Government is often unable to make its decisions effective without securing the agreement of the Länder.

Responsibility for ensuring that the Grundgesetz is observed and more particularly for delimiting the constitutional spheres of the Bund and Länder is laid on the Constitutional Court at Karlsruhe. (This is distinct from the Federal High Court in the same city, which is the last instance of appeal in non-constitutional cases.) Appointments to this Court are made alternatively by the Bundestag and Bundesrat from a list drawn up by the Federal Ministry of Justice; this includes people with legal training who have made a name for themselves in politics, administration or the universities, since only a quarter of the seats in the Court are filled by professional judges. Besides reviewing legislation, the Court deals with complaints from individuals who consider that rights guaranteed to them by the Basic Law have been infringed. But on the major issue of the Federation's right to legislate in the concurrent field, the Court is not entitled to do more than examine alleged abuses of discretion; it may not challenge the need for a particular piece of legislation.

The net result of these provisions is to give the last word on a number of issues to the Court rather than to Parliament. If the Court appears to be frustrating the popular will, its judgement can be reversed only by securing an amendment to that clause in the Basic Law on which the judgement has been based. But amendments to the Basic Law require the approval of two-thirds of the members of the Bundestag and two-thirds of the votes of the Länder delegations in the Bundesrat. They are therefore not easily carried out so that the provision gives a conservative tone to the German political system. No amendment is admissible at all which alters the federal character of the state, the rights of the Länder to co-operate in law-making, the democratic basis of the state or the human rights recognized in the opening Articles (although amendments have been allowed which amplified or clarified those rights).

A final Article said that the Basic Law would lose its validity on the day on which a Constitution came into force which had been resolved on in a free decision by the German people. At one period in 1990 it was thought that the Article might be used to effect reunification but in the end Article 23 was invoked instead. The Treaty which laid down the terms of reunification provided for the insertion, after the words 'Basic Law' in Article 146, of the extra words 'which is valid for the whole German people after the completion of the unity and freedom of Germany'.

The Basic Law represents a determined effort to learn from experience and is a good deal more down-to-earth than the Weimar Constitution. Its framers sought to provide against the paralysis of the legislative by the inability of the Assembly to agree, against the consequent resort on a lasting basis to government by emergency decree, against the growth and agitation of anti-democratic radicalism and against the victory of anti-democratic forces in a single Land. Critics have alleged that, if it had been in force in the 1930s, it would not have prevented Hitler from coming to power. The present document would, however, seem to give more opportunities than did its predecessor to anyone who is prepared to defend the kind of system which it has instituted – and that must always be a principal test of any paper formula.

(For a fuller description of Federal election procedure today, see p. 247.
An English translation of the text of the Basic Law, with amendments, is published by the Press and Information Office of the Federal Government in Bonn.)

GERMANY GETS GOVERNMENTS AGAIN

The Parliamentary Council had found life pleasant in the small and relatively undamaged university town of Bonn and when the time came to choose a capital for the Federal Republic, felt that it had many advantages over Frankfurt which, although bigger and more important, was for that reason badly bombed and full of Americans. The popular story is that Adenauer got Bonn chosen because he happened to live just across the river but a more likely explanation of his advocacy is the fact that Schumacher preferred Frankfurt and, after the advantage which the SPD leader had gained over the question of standing up to the Military Governors, the CDU leader welcomed another issue on which to assert his authority. But the alleged Schumacher statement that 'the selection of Frankfurt would be a defeat for the CDU', which is said to have played some part in getting the CDU to vote for Bonn, is believed to have emanated from two newspaper correspondents who were in love and wanted money to set up house. Another factor which played a part was the argument that Bonn would be easier to abandon if Berlin ever became available again. Indeed the transitory character of the Republic was for long reflected in many of the buildings in which the Federal institutions were accommodated. But as the prospects of reunification faded, much was done to refashion Bonn for a long-term function and by the time of reunification it was well on the way to being a handsome and efficient modern capital (although there are still a surprising number of level-crossings!). The choice, however, underlined the character of the Federal Republic as a West European state under Catholic influence.

The General Election on 14 August 1949 brought the CDU/CSU 139 seats, the SPD 131, the FDP 52, the Bavarian Party and the German Party 17 apiece, the Communists 15 and others 31. In the light of these figures, the Socialists favoured a 'Great Coalition' with the CDU, as did the left wing of the CDU. The Ministers-President also favoured a Great Coalition which they guessed would leave them more power. Adenauer on the other hand was on bad terms with Schumacher but pleased with the results which had thus far followed from CDU/FDP co-operation (see p. 122) in the Bizonal Economic Council. Indeed the CDU had largely fought the election on the economic policies of Erhard (who had only recently joined the Party) but these aroused little enthusiasm in the groups favouring a Great Coalition. Adenauer inclined instinctively towards the more conservative solution of a 'Little Coalition' with the FDP and the German Party which not only would be anti-Socialist but also would be sufficiently far to the right to deprive any more reactionary groups of their allure and so reduce the danger of anti-democratic elements exploiting their social and economic positions to turn the bureaucracy and professional classes against the Republic. He must also have seen that his influence in his own Party would be greatest if he could act as a balancing factor between two divergent wings, and that he would be more likely to hold this position in a Little Coalition since in a Great one he would himself belong to the right wing. Moreover in a Little Coalition the CDU/CSU would be the dominating partner.

His behaviour in these circumstances was characteristic. A week after the Election, he held a tea-party at his home for a hand-picked group of twenty-five CDU members including some on whom he thought he could count and some on whom he felt he would need to count. Arnold, although CDU Minister-President of the Land in which the gathering was held, was not invited. Kaiser, on the other hand, was a key figure who at an early stage was talked into supporting the Adenauer solution. Some of the opponents of this course made the mistake of going away early and thus leaving the way open for the impression to be created by adroit handling of the journalists waiting at the gate that all those present had come down in favour of a Little Coalition. Soon afterwards Adenauer secured the support of the FDP by promising his backing for their leader Theodor Heuss as President of the Republic, and of the CSU by promising in a similar way to back Ehard, the Minister-President of Bavaria, for the chairmanship of the Bundesrat. By the time the rank-and-file Deputies of the CDU got to Bonn, they found that the die had been virtually cast. The delegation from North Rhine-Westphalia, however, voted not for Ehard but for their own leader Arnold, who was in consequence elected. The CSU were furious and if any acceptable CDU candidate had been standing for the Presidency would probably have voted for him, since Heuss was too liberal for their tastes. But the only alternative was Schumacher, who had insisted on standing, and he lost to Heuss on the second ballot. Heuss nominated Adenauer as Chancellor and on 17 September his appointment was confirmed by a majority of one – when asked if he had voted for himself, he replied 'of course'. He told his followers that they must contrive to hold office for eight years.

Earlier planning had contemplated only eight Ministries – Finance, Economics, Justice, Interior, Food, Agriculture, Labour and Posts. Adenauer added Ministries for Bundesrat Affairs, All-German Affairs, Refugees, Housing and the Marshall Plan, thus enlarging the number of people he could reward. (A disarmed Germany naturally had no Defence Ministry and as long as Foreign Affairs consisted of relations with the Occupation Authorities, they were kept in the hands of the Chancellor.) Adenauer gave five of his thirteen posts to the CDU, three to the CSU, three to the FDP and two to the German Party. The CDU left wing, along with those members of the Party who had been prominent in Land Governments, or in the Bizonal Administration, were passed over. Kaiser was made responsible for All-German Affairs but found it a back seat. Except for him, the Cabinet contained nobody who had offered serious opposition to Adenauer's views. It soon fulfilled its promise of being an obsequious body.

Meanwhile those in charge of the Soviet Zone had been following step-by-step behind the West. In March 1948 a deliberative body of 400, the People's Council, was set up by a People's Congress and in March 1949 (during the blockade) approved the constitution of a German Democratic Republic (DDR). In May 1949 a third People's Congress was elected on a single party list and this in turn elected a second People's Council. In the month following Adenauer's assumption of office this constituted itself a Provisional Government. This, however, did not imply any significant relaxation of the Russian grip on the territory.

9

REARMAMENT AND THE RESTORATION OF SOVEREIGNTY: 1949–1955

SAAR AND RUHR

The establishment of a German government logically implied the end of foreign rule and the Western Occupying Powers had therefore agreed, as an integral part of the deal, to change the Control Council into a High Commission and give written definition in an 'Occupation Statute' to their rights and obligations towards the new German authorities. The three High Commissioners at one stage intended to deliver the Occupation Statute to the Federal Government in a solemn ceremony and suggested to Adenauer that he should formally present his Cabinet to them at the same time. He, however, demurred: an 'Occupation Statute', though an improvement on the situation in which the Germans had no defined rights, was still in his eyes a disagreeable document and its presentation no occasion for festivities. The High Commissioners therefore decided to hand over the Statute on 21 September 1949 in a formal but private ceremony on the Petersberg above Bonn (where Chamberlain had stayed during the Bad Godesberg talks with Hitler in September 1938).

They would stand together on a carpet while Adenauer waited in front of them and listened to an address by their French Chairman. After the speech was over, Adenauer was to step on to the carpet and be given the documents. When, however, Adenauer entered the room, the Chairman took a step forward to greet him. The German went towards the Frenchman and so brought himself on to the carpet before the address had begun. The incident symbolizes the way in which the new West German Chancellor exploited every opening given to him for extending the scope of the powers which the Allies had granted. In yielding to one of his demands during the negotiations soon to be described, the American High Commissioner was to say 'All right then. This is now the 122nd concession we have made to the Germans.' Nobody could complain that the Occupiers were committing the frequent mistake of 'too little and too late'.

Yet at the same time fairness calls for a tribute to the extent to which Adenauer worked with the Allies and tried to meet their wishes. There were no doubt two reasons for him to do so. One was that the basic Allied policy of resisting Russia and integrating Western Europe coincided with his own desires and his ideas of what was good for Germany. But in addition he believed, as Stresemann had done before him (see p. 46), that co-operation was likely to release West Germany from her limitations and penalties more rapidly than resistance would do. This attitude involved him in a considerable amount of criticism, particularly from the Social Democrats; Schumacher once taunted him with being 'the Federal Chancellor of the Allies'. But the High Commissioners in the ceremony on the Petersberg had given an unmistakable hint that early changes in the Occupation Statute would be possible if the Federal Government observed their side of it. The Statute itself talked of revision in twelve to eighteen months. The Chancellor, however, lost no time in driving home the argument that, if the Allies really intended to develop West Germany as a prosperous member of the European Community, further demolitions of factories made no sense. The truth was that Allied policy, as so often where several countries are working together, was evolved not so much as a logical whole but as a succession of compromises between different points of view. The transition from the policy of holding Germany down to that of building her up had therefore to be gradual and while it was in progress, contradictory things were capable of happening at the same time. Yet a policy which is patently inconsistent is not easy to defend and by his pressure on this weak point Adenauer not surprisingly obtained quick concessions.

Another sore point concerned the Ruhr. Talk of 'internationalizing' this area was of long standing and, in agreeing to hand the government of West Germany back to its inhabitants, the Western Foreign Ministers had sought to allay the fears which this step aroused abroad by including in the package a 'Ruhr Authority'. This body was to include representatives of the USA, Britain, France and the Benelux countries, along with one German. It was to allocate the coal, coke and steel output of the area between the German home market and exports, so as to prevent the Germans from satisfying their own needs at the expense of their neighbours. It was also authorized to fix prices and transport arrangements. Such an interference with liberty, which was moreover to last until a peace treaty was signed, aroused much resentment in Germany and indeed the Authority would probably have belied its name if the West German Government and public had chosen to thwart it. (What the advocates of internationalism in such circumstances overlook is that the establishment of such a body against the will of the inhabitants is inconsistent with democracy.) Much pressure was put on Adenauer to refuse to nominate a German member. He, however, took a wider view, expressing the hope that the Ruhr arrangement would gradually grow into an organization embracing the basic industries of other countries besides West Germany, with an underlying hint that otherwise it could not last. Moreover he realized that in this field the decision rested with the

French, since it was their desire for security which lay behind both the Authority and the dismantling policy: they too would be the people with the most to contribute, after the Germans, to any organization of West Europe's basic industries. To win their confidence was imperative and the best way of doing so would be to take part in the Ruhr Authority instead of boycotting it.

There was, however, another apple of discord between the two countries in the shape of the Saar, the area with the second largest exports of coal in Western Europe. France had tried to get possession of it in 1919 but had obtained control only over the mines; the actual territory had been placed under the League of Nations and had been returned to Germany after a plebiscite in 1935. Immediately on occupying it in 1945, the French had made it into a separate unit and set about detaching it from the rest of their Zone, since their industry was vitally dependent on its coal. On 21 December 1946 a Customs Union was proclaimed between the Saar and France (see p. 98) and the area was given a currency of its own (rather than the franc) when the Deutschemark was introduced in the following June. An election in October 1947 gave an 87 per cent majority to parties favouring independence from Germany and close association with France. In March 1950 the resulting Government was induced to sign a convention giving France a fifty-year lease of the mines. While the Americans and British did not much like these arrangements, they preferred tolerating them to meeting French wishes for an independent Rhineland. The Germans resented French behaviour and argued (as events were to show, with justice) that the election results did not represent the considered wishes of the population. Moreover Adenauer, with the full support of the SPD, enunciated over the Saar a doctrine which had even more significance when applied to the East, namely that the Four-Power declarations of 5 June 1945 (see p. 83), had left unaffected the continued existence of Germany as a state within the frontiers of 1937 (i.e. before the annexation of Austria and Czechoslovakia) and that no part of the area could be legally and permanently transferred to another state unless the government of a free and united Germany gave its consent.

German feelings were therefore very mixed when the suggestion was made that the Federal Republic and the Saar should simultaneously become associate (rather than full) members of the Council of Europe which had been set up in May 1949 and held its first meeting the following September. On the one hand West German ability to attend meetings would be a step forward, yet for the Saar to receive the same treatment might imply an admission that the area was no longer German territory. In the end the whole complex of outstanding problems was brought together in the Petersberg Agreement of 24 November 1949 between the High Commission and the Federal Government. West Germany accepted the offer of association with the Council of Europe and agreed to take her seat on the Ruhr

Authority. The Saar also became associated with the Council but there was agreement that a final settlement of the area's status could occur only at a Peace Conference. The West German Government was allowed to open consulates (but not embassies) abroad and send its own officials to the OEEC (instead of being represented by the High Commission). Dismantling for reparations and disarmament, although not altogether wound up for another two years, was reduced to a very small scale.

To obtain so many concessions within two months of the entry into force of the Occupation Statute was a distinct score for Adenauer, though the Opposition preferred to concentrate on what he had given rather than on what he had won. Gradually too his longer-term calculations began to work out.

The more far-sighted French statesmen were coming to realize that the chances of pushing through the policy towards Germany advocated by de Gaulle after the war were, in face of American and British determination to rebuild that country, virtually nil. France needed dollars too badly to withhold her co-operation from the Anglo-Saxons and if West Germany was to be allowed to recover, she must be prevented from swinging into hostility to France. In both countries there was a widespread desire, nourished by the mutual experience of defeat and occupation, to end an antagonism which had done so much to disturb and weaken Europe. With this went a belief that such an ending could be achieved only inside the framework of a closer European association. Moreover France needed both German coal and an outlet for some of the steel, surplus to her requirements, which an ambitious investment programme had just put her in a position to produce.

Such was the background which led on 8 May 1950 to the receipt by Adenauer of a letter containing a proposal for a Franco-German Coal and Steel Community, signed by the French Foreign Minister Robert Schuman, himself a Lorrainer who had been born in Luxembourg. As Schuman was well aware, his Plan fitted so closely to Adenauer's desires as to be certain of a sympathetic reception from the West German Government. It was, and was intended as, a first step towards integrating Europe and reconciling France with Germany; it got rid of the Ruhr Authority, nullified the main advantages of the Customs Union between France and the Saar and restored to the Federal Republic some measure of international equality. The Allied Governments further promised to remove the limitation on West German steel production as soon as the Community was in being. The idea of having to compete with the Germans without tariffs or quotas and on equal terms frightened the French steel industry, although a German industrialist described the Plan as an effort to overcome the difficulties of that industry. The West German Social Democrats attacked the proposal on the ground that it would continue Allied controls in a new form and make reunification harder, but they were fighting against the tide and did not have the trade unions behind them. Within six weeks of Schuman's dramatic step, negotiations were opened to give the Plan concrete shape. The Benelux countries and Italy accepted the invitation to join in, though Britain held aloof, and on 18 April 1951 Adenauer for the first time left the territory of the Federal Republic to sign in Paris the Treaty establishing the Community. Before he did so, however, he insisted on Schuman exchanging with him letters by which the French Government recognized that German signature did not imply definitive acceptance of the Saar's status.

THE DEFENCE OF WESTERN EUROPE

Discussions on the Schuman Plan had hardly begun when the whole world situation was changed by the launching of a Communist attack on South Korea. Reinforcements, nominally under the United Nations flag but in practice consisting of 85 per cent of American troops, were rushed to the victim of aggression and quickly succeeded in carrying the war into Communist territory. The result in November 1950 was the entry of Chinese troops into the fighting and the prolongation of the war for nearly three years.

Not unnaturally, though not necessarily with justification, the Communist initiative made many statesmen consider the possibility of its being repeated in other continents and look anxiously to their defences. In such a survey, the West's weakness in Europe leapt to the eye. Since the first atom bomb exploded, the West Europeans had in effect been relying on American nuclear predominance to keep the Russians from risking a forward move. In the summer of 1950 there were only twelve divisions in the area, mostly incompletely equipped, whereas in East Germany or within easy call, the Russians had 175. Not only was Russia known to possess her own fission bombs, even if in far fewer numbers than the USA, but also the Korean experience emphasized how unsatisfactory it was to rely on so devastating a weapon to meet all types of warlike situations. There was a widespread agreement that the West must greatly improve its strength in 'conventional' weapons if its determination to resist aggression was to be made 'credible' to the East. A production programme was set in hand, the economic effects of which have already been described (see p. 114). The North Atlantic Defence Treaty (see p. 109) was transformed from an Alliance into an organization, with an integrated staff and troops permanently under its command; in December 1950 General Eisenhower assumed office as Supreme Commander of Allied Forces in Europe. The divisions in Germany were brought up to full readiness and reinforced, but it was clear that they would still be no match for the Russians.

None of the NATO countries was prepared to dislocate her economy and cut her living standards so as to divert into the armed forces the personnel needed to match the Russians in numbers. This was not entirely due to selfishness. Both Britain and France had many of their forces tied down by commitments outside Europe; the USA could finance the rearmament of others only as long as she was prosperous herself. No country could become poorer without risking political upheavals which would play into the hands of the Communists. Only one alternative solution was in sight and that was to rearm the Federal Republic. At this stage her productive capacity and technical skills were of secondary interest, except for the need to keep them out of Russian hands. What the West wanted was people to fight. Ever since 1947 the War Department in Washington had been pressing for such a policy; now at last they succeeded in overcoming the political objections of the State Department. At a NATO meeting in September 1950 Dean Acheson, the US Secretary of State, made it clear that his Government's willingness to remain in Europe was contingent on agreement to rearm West Germany as a matter of urgency.

The proposal met on all sides with considerably less than enthusiasm, particularly among the other members of NATO. Many Europeans were deeply disturbed at the idea of giving arms back to a nation which had in the past put them to such brutal and destructive purposes. A Germany with access to nuclear weapons was a particularly unpleasant thought. A wave of pacifist revulsion, partly spontaneous, partly the outcome of Allied indoctrination, swept through West Germany itself. There was little eagerness to provide the West with cannon-fodder. The catch-phrase of the time was *ohne mich* or 'include me out'. Rearmament would imperil the economic revival, increase the risk of the area becoming the first theatre of any East–West clash and above all reduce the likelihood of reuniting the Federal with the Democratic Republic, especially as the Russians had already increased the paramilitary 'People's Police' in the DDR to 55,000 and equipped them with tanks and artillery. Yet these dangers would not necessarily be avoided by remaining disarmed, and the plain facts remained that the rearming of West Germany was the price demanded by the Americans for continuing the protection which the Western Europeans thought essential, and that the Germans were therefore themselves in a position to demand concessions as the price for their consent.

The influential groups of enthusiasts for European integration saw in this situation an opportunity for carrying their aims a large step closer to realization. In August the Assembly of the Council of Europe, with the encouragement of Churchill, called for the formation of a European Army, subject to democratic control. On 24 October 1950 Monsieur René Pleven, the French Prime Minister, followed the example of his colleague Schuman and proposed to the European Council the creation of 'a European Army attached to political institutions of a united Europe', with a European Minister of Defence.

Adenauer had repeatedly assured the Allies that he did not want to see Germany rearmed, though he also lost no opportunity of emphasizing to them how insecure and exposed he considered the Federal Republic to be.

He had pressed for authority to establish a Security Corps to match the People's Police and hinted that, if anything more was to be done, it should be inside a European framework. Shortly before the NATO meeting he indicated that, if an international West European Army were to be formed, he would support the inclusion of a German contingent, but at the same time he made it clear that the price of this contribution would approximate to the complete restoration of German sovereignty; any German troops must be on a footing of equality with those of other countries.

On 19 December the Foreign Ministers of America, Britain and France agreed in principle to the idea of a West German defence contingent, and negotiations began to work out what the Pleven Plan would mean in practice. The Occupation Statute was revised in March 1951, eighteen months after its inauguration, to restore to the Federal Republic control of its foreign policy. West German civilian and military representatives took part on a footing of equality in the discussions about the European Defence Community (EDC). These dragged on for over a year and it was not until May 1952 that the Treaty of Paris embodying their result was ready for signature.

Parallel with these discussions others went on between the Federal Republic and the Occupying Powers. They produced as preliminary results a declaration of 9 July 1951 bringing to an end the state of war between the negotiating parties and on 14 September 1951 a resolution favouring the inclusion of a democratic West Germany on an equal basis in a Community covering continental Europe. They were, however, held up by arguments about the repayment of German debts and the status of the Saar. The French wanted not only British membership of the Defence Community but also British and American guarantees of protection in case a rearmed Germany were ever to quit the EDC. Not only the British Labour Government but also, to continental surprise and disappointment, Churchill's Conservative Ministry which took its place in October 1951 refused to go more than a limited way to meet these wishes. All the same, a Treaty was laboriously worked out and was ready for signature in Bonn on the day before that of Paris. It restored sovereignty to West Germany, cancelling the Occupation Statute and winding up the High Commission. Arrangements were included for the continued stationing in the Federal Republic of American, British and French troops as a matter of mutual security, and for the reassumption of control by the Occupying Powers in the event of an emergency (until the Germans worked out suitable crisis plans of their own). The same Powers retained their status in Berlin, which was to remain outside the Federal Republic, but promised to consult the Bonn Government about the use of their rights in the city. An important article provided that an essential aim in the common policy of all four states would be a 'peace settlement for the whole of Germany freely negotiated between Germany and her former enemies. The final delimitations of the boundaries of Germany must await such a settlement.' Pending its conclusion, all four states would co-operate to achieve, by peaceful means, their common aim of a unified Germany enjoying a liberal-democratic constitution like that of the Federal Republic and integrated within the European Community.

The two Treaties of Bonn and Paris were complementary and it was provided that the first would come into force only when the second did. Moreover, although both had been signed, both required ratification by the Parliaments of the states concerned.

In West Germany ratification was never seriously in doubt, and Adenauer had pressed ahead with little reference to his colleagues and almost none to the Bundestag. His Minister of the Interior, Heinemann, who had shown himself a man of principle during the Third Reich and owed his position largely to his influence in the Evangelical Church, resigned on anti-military grounds. The Social Democrats, led by Schumacher and after his death in August 1952 by Ollenhauer, objected not simply because they disliked rearmament but because they believed that Germany was more likely to be reunited by a policy of co-operating with the East than by one of combating it. Adenauer's reply was that the only thing which the Russians understood and would yield to was force, so that the best prospect of reuniting Germany lay in building up the strength of the West until it was great enough to 'roll back the Iron Curtain'. As he put it in a speech in March 1952:

> The aim of German policy today as yesterday is that the West should become strong enough to conduct reasonable conversations with the Soviet Union. We are firmly convinced that if we continue in this path the moment will not be too distant when Soviet Russia will declare itself ready for reasonable negotiation.

This policy, however, proved to be based on a false assumption, for the plans to strengthen NATO were never fully realized. The eighty-five divisions originally said to be required were scaled down in 1951 to forty-three with thirty on the central front. In fact the last figure never rose above twenty-two. Arguments could be reasonably advanced to suggest that such a force might be able to resist a Communist attack. But there clearly could be no question of it initiating a successful attack on Communist territory. The post-war years had already shown how impossible it was for the United States to use their monopoly of nuclear weapons to compel Russian compliance with their wishes, and in any case that monopoly was in rapid process of being converted into an 'equivalence of terror'. In fact the West had probably reached the peak of its strength at the juncture when Adenauer made the speech just quoted.

From the point of view of West German internal politics, there was much to be said for Adenauer's policy of integrating the young Federal Republic as closely as possible into the West and thereby making it as hard as possible for an aggressive anti-Western nationalism to develop again there. Moreover this policy, which so well met the wishes of the most powerful nation in the world, was far more likely to result in a prosperous West Germany than would have followed from either an attempt to remain neutral or co-ordination with the controlled economies of the East. A break with the United States might also have halted West Germany's progress towards the recovery of sovereignty and equality. But such was the importance of refugees in Adenauer's political calculations and such the emphasis which the West German people had been encouraged to place on reunification, that the Adenauer policy could not be sold to the public on its genuine merits alone. For it to be acceptable, they had to be given misplaced hopes of what it would produce in relation to the East. In the long run, this was bound to become obvious and, when it did, to damage the public standing of the Party which had advocated it. But the death of Stalin in 1953 and the uncertainties of the Khrushchev epoch postponed the date at which this would happen until its main author was leaving the political stage.

Even in the short run, however, the policy was put in question by the Soviet Government which clearly saw their worst fears realized in the action of the capitalist world to rearm West Germany. In March 1952, three months before the Treaties of Bonn and Paris were signed, the Russians sent to the three other Occupying Powers two notes suggesting terms for a Peace Treaty to bring about German reunification on a neutral and democratic basis. These notes, which certainly arrived at a rather late stage of the Western negotiations, cannot be said to have been seriously considered. Instead they were regarded as a sign that the policy of 'negotiating from strength' was beginning to yield results and, if pursued, would result in still more conciliatory offers. The Allies argued that they should not therefore allow themselves to be deflected from their purpose by what seemed to them intended as a 'delaying bid'. The Allied reply insisted that free elections throughout Germany were a necessary preliminary to a Peace Treaty and negotiations bogged down in argument as to which should come first. Was this reaction justified or was a real chance of settlement missed?

The Russian proposals provided for a guarantee of democratic rights to the German people so that all Germany could enjoy the rights of man and the basic freedoms. All democratic parties and associations were to be allowed freedom of activity, including liberty to meet, publish and decide on their own international relations. Organizations inimical to democracy and to the maintenance of peace were not to be permitted. Civil and political rights were to be available to all former members of the armed forces and to all former Nazis other than those serving sentences for war crimes. There were to be no limitations on economic activity and Germany was to be free to join the United Nations. She was to have such national armed forces of her own as she needed for defence, and was to be allowed to produce arms, though the quantities and types of these were to be prescribed in the Treaty

144

setting up the arrangement. But she was to promise not to enter into any kind of coalition or military alliance directed against any state which had fought her between 1939 and 1945. All Allied forces were to be withdrawn within twelve months and all foreign military bases on her territory were to be destroyed.

At first sight nothing could have sounded more reasonable, even though the organizations to be assured freedom were obviously going to include the Communist Party. Perhaps too the presence of big and undefined words like 'peace-loving' and 'democratic' might have roused the suspicions of those who remembered the controversies which had flowed from different interpretations of such words in the Control Council. The Russians could get troops back again from Poland more easily than the Americans from across the Atlantic. The Russian offer may well have been seriously intended. But it involved many opportunities for dissension and delay so that its acceptance might have meant the West finding themselves after five years or so back where they had started in 1947–9. The proposal seemed obviously put forward to prevent the Federal Republic from binding itself to the anti-Communist bloc but could have been accepted only by someone willing to take the risk of a reunited Germany coming under the control of the pro-Communist bloc. German production and personnel could make too much difference to the balance of power for either side to trust the other at that stage to let the reunited country remain genuinely neutral. Such an act of faith was certainly not to be expected from an elderly man who not only was a convinced European and anti-Communist but also had staked his political reputation on a policy which involved binding his country to the West. By the time the offer was made, things had gone so far that a much higher bid would have been needed to make a reversing of engines seem justifiable to those responsible for Western policy, and so high a bid would have been too much for the East to contemplate at that stage.

The East Germans answered the Bonn and Paris Treaties by establishing a security strip along the inter-Zonal frontier and ending except at a very limited number of points the relatively free local traffic across it which had existed until then.

DISASTER AND RECOVERY

The attitude of West Germany towards the European Defence Community (EDC) could be decided by the obstinacy of a single individual but unfortunately more was needed to bring the Community into being. The Treaty signed in Paris in May 1952 required six ratifications in order to come into force; it received only five. The inroads which the proposal made on national sovereignty, though designed to allay French fears of Germany, proved more than the French, deeply divided as they were at the time by many other issues, could bring themselves to accept. The prospects of obtaining a majority for the Treaty in the French Parliament were so slight that its presentation kept on being put off, while world conditions changed and its main authors lost office. In August 1954 Mendès-France, the then Prime Minister, finally took the plunge but without showing any enthusiasm for the proposal, since if he had, he would have been brought down by his own Cabinet! A large majority accepted a motion agreeing to postpone consideration indefinitely. The country which had sponsored the idea had ended by turning against it; Adenauer's plans appeared to be in ruins.

Although the Treaty of Bonn was supposed to come into force only when the Treaty of Paris did, the world had too easily taken the ratification of the latter for granted. For over two years the Western Occupying Powers had been increasingly treating West Germany, and West Germany had been increasingly behaving, as a sovereign state, except that it had halted its preparations for raising armed forces. Here was a clock which could not be put back. The French had professed themselves nervous about the EDC for fear of it allowing West Germany to become too strong: they had as a result created a position where there would soon be little but good faith towards her allies to prevent her from rearming in total independence of all controls.

The blame for this predicament was, however, as widely laid on Britain as on France since the British reluctance to join the Community was said to have swung the balance against French participation. Though it is hard to believe that British aloofness was more than a contributing factor, it was Britain which now came to the rescue by proposing in October 1954 an organization of sovereign states, a Western European Union (WEU), instead of a move to a supra-national plane. A Secretariat replaced the proposed Commission and the Assembly (though empowered to take certain decisions by a two-thirds majority) was allowed only consultative rights. Britain undertook to keep four divisions and an air fighter force on the continent until 2000 AD. Meanwhile the Communist states replied to the WEU by establishing in the Warsaw Pact a military alliance which was clearly intended as a counterpart to it and which included the Democratic Republic among its members.

In some respects WEU was an extension of the Brussels Alliance of 1948 which had preceded NATO (see p. 109), but that Alliance had been directed against the possibility of a resurgent Germany and not only was this animus now removed but also West Germany and Italy were admitted to the Union. The Federal Republic was, however, required to incorporate all its forces in NATO, whereas no other member did so. It also renounced the right to manufacture on its territory (though not to acquire or control) atomic, biological and chemical (ABC) weapons. Moreover it undertook never to have recourse to force to achieve reunification or the modification of frontiers. In return the Americans, British and French recognized the Government of the Federal Republic as the only German Government 'freely and legitimately constituted and therefore entitled to speak for

Germany as the representative of the German people in international affairs'. They went on to reaffirm that a peace settlement for the whole of Germany freely negotiated between Germany and her former enemies, which should lay the foundations of a lasting peace, remained an essential aim of their policy. The final delimitation of the frontiers of Germany must await such a settlement (a standpoint which was widely taken in West Germany to mean that, failing such delimitation, the legal frontiers remained those of 1937). The Federal Republic was to contribute 500,000 men to NATO (the size of the army of a united Germany when Hitler reoccupied the Rhineland in 1936) but would not maintain a separate General Staff.

For some time a faction in Moscow led by Malenkov and Beria had taken the view that the Russian Zone was in the long run bound to be absorbed into the rest of Germany and meanwhile was a potential liability since intervention to keep it subservient might lead to conflict with the West. The main aim should therefore be to get as much out of it as quickly as possible. There are various estimates of the amount extracted before reparations were suspended in 1954 but it would seem that the total was about seven times as much as was taken from West Germany and came close to the $10 billion for which Molotov asked at Yalta (Sir Alec Cairncross, *The Price of War*, p. 219).

Ulbricht and the other German Communists were well aware that they were regarded as expendable and set out to make themselves valuable to the occupiers, much as Adenauer was doing in the West. The SED was changed into being an elite on the traditional Communist model. A Five-Year Plan of industrial development was introduced to fill the gaps where the Soviet Union in the past had depended on imports from the West. This made the Democratic Republic less vulnerable to being exploited and better able to exploit.

The year 1953 saw a general relaxation throughout Communist Europe due to a wish on the part of Stalin's successors to gain the good-will of their publics. When Ulbricht tried to resist this policy in East Germany, Berlin workers staged what amounted to a general strike. The police could not cope with the situation and two Russian divisions had to be called in. Although they behaved with restraint, twenty-one people were killed. Persons variously described as 'interested spectators' and 'agents provocateurs' came from West Berlin to see what was going on but the whole affair was over before the Western Governments could decide how to react. The mood of the workers seemed to bear out the warnings of those who argued that a relaxation of Communist discipline in East Germany would mean losing the Republic to the West. Either by good luck or by deliberately provoking a show-down, Ulbricht survived. Three years later he weathered another storm set off by Khrushchev's denunciation of Stalin at the Twentieth Party Congress. The Kremlin would seem to have decided that he was the person who could best be relied on to keep the situation in control.

147

10

ADENAUER'S HIGH NOON: 1955–1961

Germany will blossom as never before. Her destroyed landscapes will be rebuilt with new and more beautiful towns in which happy people will live. The whole of Europe will participate in this upsurge. Once more we shall be friends with all nations who are of good will. Together with them we shall let the deep wounds heal which disfigure the noble face of our continent. In rich cornfields the daily bread will grow, banishing the hunger of millions who are needy and suffering today. There will be plenty of work and out of it as the deepest spring of human happiness there will come bliss and strength for all.

This remarkable vision of the Federal Republic in the 1950s dates from the dark days of April 1945; it comes from Goebbels's last broadcast on Hitler's last birthday! Its idyllic word picture was intended to show the Germans what they might achieve by victory. That the dream should instead have been realized as the result of defeat was not entirely due to Soviet intransigence, for it is wrong to suppose that the liberality of the USA was exclusively inspired by the wish to save Europe from Communism. The International Monetary Fund, the World Bank and the International Trade Organization/General Agreement on Tariffs and Trade, the instruments with which the Roosevelt and Truman Administrations sought to create an open world, predated the Cold War. Indeed that war was precipitated by American insistence that aid would be forthcoming only for countries which adopted liberal trade policies. And it was that insistence alone which induced German industrialists – unwillingly at first – to abandon the attitudes of a lifetime and take part in the Organization for European Economic Co-operation, the European Coal and Steel Community and the European Economic Community. These were the institutions which made possible the widening markets characterizing the post-war worlds. And without these markets it is hard to see how there could have come into existence the 'virtuous spiral' (see p. 115) on which West German export-led prosperity rested.

No comparable openings had existed since the years before 1914 and it was equally long since Germany had made comparable efforts in foreign markets. The West German share of the world trade in manufactures rose from 7 per cent in 1950 to nearly 19 per cent in 1959, which had been approximately its level (allowing for partition) in 1913 whereas in 1937 the figure had been only 16.5 per cent. The consequence was that the Federal Republic's export surpluses became embarrassing. So far from needing to conduct an 'export drive' like the British, the Government was under pressure to get the favourable balances reduced since their accumulation inside the country could not but have an inflationary effect.

One solution to this problem was found in the removal of import quotas and the lowering of tariffs. The population was thus enabled to live better and more cheaply. Arrangements were made to pay off all outstanding external debts. Another step was a Treaty concluded in 1952 by which West Germany undertook to pay to Israel DM 3,000 million to be used in compensating Jews whom the Nazis had driven out of Europe: a further DM 450 million was made available for the same purpose in other countries. From 1953 onwards increasing sums were made officially available in the form of loans at low rates of interest for the benefit of developing countries until by 1962 annual expenditure on this head was running at about the same rate as Britain. Nearly all of this expenditure came back to West Germany in the form of orders but, while it thus increased the income of manufacturers and workers, it did not necessarily add to the country's material resources as much as its use in other directions might have done.

None of these measures proved adequate and in March 1961 the Deutschmark was revalued upwards by approximately 5 per cent. Devaluations of currency have been distressingly frequent in the world but this deliberate move in the opposite direction was almost unprecedented. The step was strongly opposed by the Bundesbank, which would have preferred to see the rest of the world devalue instead, and by industrialists who feared that selling abroad would become harder and competition at home from imports fiercer. It turned out, however, that West German goods sold on quality, delivery and servicing as much as on price while export markets had become so important that manufacturers made an even greater effort so as to retain them, with the result that this and subsequent revaluations had only a temporary effect on the surplus. The truth is that, to make an international monetary system function smoothly, a country which is a persistent creditor must get rid of its surplus by lending abroad and this the Federal Republic was slow to do; whereas her cumulative surplus over the years 1951–61 amounted to DM 24,000 million, her overseas investments in 1966 only totalled DM 8,500 million. One reason for this was the vast amount of capital needed for reconstruction at home. By 1964, 8 million houses had been built (as against 4.8 million in Britain). By 1967 over half the dwelling-units in West Germany were post-war. Over half of the cost was in effect borne by the public authorities either in the form of loans or tax remissions so that the necessary funds could be raised without having to put up interest rates to a level which made rents prohibitively high. (Building societies of the British type do not exist in West Germany.) Similar tax remissions encouraged individuals and firms to plough back large parts of their earnings into development. The Government is estimated to have been responsible for 43.5 per cent of total net investment between 1948 and 1957.

Thus the background to the West Germany of the 1950s was one of great and growing prosperity, a situation all the more gratifying because it was unexpected. For the first time in German history democratic government came to be associated with success and the world owes to Adenauer and Erhard a considerable debt of gratitude for having proved that such a conjunction was possible. A preoccupation with material well-being absorbed the country, illustrated by the story of the girl who said that the two books to have had most influence on her life were her father's cheque book and her mother's cookery book. Nor was it only the rich who profited, in spite of some appearance to the contrary and of the frequent assertions of foreign critics. Germany had led the world in devising social insurance (see p. 16) and a generous system of social security was now built up until the West German people were in this respect the best cared for in the world. In particular a scheme was introduced in 1957 for 'dynamic pensions' which rose automatically with the cost of living. Although much of the finance for these services came from contributions by employers and workers, the amount spent by the state trebled between 1950 and 1962, while Land and communal governments spent even more. A not surprising result was that the level of taxation also became as heavy as any in the world.

Control of firms in the Federal Republic, as in much of Western Europe, is divided between a Supervising Council (*Aufsichtsrat*) and a Management Board (*Vorstand*). The former meets four or five times a year, appoints the Management Board, supervises the firm's balance sheet, and decides on such matters as mergers, take-overs, major expansions or closures; the latter conducts the day-to-day business. During the occupation period (see p. 112) workers in the coal and steel industries secured equal representation with the shareholders on the Supervising Councils (the two groups then combining to elect a chairman). In the rest of industry a law of 1951 gave the workers one-third of the places on the Supervising Councils. Moreover, every firm with more than five workers is required to have a Works Council, elected by the entire labour force (and not merely the union members) in a secret ballot: this body has a right to co-decision with the management in such matters as job evaluation, wage structures, working hours and holidays, training and welfare schemes. Wages are settled by collective bargaining between an industry and the union which represents all the workers in it, usually on a regional basis; once concluded, such agreements are legally binding on both sides for the full period which they cover; strikes are permitted only when an agreement has expired and then only if three-quarters of the union members concerned have voted in favour in a secret ballot. An elaborate but cheap system of labour courts exists to decide disputes between individual workers and their employers. The net result has been a high level of peace and orderliness in industry. It is hard to say how far this is due to the existence of a fixed and unchallenged legal framework, how far to workers' awareness that they have spokesmen for their interests at the top.

The victims of the war, including those on whom the Currency Reform had borne harshly, were not forgotten when the benefits of prosperity came to be distributed. After a temporary measure in 1949, a Law for the Equalization of Burdens was passed in 1952. This combined a capital levy, capital gains tax and a levy on mortgages, intended to amount to 50 per cent. From the fund thus created, a variety of compensation payments were to be made. Obviously, however, it was impossible to raise so large a levy at one blow and arrangements were made to spread its collection over twenty-seven years, though loans were raised on the strength of the initial contributions so as to allow hand-outs in anticipation of the income. By the end of 1964 benefits totalling over DM 40,000 million had been distributed to communal enterprises of social importance as well as to individuals. Another law of 1953 made the handling of refugees into a Federal rather than a Land matter, so that all should receive comparable treatment, irrespective of where they had come from or of what part of Germany they had gone to. A law passed two years earlier provided for the payment of compensation to those who had suffered at Nazi hands, as well as for their reinstatement in their old posts or pensioning in accordance with the rank which they would have reached had they not been dismissed.

Considerable comment was, however, aroused both inside and outside Germany by the fact that this law was accompanied by another passed under heavy pressure from the organizations representing civil servants and ex-members of the armed forces. Article 131 of the Grundgesetz called for legislation to regulate the position of all who had been in public service on 8 May 1945, and had since been removed from office for reasons not laid down in the service code. This was now interpreted to require the reinstatement in office at their former rank of all except those actually serving prison sentences as a result of the denazification procedure; it was argued that to do anything else would be to punish them twice. Their replacements, often victims of Nazism, had in many cases to make way for them. Any who had passed the age of retirement were awarded their normal pensions, as were all who had belonged to the armed forces before 1935. This single act undid much of the work achieved by the Occupying Powers (already considered by many to have been inadequate) of eliminating from positions of responsibility men who had shown by their attitude to Nazism that they could not be relied on as friends of democracy or humanity. Every second

151

senior civil servant in West Germany in the early 1960s had worked for the government under the Third Reich. Between December 1949 and June 1950 twenty-three ex-Nazis were recruited into the Ministry of Economics. In March 1952 thirty-nine out of forty-nine senior officials in the Foreign Office proved to have been Nazis. A grotesque situation was disclosed when, as a result of publicity from Poland and Russia, it emerged that the Baden-Württemberg Government had in 1958 appointed to the Directorship of the Central Office for the Investigation of Nazi Crimes a man whom they knew to have been a Storm-Trooper and Party member.

Adenauer showed himself insensitive to the undesirability of employing in high office people whose record in the Third Reich had been unsatisfactory. His 1953 Cabinet included as Minister of the Interior Gerhard Schröder, who had been a Party member; as Minister for Refugees, Theodor Oberländer, who had belonged to the SS; and as Minister of Transport, Hans Christian Seebohm, a prominent protagonist of the Sudeten Germans who was later to define Germany as including all areas where Germans had ever settled and make many similar utterances without being seriously reprimanded. Hans Globke, the State Secretary at the head of the Chancellor's Office, although not a Nazi, had written the official commentary on the anti-Jewish laws and the other heads of Departments included several who were similarly compromised.

The tolerance was undoubtedly deliberate. The Chancellor was sufficiently a German and sufficiently a conservative to have a good deal of sympathy with the attitudes of old-fashioned nationalism. Moreover he realized that, if such elements in the nation were cold-shouldered by the regime, they would turn against it. One of the reasons for the failure of the Weimar Republic has been seen to be the hostility, amounting to disloyalty, of many who had formed the pillars of society under the Hohenzollerns. It was important that this should not happen again. There is a good deal of evidence indicating that, even at the end of the war, 10 per cent of the adult population, or 4 million people, were hard-core Nazis (see p. 94). The members of the Nazi Party and affiliated organizations had numbered 12 million. The 8 million or so refugees and expellees from the East in the Federal Republic were all potential recruits for radical policies. To give the CDU a character which enabled it to appeal to such people was not merely shrewd political tactics (though undoubtedly this aspect was not lost on its leader), it was also calculated to keep within limits the growth of parties further to the right. There can be no doubt that as a result of Adenauer's policy a number of people who might otherwise have sabotaged the democratic experiment were induced to tolerate it until its very success made them think that it might after all have merits. How do you run a liberal democracy if the supply of competent and convinced democrats is inadequate?

Nevertheless West Germany had to pay a price for the Adenauer era. In too many directions it amounted to a restoration of the kind of society which its leading figures had known in their youth. Thus the civil service unions were able to frustrate most of the half-hearted measures taken by the Occupying Powers to reform the administrative corps by widening the area of recruitment in terms both of class and intellectual background. Preference continued to be given to those whose parents had paid for their education and who had then passed an examination in law. In education the British and Americans had deliberately refrained from trying to enforce changes, only to see their advice and example largely disregarded and little done to overhaul the system either as regards curriculum or as regards equality of opportunity. The universities still concentrated on training students by specialist research and were slow to recognize the need of modern society for large numbers of people with a general higher education. The chief step towards change was taken by President Heuss, who in 1957 had set up a Council for the Humanities and Sciences (*Wissenschaftsrat*) to give advice about higher education. It was more like a British than a German institution in that it had no legal existence and its conclusions bound nobody. But its members were distinguished and wise so that what they said was often listened to.

In its treatment of criminals and in its laws on such matters as divorce and abortion, the Federal Republic remained old-fashioned. As a result she increasingly failed to meet the wishes and needs of the generations who came to maturity in her. Had she lasted only a decade, this might not have mattered, especially as her rightward character meant that any change was almost bound to be towards the left. But the success of the 'Miracle' made its beneficiaries reluctant to move away from it and this resulted in an estrangement between the generations which created an explosive situation.

The initial satisfaction of the West German people with the general policy of their government was convincingly demonstrated in the elections of 1953 when the CDU/CSU won 243 of the Bundestag's 487 seats. Adenauer, however, preferred to keep his former allies of the FDP and German Party in the Cabinet, so as to maintain a united anti-Socialist coalition. He even brought into that coalition, and in due course absorbed into the CDU, the Refugee Party which had been established in Schleswig-Holstein in 1950.

Among minor parties without representation in the Bundestag, some attention was attracted by the Socialist Reich Party – a right-wing group centred in Lower Saxony – and the Communists. The first of these was, however, declared by the Constitutional Court in 1952 to contravene Article 21 of the Grundgesetz forbidding parties which sought to alter the democratic character of the State; the second suffered the same fate, on the initiative of the Federal Government, in 1956. There were those who thought it a mistake, particularly with the Communists, to drive them underground where their weakness could not be demonstrated.

The CDU/CSU contested the 1957 Elections with great vigour and spent over £3 million (five times as much as the British Conservatives in the

General Election of 1955) in support of the slogan 'No Experiments'. An analysis before this election suggested that there were in the Republic 8.5 million firm CDU/CSU supporters and 3.25 million lukewarm ones, 9 million firm SPD supporters and 3.25 lukewarm ones, 1 million firm supporters of the minor parties and 2 million lukewarm ones, with 3 million voters undecided. In the event most of the lukewarm and undecided voters (many of them women) would seem to have played for safety with the result that Adenauer received an even greater majority than before in the highest poll yet known in Germany (disregarding 1933), while the Refugee and Centre Parties disappeared from Federal politics.

Adenauer was at the height of his prestige. His success presented a serious problem for the Social Democrats. Their Party was taking an active share in several Land Governments, notably Greater-Hesse, Hamburg and Bremen, as well as West Berlin, and it was at this level that their ablest leaders, such as Brauer, Kaisen and Willy Brandt, were deployed. On the Federal plane, however, the CDU/CSU appeared to be so firmly in the saddle that the SPD looked like being condemned to permanent opposition, which in a democratic state is tantamount to slow extinction. The prospect caused the intellectual leaders of the Party, in particular Herbert Wehner, Fritz Erler and Carlo Schmid, to insist that the programme must be drastically revised to take account of the Welfare State and the Communist threat. This meant not only committing the Party to the support of the free democratic order – which after all had been the Socialist position for many years – but also ending its identification as primarily a working-class and Marxist body, which sought the public ownership of key industries. Prosperity was bringing nearer to completion a social process which had been intermittently under way since 1933 and giving to the workers an outlook hitherto characteristic of the middle classes. Unless the Party could be made not merely compatible with, but positively attractive to such an outlook, it would have small hope of picking up the essential marginal votes needed to give it a majority. Moreover the time had come to realize the growing affinity between the Party and the increasing social awareness shown by many members of the Churches; to this the materialism of Marxist doctrine was an obstacle. Finally the Party saw no alternative but to admit that Schumacher's opposition to Western integration had been a costly mistake. In 1957 the SPD voted for entry into the Common Market (see p. 157) and in June 1960 Wehner, speaking in the Bundestag, announced the Party's acceptance of Adenauer's foreign policy in its broad principles. Meanwhile the new look of the Party had in 1958 found expression in the Godesberg Programme. The key slogan in the economic field had already been coined by Professor Schiller, 'Competition as far as possible – planning so far as necessary.'

In the Godesberg programme, the SPD became a Party like the others and ceased to consider itself as a community of political saints.

Parliamentary democracy was no longer a halting-place on the road to true Socialism, economic policy no longer a short-cut to nationalisation, the class struggle with the victory of the proletariat no longer the sole way to save the world. Since Godesberg the SPD has sought its justification not in true faith but in good works.

(Rolf Zundel in *Die Zeit*, 18 April 1969)

By 1957 Adenauer was 81 and, though remarkably lively for his years, was growing ever more autocratic and high-handed. His success in managing the West German people led him to believe that any change of leader could only be for the worse. Various possible successors were considered but given no real chance to show their paces and then discarded. Particular difficulty was caused by Adenauer's fixed and, as events proved, justified belief that the most successful of his assistants, Ludwig Erhard, was too genial and unsubtle for the post of Chancellor. He therefore determined to ditch him if he could.

In 1959 an opportunity for change arose. Theodor Heuss had for ten years filled the post of President with a good sense, modesty and impartiality which deservedly won him respect and affection. The Grundgesetz laid down that a President could be re-elected only once; Heuss characteristically refused to allow the Law to be modified in his favour so that a successor had to be found. Adenauer failed in an effort to talk Erhard into taking the job, and was then induced to announce his intention of standing as a candidate himself. But he also made remarks in public and private which suggested an intention to exert more political influence than Heuss had done, and to secure the succession to the Chancellorship for a former industrialist Etzel rather than Erhard. Considerable opposition was at once evident to a step which would undo much of Heuss's achievement by bringing the Presidency back into party politics. The CDU flatly refused to consider Etzel for the succession and Erhard flatly refused to refrain from standing as a candidate for it, while close study of the Grundgesetz seems to have convinced the 'Old Man' that a President did not have the powers which he would want to exert. He therefore withdrew his candidature as abruptly as he had announced it, proposing instead Lübke, the Minister of Agriculture. Lübke was duly elected but the impression was given that the CDU leadership thought a second-rate man, and one with strong party affiliations too, good enough for the Presidency. As it was to prove, Adenauer would have done much better for his own reputation if he had withdrawn while his prestige was still intact; his behaviour was the first step of a series which were to cast a shadow over his closing years.

INTRANSIGENCE ABROAD

A minor casualty of the French failure to ratify the EDC had been the idea of using the Community's existence to settle the question of the Saar.

Instead, the 1954 Paris Agreement included a Franco-German deal by which the Saar, until the conclusion of a definitive Peace Treaty, was to be administered as an international territory under a European Commissioner responsible to WEU. The population was asked to confirm this imaginative and conciliatory arrangement but was also given the option of joining the Federal Republic. Times had changed since the bleak days after the war when an overwhelming majority had voted for close association with France. Life in prosperous West Germany had recovered its attractions to such an extent that two-thirds of the electorate thought it preferable to becoming a guinea-pig for a federated Europe. There was nothing for the French Government to do but 'faire bonne mine au mauvais jeu' and at the beginning of 1957 the Saar became the tenth Land of the Federal Republic.

The summer of 1955 was eventful. In July, at Geneva, the leaders of the USA, USSR, Britain and France held the first summit meeting for ten years. The chief problem was German reunification, on which neither side was prepared to depart from its prepared position. Consequently neither that meeting nor a Foreign Minsters' Conference which followed it in the autumn achieved in this field anything more than sterile argument. What the summit did do was to reveal to each side that the other realized what an atomic war would mean and had no intention of starting one if it could avoid doing so. Though few at the time appreciated the implications of this discovery, it was fatal to the policy of reunification through strength.

In the following month Adenauer, against the advice of his experts, decided to try his own hand at negotiating and accepted an invitation to visit Moscow. On arrival, he proposed two subjects for discussion with his hosts – reunification and the return to Germany of German prisoners-of-war still in Russian hands. He made no progress whatever on the first and for a limited verbal undertaking on the second had to agree to the establishment of diplomatic relations between the Federal Republic and the Soviet Union. To prevent such relations from being interpreted as implying West German recognition of the 1945 territorial arrangements, he insisted on the Russians accepting from him a note saying that this was not so, though even then the Russians published the note accompanied by a statement joining issue with it. The prisoners – or some of them – later came back, but two days after Adenauer left, a DDR delegation arrived to conclude a Treaty which gave sovereignty to their Government and authorized it to enter into diplomatic relations with other states.

Adenauer's chief justification for making this somewhat unhappy excursion had been that, as reunification was a matter for the Four Powers rather than for the two Germanies, the Federal Republic must have direct relations with the Russians. But by his action he had created the danger that other states would follow the Russian example and establish diplomatic relations with the DDR as well as with the BRD. To counter this the Bonn Government promulgated in December 1955 the Hallstein Doctrine (called after the State Secretary of the Foreign Office) according to which recognition of the DDR by any state would be regarded by the Federal Republic as an 'unfriendly act', since it would involve recognition of the division of Germany into two states for which there was (in Bonn's eyes) no legal justification. When in 1957 the Yugoslav Government accepted a DDR legation, the Federal Republic broke off diplomatic relations and moreover, until February 1967, it did not establish such relations with any of the USSR's allies in view of the fact that they possessed relations with the DDR. The main targets of the 'Doctrine', however, were the non-aligned states of Asia and Africa and there can be no doubt that, supported by Bonn's extensive programme of aid (which owed a good deal to such political calculations), nearly a hundred states were for some ten years dissuaded from recognizing the DDR. On the other hand the Doctrine gave to any neutral state which wished to extort concessions from Bonn a convenient handle for doing so in the shape of a threat that it would otherwise come to terms with the rival.

West Germany did not rest content with the Hallstein Doctrine but proceeded, with that methodical thoroughness which is such a notable national characteristic, to draw all possible consequences from the theory that their neighbours to the east had no right to exist. For one thing, use of the term 'Deutsche Demokratische Republik' was turned into an action tantamount to treachery; if employed at all, it was always prefaced by the adjective 'so-called' and as a rule the term 'Russian Zone of Occupation' was substituted for it. Indeed in many nationalist quarters the favourite description of that section of the country was 'Middle Germany' with the obvious implication that the areas taken over by Russia and Poland within the 1937 frontiers still constituted 'East Germany'.

A more constructive development also began in the summer of 1955 with the decision taken by the Foreign Ministers of the Coal and Steel Community, meeting at Messina, to set up a Committee under a 'political personality' (who proved to be M. Spaak of Belgium) with the task of working out proposals for closer European integration in the economic field. This initiative led to the scheme for the European Economic Community which achieved concrete realization in the Treaty of Rome (25 March 1957). The elaborate provisions of the Treaty combined respect for the rights of member states with an inexorable advance to a situation in which decisions on such matters as agricultural prices, tariffs, and commercial policy would have to be taken collectively. Once signed, the Treaty allowed for no going back. It has sometimes been described as a compromise between German industry and French agriculture; this is too sweeping but it was largely a bargain between West Germany and France and represented in many ways the culmination of Adenauer's policy. West Germany was henceforward to be mixed with the rest of Western Europe in a way which would be difficult to unscramble. When critics suggested that the course might prove an obstacle to reunification, the habitual answer was that, on the contrary, only in the context of an integrated Europe would reunification become possible. A little-noticed proviso, however, allowed the Federal Republic to treat the Democratic Republic as an associate of the Community, in that goods passing from one to the other did not have to pay duties. A minor advantage of the Community has been that it enabled the vexed issue of decartellization to be transferred to a European plane. At such a level the question whether a single West German firm holds too big a share of the market changes its character since such a firm must expect to withstand competition on level terms from similar giants in other EEC countries. The job of seeing that these giants did not in turn concert to fix prices or share the market was made the responsibility of the Community (though West Germany has its own legislation against restrictive practices, introduced by Erhard against the wishes of industry).

Meanwhile the Federal Republic put in hand the recruitment and organization of the armed forces (*Bundeswehr*) needed to fulfil its obligation as a member of NATO. The process was carried through even faster than it had been in 1935–9. Curiously enough the victor nations which had made such a fuss about disarming Germany in 1945 made no contribution to the problem of how to rearm Germany without reviving militarism. It was the Germans themselves who, with the warning of the Weimar Republic in mind, devised precautions to ensure that the new troops should be loyal to the democratic state; these largely corresponded with current thinking about the kind of people needed in a modern technological army. The soldier was to be the 'citizen in uniform'; in a considerable break with German tradition, soldiers did not wear uniform off duty. Drill was reduced to a minimum, instruction was given in civics and everyone from general to private was free to join a trade union (as the Grundgesetz required). Full authority over the armed forces rests in peace time with the civilian Minister of Defence, who has on several occasions removed high officers from their posts for talking out of turn. The Defence Committee of the Bundestag was given permanent status. A civilian Personnel Committee was set up to go into the record of each senior officer before appointment and the Bundestag was authorized to appoint a Defence Commissioner with the job of watching over the maintenance of parliamentary control, investigating alleged infringements of basic rights and acting as a sort of Ombudsman for any members of the forces who felt themselves aggrieved. The first few choices for this office were not wholly happy and the safeguards, taken as a whole, are so thorough as to make it a question whether they may not in due course provoke a reaction by impeding military efficiency; they have already undergone some modification. Relations between Government and Bundeswehr are, however, very different from what they were under the Weimar Republic.

The original target had been to have 95,000 troops under arms by the end of 1956 and 270,000 by the end of 1957. Long before those dates, however, complications had set in. The aim of the NATO allies had been to raise in West Germany the personnel whom they were not themselves prepared to spare from their peace economies (see p. 141). But as the Economic Miracle got under way the prospect of some 500,000 people being removed from the labour market began to fill German industrialists with alarm. While there was some doubt as to whether the weapons needed to arm the Bundeswehr (which at this stage would have to be largely imported) could be paid for without either inflation or massive US help, the real fear was that an artificially induced labour shortage would make it impossible to hold wage claims in check. As the Ministry of Defence under Theodor Blank paid little attention to their representatives, the bosses turned elsewhere and found a more receptive ear in the Minister of Nuclear Power, Franz Josef Strauss, an exceptionally intelligent butcher's son and ex-bicycling champion of 40 who was working his passage to the top of the CSU.

As early as November 1955 Strauss was publicly attacking his colleague Blank's arrangements. In July 1956 the Bundestag Defence Committee, whose chairman belonged to the same party as Strauss, cut out of the draft bill for raising conscripts the figure stating the length of time (eighteen months) which they were to serve. In mid-September 1956 the CSU leaders laid down principles of rearmament which hardly squared with those of the Government and at the end of the same month the Budget and Defence Committees of the Bundestag combined to cut out of the Defence Estimates the provision for equipping all units with tanks. Adenauer's majority was not such as to let him dispense with CSU support and in October he replaced Blank by Strauss. The new broom immediately cut down the numbers to be raised to 76,000 at the end of 1956 and 120,000–135,000 twelve months later. By the end of 1958 only 180,000 were to be in service, of whom only 45,000 had to be conscripts. Conscription was reduced to twelve months and it gradually emerged that the final target was to be 350,000 instead of 500,000 while even this level was not to be reached until 1961 (G. Brandt, *Rüstung und Wirtschaft in der BDR*).

The apprehensions of the industrialists were thus allayed. The Federal Republic had paid the rest of NATO back in their own coin, refusing in turn to allow the economy to be disrupted and the tide of prosperity checked by the need to compete with the Russians in numbers. Nor was this all. The reduction in numerical strength could be justified only if the fire-power of the remainder could be increased. Just at this stage technological advances in the construction of nuclear weapons enabled them to be made in small sizes and used much as artillery. American and other strategists, convinced by German developments and by the response of the rest of NATO that the original target of ninety-six divisions could never be realized, argued that the use of such 'tactical' weapons offered the only means short of full-scale atomic war by which the West could hope to offset Communist superiority in personnel and conventional weapons. West

German industry saw in this development the chance of manufacturing under licence a wide range of modern weapons and thereby gaining not only profits and government help with research but also know-how which could be turned to effective civil use. Strauss on occasion argued that, as West Germany was on a footing of complete equality with her NATO allies, the Bundeswehr must get nuclear weapons. The Americans, however, insisted that, while all troops should be equipped with means of firing such weapons and trained in their use, the actual warheads must remain under US control – and American theatre commanders were required to refer to the President before authorizing the small bombs to be used. There was soon, however, every sign that an attempt by the President to withhold his sanction would throw the entire defence arrangements of the West into disarray. The paradox of course was that the case for rearming West Germany had rested on the need to match up to the Russians in conventional weapons; as things worked out, German rearmament was accompanied by a decision to abandon for all practical purposes the idea of defending the West conventionally, while the danger of a deliberate Russian attack on Western Europe was becoming steadily more questionable.

But a NATO decision, taken in December 1957, to authorize the use of tactical nuclear weapons in Central Europe precipitated a flood of controversy. For, though smaller than bombs delivered by aircraft or missiles, they were clearly going to be extremely destructive, and the knowledge that the West was equipped with them would almost certainly (and in practice did) lead to the East following suit. Any incident on the East–West frontier, whether provoked deliberately or by accident, would be capable of escalating rapidly into a situation in which atomic weapons devastated considerable areas, and the areas most likely to be devastated lay in Germany. The result was a West German clamour for the stationing of such weapons on German soil to be forbidden, reinforced on the part of many past victims of Germany by a clamour against putting such lethal weapons into the hands of German soldiers under any circumstances.

Adenauer and Strauss refused to make any concessions to this outcry. According to their arguments the knowledge that tactical nuclear weapons were available would in itself be enough to prevent incidents from occurring. When fifteen distinguished scientists from Göttingen University pressed that the Federal Republic should renounce all use of nuclear weapons, Adenauer disparaged them in public, while he was able to quote in his own favour a strong statement by General Norstad, the American NATO Commander. A vote in favour of nuclear arms was forced through the Bundestag in the spring of 1958, largely by the argument that such a step was vital to West German and European security; when the SPD put their opposition to the test in Land elections in North Rhine-Westphalia in July, they were decisively defeated.

Yet though inside West Germany the issue had been decided, the fears of

Germany's neighbours remained. Communists were not loath to stoke the fires of disquiet, and the period saw a proliferation of plans for the creation of a nuclear-free or even armament-free zone in Central Europe. Adenauer and Strauss poured scorn on any such suggestion, especially when it was accompanied by proposals for a fresh approach to reunification initiated by direct talks between the two German states. They persuaded the Americans to treat the overtures as mere devices to stop the introduction of nuclear weapons into NATO and were rewarded by accusations that their own ultimate aim was to make the Federal Republic a nuclear power in its own right. East and West showed themselves suspicious that the other would somehow evade its undertakings about disarmament, would use provisions for inspecting the genuineness of disarmament to carry out espionage or subversion, and would manage to exploit a disarmed zone for its own purposes. The question whether disarmament should precede or follow reunification also provided a fruitful source of dissension. The actions of both sides had built up an atmosphere of distrust which virtually precluded agreement and there is no point in trying to chronicle negotiations which were doomed from the start. Mutual obstinacy had led to an impasse.

Unfortunately the East could not afford to let things go on as they were. Conditions in the DDR had undoubtedly improved since 1953. Reparations were stopped in 1954 and occupation costs ceased to be levied after 1959. Food rationing was given up in 1958. The Republic was in the process of becoming the biggest producer and exporter of manufactured goods among all the communist satellites and was at last being paid for its deliveries, even if at low rates. Gross National Product rose above the 1936 level (though long after it had done so in the West and chiefly as the result of increased output of capital goods). In 1958 personal consumption per head at last got above the pre-war level. But by that time it was half as high again in the western part of the country, and the contrast between the two economies, when combined with the Communist limitations on personal freedom, provided a strong incentive to migration. Over the nine years from 1952, an average of around 600 people crossed to the West (mainly through Berlin) on every day of every year, the total loss coming to over 2 million; and it was mainly the young, the enterprising and the skilled who left. No state can face such a drain and survive. The policy of combating Communism by making the West strong and prosperous was succeeding only too well. Its fallacy lay in supposing that counter-measures could not and would not be devised.

In August 1957 the Soviet Union was reported to have launched a missile with an atomic warhead. In the following October came the first 'Sputnik' (i.e. traveller) which gave evidence of a capacity to carry such a warhead from Warsaw to Washington in twenty minutes and guide it with enough accuracy to destroy a target as limited as the Capitol building. For various reasons the Russians were not as far ahead, nor the Americans as far behind, as was first thought. But the revelation cast doubt upon the long-term willingness of the Americans to use nuclear weapons in the defence of Western Europe since henceforward such an act was going to invite similar retaliation on America. Khrushchev, who was under some criticism at home for his renunciation of Stalin's policies, seems to have decided to exploit his temporary advantage by pressing for a European settlement. The Russians made no response when Adenauer on three occasions in 1958 secretly suggested the application to the DDR of the neutrality formula which in 1955 had made possible the restoration of Austria's independence. Instead Khrushchev in November 1958 made a threatening speech in which he said that the time had come for the signatories of the Potsdam Agreement to 'renounce the remnants of the occupation regime in Berlin' (which had not in fact been mentioned at Potsdam) and thereby make it possible to create a normal situation in the 'capital of the DDR' (a description incompatible with the agreements which had actually been made as to Berlin). Seventeen days later his underlings followed him up by a more accurate but equally sinister note saying that the Russians regarded the pre-surrender agreements regulating the status of Berlin (see p. 81) as obsolete. It then proposed that West Berlin should be made into a demilitarized free city under Four-Power guarantee and threatened that unless the West accepted such a solution within six months, control over communications between the city and West Germany would be handed over to the DDR authorities. Apart from the fact that to get into the city thereafter would involve the West in giving practical recognition to the DDR, the authorities of that Republic could be expected to act more provocatively than the Russians, so that the chances of an armed clash would thus become distinctly greater.

The Western Powers replied in effect that their right to be in Berlin derived from the same pre-surrender agreements which gave the Russians a right to be in Germany at all, and which could not be ended by unilateral repudiation. The Soviet Union was not entitled on its own initiative to transfer its responsibility to any other government, let alone one which its co-signatories did not recognize. No doubt was left about the intention of the West to maintain its position in Berlin, if necessary by force. This show of firmness, which was accompanied by expressions of readiness to discuss Berlin in the wider context of Germany as a whole, had its effect. After pressure had been put on the Russian leader Mikoyan when he visited the USA in January 1959 and after arguments had been deployed by the British Prime Minister Macmillan when he visited Moscow the following month, the Russians began to abandon the time limit and in May the four Foreign Ministers met in Geneva.

Whereas the Bonn Government were delighted with the three Western Powers for standing firm, they were distinctly less enthusiastic over the idea of negotiations, and particularly negotiations in which they could not directly take part. Reunification was becoming so improbable that they attached ever-increasing importance to Western pledges of support for it and deprecated any overtures which might suggest a willingness to compromise. Macmillan's trip to Moscow earned him a black mark in Adenauer's books, while German faith in the USA was never the same after the retirement and death of John Foster Dulles in 1959. The British and American leaders were, however, under increasing pressure from their publics which, while ready to protect West Berlin and West Germany against Communist encroachment, were much less concerned than the Germans about reunification and insistent that West German opposition to negotiations should not result in a slide towards atomic war.

The Foreign Ministers argued for four months and at one stage seemed on the verge of agreeing on at least an interim settlement for Berlin. Their failure to do so was chiefly due to disagreement as to whether, at the end of the interim, Western rights in the city were to continue until reunification or to lapse. In the autumn Khrushchev visited the USA and agreed with President Eisenhower that another attempt should be made to settle the problem. But the Summit conference at which this was to be set in train was delayed by de Gaulle and, when it was finally convened in Paris in May 1960, was broken off by Khrushchev, ostensibly because of the shooting-down of an American spy-plane but probably because he saw no prospect of emerging from it with any settlement which his colleagues at home would tolerate. Thereafter he refused to negotiate as long as President Eisenhower was in office and the whole question smouldered till May 1961 when, meeting President Kennedy in Vienna, Khrushchev revived his threats and again talked of time limits.

Kennedy, on taking office, had initiated a radical re-examination of NATO's strategic plans, for he shared widespread fears that the West had been preparing for the wrong kind of emergency. A deliberate attack in strength by the East on the West, the spectre of the early 1950s, was coming to seem less and less likely. What were possible were minor probes or border raids, either deliberate or provoked by misunderstandings. Yet if these were met at the outset by tactical nuclear weapons, there seemed a real danger that the situation would get out of hand through escalation. The Kennedy administration set out to develop the theory of the flexible response, which called for the presence of sufficient ground forces, equipped and trained to fight on conventional lines, to hold an attack until its true scale and object became clearer. The efforts to raise NATO's conventional forces were not very successful but in the late 1950s the Russians reduced their strength in Eastern Europe and it became not unreasonable to suppose that as a result the divisions in Western Europe would be just enough to make a Communist attack from immediately available forces a risky business. If, however, one should occur on a full scale, the West's plans still required NATO to be the first side to use nuclear weapons.

The new policy was, however, unwelcome to Adenauer, Strauss and

German industry. Not only did it undermine the Minister's position with their home public, to whom they had multiplied assurances that tactical nuclear weapons were essential, but also it seemed to involve abandonment of defence in forward areas for defence in depth, which was likely to make the whole of the Federal Republic east of the Rhine into a battleground. Adenauer would have agreed with Bismarck's view that 'Russia must be treated like bad weather till things are different.' He considered Kennedy a brash young man who was mistaken in preferring politics of movement to those of stone-walling; he once described him as 'a cross between a junior naval person and a Roman Catholic boy-scout'.

During the weeks succeeding the Vienna meeting, however, Kennedy took the lead in combining firmness with conciliation. American troop strengths in West Germany were increased and the Bonn Government announced its intention of raising the Bundeswehr to its original target of 500,000. But at the same time the West made clear that negotiation would be possible if the Soviet Union would accept the freedom of West Berlin, the principle of free access from West Germany to it and the maintenance of the Western garrisons in it as a guarantee of these freedoms. Significantly, nothing was said about reunification and nothing about free access to West Berlin from the East.

The Soviet leadership would seem to have concluded that the West was not to be cajoled or intimidated and that, as a solution involving attacks on West Berlin and the access routes was likely to be met by force, it must be discarded as too risky. Something, however, had to be done to stop the exodus from the DDR which was swelling to a flood as potential emigrants decided that, if they waited any longer, they might find it too late. Pressure from Ulbricht resulted in a decision to put into practice the least risky solution (for which indeed preparations had been begun some time previously). On 13 August 1961 a barbed wire fence, soon converted into a wall, began to go up hermetically sealing East Berlin from the rest of the city (except at a few controlled crossing-points). On 22 August West Berliners (as distinct from West Germans) were barred from entering the Russian sector without passes and, as the West Berlin authorities refused to allow those passes to be issued on their side of the city, traffic came to a halt. Henceforward Germans had to learn to live with an extra obtrusive symbol of the country's defeated and divided condition.

The people, and possibly the Government, of West Germany were disillusioned to find that their Western Allies took no steps to interfere with the building of Berlin's Wall, or to secure its demolition once it was built. But any attempt by them to use force on the eastern side of the boundary might have provoked Ulbricht into interrupting their communications with West Berlin and thus might well have developed into all-out war. The free world regarded the Wall as an act of unprecedented and inhuman barbarism. But such a reaction was naive. Not merely did it overlook the probability that the alternatives would have been harsher and more dangerous. It overlooked the alternatives because it assumed that an opponent who was conventionally regarded as ruthless and materialistic would act out of character by remaining inactive when pressure was applied to a key point in his system. What the building of the Wall demonstrated was the determination of the Russians to hold on to the parts of Germany which they had won and the inability of the West to shake their grip. Thereby it also seemed to demonstrate that the policy of undermining the foundations of the Democratic Republic was as futile as that of rolling back the curtain. There were in any case those in the West who had no objection to Germany's strength being reduced by partition provided it could be prevented from leading to war; a Frenchman said, 'J'aime tellement l'Allemagne que je suis heureux qu'il y en a deux.'

11

THE ERHARD INTERLUDE:
1961–1966

ADENAUER PROVES HIS OWN WORST ENEMY

Just over a month after the building of the Wall, on 17 September 1961, West Germany went to the polls. The growing disillusionment with Adenauer was reflected in the loss by the CDU/CSU of twenty-eight seats, which involved into the bargain the loss of their absolute majority. The German Party, which had been their coalition partner, fared even worse; it won only 2.8 per cent of the poll and as a result disappeared from federal politics. The SPD, fighting under the leadership of the young Lord Mayor of Berlin Willy Brandt, gained twenty-one seats, the FDP twenty-six. Many people inside and outside Germany had hoped that the venerable Chancellor would take the occasion to retire. There were those in his own Party who wanted to see him replaced by Erhard because, although they thought Erhard would make a bad leader (as he did), they reckoned for that reason on being able to get rid of him more easily than Adenauer and to open the way for one of themselves. But Erhard refused to be a party to such intrigues or put himself up against Adenauer while Adenauer, on whom such calculations were by no means lost, regarded the situation as so serious and his colleagues as so unsatisfactory that on the morning immediately follow-ing the Election, he announced his intention of continuing in office. To do so, however, he needed the support of a second party – and by now the Parties in the Bundestag had been reduced to four (counting the CSU as distinct from the CDU). The chief gainer at the Election had been the FDP but it owed this success in large part to a promise by its leader Dr Mende not to join in any coalition as long as Adenauer remained at the helm. The alternative of a 'Great Coalition' with the SPD had adherents in many quarters but its opponents in both Parties on this occasion won the day. A coalition between SPD and FDP was at the time ruled out by the Confederation of German Industry which financed the FDP and was not convinced that the SPD had genuinely renounced socialization. In the end, after seven weeks of bargaining, a CDU/CSU/FDP coalition emerged, Mende atoning for his rash commitment by forswearing office. A promise was, however, extorted from Adenauer that he would retire in 1963 at the latest.

The building of the Wall did not end the Berlin crisis, which continued to simmer for another eighteen months. Kennedy made clear that he was still ready to discuss solutions which did not impair the fundamental determination of the West to protect West Berlin; as a result he went a long way towards alienating Bonn without quite conciliating the Kremlin. At one point Grewe, the German Ambassador in the USA, felt compelled to appeal to the Article in the 1954 Paris Treaty by which the West had committed itself to seeking a freely negotiated peace settlement for the whole of Germany; at another, great offence was taken in Bonn when Washington suggested making concessions to the East and in Washington when Bonn sought to torpedo the move by deliberately leaking the US proposals. Grewe himself had later to be removed on account of incompatibility with Kennedy and the State Department. Relations improved slightly as East and West measured up to the confrontation which was precipitated in October 1962 over Cuba. The demonstration that Kennedy was not to be intimidated but was anything but brash earned him widespread respect in West Germany. The crisis had clear implications for Russian policy regarding Berlin and Germany; that Khrushchev had learnt them was suggested when on 16 January 1963 he told the East German Party Congress that the problem of the German Peace Treaty was not what it had been before defensive measures (including the building of the Wall) were taken. Thereafter, for the time being at any rate, the chief Russian aim seemed to be to harass sleeping dogs with nothing more than tintacks.

Since the election of Kennedy the US administration had given Adenauer little encouragement for pursuing his hitherto unyielding line. His disillusionment with the country which he had made one of the two main foundations of his policy inclined him to pay all the more attention to the other and helps to explain the friendship which was struck up from the autumn of 1958 onwards between himself and de Gaulle. The General's previous record towards Germany should hardly have disposed the Chancellor in his favour. His hostility to the EDC and, as was to become evident, to the supra-national conception of the EEC might have been thought to show a radical difference of approach. Moreover de Gaulle had as early as March 1959 committed the sin, usually regarded in Bonn as unforgivable, of saying that present frontiers (including presumably the Oder–Neisse line) must be maintained; he also insisted on keeping in touch with the Russians because of his hope that France could prove she was still a Great Power by mediating between East and West. But both the French and the German statesmen were elderly, both Catholic, both inclined to behave as autocrats; their homes were within two hundred miles of one another. Each of the two combined a respect for tradition with an astute eye for political advantage. De Gaulle could have no hope of realizing his ambitions in Europe, involving as they did the reduction of American influence, unless he could secure at least one powerful ally and, in her current mood of disappointment, West Germany must have appeared a more likely recruit than Britain. Another factor which could be counted on to work in the same direction was Adenauer's well-known desire to end Franco-German animosities for good and all. The Germans may well have appreciated that France's reasons for disliking the USA were by no means the same as their own. But the French policy of building up Europe as a 'third Force' must have appeared to Adenauer to offer a chance of maintaining towards the East the unyielding line which seemed otherwise doomed by the withdrawal of American support.

For the rest of the period covered by this chapter, two alternative schools of thought contended inside Bonn government circles for the control of foreign policy. One, represented by Adenauer and Strauss, denied that there had been any fundamental change in Russia's desire for world domination and therefore sought to maintain with as little alteration as possible the attitudes of the Cold War. But they now sought to achieve this policy in association with France rather than the USA and by building up a 'Europe des patries' which, although composed of states still essentially sovereign, would co-operate sufficiently to overcome the inadequacies of sovereign states in the modern world, notably as regards the possession of nuclear weapons. The other school, of which Erhard and Schröder were the protagonists, argued that for the foreseeable future West Germany must continue to depend for her defence on American nuclear might, and that, to maintain American good-will, some (but not too many) concessions must be made to the American desire for a reduction of East–West tension. If Erhard's tenure of office had been more auspicious as a whole, he and Schröder might have been able to make their views prevail. But as it was, they had to make so many concessions in order to carry their Party with them as to remove any real chances of success. Thus the 'Peace Note' which they circulated to all friendly Powers in March 1966 was far too cautious to melt any Eastern ice. But the German Gaullists for their part were frequently embarrassed by the unwillingness of their patron to consider any German interests which did not suit him, as well as by the failure of various proposals to evolve a European deterrent.

The SPD not only agreed with Erhard that there was no future in stone-walling but also had positive reasons for favouring a positive approach. Their attitude was well expressed by a speech made in 1963 by Egon Bahr, the press officer and policy adviser of Willy Brandt:

The American strategy for peace can be expressed by the formula that the Communist domination has got to be transformed rather than superseded.

The first consequence of applying the Strategy for Peace to Germany is that the policy of all or nothing has got to stop. Today it is obvious that reunification is not to be a once-for-all affair but a process with many stages and many pauses. There is no need for us to be handicapped by our refusal to recognize the Zone as a lawful state. This goes without saying and without serious challenge. Our first concern must be with human beings and with the exploration of every conceivable and defensible means of improving their situation. An improvement in material conditions in the Zone must lead to a relaxation in tension.

Such a policy can be summed up in the phrase, 'Nearness will bring change'.

Bahr's attitude was regarded by the 'hard-liners' of the CDU/CSU as incapable of arousing any response on the part of the East and therefore as involving a gratuitous display of weakness.

This background helps to explain the commotion caused in West Germany towards the end of 1962 by the 'Spiegel Affair'. Der Spiegel is a weekly paper which had often given publicity to topics hushed up by the Government. It performed during the Adenauer era the useful function of forcing on public attention issues and scandals which politicians preferred to keep wrapped up. Besides being frequently critical of Adenauer himself, it had on several occasions spotlighted actions by Franz Josef Strauss of distinctly questionable propriety, although he afterwards explained them to the satisfaction of the Bundestag majority. They included a report that, on one of the crucial nights of the (then recent) Cuba crisis, the Minister of Defence had been the worse for drink. At almost the same time Der Spiegel published an article on the position of the Bundeswehr in NATO which not only contained privately obtained information as to future plans but claimed that at the Minister's instigation so much attention had been given to the use of tactical nuclear weapons as to impair the efficiency of conventional training.

Over a fortnight later police raided the office of Der Spiegel and the homes of some of its senior staff, on the pretext that there had been a leakage of vital defence secrets. Eleven arrests were made; that of Conrad Ahlers, the author of the article, was effected by the Spanish police, at the request of the German Embassy, while he was on holiday. Rudolf Augstein, the paper's publisher, was kept in jail for fourteen weeks.

In the subsequent controversy both Adenauer and Strauss at first attempted to minimize their parts, only to have it demonstrated that they both had told lies to the Bundestag. In particular a telephone call to the Madrid Embassy was shown to have been made by Strauss himself, though he subsequently claimed to have been acting on the Chancellor's behalf. Adenauer, who on the whole despised his Cabinet colleagues, recognized in Strauss something of the flair for political manoeuvre on which he prided himself. He would probably have liked to keep the offender in his Cabinet

169

but was precluded from doing so by the FDP, whose Cabinet representative, Heinemann, the Minister of Justice, had by Adenauer's orders been left in the dark in a matter involving his Ministry. Adenauer's first expedient was to dismiss the two senior officials who had done as they were told but this did not suffice to stop the FDP Ministers from resigning in a body and indicating that they were no longer prepared to serve with Strauss. Before they returned, the Cabinet had to be reconstructed, Strauss had to resign and the Chancellor had to confirm his intention of retiring in 1963. The FDP Minister of Justice was, however, left out of the new Cabinet. Meanwhile in the middle of the row the people of Bavaria had gone to the polls and voted for the return to office with an increased majority of the CSU who had in the previous spring chosen Strauss as their Chairman.

Hardly was the Cabinet reconstructed than Adenauer in January 1963 visited Paris to put the coping-stone on to his policy of reconciliation by signing a Franco–German Treaty of Friendship. The auspiciousness of the occasion was somewhat impaired by its occurrence midway between the press conference at which de Gaulle questioned the qualifications of Britain for joining the Common Market and the meeting in Brussels at which the British application for membership was finally on French insistence suspended. Had Adenauer made his signature of the Treaty conditional on British entry, as some of his colleagues wished, much might have altered. But the development and maintenance of Europe was always his first priority, while for Britain he had at best respect, never affection. British attitudes towards disarmament, nuclear free zones and a compromise with the East smacked altogether too much of appeasement for his tastes. The Bundestag, however, when ratifying the Treaty, insisted on adding a preamble which reaffirmed the German desire to maintain the Atlantic Alliance and strengthen the European Community by the inclusion of Britain. They thus ruled out the use of the document to support Gaullist policies.

THREE YEARS OF FUMBLING

Adenauer finally retired in October 1963. In spite of all his efforts, Erhard was nominated by the Party as his successor. But they allowed him to remain Party Chairman and he did not resign from the Bundestag. From these positions he kept up a running fire of comment about the policy of the new regime and at an early stage a remark that 'I can no longer endure the miserable talk of relaxation' began to make the rounds. Schröder, as Foreign Minister, inaugurated a 'policy of movement', the chief feature of which was the development of trade with, and the establishment of trade missions in, the five Communist satellites whose recognition of the DDR made impossible under the Hallstein Doctrine the establishment of full diplomatic relations. In the documents effecting this development, the terms offered by the Federal Republic were said to apply throughout the currency area of the Deutschmark; this formula neatly evaded the controversial question of the Republic's right to act on behalf of West Berlin.

A similar evasion was resorted to at Christmas after the DDR Government had offered to allow citizens of West Berlin facilities for visiting relatives in the east part of the city. A representative of the West Berlin Senate at the last moment negotiated an arrangement which, rather than use terms with implications unacceptable to one or the other side, opened with an admission that the two negotiators had been unable to agree on how to describe their respective areas, superior authorities or positions! The Bonn Government disliked the development but lacked the courage to veto a step which could bring happiness to many, and almost 1 million people passed through the Wall. The arrangement was repeated in 1964 and 1965 but grew more and more unpopular with the hawks in Bonn who feared not only that the very act of negotiating with DDR officials might be exploited as involving recognition but also that any steps which eased the evils of partition might weaken the determination to get it abolished completely. The DDR, observing this, thought that they saw an opportunity of putting the hawks at cross-purposes with the doves and, when the 1966 negotiations started, insisted on spades being called spades. As a result no agreement was reached and no visits exchanged.

The virtual cessation of traffic between the two sides of the city was not merely a human tragedy. It called into question the functions which during the 1950s the Western side had been performing of show-window, listening post, reception centre and propaganda factory. Moreover with the ending of replenishment from the East, West Berlin's labour force began to fall and the proportion of pensioners in the population to grow abnormally high. To maintain employment the Federal Government, on top of other financial aid, provided subsidies which enabled raw materials to be brought from the West, made into finished goods in the city and taken back to the West for sale. Even so there were signs of a drift of work, talent and control to West Germany. The unbroken monopoly of political power which the SPD enjoyed began to have its usual corrupting effects. The beleaguered bastion of liberty was showing signs of degenerating into a dead end.

Erhard and Schröder remained faithful to the Atlantic Alliance and their relations with France failed to live up to the aims professed in the Treaty of Friendship. The USA's attention and resources became increasingly strained by the Vietnam War and after Kennedy's assassination few initiatives were taken in Europe. US expenditure on aid combined with extensive overseas investment and the rising outlay on Vietnam to create a serious overall deficit. Britain had for some time been endeavouring to make the Federal Republic choose between contributing more to the cost of maintaining British troops in Germany or seeing their numbers reduced, and now the Americans, in search of economies, adopted the same line. De Gaulle made increasingly clear his determination to wreck NATO which had for so long been the sheet anchor of West German defence policy. In the summer of 1965 his high-handed attempt, in defiance of the Rome Treaty, to reshape the Common Market more to his liking added another ground for dissension, since the West Germans stood firm in solidarity with the Italians, Benelux and the EEC Commission. The policy of seeking reunification through a relaxation of tension seemed productive of problems rather than results.

Nor was foreign policy the only field in which things were going wrong. In the economic field much had changed since the early days of the 'Miracle'. Many of the initial advantages had faded away. People who had rebuilt their fortunes no longer felt the same need for effort; by 1966 the average working week in West Germany was 2.5 hours shorter than in Britain. Workers who had tasted the pleasures of the affluent society grew eager for the money and leisure needed to enjoy more of them; in particular the practice grew of taking expensive holidays abroad. The building of the Wall, by stopping the flow of workers from the East, made labour for the first time scarce; the workers who came instead from Southern Europe, besides being less skilled, sent back much of their earnings to their families at home. The West German trade unions began to demand and obtain higher annual wage increases. In 1963 an export boom set in, producing such prosperity that prices and imports began to rise alarmingly. In 1965 the country had a deficit on current account of DM 6,500 million (£550 million), and whereas Britain was accustomed to cancel out her traditional deficit on visible trade by a surplus on invisibles, the Federal Republic was coming to need a substantial visible surplus to offset the expenditure of her tourists, the remittances of her foreign workers and the considerable sums which she was paying as development aid.

Deficits were not confined to foreign trade. In the prosperity of the 1950s, a readiness had developed to quiet the complaints of pressure groups by handing out public money. Pensions had been made up on a lavish scale; many people received 60 per cent of their final salary. Subsidies were given to encourage building, the unnatural economy of West Berlin was bolstered up, compensation paid to all affected by the war, uneconomic industries like textiles, coal-mining and ship-building kept in being. The fact that some of these expenditures were sensible did not prevent them from being costly. Such generosity at the expense of the taxpayer was not confined to the Federal Government which incurred only 20 per cent of total public expenditure; many social services in West Germany are the responsibility of the Land Governments, others that of the cities and communes. Extravagance was just as noteworthy here. Moreover the system of government, and in particular the allocation of tax revenues (see p. 131) would have made it impossible for the Federal Government to control expenditure elsewhere, even had the desire to do so existed. As the 1965 election approached, the largesse became more lavish than ever; a particularly untimely step (not unknown in Britain in similar circumstances) was a cut in income tax. The praise accorded to the 'Social Market Economy', by making 'planning' a dirty word, discouraged people from asking how the Budget was going to be balanced or what levels of expenditure would be involved in future years by the commitments already entered into.

Curiously enough, the election campaign of 1965 did not lead to any real debate on the problems facing West Germany in the fields of economic and foreign policy. The Government was too fundamentally divided to encourage discussion, while the Socialists, fighting again under the leadership of Willy Brandt, seem to have feared that talk of the need to economize or suggestions of a more conciliatory policy towards the East might lose them votes. They hoped to win victory by promising to do the same things as the Government but to do them better. These tactics did not pay. Their gain of twelve seats fell far short of their expectations, whereas the CDU/CSU, who had been afraid of losing ground, returned three seats stronger. The real losers by eighteen seats were the FDP; no other parties gained any representation at all. Although there was once again talk of a 'Great Coalition' (principally by people who wanted to get rid of Erhard), the Chancellor insisted on keeping the FDP as his partner in government and they were still content to play that role. With their help he beat off attempts to bring Strauss (now leader of the CSU in the Bundestag) back into the Cabinet and to evict Schröder from the Foreign Ministry.

In the succeeding twelve months, however, things got worse rather than better. Dissatisfaction mounted with the lack of progress over reunification. The 'German Gaullists' remained opposed to gratifying American desires for negotiation with the East, but their resistance to all forms of relaxation grew increasingly difficult to reconcile with their advocacy of close co-operation with France and the development of an independent Europe, since de Gaulle showed himself almost as anxious as the Americans to improve relations with the East. The choice open to West Germany began therefore to be seen, not as one between rigidity and movement but between the Social Democratic solution of trying by negotiations with the rulers of the DDR (short of formal recognition) to secure minor alleviations for their population and on the other hand the official preference for trying by negotiations with other Communist states to isolate and undermine the rulers of the DDR. It became, however, increasingly clear that Erhard was too genial, too much of a technical expert and too little of a politician to impose his authority on his colleagues. He did not dare to threaten resignation because he knew (especially after the Election of 1965 had been won) that many people would have been glad to see him go. Consequently West German policy remained one of little steps because Ministers could not agree in what direction to make big ones.

Much the same story was repeated in economic affairs. The boom of 1963 was gradually waning. In particular the programme of housebuilding, which hitherto had been a major source of growth, was at last beginning to slacken as supply caught up with demand. But there was still a certain amount of inflationary pressure in the economy. The Bundesbank, which was required by its Charter to give overriding priority to maintaining the value of the Mark, had not yet realized how much time modern economies take to answer the monetary helm and insisted on maintaining a deflationary course for longer than was appropriate. Interest rates were kept high, industry became reluctant to borrow, orders began to fall and business confidence to be shaken. As the Bank had been deliberately so constituted as to be independent of official control, the Government could not enforce a change of policy and failed to achieve one by persuasion. The fall in tax revenues further impaired the balance of a budget already upset by the lavish expenditure. Various proposals for savings had no practical result and even the expedient of forming five Ministers into a *Streichquintett* to strike out proposals for expenditure came to little because the Ministers affected by the cuts persuaded the Cabinet to cancel most of them; party discipline was not strong enough to prevent the representatives of pressure groups from getting other economies rejected when they came before the Bundestag. An attempt to reduce defence expenditure was stamped on by the Americans. The Government was therefore unable to comply with the Basic Law's requirement that the Budget must be balanced. The symptoms of a crisis were thus unmistakable. They even induced Erhard to overcome his objections to attempts at guiding the economy and allow his Economics Minister Schmücker to introduce a Stability Bill giving the Government powers to accelerate or slow down the rate of expenditure at Land and local levels as well as centrally. The project, however, evoked numerous objections, not least from the Land Governments, and became bogged down in Bundestag debates.

When a Bundestag Deputy dies or retires, his place is filled automatically by the next available man on his Party's list for election by proportional representation (see p. 125); thus there are no by-elections. As a result, it is elections for Land Governments which in the Federal Republic perform the role of recording changes in public attitudes towards the Government. In July 1966 such elections fell due in North Rhine-Westphalia, and in them the SPD came within two seats of winning an absolute majority. This was an omen which the CDU could not afford to disregard. Dissatisfaction with Erhard ceased to be confined to political opponents and personal enemies; even for those who had hitherto supported him, he began to seem more a liability than an asset. The FDP in particular began to worry whether in their electoral position they could afford to be associated much longer with a discredited regime. But Article 67 of the Grundgesetz (Constructive Vote of No Confidence, see p. 129) makes any Chancellor difficult to dislodge, and all the obvious CDU/CSU aspirants for the succession had determined enemies. It took a double manoeuvre at the end of October 1966 to evict Erhard. In the first place the rank-and-file of the FDP Deputies insisted on their representatives in the Cabinet vetoing proposals for balancing the Budget by higher taxes; they hoped by this means to force the CDU/CSU into facing fundamental policy decisions. The rank-and-file of the CDU/CSU, led by Strauss, saw their chance and, by insisting on their Cabinet representatives standing firm, provoked the FDP Ministers into resigning. Though Erhard tried for a time to weather the storm, it became clear that he could not fill the vacancies, that he would therefore have to resign and that a new Cabinet would have to be formed under a new Chancellor. But who should compose it?

The urgency of the situation was underlined by elections in Hesse on 6 November and in Bavaria on 23 November. Not only did the FDP lose ground in both, being completely deprived of representation in the Bavarian Landtag, but also the right-wing 'Neo-Nazis' or National Democratic Party (NDP) – which had obtained no seats in the 1965 Federal Election – made striking gains, polling 7.9 per cent of the votes (with eight seats) in Hesse and 7.4 per cent (with fifteen seats) in Bavaria. Some voters were losing patience with democracy.

The first step towards the resolution of the crisis was taken when the CDU/CSU decided, largely on the initiative of Strauss, to bypass all the more obvious rivals for the succession and call back to Bonn, as its candidate for the Chancellorship, Dr Kurt Georg Kiesinger, a former Bundestag Deputy who, after Adenauer had dashed his hopes of becoming Foreign Minster, retired to his native Land of Baden-Württemberg as its Minister-President. The most obvious objection to his appointment was that he had not only joined the Nazi Party in 1933 but also remained a member, even if a relatively inactive one, throughout the Third Reich, with a post as liaison officer between the Foreign Office and the foreign services of the Reich Broadcasting Company; this at least seemed to justify a charge of conformism and thereby to impair the good impression made by his post-war record.

Both the CDU/CSU and the FDP regarded with distaste the idea of working together again. The character of the new Government was thus made dependent on the preference of the SPD. While they still differed from the CDU/CSU on many issues, the gap between the two Parties had been narrowing ever since the Godesberg Programme (see p. 154), while the Social Democrats could not be said to see eye to eye with the leaders of the FDP. The greatest objection to a 'Little Coalition' lay in the fact that it would have a majority of only six and there was considerable doubt (to be justified by experience after 1969) as to the loyalty of some members of the FDP right wing. In a 'Little Coalition' the main responsibility would have rested with the SPD and they were afraid of being discredited, on at last achieving office, by failure to discharge it effectively. Yet if they refused office altogether, they would face criticism for shunning responsibility. They also feared that, in face of an SPD/FDP government, the CDU/CSU would move to the right and criticize Ministers for lacking patriotism, as after 1918. There also seemed to be a good deal in the argument that only a Great Coalition would be strong enough to overcome the difficulties facing the new government abroad and restore business confidence at home.

For all these reasons, under the strong promptings of Herbert Wehner, but against the inclinations of many ordinary party members, and to the disillusion of the young, the SPD Deputies came down at the end of November 1966 in favour of a Great Coalition. The CDU/CSU were delighted with a solution which spared them the unpleasant necessity of giving up office. Under Kiesinger as Chancellor, Brandt became Foreign Minister, Schiller (a Professor of Economics who had distinguished himself as an SPD Senator in Hamburg) Economics Minister, Strauss Finance Minister, Schröder Defence Minister and Wehner Minister for All-German Affairs. In total, the CDU held eight posts, the CSU three and the SPD nine. The first, and as it proved, decisive step had been taken towards ending the domination of Federal politics by the CDU/CSU.

12

THE GREAT COALITION:
1966–1969

RESTORING CONFIDENCE AT HOME

The main domestic task of the new Government was to restore confidence
in West Germany's continued economic prosperity. But this could best be
achieved by success in two other tasks. The first was to reverse the policy
of deflation and get the economy expanding again. This was all the easier
because by the time the Great Coalition took office, there was unmistakable
evidence that the boom had run its full course. Whereas in October there
had been 300,000 more unfilled jobs than unemployed, by December the
second exceeded the first. The Bundesbank was thereby helped to overcome
its hesitations about reducing the interest rate, a step which it was all the
readier to take because the very formation of the Coalition was evidence of
an intention to tackle the other main source of inflation, namely the Budget.
To believers in the Keynesian principle of working against the cyclical trend,
the very fact that this was unbalanced was a recommendation in its favour.
Not only did the Grundgesetz require it to be balanced, but also the inbred
fear of rising prices and mounting debts, due to memories of 1923 and 1948,
made the crude form of deliberately incurred deficit out of the question.

This was where the Great Coalition did most to justify its formation. The
presence of two parties in the Cabinet and the division of responsibility
between two Ministers (Strauss and Schiller) allowed the problem to be
solved by pursuing two policies at once. Strauss pleased the CDU/CSU by
balancing the Budget through the orthodox remedy of taxing more and
spending less; Schiller pleased the SPD by pursuing a counter-cyclical policy
of 'moderated expansion' (*Aufschwung nach Mass*) with a special programme of capital expenditure on communications, public building and the
provision of similar 'infrastructure' which had been neglected in previous
years and could quite properly be paid for by running into long-term debt.
Each Minister backed the other up, so that the performance was said to
have 'words by Schiller, music by Strauss', and Kiesinger backed both:
their combined weight was sufficient to get the programme through the
Cabinet and Bundestag more or less intact. The unions, anxious to avoid

unemployment, agreed to co-operate by moderating their demands for higher wages and making the new rates run for two or three years.

The cure was completed by steps to prevent the disease from recurring. July 1967 saw the passing into law of a revised version of Schmücker's Stability Bill (see p. 174). It set as the targets of government policy the 'quadrilateral' whose all-round achievement has often been thought impossible – stable prices, full employment, adequate growth and a reasonable external surplus. It allowed for 10 per cent adjustments up or down to be made in certain taxes without Bundestag approval being necessary. Both the Federal and Land Governments were authorized to freeze revenue in booms and release the money in recessions; they could also remit taxes on companies to encourage investment or suspend allowances to deter it. As no increase in Federal authority over expenditure had a hope of being accepted by the Bundesrat, a 'Business Activity Council' (*Konjunkturrat*) was set up to steer the economy, on which the Federal and Land Governments, the Communes and the Bundesbank were all represented. A Council of (five) Experts had already been set up in 1964 to provide economic forecasts and suggest action; the Government was now required to report annually to the Bundestag its reactions to these suggestions. The joke that the country was becoming a 'Republic of Councils' (*Räterepublik* – what the left wing had wanted to set up in 1919) was encouraged by the creation of yet another one to produce rolling forecasts of overall income and expenditure in the public sector for the next three years (*Mittelfristigesplanung*). A Council of Government, Employers and Unions (*Konzentierte Aktion*) was set up to produce in concert forecasts of growth and, in the light of these, recommendations as to the size of wage increases which could be afforded. Finally the Government was required to publish annually a list of all the subsidies which it was paying.

The other notable achievement of the Great Coalition in the economic field was its reorganization of the coal industry. The drop in demand for coal, highlighted early in 1967 by the near-bankruptcy of Krupps, meant that, if the industry was to remain profitable, it must be reduced in size. But as long as the pits remained in separate hands, often owned in conjunction with enterprises in other fields, diversity of interest would prevent the framing of any rational plan for contraction. Ideology made straightforward public ownership out of the question and only the obstinacy of Schiller brought about the formation at the end of 1968 of an overall Company for the Ruhr Coal Industry, which took over the mining activities of forty-seven companies, in return for generous compensation to be paid over a long period. Schiller also saw to it that elaborate plans were included for compensating and retraining redundant miners, thereby avoiding obstruction by the unions. He had less success in his efforts to form a single German oil company large enough to compete with Esso, BP and Shell, which dominate the market. An ambitious scheme by the Minister of Transport to

178

transfer heavy long-distance loads to the railways fell foul of the road transport lobby. The idea of extending workers' co-determination was as unpalatable to the CDU as it was dear to the SPD and, as a compromise, a commission was given the job of formulating precise proposals. While many favoured the idea of revising the financial relationships between Bund and Länder, everyone had different ideas as to the form which revision should take, so that the most achieved in the end was minor tinkering. In 1969 amendments were passed to the Basic Law giving the Federal Government power to work with the Länder (mainly by contributing cash) on higher education, scientific research, town planning and hospital construction.

Novel as the idea was that the economy could and should be deliberately steered by the Government, the CDU/CSU members of the Coalition came to accept it. What they and still more their SPD colleagues overestimated was the ease and speed with which it could be done. In 1967 progress was slow, largely because the local authorities found it hard to accustom themselves to the idea that the right way to counter falling revenues was to increase expenditure. By July industrial capacity was only 75 per cent employed and Schiller secured authority for a second investment programme. Most of the increasing production went into exports, which led to a favourable trade balance of DM 9.5 billion. After the New Year, however, home demand began to pick up and by mid-1968 the economy was once again at full stretch. No trace remained of the anxiety which had been so much more widespread than people outside Germany had realized. The budget was back in balance; the growth rate, instead of the forecast 4 per cent, reached 7 per cent while exports were up by 13 per cent (as in most other countries of Western Europe). Everyone who had a chance of holding Marks took it. Money poured into the country, with inflationary results.

The US and British Governments, which were struggling with deficits, called on the West Germans to help by revaluing the Mark upwards. Strauss and Schiller were ready to consider a small rise as part of a general international adjustment. But when this was blocked by de Gaulle's refusal to devalue the franc, Strauss refused to handicap exporters and farmers by making the Mark more expensive abroad. The Bundesbank, giving priority as usual to preventing inflation, wanted a unilateral revaluation. Schiller's concern for the consumer made him sympathetic, but the most he could get his colleagues to accept was a scheme of taxes and rebates on foreign trade which had much the same effect as a revaluation.

But although this resolved the political deadlock, it did not remove the economic difficulty; the trade surplus continued to grow. By March 1969 Schiller was telling the Chancellor that revaluation was inevitable, but he had not got far towards securing agreement on such a step when at the end of April de Gaulle's resignation seemed to remove the obstacle to an international solution. Strauss tried to precipitate one by saying that the Mark needed to go up by 8 to 10 per cent, an ill-considered remark which caused the amount of foreign money in Germany to double within a week. Action by further countries, however, was not forthcoming and the Cabinet therefore decided to remain inactive too, a decision which produced a protest from sixty-one Professors of Economics but was approved by 87 per cent of the electorate! The Cabinet spokesman into the bargain described it as being valid 'for ever' (*auf ewig*), a time limit which most observers interpreted as meaning until after the election due in September, and even in that sense considered foolhardy. Schiller disowned responsibility for what might happen in the interval but did not resign since he would thereby have almost certainly broken up the coalition and left a minority government to caretake for five months. The close collaboration between the two Ministers had been ended by the very success which it had made possible. The views of the two Parties had become diametrically opposed and, although this was partly due to discrepant guesses as to which line would bring most votes, the chances of them ever being able to work together again harmoniously seemed small. Paradoxically it was the SPD who favoured leaving market forces free to act and the CDU/CSU who wanted them to be directed by the Government.

SMALL STEPS ONLY GET A SMALL DISTANCE

In its policy towards Communist East Europe (*Ostpolitik*), the Coalition professed an intention to advance by a series of small steps, which the Democratic Republic unkindly rephrased as 'aggression in carpet slippers'. From the outset there were two distinct ideas about how to pursue this. One school of thought wanted to build on the foundations already laid by Schröder of developing relationships with all the non-German satellite states, hoping in this way to weaken the ties between those states and the 'hard-line' regimes in Russia and East Germany. The other, considering this tactic too obvious and therefore doomed to failure, favoured approaches to all states at once. Kiesinger, in his initial declaration of policy, had said that 'we want to relax rather than stiffen, to bridge differences rather than deepen them'. He offered to establish diplomatic relations with all states which did not demand unacceptable conditions in return. But that was precisely what the Russians and East Germans did, making clear that as an essential to any progress the Federal Republic must recognize the Democratic Republic and the 1945 frontiers.

Only the Romanians showed themselves more amenable. The Federal Republic had already become their largest supplier after the Soviet Union and, true to their Latin origins, they were showing in the Warsaw Pact much the same independence as the French were doing in NATO. In January 1967 they agreed to the upgrading into full-scale embassies of the trade missions in the two countries. They allowed a clause to be inserted in the agreement which explicitly recorded that its conclusion did not imply any change in

Bonn's views about the illegality of the DDR. This, and the invention of a theory that Romania could not be criticized for recognizing that state since she had never been left any choice by the Russians (*Geburtsfehlertheorie*), enabled Kiesinger to conciliate the more intransigent members of his right wing.

Ulbricht for his part had hoped to use West Germany's desire for trade with south-east Europe as a lever for forcing the members of the Atlantic Alliance to recognize the existence of his own state. His party paper minced no words about Romania's sale of the pass; the Romanian party paper replied, at four times the length, to the effect that that country's leaders intended to run their own foreign policy. They further refused to go to East Berlin for a conference to co-ordinate action, though they were not able to prevent a later conference in Czechoslovakia from vowing never to follow their example. Feelers which Bonn had been putting out, particularly towards Hungary, were as a result rebuffed. This outcome bore out the misgivings of those West Germans who had questioned the wisdom of approaching the Eastern bloc through its deviant member – but no other approach had at that juncture any better prospects.

In April 1967 Kiesinger proposed to the DDR a sixteen-point programme for easing mutual relations. No immediate answer was made but in May a letter arrived at the Chancellor's office containing an offer from Willi Stoph, the East German Prime Minister, to meet Kiesinger with a view to creating 'normal relations' – what Willy Brandt at about the same time described as 'regulated co-existence' (*geregeltes Nebeneinander*). A pre-condition, however, was that the Federal Republic should give up its claim to represent all Germans. As all previous letters of the kind had been returned unopened, the very reading of this one was an advance. But the problem of what to say in reply and even of how to address the writer (who could hardly be called Prime Minister if his state did not officially exist) meant that a month went by before an answer was dispatched to the 'Dear Chairman' (of an unspecified body) suggesting that, at any rate to begin with, conversations would be best left to subordinates, and adding that if Herr Stoph insisted on prior recognition, Dr Kiesinger would be obliged in return to demand a secret plebiscite of all Germans about their future. Stoph returned to the charge in September but with an 'all-or-nothing' demand which showed that Bonn had to choose between changing its attitudes altogether and making no progress. Meanwhile Moscow and East Berlin dilated on the electoral successes of the National Democratic Party (see p. 175), while the more that the CDU leaders tried to calm their hawks by saying that the new policies meant a change only of methods and not of aims, the easier it was for Communist publicists to argue that the capitalists were as dangerous as ever.

There remained Yugoslavia, which sent so many workers to the Federal Republic and entertained so many tourists from it as to make the absence of formal diplomatic contact between the two countries (see p. 157) exceptionally nonsensical. But although there was wide agreement that enforcing the Hallstein Doctrine in this case had been a mistake, the reversal of that step would imply abandoning it as a principle, and this the right wing of the Coalition was reluctant to do. Late in 1967, however, the Yugoslavs lost patience and induced Brandt to follow suit. In January 1968 he insisted on concluding an agreement with Belgrade which, in spite of a face-saving clause, effectively admitted that West Germany no longer objected to other states recognizing two Germanies at once.

For the next nine months attention was dominated by events in Czechoslovakia, which themselves indicated the successes and limits of the new Ostpolitik. There could be no doubt about the desire of the Dubček regime to take up the West's offers of closer relations. But it was precisely for that reason that the Russians (egged on throughout by Ulbricht) set limits on the relaxation which they would permit. Early in the summer a couple of West German politicians went to Prague and there seems to have been talk of a West German loan. But Brandt left unheeded Czech hints that a visit from him would be welcome, while in July he persuaded Kiesinger to shift away from the Czech–Bavarian frontier manoeuvres which were planned to take place there in September, so as to give the Russians no ground for using a supposed threat from the West as an excuse for intervening in Czech affairs. When nevertheless they did intervene, the revulsion throughout the free world was such that efforts at relaxing tension became for a period futile.

During the same summer, much play was made by the Communists about West Berlin being no more than a temporary Allied enclave on East German territory and not, as Bonn maintained, an integral part of the Federal Republic. Severe limitations were imposed on the passage of West German (though not of Allied) nationals over the surface access routes to West Berlin, culminating in a refusal to allow members of the Federal Convention to go there for the Presidential Election in March 1969 (see p. 187). But as the Allies regarded the choice of the city for that Election as possibly illegal and certainly tactless, and as it was always possible to get there unimpeded by air, no show-down resulted.

Soon afterwards Cambodia, Iraq and the Sudan recognized the DDR; the CDU/CSU pressed for diplomatic relations with them to be broken off and aid to be stopped but the SPD were not to be lured into exasperation. Brandt for his part paid more attention to overtures from Poland than Strauss thought appropriate. Both Parties were by this time angling for votes, with opinion polls suggesting that over half the population saw no point in continued intransigence, so that the SPD's attitude was more likely to win them than the CDU's. Everything moreover went to show that no real improvement with the East was possible until the Federal Republic accepted that the 1945 settlement was lasting, if not permanent. The Great Coalition could not do this for, had the CDU and CSU Ministers agreed, they would have split their Parties.

THE OPPOSITION GOES OUTSIDE PARLIAMENT

The overwhelming majority which the Great Coalition possessed in the Bundestag deprived opposition inside Parliament of much of its point but stimulated opposition outside Parliament on both extremes, a development which may have been inevitable in any circumstances. Fortunately neither radical left nor radical right produced a leader of any real ability. The NDP won 5.8 per cent of the vote in the Schleswig-Holstein Land elections in April 1967, 6.9 per cent in the Rhineland-Palatinate ones in the same month and an ominous 9.8 per cent in Baden-Württemberg a year later. The imminent prospect was that they would win more than 5 per cent in the Federal Election due in September 1969 and consequently enter the Bundestag. There was as a result much talk about the desirability of changing over to a British-type electoral system with single-member constituencies, since this was expected to prevent the NDP – and the FDP – from winning any seats at all. But the SPD were afraid that such a change would provide the CDU/CSU with a permanent majority and in 1968 decided to postpone a decision on the matter until 1970. Attention then switched to the desirability of banning the NDP as unconstitutional.

In the summer of 1967 the Government stirred up a hornet's nest of controversy by trying to solve the problem of an Emergency Law. In the 1952 settlement (see p. 142) the Western Occupying Powers had reserved the right to reassume authority if any emergency threatened to undermine the security of West Germany before the Federal Government had passed legislation enabling it to deal with such a contingency. Although there had ever since been a natural desire to expunge this last vestige of a subordinate status, the Parties had been unable to agree on the kind of legislation which would be appropriate and the circumstances in which it could be applied. A nuclear war or Russian attack might obviously make it impracticable to observe all the due processes of law but memories of how such legislation had been applied in 1930–2 (see p. 50) made many people reluctant to renew it. In the end the Government proposed that the Bundestag should elect an emergency committee of twenty-two members, to whom the Bundesrat would add one representative from each Land. This body would have the right to decide by a two-thirds majority that the Bundestag was incapable of acting, after which it could proclaim an emergency and bring into operation some forty previously prepared (and debated) decrees. The task of enabling a government to act effectively in a crisis without thereby enabling it to act arbitrarily is always delicate and was in this case complicated by the national predilection for precise definitions. The difficulty found in reaching a compromise illustrates the healthy suspicion with which many Germans have come to view their rulers.

The agitation and demonstrations against the Emergency Law were only one aspect of a disenchantment with the established affluence which was boiling up among the young. This was not of course confined to West Germany but special reasons fostered it there. The generation which was coming of age had been born in the chaotic years 1943–9 and had often been neglected in their 'teens by parents whose long hours of work had been so important in achieving the 'Miracle'. As has been said (see p. 152), the Federal Republic was basically fortunate in starting her existence under a government of a decidedly right-wing complexion but Adenauer's over-long tenure of power had meant that many reforms needed to modernize society had gone unmade. Now, instead of a Socialist government turning out the old order and embarking on a thorough programme of reform, the SPD appeared to have come to the rescue of their opponents, to be gratuitously prolonging the CDU/CSU hold on power and as a result to be themselves debarred from making changes. Many of the young, accepting the world's condemnation of the Third Reich, found the record of their parents during it and the toleration of ex-Nazis in high places hard to stomach. They were not prepared to take for granted the revulsion felt by their elders towards Communism or to regard recognition of the status quo in Eastern Europe as unthinkable. The Western Alliance was seen as linking them with a country which in Vietnam was behaving much as the Nazis had done. The less lovely aspects of the Affluent Society were felt to cancel out its advantages.

The focus of discontent was to be found in the institutions of higher education. A higher proportion of each age group than ever before was seeking such education and tradition required that everyone who had a grammar-school leaving certificate (*Abitur*) was entitled to enter whatever university he or she chose. The expansion of the universities was, however, one of the things which had been neglected. To help the professors teach the extra numbers, many junior posts had been created. But decisions about appointments to such posts and about the research to be done in each faculty had been left in the hands of the professors. Junior staff were consequently dissatisfied about their lack of say in their conditions of work, while students complained about overcrowding, lack of guidance from and contact with their teachers and the irrelevance of many courses to contemporary life. Demonstrations and sit-ins were regular events. The chief degree conferred by universities remained the doctorate, though this was mitigated by the large variety of diplomas which were issued, often by official bodies. Reasonable changes had been too long resisted, with the result that the politicians intervened. Laws reforming the system began to be passed in one Land after another, led by those where the SPD was in power. New universities were founded with more liberal constitutions. The most radical novelty was a tripartite scheme by which the teaching staff (including juniors along with professors), the non-teaching staff and the students were given an equal say. This was not unnaturally unpopular with professors (who often migrated to universities where it was not in force) and damaged standards of thoroughness and objectivity.

In 1961 an epoch-making stimulus to the task of rethinking Germany's past had been provided in a book by a Hamburg Professor, Fritz Fischer, *Germany's Aims in the First World War* (*Griff Nach der Weltmacht*). This challenged, in the light of official documents which had only recently become available, the established nineteenth-century doctrine (see p. 27) that Germany's position in the centre of Europe, surrounded by jealous enemies, made it essential for her to have a 'strong' (i.e. authoritarian) government and strong armed forces. Internal policy was dictated by external pressures. Fischer argued that, on the contrary, external policy had been dictated by internal considerations. Germany's behaviour had been motivated by her ambition to become a World Power, something which could be achieved only at the expense of those who already held power. A fundamental reason for this ambition was the fear of the German ruling classes lest they be forced by popular pressure to surrender privileges. This explanation of German aggressiveness had been held for long among Anglo-Saxon historians and it is the view which is on the whole taken in this book. But it created bitter controversy when first presented by a German and supported by German documents. Fischer was even refused permission to lecture in the USA. By now (1992) many other historians, German and non-German, have carried research and evaluation further. Fischer's views cannot be accepted without modification but the crude dogmas which prevailed before 1961 have been permanently discredited. When combined with the indisputable crimes of the Third Reich and the loss of both wars, this has led to a fundamental reappraisal of Germany's place in the world.

When the Shah of Persia visited Berlin in June 1967, a demonstration against him was organized, in the course of which a student called Bruno Ohnesorg was shot. This was one of many occasions when charges of high-handed action were made, as it would seem with some justification, against the police. There was a further crisis in the city at Easter 1968 when a young man who could not abide Communists (but fortunately had no other traceable political connection) tried to assassinate the student leader Rudi Dutschke. Prominent among the targets of the ensuing riots were the papers and premises owned by Herr Axel Springer, who was resented not merely as an outspoken anti-Communist but even more as the owner of 80 per cent of the daily papers with nation-wide circulation (three-quarters of which was provided by the tabloid illustrated *Bild*).

In the end the Emergency Law was got through the Bundestag after a number of safeguards had been added but without drastic modification. Kiesinger lived up to his reputation as an adroit conciliator; he was not unfairly described as a 'Super-Erhard'. There were those in his own Party who criticized him for not pressing their preferred policies more strongly, oblivious of the fact that, had he done so, he would have broken up the Coalition. To begin with, however, relief at not finding themselves ousted from office reconciled the CDU/CSU to the unpleasant necessity of making concessions to the SPD, while later their ability to keep those concessions limited had much the same effect. Whereas hitherto the CDU had almost exalted its lack of a formal programme into an actual programme, it now realized the need to establish a profile distinct from those of the other Parties and in 1967–8 formulated the Aktion (or Berlin) Programme which, on matters of social and economic policy, and even on relations with the East, showed a distinct liberalization of outlook. The Party's aim was said to be the promotion of freedom, justice and peace. The pride of place which had once been assigned to Christianity now went to efficiency.

The Socialist rank-and-file at first found it highly uncongenial to be running in harness with their habitual opponents. At a Party Congress in March 1968 they refused to bless in retrospect the decision to enter the Great Coalition and approved by only 147 votes to 143 the way their leaders had conducted themselves inside it. Particular resentment was aroused by the tendency of the CDU/CSU to annex credit for an economic recovery which owed more to Schiller than to anyone else. Few appreciated how much their Party had gained by taking office (and thereby acquiring experience) for the first time in circumstances which inhibited the backwoodsmen of the right from accusing it of betraying national interests for fear of involving their own leaders in that charge. As time went on, however, confidence in Social Democratic ability to govern grew hand in hand with credit for Social Democratic achievements in governing. The SPD began to think that they would like to go on governing without having to bother about CDU/CSU susceptibilities.

As 1968 passed into 1969, the two major Parties came increasingly to resemble a cat and dog tied together by their tails. The closer that the election came, the greater was the repugnance on both sides against renewing the Coalition. The chances of avoiding such a fate would, however, be reduced if, as seemed well on the cards, the NDP surmounted the 5 per cent hurdle and as a result had twenty-five or more Deputies in the Bundestag. For their presence would reduce the strength of the other parties and make it less likely that any could obtain an outright majority. As the idea of a government dependent on NDP votes was by general consent ruled out, the only alternative to a Great Coalition would be one with the FDP. But the FDP was itself being gradually transformed. It had long been a marriage between liberal (and anti-clerical) idealists and middle-class (and often reactionary) property owners; as has been mentioned (see p. 166), it had depended for part of its funds on contributions from industry. But the younger generations of well-to-do bourgeois were gravitating to the CDU as their natural home. The FDP's role in opposition made it want to find some way of looking different from both the governing Parties. To try to overtake the Great Coalition on the right would have lost it its left-wing members. Consequently the obvious tactic was to overtake on the left, with a programme of individualist radicalism. The move in that direction was personified towards the end of 1967 when Erich Mende was replaced as leader by Walter Scheel, since Scheel, though no revolutionary, was open to new ideas and quick to spot tactical opportunities. His main problem was whether he had enough authority over his rank-and-file to deliver their votes in whatever direction he might promise them.

This question seemed to receive a clear answer in March 1969. About a year earlier, stories began to be put about from East Germany that President Lübke had during the war been involved in building death camps. Though largely malicious lies, they had a small substratum of truth. Lübke mistakenly began by blanket denials only to be forced later into partial admissions. Calls were made for his resignation and in the end he agreed to go before his (second) constitutional term was up; this had the extra advantage of avoiding a close conjunction between a Bundestag election and a Presidential one. The CDU put up Schröder as their candidate, the SPD Gustav Heinemann (see pp. 143, 170) who, as the Great Coalition's Minister of Justice, had carried through a number of liberal alterations to the penal laws; his general attitude can be gathered from his statements that 'Christ died for us – not against Marx' and 'I love my wife – not the state.' The FDP were persuaded to back him, whereas the twenty-two NDP votes in the Electoral College went to Schröder. On the third ballot, where a plain rather than a two-thirds majority was called for, Heinemann was elected. His comment that a clear shift of power had been brought about by democratic methods did nothing to reconcile the CDU/CSU to their defeat. But the SPD saw in the episode ground for reassessing the doubts about the FDP's reliability which had kept them from forming a coalition with the Party in 1966. They showed good-will and gratitude by dropping finally the idea of eliminating proportional representation (see p. 183).

The Great Coalition performed a useful function which had much influence on the subsequent course of politics, but its final months were inglorious. *Geregeltes Nebeneinander* applied just as much, and had as many imperfections, at home as abroad. The Parties constituting it could agree on practically nothing except to extend for a further ten years the period during which Nazi crimes could be punished. The proposal to ban the NDP was dropped, while an international treaty renouncing the acquisition of nuclear weapons had to be left unsigned. As the elections came closer, pressure on the Mark increased while the refusal to revalue meant that imports cost more. Thanks to the moderation shown by the unions in 1967, the workers had fallen behind in the race for purchasing power and their resentment over the rising cost of living led to a sudden wave of spontaneous strikes. Everything suggested that Schiller had been right in urging revaluation as compared with Strauss who had opposed it. This impression became even stronger immediately before polling day when foreign demand for Marks led to the exchanges being shut until the voting was over.

13

THE BRANDT GOVERNMENT:
1969–1974

THE TRANSFER OF POWER

In the election held on 28 September 1969, the SPD won 224 seats, the CDU 192, the CSU 50 and the FDP 30. To the general relief, the NDP obtained only 4.5 per cent of the votes overall, so that they remained unrepresented in the Bundestag; the support which they received in the southern Länder failed to outweigh their weakness in the north and above all in North Rhine-Westphalia.

Although the FDP had won its presence in the Bundestag only by the narrow margin of 0.8 per cent, it was the party in a position to decide the character of the new government. The indications which Scheel had already given as to what this decision would be enabled Brandt to tell President Heinemann forthwith that he was prepared to accept office. The CDU/CSU (who are in the happy position of being able to represent themselves as one party or two according to the convenience of the moment) made a show of protesting that the President's first approach should be to them, as the strongest party. But, in spite of the strenuous efforts which they made in all sorts of ways to lure over the FDP's right wing, their prospects of securing a majority were never firm enough to justify a formal claim to power. After more than three weeks of negotiation (a lapse of time more usual on the Continent than in Britain) Brandt obtained 251 out of 496 votes, with three FDP Deputies abstaining. Scheel became Foreign Minister and Genscher Minister of the Interior while the post of Minister of Agriculture went, with lasting results for the EEC's Common Agricultural Policy, to the right-wing leader of the Bavarian FDP, Josef Ertl; Schiller, who had done as much as anyone to win the victory, remained Minister of Economics. Helmut Schmidt became Minister of Defence while his previous post as leader of the SPD Parliamentary Party (*Fraktion*) was taken over by Herbert Wehner, whose strategy for obtaining power through a Great Coalition had been triumphantly vindicated (though only because the FDP had changed sides). The extent to which the German civil service takes part in politics was illustrated by the fact that 13 out of 26 permanent State

Secretaries were changed, though only 11 out of 110 officials at the next level down (*Ministerialdirektor*).

The election thus marked the close of a chapter in German politics. The Federal Republic obtained – for the first and presumably the only time in its history – a President and a Chancellor simultaneously who had both been actively associated with the Widerstand to the Nazis (see p. 57); Brandt is said to have remarked as the results came in that 'tonight, finally and for ever, Hitler lost the war'. Such a remark may sound unfair to the Adenauer and Erhard regimes, but both had been more prepared to be reconciled with ex-Nazis than with the full consequences of defeat. The vital question for the future had hitherto been whether a majority could be found for a left-of-centre regime or whether (as in Italy) the right was to be a permanent element in government. For the next three years Brandt's position was to be precarious but in fact he had on his side the factor which came to be known as 'Comrade Trend'. In each of the elections of 1965, 1969 and 1972 the SPD share of the vote grew by 3.1 per cent.

To counter the impression that external affairs would get prior attention, Brandt described himself as 'a Chancellor of inner reforms', but in practice he was able to achieve disappointingly few of them. Some were blocked by the FDP, the most notable being the extension of parity in workers' co-determination from coal and steel (see p. 150) to the whole of industry, though the Plant Constitution Law (*Betriebsverfassungsgesetz*) of 1972 considerably extended the range of matters over which management were required to consult Works Councils. Other reforms, particularly in the field of taxation, required the co-operation of Land Governments whose inherent suspicion of the centre was reinforced in half of them by CDU/CSU participation in their Ministries. A number of schemes to benefit the weak and poor had to be shelved for lack of cash. A final group of social reforms (e.g. divorce and abortion) might be cheap but were disproportionately controversial and needed Bundesrat approval which was often not forthcoming.

Two days after the election, the Kiesinger Government, as still legally in charge, announced that the Mark would be left to float. After it had done so for twenty-six days the Brandt Government fixed its value again 8.5 per cent higher. This was a logical consequence of fidelity to a free market system by a country distinguished from its neighbours through an exceptionally low rate of inflation and an abnormal bias towards exports, particularly of capital goods. The home public's readiness to co-operate in keeping prices down increased the competitiveness of West German goods abroad and swelled the export surplus. Unless the Mark's value was continually adjusted upwards in compensation, foreign demand for Marks increased the money supply and thereby threatened to cancel out the achievements of domestic restraint. West Germany had become so dependent on exports that she could not afford to isolate herself from the outside world, even if her rulers had not been dominated by a belief that this was a wrong thing to do. But as long as that world was living beyond its means, the Federal Republic's attempts to do otherwise meant a continual struggle against the stream.

Schiller had hoped to balance the revaluation by relaxing credit so as to increase home demand at the same time as the rise in their prices was discouraging sales of West German goods abroad. This strategy assumed that goods made for export could be equally well disposed of domestically; in reality any extra home demand would more probably have been in other directions (e.g. consumer goods and services), so that, for the policy to succeed, a long-term shift in resources would have been needed. Moreover the revaluation came too late (or alternatively was not big enough) to shield the home economy from the inflation going on outside. Between the autumn of 1969 and the spring of 1971 prices rose at an annual rate of 4.5 per cent. This imported inflation was reinforced by a 'home-made' variety when the unions, feeling that their moderation had been exploited, insisted for the first time on wage rises which outstripped gains in productivity. The Bundesbank and the public, to whom any inflation rate over 3 per cent was high, demanded controls halting expansion at home while the continued ability of exporters to make profits abroad removed the incentive to shift their sales efforts. Yet if in the struggle against inflation interest rates were pushed too high, employment might suffer and unwelcome foreign money be drawn in. The federal policy-makers had to pick a precarious path between risking inflation and risking unemployment.

THE OSTPOLITIK SCRAPES THROUGH

Even if there had been more room for manoeuvre at home, the lion's share of attention during these years would have gone to the main unsolved problem in the Federal Republic's affairs, namely relations with the Communist world. Not that relations with the West were neglected. Brandt repeatedly emphasized that conciliation with the East was possible only for a Republic securely integrated with the West. At a Prime Ministers' meeting at The Hague in December 1969 he played a leading part in opening the way for Britain to join the Common Market. In his initial declaration of policy, he expressed the wish to prevent a further 'growing apart' between the two German Republics so that 'regulated neighbourliness' could operate. His aim was to advance from conflict through co-existence to co-operation (*vom Gegeneinander über ein Nebeneinander zum Miteinander*). He made no mention of reunification or sole representation or the Hallstein Doctrine, and described the DDR as a state, though adding that, if there were two German states, their relationship must be of a special kind, as was the case between members of the British Commonwealth. Before 1969 ended Moscow had accepted his offer to negotiate an undertaking that neither the

Federal Republic nor the Soviet Union would attack one another, while Warsaw had agreed to talks on Polish–West German relations. Both sets of negotiations started early in 1970. They proved detailed and laborious but not wholly unpromising.

The man in the brake-van, however, was Ulbricht, who clearly found the whole business unpalatable. This last-surviving Stalinist had long been holding together the inhabitants of his Republic by presenting them with a picture of an unregenerate, revengeful and dangerous next-door neighbour – what the Germans call a 'Boo-man'. Brandt seemed set on depriving this presentation of its credibility. Shortly before Christmas, an East German draft for a Treaty was sent to Bonn. It began by insisting on the DDR being recognized as a foreign state in international law – the one thing which Brandt had declared to be impossible. It went on to demand that West Germany should repeal all laws contrary to the proposed Treaty – a stipulation which could be read as requiring the Federal Republic to leave NATO and the EEC. The terms were such as to be politically impossible for Brandt to accept and seemed deliberately intended to provoke a refusal. Realizing that such a reaction would be exploited to put the blame on him, Brandt carefully refrained from making it but instead reiterated his desire to negotiate.

At this point the advantage of dealing with the Soviet Union, Poland and East Germany simultaneously was demonstrated. The talks in Moscow and Warsaw went forward too well for Ulbricht to be able to rely on them breaking down, but if they were going to succeed, he could not afford to be the only man left out. Accordingly Brandt was invited to visit East Germany and on 19 March met Stoph, the DDR Prime Minister, at Erfurt. The most remarkable feature of the visit was a silent but unmistakable demonstration of welcome by the population. Whereas the Eastern Willi repeated the demand for full recognition, the Western Willy emphasized the need to mitigate the human hardships caused by partition. But the only thing on which they could agree was to meet again at Kassel on 21 May and, when they did, to the accompaniment of noisy demonstrations from both neo-Nazis and Communists, they found the going even tougher than ever. Both sides decided that a pause for thought was advisable.

In the Kremlin, however, desire for better relations with the West, presumably fed by worry over economics as well as over China, was gaining the upper hand. The Politburo realized that no subsequent Bonn government was likely to be more conciliatory than the existing one while a rebuff to it would increase the chances of a successor being more hostile. The idea was floated of the general Security Conference which in due course was to meet in Helsinki. But the Western governments stood firmly together in saying that a German settlement must come first. With great dexterity a formula was evolved to which both Bonn and Moscow could agree without eating too many of their previous words and in August 1970 a Treaty of Non-Aggression was signed.

Both sides promised to 'promote the normalization of the situation in Europe, taking as their starting point the actual situation existing in the area'. They agreed to 'acknowledge that peace can only be maintained if nobody infringes the present borders' and to 'respect without reservation the territorial integrity of all states in Europe' in their borders of today. In addition to declaring that they had no territorial claims against anyone and would not raise any in future, they described the borders of all states in Europe, including the Oder–Neisse line and the BRD–DDR frontier, as 'inviolable'. In addition, however, the Russians agreed to accept a letter saying that, in the West German Government's opinion, the Treaty did not conflict with the political goal of a state of peace in Europe in which the German people regained its unity in free self-determination. In other words, the Treaty did not close the door to reunification by agreement (however distant such a prospect might be) but only to the possibility of one side imposing it on the other (something which the experience of the previous twenty years had shown to be impracticable). The Federal Republic was also authorized to tell the United States, Britain and France that in the opinion of both signatories the Treaty did not affect the rights and responsibilities in Germany (and particularly in Berlin) of the four Occupying Powers. Finally the Russians were given unmistakably to understand that the Treaty's ratification would depend on a Four-Power Agreement being reached about Berlin. An unmentioned attraction of the Treaty for the Russians was undoubtedly the prospect of easier access to German credits, industrial skills and equipment; the preparatory negotiations had been given a 'sweetener' in the shape of a contract for oil pipes on favourable terms.

Next came Poland. Here agreement was complicated by the West German insistence that Polish citizens of German extraction must be allowed to leave for the West if they wished to go. The Poles did not reject the demand but held back from making any promises until the actual Treaty had been concluded. The vital clause in this contained Bonn's admission that the Oder–Neisse line constituted Poland's western frontier and was 'inviolable'. The text, however, was so drafted as to avoid use of the word 'recognition'. The Anglo-Americans were left free to maintain their Potsdam provision that a final settlement of the frontier must await a peace conference, but the sting of this had been drawn by clear indications from them that they did not intend at such a conference to press for any revision. The Poles then issued a statement that 'people of indisputably German nationality' who wished to emigrate to either German Republic could do so if they respected Polish rules and regulations. In December 1970 Brandt went to Warsaw for the signing of the Treaty and, during a visit to the site of the Jewish ghetto (see p. 79), dropped on his knees in front of a memorial to the victims. This courageous gesture received more widespread acclaim outside the Federal Republic than inside.

As regards Berlin, the Bonn Government insisted that prime responsibility rested not with itself but with the Four Powers. Their ambassadors had indeed met to discuss the problem on various occasions since March 1970 but without making much progress. Even when the signature of the Moscow and Warsaw Treaties put a premium on agreement, it failed to emerge. The whereabouts of the impediment became clear when at the end of April 1971 Ulbricht, then aged 77, was 'promoted' from being First Secretary of the Party to a post which looked purely honorific. It was not only in West Germany that there had to be a change of leadership before an agreement could be reached. Ulbricht's successor Erich Honecker was to prove almost as obdurate. (More recent evidence claims to show that the Russians installed Honecker because they could not trust Ulbricht to stand firm.)

Two months later the ambassadors announced what was in effect a compromise. The three Western ones had stood out for what became known as the three Zs: *Zugang*, unimpeded movement between West Berlin and West Germany for West Berliners and West Germans as well as for Americans, British and French; *Zutritt*, the extension to West Berliners of the facilities allowing West Germans to visit East Germany; and *Zuordnung*, recognition by the East of the fact that West Berlin was tied to West Germany (as against the East German thesis that it was merely a special enclave in the territory of the DDR). All three demands were recognized in the agreement. The three Western Governments declared, however, that 'the ties between the western Sectors of Berlin and the Federal Republic of Germany would be maintained and developed, taking into account that these Sectors continue not to be a constituent part of the Federal Republic and are not to be governed by it'. The last twenty-four words corresponded with the position which the Allies had steadily maintained over West Berlin but contradicted the West German position as stated in the Preamble to and Article 23 of the Basic Law and the West Berlin Constitution. The Federal Convention to elect the President was not henceforward to meet in West Berlin, while the Bundestag and Bundesrat and their committees could do so only to discuss matters directly affecting West Berlin. On the other hand representatives of West Berlin might continue to sit (but not vote) in both bodies and West German laws could still apply in the city, provided they had been adopted (at least tacitly) by the Senate of West Berlin. The Federal Republic was authorized to act for West Berlin in dealings with foreign countries. Federal institutions such as the Cartel Office already established in the city might stay there (at considerable inconvenience). Finally the Russians were allowed to open a consulate in West Berlin to deal with the commanders of the Western forces, which implied that they no longer had any responsibility themselves for governing the area, whereas their retention of such a responsibility in East Berlin was their justification in international law for being in the city at all. The Four-Power agreement was supplemented four months later by three separate inter-German ones. Between them the documents amounted to little more than a confirmation of the status quo but gave to that status a precision which it had hitherto lacked (but which was to prove, perhaps inevitably, rather short of absolute).

To work out such a package deal was a considerable achievement. Although Brandt left the detailed work to others, notably Egon Bahr, it was his determination to reach a settlement which led to compromise formulas being found. But the package could still be frustrated if the Bundestag were to refuse ratification. The CDU/CSU were of course hostile. They complained that the vital cards which West Germany held for bargaining, consisting essentially of refusal to recognize the 1945 settlement, had been played without anything being obtained in return other than imprecise assurances of good intent. The SPD answer was that after twenty-five years the settlement was so well established as to deprive the refusal to recognize it of almost all political value, while the only way to improve relations and get concessions was to behave reasonably and hope thereby to encourage reasonable reactions. A great deal thus hung upon the FDP. Although their leader Scheel had played a large part in negotiating the agreements, the Party had showed up badly in Land elections early in 1970, which its right wing attributed to its association with Socialist policies. In October Mende and two other Deputies went over openly to the CDU (which promised to put them on its list at the next election). With the Government's majority thus reduced to six, the doubts expressed by three more FDP Deputies became a crucial matter. A further complication was that in the Bundesrat the CDU/CSU had a majority of twenty-one to twenty (largely because the number of votes possessed by a Land did not correspond exactly to its population (see p. 128) and had all to be cast in the same direction). To overcome an adverse vote in the Bundesrat, the Government required an absolute majority of all members of the Bundestag (and not simply a majority of those voting).

Parliamentary discussion of the agreements began late in 1971 and the crucial vote was due in the following April. Kiesinger's skill in achieving compromises had become less of an asset when the CDU shifted into opposition and he had been succeeded as leader by Rainer Barzel, a nimble tactician and articulate critic rather than a forceful commander. In April Barzel seems to have thought that some FDP Deputies could be prevailed on to defect and therefore tabled for the first time in the history of the Republic a 'constructive vote of no confidence' (see p. 129). While demonstrations in favour of the agreements filled the streets, most of the SPD Deputies, in obedience to orders, abstained from voting. On 27 April the motion obtained 247 votes against 10, two short of the majority of 249 which it needed. Three Deputies abstained and two FDP ones voted for the motion, so that at least one CDU or CSU Deputy must have voted against it. Just over a year later, a newspaper named as the culprit a none-too-reputable CSU Deputy. Further 'investigative journalism' strongly suggested that he had received some £25,000 as an inducement from an SPD Whip, Karl Wienand. The latter denied the story and was shielded by Wehner, so that a Bundestag inquiry failed to reach any conclusion. But in another more or less contemporary scandal Wienand was shown not to be a witness of truth and a few years later had to quit the Bundestag under a cloud. The episode left an unpleasant taste but there were equally strong stories, to which Willy Brandt gave support in the autumn of 1972, that bribery had been used by the Opposition to induce the FDP desertions.

Barzel's fiasco did not improve the Opposition's prospect of defeating the Treaties. Moreover he and some of the more realistic CDU members were belatedly beginning to examine their strategy. The Russians were making clear that no regime responsible for frustrating the settlement could expect any co-operation from them thereafter. West Germany's NATO allies left no doubt of their desire for ratification. Opinion polls suggested that a majority of West German voters were ready to accept it. The alternative to ratification would not be a return to the 1970 position but to something more strained in which the chances of getting alleviations for the inhabitants of the DDR would be minimal. Barzel accordingly negotiated with Brandt and Scheel a declaration 'interpreting' the Treaties in a way which left a door open for the German nation as a whole to be free at some date in the future to determine its form of government and for the existing frontiers to be capable of adjustment at a Peace Conference. The Russians raised no objection to the declaration, though pointing out that what counted in international law was the text of Treaties and not that of unilateral statements!

Barzel had originally intended that his followers should, on the strength of the declaration, vote for the Treaties. But some of them, and still more of the CSU, objected so strongly that he had to be content with their abstention and on 17 May the Treaty with the USSR was accepted on this basis by 248 votes to 10 and that with Poland by 248 votes to 17. The Bundesrat decided to abandon opposition and the Brandt Ostpolitik could thus take effect. Barzel had hardly cut an impressive figure but the real blame for defeat must rest with the backwoodsmen of his Party and still more with Strauss and the CSU. They had refused to face up to the consequences of a lost war and had shut their minds to the way politics were developing outside the Federal Republic. Too much emotion had been attached to the so-called 'Right to the Homeland' and to the idea that members of an individual nation have an exclusive right to settle its frontiers, with the result that the practicability of exercising such rights was disregarded. But some blame attaches to the Americans and British who, in their anxiety to secure West German support in the Cold War, had encouraged such intransigence and given a false impression of the extent to which they would support it.

Although the Treaties had been passed, the Bundestag remained in deadlock. A vote on one part of the Budget resulted in a tie, suggesting that the Government could no longer get its proposals passed into law. The natural way out was a dissolution followed by an election. But Article 68 of the Grundgesetz provided that a Chancellor could ask for a dissolution only if defeated on a vote of confidence and then only provided that the Bundestag did not with a majority of its members vote confidence in an alternative Chancellor. But if the Opposition were strong enough to defeat a motion of confidence, what would there be to stop them from using their strength to vote Barzel into power? The position was further complicated by the establishment a few years previously – after a Deputy's widow was found to be practically penniless – of a generous pension scheme which rose sharply with each year of service. This made the members of the Bundestag, irrespective of party, reluctant to bring about an election before the maximum term of four years had run out. Barzel at first refused to make any promises as to what he would do if Brandt, in order to secure a dissolution, engineered his own Party's defeat. But the Opposition would then have come into office, if at all, with as tenuous a majority as was already making the task of government difficult and the disadvantages of taking power in such circumstances were so clear as to induce Brandt to run the risk. By the time the Bundestag went on its summer holidays, an election in the autumn was taken for granted.

Before it occurred, however, a distraction was created by Karl Schiller. The Economics Minister had as time went by become increasingly high-handed and made himself unloved by many, including most of his colleagues and the French Government. In the summer of 1971 the Finance Minister, frustrated by his inability to secure desirable but drastic reforms in the taxation system, was provoked by a dispute with Schiller into resigning. Brandt, to ensure a unified economic policy, invited Schiller to take over the Finance Ministry while keeping his own, thus making him to all appearances the second most powerful man in the Cabinet. In 1972 a fresh wave of prosperity renewed the need to choose between risking more inflation and risking more unemployment. Schiller staked his position on the former and the general view was that the Government would not be able to afford his resignation. But the Governor of the Bundesbank, whom Schiller himself had appointed, persuaded the other Ministers to restrict instead the freedom of foreigners to increase inflation by buying German securities. Brandt put up no fight for his 'Super-Minister' and Schiller resigned, being replaced in his double function by Helmut Schmidt, whose record at the Ministry of Defence had greatly enhanced his reputation. The expected crisis of economic confidence did not occur.

In the meantime negotiations had been proceeding in Berlin between the two German Republics and on 8 November a Basic Treaty between them was initialled. It was described as taking for its point of departure 'historical facts' without prejudice to the differing views of the signatories on fundamental questions including the national one. The two Governments declared that they would develop good relationships with one another on the basis of equal rights, that they would solve their disagreements only by peaceful means, that present frontiers were 'inviolable both now and in the future' and that neither would interfere in the affairs of the other. They affirmed their intention to abide by the principles of the UN Charter, in particular the sovereign equality of all states, respect for independence, autonomy and territorial integrity, the right of self-determination, the protection of human rights and non-discrimination. They would proceed on the assumption that neither of the two states could represent the other internationally or act in its name. They undertook to conclude further detailed agreements on such matters as science, traffic, postal communications, health, sports and environmental protection. The exchange of 'permanent representatives' (rather than ambassadors) was also provided for in one of seventeen appendices. Both sides agreed to apply for membership of the United Nations (hitherto blocked by the vetoes of one or other of the Great Powers).

The basis on which settlements had been reached with Russia and Poland was thus extended to inter-German relations. The Federal Republic, except that it did not explicitly 'recognize' the other state, abandoned almost completely the positions which it had been maintaining since the creation of that state. The Democratic Republic on the other hand gave up its insistence on being explicitly recognized as a foreign state in international law (though continuing to maintain that it was one). West German voters were thus enabled to go to the polls with their eyes open to the full range of concessions which they were being asked to approve.

For at the end of September Brandt tabled a motion of confidence and, when the time came to vote on it, refrained in common with the other Ministers from supporting his own Government. The Opposition mustered their full strength with the result that the motion was rejected by 248 votes to 233. This extraordinary manoeuvre, rendered necessary by the fact that the Basic Law had been designed for a Republic with many rather than with few parties, opened the way for the President to dissolve the Bundestag. In a 91 per cent poll on 19 November 1972, the CDU, even taken in combination with the CSU, found itself replaced as strongest party by the SPD, winning only 225 seats as against 229. The FDP rose from 30 seats to 42; the NDP obtained only 0.6 per cent of the poll. Brandt may have been described by his critics as the 'Chancellor of renunciation' but his policy of facing unpalatable realities had been endorsed by the West German people. Moreover German employers could no longer count on their friends in the Bundestag being strong enough to prevent co-determination being applied throughout industry. Both at home and abroad turning-points had been reached.

NO LONGER THE MAN FOR THE SEASON

As so often, however, triumph soon turned sour and the next eighteen months were a time of anti-climax in which little went right for Brandt. His Party's unity was threatened, reform at home remained elusive and the results of the Ostpolitik fell short of expectations.

After the unrest of 1968, the more moderate of the young intellectuals decided that they were unlikely to succeed in transforming society by revolution and must therefore set out on 'the long march through the institutions' so as to win a position where they could effect reforms peacefully. The old-established members of the Party were lethargic by comparison and baffled by the sociological jargon in which they now found political arguments being clothed. The young socialists (*Jusos*) thus gained a prominence disproportionate to their numbers and dominated the organization to which every SPD member under thirty-five automatically belonged. Their support for the Ostpolitik had been welcome; their increasing concentration on internal problems proved less so. They were not content with modifying the existing order of society but wanted to sweep it – and private enterprise – away. Yet, although they admitted to being Socialists rather than Social Democrats, bureaucracy and centralization figured high among their bug-bears. Their ideal was a society which in all its manifestations, political, economic, and social, was controlled by the rank-and-file. Whether, if choice were inevitable, liberty or equality should come first was not a question to which they much addressed themselves.

The SPD, however, would never have achieved their victories of 1969 and 1972 if they had not jettisoned their tradition as a Marxist party devoted to the interests of the working classes and, by becoming instead a popular party (*Volkspartei*) of pragmatic reform, won over a substantial proportion of the 'middle ground' (which was of course coming to include more and more affluent workers – the 'new bourgeoisie'). The Jusos, along with various groups among the over-thirty-fives, were challenging this transformation and thereby creating an obvious danger of alienating the essential middle vote. There was the further danger of estranging the FDP, who believed with much justification that the extra votes won by them in 1972 had come from people who wanted a government which was neither reactionary nor radical and looked to them to hold the SPD left wing in check. As one of them put it, 'the economic system may not be a sacred cow but neither is it a lamb waiting for slaughter'. In the past German parties, and particularly those in the middle, had resolved their internal quarrels by splitting in two. The damage which this had done to good government, however, had brought the 5 per cent rule into existence to discourage it. But if parties are not to split, then they must act as umbrellas sheltering a variety of views within their ranks. But this is a situation unpalatable to enthusiasts who are reluctant to make the compromises needed to sustain it.

To the Jusos the SPD was the dominant partner in the Coalition and as such entitled to decide its policies. They discounted the danger of the FDP changing partners again on the ground that another turnabout would do the Party such discredit as to bring it below the 5 per cent line. They argued further that for a progressive party to stop introducing changes meant stagnation, which would soon lead to votes being lost to parties more on the left. Brandt saw the force of this argument. He had done his best to reduce the gulf of distrust between the generations which had appeared so alarmingly during the Great Coalition and he did not wish such success as he had achieved to be dissipated. He described the Jusos as 'the salt in our soup' and, though adding 'we must see that they don't make it too salty', exerted himself, as did Wehner, to keep the enthusiasm of the left wing harnessed to the Party's cause. As a result he was accused by the right wing, and still more by the Opposition, of weakness in the face of crypto-Communism.

The atmosphere in the CDU/CSU was hardly more harmonious. There too a familiar struggle was in progress between those who argued that the Election had been lost by too much moderation and those who argued that the mistake had lain in not being moderate enough. Strauss had reacted to the defeat by calling for 'the helmet to be bound on more firmly'. He believed that the way to attract votes was to be more aggressive, pointing out that in Bavaria and Hesse where this had been done, the Party had fared best. He denied that the Government had settled the German problem – and events soon began to suggest that he was right. He argued that a lasting solution could be found only within a European context, by bringing about a Federation embracing the whole of Europe – an echo of de Gaulle's 'from the Atlantic to the Urals' which seemed to imply that the Curtain could be rolled back. How far he was in earnest is hard to say. He has been described as one of those tragic figures who cannot find the place in history to which their abilities entitle them. He seemed unable to reconcile himself to the fact that the causes in which he invested his emotions were not those which a majority of his fellow-countrymen were prepared to back. With such a handicap, his energy and eloquence made him a disturbing influence in any organization to which he belonged. The position was complicated by the unusual relationship between the CDU and CSU. Although the latter claimed to be a separate party with views of its own, its activities were confined to Bavaria, so that it could not hope to obtain more than about one-third of the number of seats obtained by the CDU; in consequence the common assumption for long was that it could not provide the right-wing candidate for the Chancellorship. (Both Bavarians in general and Strauss in particular were in addition viewed with suspicion in other parts of Germany, somewhat as Welshmen are in Britain.) Although Strauss accepted this bar, it did not prevent him from constantly belittling the man who was chosen instead and from trying to dictate to the CDU on matters of policy.

In May 1972 Strauss had embarrassed Barzel by rejecting the compromise over the Treaties which he had helped to work out and insisting that the joint Parties abstain in the vote. When in the spring of 1973 the Basic Treaty came before the Bundestag, Barzel found his advice as to its treatment rejected by his own Party who preferred to follow Strauss up what proved to be a blind alley. Coming on top of the lost election, this was a bad enough rebuff to provide in itself adequate reason for his resignation from the post of Party Chairman although eleven years later it was to emerge that other inducements had played a part as well (see p. 224).

Barzel's successor was Helmut Kohl, a man of 43 who had made a considerable name for himself as Minister-President of Rhineland-Palatinate. Kohl is a big block of a man – some would say a blockhead. (The everyday meaning of the word 'Kohl' is 'cabbage'.) Most attacks on him are brushed aside without leaving any apparent effect. He is a better administrator than speaker. He likes to be known as Adenauer's grandson but he lacks Adenauer's subtlety in dealing with individuals. He prefers settling questions by man-to-man talks rather than in meetings. His favourite method of dealing with problems is to play for time in the hope that they will go away. But some of those who have counted on his immobility have been caught out by the speed, shrewdness and lack of consultation with which he can act when he sees the need.

A fresh bout of inflation developed in 1973 but unlike earlier ones this was largely home produced. For in the spring the Mark had been set free to float, in common with other Common Market currencies and following the breaking of the link between the dollar and gold in 1972. The Bundesbank reacted by pushing up interest rates and thereby checking the incentive to invest at home. But this effect was counterbalanced by a flow of funds into the country and by union demands for wage increases exceeding the natural rate of growth. The Union of Public Servants secured by the threat of a strike a rise which for the first time in West German history went into double figures. There was much talk about Germany catching the English disease and the widespread belief that the Government had given way too easily strengthened the impression that Brandt was too kind.

The principal internal reforms which the Government succeeded in carrying through in its first year of existence were those establishing the breakdown of a marriage as the sole ground for divorce and exempting pornography from prosecution unless it caused social offence. Although both changes scandalized the old-fashioned, they had been virtually agreed by all the Parties before the election. In January 1974 the FDP finally gave way to SPD insistence that workers' co-determination (*Mitbestimmung*) must be extended to all firms employing more than 2,000 persons (see pp. 150, 189). After 1976 Supervising Councils in such firms were to consist of shareholders and workers' representatives in equal numbers, but the SPD and trade unions agreed reluctantly to a requirement that one of the seats on the workers' side should go to a representative of the senior executives. Controversy continued, however, as to how the workers' representatives should be chosen and how deadlocks between the two sides were to be resolved. The employers (led by their chairman Hans-Martin Schleyer) challenged the legality of the law. In due course the Constitutional Court pronounced against them but in the meantime the unions, out of resentment against the refusal to accept a parliamentary decision, withdrew from the *Konzentrierte Aktion* (see p. 178). The FDP also accepted a scheme by which firms were to pay part of their profits into a central fund which would then pay out to some 24 million workers 200 Marks annually in the shape of certificates to serve as capital. Agreement could not be reached, however, on a proposal to tax increases in land values and subject property owners to closer social control.

To the left-wing SPD and Jusos, these reforms were temporary palliatives rather than final solutions. To give workers a say and share in their firms was not considered enough. What it was held that they should have was sole control and exclusive ownership. Indeed the limited reforms were regarded as questionable in case they damped down the demand for further-reaching ones. To get a majority for such sweeping changes was of course out of the question but the awareness of this only made the radicals more impatient with the FDP – and indeed with the Government as a whole. A further cause of strife was the 'Radical Decree' (*Radikaler Beschluss*). The complex story of this matter merits explanation, not least because of the light which it throws on the Federal Republic generally (G. Braunthal, *Political Loyalty and Public Service in West Germany*).

Article 21 of the Grundgesetz branded as unconstitutional any parties which by their aims or by the behaviour of their members set out to influence or set aside the free democratic order. In a consequential spirit, the law regulating the public service (in Länder and communes as well as at federal level) confined appointments to persons who demonstrated that they could be relied on at all times actively to support the free democratic system established by the Basic Law. This concept was inherited from a law passed in the Weimar Republic after the murder of Erzberger and Rathenau (see p. 43). The requirement came into prominence during the spring of 1972 when, as part of the dispute over the Eastern policy, the Opposition were making much of the left-wing sympathies of the SPD and the danger of Communists being among those who were starting on 'the long march through the institutions'. (The Communist Party, having been prohibited under the Basic Law in 1952 (see p. 153), had been allowed to re-establish itself in a slightly different form in 1968.) The Constitutional Court had laid down that nobody should be disqualified simply for belonging to a party which had not itself been proscribed; activity rather than membership was to be the criterion. At a meeting between Brandt and the Ministers President of the Land Governments in January 1972, it was decided that, in order to establish uniformity of practice throughout the country, every applicant for appointment as an established official (*Beamte*) must be examined as an individual case, that membership of an organization hostile to the Constitution raised doubts as to the loyalty of the individual concerned and that such doubts as a rule justified rejection. By making 'hostility to the Constitution' rather than 'incompatibility with the Constitution' into the test, this decision outflanked the more liberal ruling of the Court. It also raised the question of who was to decide, and on what grounds, which organizations were to be classed as 'hostile'. Those Land Governments which were led by the CDU or CSU tended to be more strict than those where the SPD predominated. But all were able to answer the charge of allowing Communists to infiltrate the government machine without having to take the step, judged politically inopportune, of again proscribing the Communist Party and driving it underground.

To appreciate the repercussions of this decision, however, one has to remember that in Germany not only are the senior staff of government departments graded as Beamte but so also are the teachers, judges, engine-drivers, postal workers and grave-diggers. Many legal and medical posts require a period of preliminary training under government control. To exclude people on the ground of political opinion was therefore often equivalent to forbidding them to follow the profession of their choice; Article 12 of the Basic Law, which ostensibly guarantees freedom to choose, was regarded as less important than Article 21. Between January 1973 and June 1975 some 455,000 applications were examined; in 5,700 grounds for doubt were established and 235 rejections occurred. In 1979 the Federal Government issued 'guidelines' which eliminated automatic screening and the process might have been abandoned completely soon afterwards (as it was in the Saar under Lafontaine in 1985) but for the change of government in 1982. The FDP were, however, able to prevent the CDU from giving public order as much priority over civil liberties as the latter would have liked. To outsiders the solution might seem to lie in only requiring evidence of loyalty for specially sensitive posts. But any reform which in any way reduced the status of a Beamte would be unlikely to find favour in a Bundestag where 37 per cent of the Deputies possess that status! The Constitutional Court has in fact already ruled that such a solution would be illegal.

In May 1973 the Constitutional Court gave a fresh turn to the controversy about university government. A case was brought before it on behalf of 400 professors in Lower Saxony arguing that the establishment of threefold parity on university senates (see p. 189) was incompatible with the freedom of learning guaranteed by Article 5 of the Grundgesetz. The Court's judgement was long and, as often, couched in theoretical terms from which practical conclusions had to be deduced. It began by saying that the participation of all teaching staff (and not exclusively professors) in matters of self-government did not infringe the freedom of learning. It laid down that the state, in deciding how universities were to govern themselves, must respect the special position of 'those who are qualified and appointed to represent their field of knowledge in research and teaching'. It left open the question of whether students and non-teaching staff had a right to a voice, though conceding that such a voice was not ruled out by the Grundgesetz, but it ended by requiring that the teaching staff should have 'an authoritative voice'. This was interpreted to mean that, provided the professors were agreed among themselves (which, owing to radical influence on appointments during the immediately preceding years, they often were not) they would not be outvoted. In matters of research and appointments (two particularly tender spots), their voice was to be decisive. Junior teaching staff were thus assured of a say in university affairs but threefold parity was declared unconstitutional. The judgement chimed in with a widespread feeling that the democratization of universities had been carried to lengths at which the quality of their work was being damaged. But by handing back a limited power of veto to the people who had done most to hold up the adaptation of the universities to the twentieth century, it represented a set-back for reform.

The decade 1970–80 did, however, see progress. In 1973 the Federal and Länder Governments agreed on an educational plan (*Bildungsgesamtplan*) which allowed comprehensive schools to be started, especially where they supplemented rather than superseded the traditional tripartite system. The year 1976 saw agreement, after five years of discussions, on a Federal Framework Act for Higher Education (*Hochschulrahmengesetz*), intended to reform higher education by combining the functions of research, teaching and studies, hitherto performed by different types of institutions (universities, polytechnics and teachers' training colleges). The extent to which advantage has been taken of these provisions has varied from Land to Land, those with SPD Governments having not surprisingly gone further and faster than the CDU/CSU ones. The lack of uniformity which resulted is a tiresome complication rather than an impassable barrier and would have been greater still if there had been no agreed framework. An amending law passed in 1985 was seen by some as eliminating those parts of the 1976 Act which had worked badly and by others as a reactionary measure cancelling out some of the progress which had been achieved. There can, however, be no question but that a good deal has been done to remedy the causes of critical unrest in the 1960s.

In May 1973 Brezhnev paid the first visit that a Russian head of government had made to a non-Communist German state for sixty years. It was said, with an excess of optimism, to mark the end of both the Second World War and the Cold War. In talking to industrial leaders, the First Secretary held out rosy prospects of long-term Russo–German co-operation in exploiting Soviet raw material resources. He pictured the two countries as advancing from coexistence to interdependence, a process which would necessarily bring with it both external and internal relaxation. The underlying motive was not hard to guess. The Soviet Union needed the technical help of the West if she was to retain her military position as a Great Power and at the same time meet the desires of her peoples for better living. Nor was West German industry blind to the possibility of what had always been for it a useful market, and one which would gain in importance if a recession set in elsewhere. But at the moment Russian desires were something of an embarrassment to a country whose industry was at full stretch and whose economic problems were bound up with an excessive propensity to export. East–West trade showed a clear surplus in favour of the Federal Republic to which the Soviet Union and the Eastern bloc generally were heavily in debt. On the other hand the best prospect of getting paid lay in developing the Eastern output of raw materials and energy, which could be achieved only by further credits. The outlook was neither hopeless nor straightforward but the moment of sobriety reduced the Kremlin's willingness to twist the arms of the satellites when difficulties arose in their relations with West Germany.

With Poland these difficulties, though including similar stickiness over credits, concentrated on the question of refugees. Following the promises which the Polish Government had made at the time of, though not as an integral part of, the 1970 Treaty (see p. 192), 25,000 people of German origin had been allowed to leave the country in 1971 but in 1972 the number dropped to 13,500 and showed signs of drying up completely. Though the Bonn estimate of 250,000 anxious to leave must have included a number of people with mixed nationality (as to whom no specific promise had been given), it was hard to believe that there were no more qualified and willing to come. The Poles were not only nervous of the effect on their economy if too many skilled workers left too quickly but also loath to admit that their efforts to turn Germans and half-Germans into Poles had had little success. They raised as a distraction the question of compensation for those of their citizens who had suffered in concentration camps. The West German answer was to point to the vast areas of German territory which had passed into Polish hands and to the financial burden caused by having to support their compatriots who had fled virtually destitute from that territory. The Poles were told that they could not sell the same horse twice but this did not stop them from continuing to try and for a time negotiations languished.

With the DDR still more, a happy life ever after was proving something of a fairy tale. Certainly the number of people crossing the frontier in both directions increased, though East Germans were allowed to do so only if they were over working age, while the East's action in doubling without consultation its charge for entry permits was regarded as a piece of sharp practice. In spite of the promise to allow traffic to pass freely on the roads to West Berlin, periodical police checks were staged and difficulties made over the staff of Federal offices and over parties of schoolchildren being taken to demonstrate against the Wall. Remonstrations received the reply that searches had to be made for criminals and undoubtedly a certain number of people were exploiting the access roads in order to escape. The Bonn decision to locate the new Federal Office on Environmental Questions in West Berlin evoked a protest on the ground that, although the Four-Power Treaty had recognized existing ties with the West, it had said nothing about the creation of new ones. The decision was certainly ill-considered – it is said to have slipped through the Cabinet without its full implications being realized (the sort of thing which was rather too liable to happen under Brandt's easy-going management). Negotiations about it were complicated by the fact that the German translation of the Treaty (of which the authentic texts were in English and Russian) was not identical in the two Republics and the Eastern addition of three letters at one point (*Verbindungen* rather than *Bindungen*) reduced appreciably the scope of the clause. There were further arguments as to whether the 'permanent representatives' which the two Governments were to exchange should deal with the Foreign Office as though they were ambassadors or with the Chancelleries on the ground that they represented not foreign countries but two parts of the same nation. The squabble was settled by letting each side have its own way in its own area, but it illustrated how tenaciously each stuck to its own point of view and how little the conclusion of the Treaty had fostered the good-will and reasonableness for which Brandt had hoped. The Democratic Republic did not want relaxation but only the advantages flowing from it in such matters as international recognition.

During a visit to Moscow in October 1973 Wehner said that he considered the Federal Republic to have overdrawn its credit under the Treaties. However, the basic difficulty was that the two German regimes had contradictory aims which the agreements had not reconciled. For the West, reunification remained the ideal which it had merely agreed not to seek by force; had Brandt refused to leave open the possibility of it being achieved by agreement at some date in the indefinite future, he would never have got the Treaties ratified. The political form which a reunited nation would take was left vague, but the conversion of the Federal Republic into a Communist state hardly seemed likely. But without such a conversion, reunification must mean for the East Germans the partial if not complete dismantling of their system, which was to them unthinkable. The West hoped that relaxation would gradually lead to the disappearance of Communism, the East to its consolidation. The two sides were, as the Chinese say, 'dreaming discrepant dreams in the same bed'. Honecker's Government set out on a campaign of 'distinction-drawing' (*Abgrenzung*), doing all in its power to make its country look different from the one next door. One of these steps was to cut down the use of the word 'German', another, paradoxically, was to re-emphasize links with the Prussian tradition in such matters as army insignia. Indeed the DDR had much in common with the state of Frederick the Great.

Although the two Governments had promised that they would not interfere in one another's affairs, neither did much to reduce the efforts it had long been making to infiltrate the other's ranks, in order to discover secrets and influence policy. The situation made the checking of espionage unusually difficult. Not only did identity of language render it easier for spies to operate undetected but also absconders were positively welcomed and the Federal Republic would have been distinctly less well served if it had employed no refugees from the East. In spite of elaborate precautions and extensive organizations for counter-intelligence, a long series of agents had been uncovered in high places. The most spectacular of these came at the end of April 1974 when it was announced that Günther Guillaume, one of Brandt's personal staff whom he had taken with him on a holiday in Norway the previous summer, had admitted to being a Communist spy. Guillaume had come from East Germany in the early 1950s, ostensibly as a faithful Socialist whose prospects had been ruined by the Communists. He built up a position for himself in the SPD Party machine whence in due course he got a transfer to the Chancellor's office. If several slips had not been made during his security screening, the fact that he had been suspected of espionage in 1955 should have come to light. (It is not altogether impossible that rabid anti-Communists in the security service deliberately overlooked this so as to discredit Brandt whose policies were anathema to them.) Responsibility for the omissions rested with the FDP Minister of the Interior, Genscher (who had himself come from East Germany in 1952 as a faithful Liberal whose prospects had been ruined by Communists) or with Ehmke, the Minister at the head of Brandt's office. But on 7 May Brandt announced that he was taking the blame personally and had resigned as Chancellor. His successor was to be Helmut Schmidt.

Brandt's step did him credit but was not strictly necessary. He could well have left the consequences to be shouldered by others such as Genscher, though the position was complicated by Scheel having just announced his intention of standing for the Presidency when Heinemann retired later in the year; Genscher was booked to succeed him both as Foreign Minister and leader of the FDP. Rumours were rife that Guillaume had discovered some discreditable secret in Brandt's personal life, which he threatened to reveal if the Chancellor stayed in office. Brandt was well known to have his weaknesses but if there had been anything serious to hide, it might have been expected to leak out in the years which have elapsed since then, while his colleagues would hardly have exerted themselves as they did to make him go back on his decision. Moreover it is hard to see why Guillaume should have wanted to force him from office. A paradoxical element in the whole affair is that all Guillaume's masters succeeded in doing by their sensational infiltration was to cause the downfall of the most sympathetic Chancellor they were ever likely to have.

A more probable explanation is that Brandt was losing heart and interest in the job, in face of all the difficulties which have been described, the continual sniping at him for treating the left wing at home and Communists abroad too gently and the losses in Land and communal elections which the SPD had recently suffered. He had achieved his main object of realigning West German policy towards the East in such a way that it could never be wholly reversed. He had made the SPD into the strongest party and, in coalition, one with a clear majority in the Bundestag. He could hardly hope, by staying on, to improve his record: the previous eighteen months suggested that he would only blot it. If he judged that it was better to go at a moment of his own choice rather than wait like Adenauer till retirement was forced on him, there would be plenty to be said for the decision. A friendly critic remarked that he had put too much trust in good faith and too little in power; he had set out to rouse conviction and sympathy rather than to mobilize supporters (Rolf Zundel in *Die Zeit*, 10 May 1974).

14

THE SCHMIDT GOVERNMENT:
1974–1982

SCHMIDT SAVES THE SITUATION

The new Chancellor, 54 years old, was a man of many accomplishments, some of which, like speaking fluent English and playing the organ, are not normally expected in a workers' leader. His orderly mind enabled him to see to the roots of a problem and his fluency of speech to say clearly what he saw. Senses of responsibility and proportion added to his equipment. His chief weakness was impatience with those who saw less well, dithered more or took longer to express themselves; he had little time for proponents of plans which he considered to be impracticable in current circumstances. These circumstances included the need to find a happy medium between inflation and unemployment, to halt the clear right-wing trend in Land elections and to keep the support of the FDP. Although the Government mishandled tax changes in January 1975 and pension increases two years later, its management of affairs improved but its ambitions became more limited. The left wing and particularly the Jusos grew restive but had to face clear evidence that, where they got the upper hand in party affairs (as they did in Frankfurt and Munich), the result was loss of votes and office.

Chancellor Schmidt saw two main causes for concern about Germany's future. The first arose from the West's lack of intermediate-range Europe-based missiles. Those which had existed in the 1960s had been scrapped when the USA succeeded in developing long-range intercontinental missiles designed to exert the same deterrent function from further away. But doubts grew as to whether the Americans would in practice be ready to use these missiles in reply to anything except an attack on their own territory and would not expose that territory to bombardment simply because the Soviet Union had attacked Western Europe. The Russians, for their part, had replaced their ageing middle-range missiles with new SS20 ones to which the West had no nuclear answer for use from a European base. Schmidt called attention to this Euro-strategic imbalance in a speech in London in October 1977 and what became known as NATO's 'Two Track' policy was adopted two years later as an answer. According to this, NATO was

208

to confront the Russians with a choice between scrapping their own intermediate-range weapons and facing the build-up of similar weapons by the West as a reply. If negotiations about this deal had reached no agreement by 1983, 108 American Pershing II intermediate missiles and 96 cruise missiles were to be installed in Germany as well as 370 cruise missiles in other parts of Europe (since the Federal Republic refused to be the only West European NATO member to provide a base for weapons which the Soviet Union regarded as a major strategic threat).

The years between 1978 and 1983, however, saw the Americans under President Carter and then more emphatically President Reagan return to the Cold War attitudes which Brandt and Schmidt had abandoned in the Ostpolitik. They launched a massive rearmament programme which they justified by claiming that the Communists had regained the lead in weapons and that the resulting 'window of opportunity' must be closed. The offensive track of NATO's policy against the 'evil empire' received more attention than the conciliatory one, especially after the Russian attack on Afghanistan in December 1979. The Russians retaliated by refusing to come to the conference table, so that the installation of the new Pershing and cruise missiles began to look more and more inevitable. Demonstrations of protest filled West German streets and squares; anti-American feeling was widespread. The left wing of the SPD refused to believe in the danger of a Communist attack and showed the utmost reluctance to accept their leader's policy. Schmidt, who was closer to his opponents than to his followers, argued that the East could get its way by intimidation alone, without resort to actual war, unless the West Europeans had similar weapons of their own or could count on American nuclear aid, as to which he was sceptical.

The Chancellor saw equal cause for concern in the international monetary system. By the Bretton Woods agreement of 1944, the US Government had undertaken to change all amounts of other currencies offered to it into dollars at constant rates, thus creating a network of fixed parities throughout the capitalist world. By the end of the 1960s, however, largely because of the dollars spent on the Vietnam war, so many of them had passed into non-American hands that, if they had all been presented for exchange at once, US reserves would have run out. Accordingly in 1971, the dollar and with it all other Western currencies were left to float. Schmidt was afraid that, if this situation were allowed to continue, each country would follow her own narrow advantage and the increased uncertainty as to what each would do in the future would drastically cut the volume of international trade, on which German prosperity was becoming increasingly dependent. In 1972 an attempt was made to get a substitute system of semi-fixed currencies set up for Western Europe. Under this scheme each currency was given an exchange rate against each of the other currencies in the system. As soon as the market rate for a currency began to diverge from the rate by more than an agreed percentage, it became the responsibility of the Government and

Central Bank of the country concerned to take such remedial action as would bring the rate back within the agreed limits. This arrangement was known as 'the Snake' because of the similarity to a reptile going down a tunnel without hitting either the roof or the floor. The system allowed for revaluation up or down if a currency showed a steady tendency to go in one direction or the other. But the advantages were lost if such revaluations were too frequent and in practice the weaker countries found difficulty in staying within the limits. Some of them did not try too hard and others did not regard themselves as under any particular obligation to help. Matters were not eased by the inflation following the 1973 rise in oil prices. By 1977 the Snake had become reduced to a Deutschmark area with various Benelux and Scandinavian hangers-on.

Schmidt refused to rest content. He found a willing ally in Giscard d'Estaing, who became President of France in 1974. They both knew English so well that they could talk together in that language without any need for interpreters. They had to reckon with the fact that few of their subordinates sympathized with their objectives. The conventional criticism of systems designed to fix exchange rates between currencies is that they cannot last unless the countries belonging to them have the same economic objectives, which they rarely do for long, and that once a currency is clearly heading for a change of value, speculators can make easy money. A single country may have difficulty in keeping its currency stable, especially if it has economic weaknesses, but for other countries to help it often requires them to act against their short-term interests. Schmidt and Giscard thought that these defects were outweighed by the advantages of stability. But after they decided late in 1977 to set up a successor to the Snake, they had to conceal their plan from the numerous people who would be bound to rubbish it while they secured through private channels enough supporters to have a chance of getting it accepted in the institutions of the European Community. After last-minute hitches, it came into operation on 13 March 1979. The chief difference from the Snake was that a 'divergence indicator' took effect as soon as a currency had gone (in terms of European Currency Units based on a weighted average of the main currencies in the scheme) three-quarters of the way towards its maximum permitted spread. This would be the signal not only for intervention by the Central Bank immediately concerned but also for consultation with other Central Banks in the system. That the European Monetary System so set up should have lasted for thirteen years and should now be on the way to expansion suggests that it met a real need.

In 1976 Schmidt's freedom of manoeuvre in home politics was limited by a revolt of the Hanover SPD against a central attempt to impose a leader on them. This led to the Land Government being taken over by the CDU. But the new Cabinet under Ernst Albrecht could survive only because it was tolerated by the FDP, who later in the year accepted office in it. As the Saar already had a CDU/FDP Black/White 'Zebra' Coalition Government, this brought their number to two and gave them eight votes in the Bundesrat, where the Länder under CDU rule had eighteen and those under SPD fifteen. The FDP therefore (see p. 128) had a voice in eight casting votes and mainly used them to put back into legislation those provisions which they had been unable to induce the SPD to accept; the chances of getting radical legislation through the Upper House virtually vanished. The Mediation Committee of the two Houses (see p. 128) was increasingly called on to devise compromises; where it failed, the Government had little choice but to abandon its proposals. The FDP welcomed the chance of showing that it was no mere lackey of the SPD.

Externally the chief short-term problem (other than chronic bickering about the interpretation of the Eastern Treaties) arose from a decision of the Federal Government to yield to the Polish demands for compensation (see p. 204) so as to re-start the flow of immigrants. Both CDU and CSU condemned the bargain which for a time seemed bound to be thrown out by the Bundesrat. But Kohl, who had inherited Barzel's doubts as to the wisdom of intransigence (see p. 195) brought off a deal by which the Poles accepted some last-minute modifications in the text (something which Schmidt had declared to be out of the question) while in return first Albrecht and then even the Bavarians were induced to say 'Yes' in the Bundesrat so that the Treaty could be passed unanimously. The FDP had done much to help the compromise and Kohl undoubtedly hoped that his tactics would find favour with them and even start them thinking about changing partners again after the Election due in October 1976.

That, however, was reckoning without Strauss, who particularly resented a surrender in which his Bavarian colleagues had had a hand. He was largely responsible for the decision to make the issue of the election into a choice between Freedom and Socialism. Such a formula would have been justified only if the SPD left wing had had a major say in determining policy, which was just what Schmidt was denying them; it polarized the votes instead of attracting floating ones. All the same the CDU started favourites in a campaign fought primarily on internal issues. Kohl made superhuman efforts and 140 speeches; the SPD pulled out the stops only at the end, perhaps as deliberate tactics, perhaps because they were slow to recognize danger. They lost seventeen seats and the FDP two, but they won back 1 million of the voters who had deserted them in recent Land elections. The CDU/CSU recovered their position as the strongest Party and polled more votes than in any election since 1957 but as the overall total of votes had been increasing, their gains were not quite enough to turn the scale. The Schmidt Government was more relieved than exhilarated at the prospect of continuing in power with a majority of at best eight (in the first vote of confidence it fell to one!). The Chancellor's personal prestige had done much to decide the issue; if Brandt had still been in charge, the other side might have got its nose in front.

TERRORISM AND NUCLEAR ENERGY AROUSE PASSIONS

Terrorism dominated the next twelve months. There had been sporadic acts since 1968, with a first peak in 1972; starting from Berlin, they spread round the country and outside it. A number of bomb attacks were made on public buildings, embassies and military installations; banks were robbed to obtain funds. In the course of these actions and consequential arrests, several police-officers and still more terrorists were killed and some of the ensuing incidents were declared to be revenge. After a terrorist, Holger Meins, had died on hunger strike in November 1974 a senior judge was murdered in Berlin where four months later the local CDU leader was kidnapped just before the city elections; in spite of misgivings about paying '*Danegeld*', five terrorists were set free to secure his release. Between April and September 1977 a prosecuting counsel was assassinated in Karlsruhe, a banker, Jürgen Ponto, shot with the aid of his god-daughter in his home near Frankfurt and the employers' leader Hans-Martin Schleyer (see p. 201) kidnapped in Cologne. The police did not show up too well in pursuit of the criminals, partly because of rivalries between the Federal Criminal Office and the Land Forces. But it was a different story when on 17 October 1977 a German airliner returning from Majorca was hijacked and taken to Mogadishu. A specially trained squad of Federal Frontier Police was sent out, with the consent of the Somali Government; the plane was recaptured, the passengers freed and three terrorists killed. Three other notable terrorists, Baader, Rasper and Gudrun Esslin, who were serving life-sentences in prison near Stuttgart, committed suicide on hearing the news. Next day Schleyer's body was found in the back of a car in Alsace.

The outcome owed much to the Chancellor's determination and added correspondingly to his prestige; there were no serious acts of terrorism in the next thirty-five months. Over the whole period 1970–80, forty-one people were killed including eleven police-officers, but twenty-one terrorists lost their lives while about four hundred more received sentences.

The wave of terrorism was not, of course, confined to West Germany; indeed the German terrorists had links with gangs, particularly of Arabs, elsewhere. But most of the others had clear political objectives whereas the Germans merely claimed to be using violence in the interests of 'humanity' without any definite ideas as to what they would do if they overthrew the existing system. The terrorist epidemic is best seen as an extension of the student unrest of 1968 and a further price which West Germany had to pay for the social immobility of the Republic's first twenty years. The people involved were alienated from society and frustrated at its slowness to change. Nearly all of them were young middle-class intellectuals with psychological problems aggravated by some sort of personal failure. They were the flotsam of a generation which grew up while their parents were absorbed in the war or in achieving the 'German Miracle', so that they had not known stable family life. Women were as numerous as men. They were estranged from their elders by revulsion at the acquiescence of that age-group in Nazi crimes; they considered themselves justified in using violence against a society which had condoned it in the Third Reich and Vietnam and employed it against Ohnesorg, Dutschke and Martin Luther King. (Schleyer had held high rank in the SS.) Their hostility to the established order with its affluence made them sympathetic to Marxism and other revolutionary dogmas which provided rational justification for courses of action attractive to them on emotional grounds. They were more the children of 'Marx and Coca-Cola' than of Hitler. Moscow tried to take advantage of them but they were not under its orders.

They could have done serious damage to the Federal Republic if they had succeeded in driving it into blind repression. But when they were most active, liberal men were fortunately in power who saw the danger and refused to panic; instead they merely increased the numbers and co-ordination of the police, improved intelligence and limited the traditional right of defence lawyers to free access to their clients when this had been palpably abused. As soon as the situation seemed to be under control, the FDP Minister of the Interior, Baum, began making minor relaxations, only to be criticized by the Opposition in the election campaign of 1980. The number of active terrorists probably never reached three figures nor did that of those giving them aid and comfort reach four. They were able to exploit the vulnerability of pluralist society to ill-willed individuals but they did not find in the population as a whole the sympathy which alone could have made them a serious political threat.

Energy, however, was to prove a more intractable problem. Like most industrialized countries, the Federal Republic depends for all her oil on imports, principally from the Middle East. Accordingly the sudden and drastic rise in prices imposed by that area's producers at the end of 1973 added significantly to the import bill. Some countries such as Britain and the USA refused to alter their pattern of expenditure to accommodate the extra amounts which they needed to spend on oil, preferring to increase their money supply and let prices rise generally, thus reducing the real cost to them of the extra oil and depriving its producers of part of the gain which they hoped to draw from the higher prices. But West Germany managed to increase her exports, particularly to the Middle East, and her extra earnings, taken together with some Middle Eastern investment in her own economy, enabled her to pay for the oil without putting her overall balance into deficit or seriously raising the rate of inflation. The record 1974 surplus of DM 26,500 million sank to DM 1,000 million in 1975 but by 1978 it was back at DM 18,400 million. This success, however, increased the problems for the rest of the world, since the large surplus won by the oil producers had to be matched by a deficit somewhere else. Accordingly the Schmidt

Government came under considerable pressure from the Americans and others not to tighten credit in order to contain inflation but to keep the West German market open for other countries. The stimulus which it gave to its economy in due course resulted in it doing what it had previously managed to avoid and 1979 saw a payments deficit of DM 11,000 million – the first for fourteen years. The further rise in oil prices following the cutting of Iranian supplies drove the 1980 deficit to DM 29,000 million. The size of West German monetary reserves prevented such a result from causing an immediate crisis but would not go on doing so indefinitely.

An obvious way of easing the situation was to consume less oil and oil's share of West German energy consumption was cut from 53 per cent in 1970 to 40 per cent in 1990. But there were limits to the use which can be made of substitutes either on account of their environmental effects (as with coal) or their scarcity (natural gas and water). The only short-term alternative fuel was nuclear energy and its share consequently rose from 0.6 per cent in 1970 to 12.7 per cent in 1990. In face of the Chernobyl disaster nobody would deny that this solution involves danger, whether from accidents to reactors or from the need to store quantities of spent but lethal fuel over centuries. Yet the Government, well aware that it would be blamed for an economic break-down, was unwilling to take the risk of doing nothing; in this it was supported not only by industry, afraid that lack of contracts at home might lead to a loss of contracts abroad, but also by the unions, concerned for the jobs which would be provided if reactors were built, as well as for those which would be lost if power shortages forced close-downs. Refuge was found in the formula 'As much coal as possible; as much nuclear power as necessary'. In practice, this meant reducing the number of reactors in use or development from thirty in 1980 to twenty-one in 1990.

Opposition to nuclear expansion provided a focus for all those dissatisfied with things as they were; the student upheavals of 1968–70 were replaced by mass demonstrations at reactor-sites, some of which ended as pitched battles with the police. Every legal opening provided by the Grundgesetz and other laws was exploited. A number of verdicts were obtained delaying the building of reactors, so that the paradoxical situation arose of decisions about policy being taken by judges rather than by ministers. Feeling was strong among the SPD rank-and-file; in Hanover and Baden-Württemberg the local leadership (perhaps because it was not in office) refused to toe the central line.

But opposition was not confined to existing parties. The kind of people who had composed the 'extra parliamentary opposition' in 1967–9 were beginning to band themselves into groups known as 'the Greens' (in Berlin the 'Alternative List'). In December 1977 they set out their fields of concern as being economics, energy, transport, land use, pollution, education and technology. They found it hard to decide whether they were a pressure group or an organized party. They were reluctant to accept that a minority must in a democracy yield to a majority on a matter which it feels keenly. The rank-and-file were reluctant to accept decisions (and particularly compromises) taken for them by the leaders whom they had themselves chosen. They found their main support among young middle-class intellectuals of both sexes; the working classes were less interested. In June 1978 they put up candidates in a Land Election but failed to surmount the 5 per cent barrier. The story remained the same for the six next attempts, but in October 1979 they won 5.14 per cent and four seats in Bremen, followed five months later by 5.3 per cent in Baden-Württemberg. Even where they did not win seats, they were clearly attracting voters from the SPD and FDP. If this were to happen in the 1980 Federal Election it would mean that the CDU/CSU could get an absolute majority with only 48 per cent of the votes and an opinion poll in the late summer already gave them 47 per cent.

THE UNDOING OF FRANZ JOSEPH STRAUSS

Their prospects had, however, been complicated by Kohl's announcement in May that he would not accept nomination as candidate for the Chancellorship in 1980. He pressed instead the choice of Albrecht, the young Minister-President of Lower Saxony. This was more than the CSU could stomach since Albrecht, although full of promise, was short on experience (especially in Federal politics) and could not compare in force of character with Franz Joseph Strauss who did not need much encouragement to stand against him. In a combined vote of the two Parties, the Bavarian leader received 57 per cent. As nearly all the CSU must have voted for him, this figure showed that less than half the CDU could have done so, and the motives of many who did were questionable. For some were frightened of losing their seats if Strauss, in revenge for being rejected, should get the CSU to put up candidates for the Bundestag outside Bavaria (as he had often threatened to do). Others, sick of the way Strauss had denigrated Barzel and Kohl, and foreseeing similar treatment of Albrecht, thought that the best way of drawing his political sting was to put him up in an election which he would have difficulty in winning, for his record reinforced the habitual North German distrust of Bavarians. He was unlikely to attract floating voters and there was no chance of the FDP turning back to coalition with the CDU/CSU as long as that combination was under his leadership. These considerations did not, however, prevent some Social Democrats from fearing that during the months before the election, trouble over energy, or a revival of terrorism, or rising prices or unemployment, or a Russian violation of the Eastern Treaties could turn the crucial margin of opinion against them.

Instead, Iranian students stormed the US Embassy in Tehran, the Russians invaded Afghanistan and the Carter Administration reverted to the attitudes of the Cold War. Schmidt had already sized up Carter as a

215

lightweight and the tension between the two men was enhanced by the President's tendency to change policies suddenly without consulting his allies. The Chancellor knew that, in the last resort, the Federal Republic must stand by the United States and indeed he did not wish to do otherwise. But he was not prepared to jeopardize the achievements of the Ostpolitik without compelling reason and, although he went further than Britain in acting as the Americans wanted him to do, he doubted whether the course which they favoured would have its intended effects in Moscow. Had he done otherwise, he would have intensified his existing difficulties with his Party whose left wing congratulated him ironically for successfully maintaining the status quo. As it was he found himself supported not only by a majority of West Germans, whose dominating concern was to avoid a war fought over their territory, but also by moderate opinion throughout Western Europe. He was helped also by the obvious anxiety of the Russians and East Germans to maintain contact with him. The political shrewdness of his course was illustrated by the restraint which Strauss at first showed in attacking it and by the striking gains which the SPD made in Land Elections in the Saar and in North Rhine-Westphalia in May. In neither Land did the Greens get 5 per cent and as their indecision about what they wanted to do increased, the danger from them seemed to be on the wane; Strauss, disillusioned by the poor results of trying to play the statesman, relaxed into the more congenial role of demagogue and attacked the Government for betraying the North Atlantic Alliance. But there were no indications that the change brought him votes.

In July the Chancellor went to Moscow and persuaded the Russians to resume talks with the Americans; he justified this as a service to humanity which few other people could perform. Probably he would have liked to base his whole campaign on such a profile. But he had to cancel visits to Poland and to the Democratic Republic in September because of the 'Solidarity' strikes started in the former country; it would not have done for the leader of a free state to be a guest of people who started using violence to suppress freedom and there was no assurance that this would not happen (although in fact it did not). As a result home affairs got more attention in the election campaign and here the Government were more vulnerable, in spite of the fact that the Federal Republic with unemployment at 3.7 per cent, inflation at 5.5 per cent and growth at 2.5 per cent compared favourably with any other country in the world.

Fifty million dollars are said to have been spent on campaign publicity, much of it being paid for out of public funds. Strauss, having clearly decided that his best chance of victory lay in exciting the voters by emotionalizing the issues, accused the SPD of extravagance and of weakness towards Communism and terrorism. He launched a series of allegations, in each of which the truth was more or less twisted. But by the time his opponents had got round to putting the record straight, he had diverted the public's attention to the next charge. Personal abuse abounded, with even the Chancellor stooping to it. The left wing, its dissident factions for once united under the banner 'Stop Strauss', itself stopped at little but its victim would have gained more sympathy if he had shown more restraint himself.

The electorate would seem to have tired of the scurrilities and noticed the lack of solid argument. In a poll on 5 October a little lower than that of 1976, the SPD failed to realize either their maximal hope of a clear majority or their more modest one of becoming the strongest party again and had to be content with a marginal rise in their share of the total vote to 42.9 per cent. The CDU/CSU lost nearly 4 per cent, falling to 44.5 per cent, their lowest figure for twenty years; Strauss must bear some blame for this. The beneficiaries were the FDP who had fought a more moderate campaign, perhaps because the Opposition's fire was concentrated on the SPD; having fallen below the 5 per cent line in North Rhine-Westphalia in the previous May, they were more than a little gratified to emerge at 10.6 per cent, albeit without winning a single constituency. The Greens received a mere 1.5 per cent, suggesting that they had some way to go before they became a serious political factor.

DIE WENDE

The humiliation of Strauss opened up the cracks between his opponents which had been papered over in the common desire to stop him. Those inside each Party were almost as wide as those between them.

To the CSU the internal policy of the CDU was insufficiently authoritarian and for a few weeks in 1976 there had been serious talk of setting up as a distinct party throughout the country. This plan however never got beyond talk because it would have split the right-wing vote and still have left the possibility of a right-wing government dependent on a coalition between the two parties. Kohl, as CDU Chairman since 1973, seems to have reached the conclusion soon after the 1976 election that even in combination the CDU and CSU would have little chance of again winning an outright majority over all the other parties. He therefore tacitly set himself to win the FDP back from its association with the SPD, a shift which would have the additional advantage of reducing his dependence on the CSU. Strauss, foreseeing that this would happen, was strongly set against currying favour with the FDP

The differences inside the SPD have already been described. As time went on, Schmidt became increasingly at loggerheads with his left wing, and since it was largely a matter of a generation gap, time was unlikely to modify the trend.

The split personality of the FDP was in keeping with the traditions of German Liberalism. Two-thirds of the Party believed in maximizing human freedom and private enterprise. One-third wanted social welfare without a socialist state. The weaker group were reluctant to abandon the progress achieved towards making the Federal Republic into a genuinely liberal society but feared that this might happen in a coalition dominated by the CDU and accordingly opposed a change of partners. The stronger wing considered that West Germany had embarked on higher welfare expenditure than even she could afford and were anxious to economize. They were afraid that, if the Party were to remain much longer in coalition with the SPD, it would lose its identity. Moreover a second switch of partners could be justified on the ground that liberal democracy requires for its efficient functioning a periodic change in the personnel and policies of Cabinets. The differences between them and the more progressive members of the CDU were as small as those between the left wing and the moderates in the SPD.

A wag had, however, suggested that 'FDP' stood for *Fast Drei Prozent*, meaning that the convinced adherents of the Party amounted only to just under 3 per cent of the electorate. If that had been the whole story, the Party could never have hoped to surmount the 5 per cent barrier and obtain seats in the Federal and Land legislatures. But (as explained on p. 247) every German voter has two votes, one for a candidate in a constituency, the other (in effect) for a party at the national level. It is exceptional for a party to win an absolute majority on its own so that governments have to be coalitions. Voters can accordingly seek to modify the practice of the party to which they give their first vote by giving their second to a more moderate one. The party best suited for that purpose is the FDP, which has come to depend on being saved from falling below the 5 per cent line by the second votes of Christian Democrats who do not want too reactionary a government and of Social Democrats who do not want a too radical one. The chiefs of the two major parties are even inclined to look benevolently on the practice since it saves them from being too dependent on their own extremists. An incidental result is to make the CSU violently hostile to the FDP.

By 1981 the economic difficulties confronting the Federal Republic (see p. 214) were worsening. In August Genscher, as the senior FDP Minister, circulated a letter showing how the financial situation was deteriorating. Apart from the adverse Balance of Payments, the public debt had risen during the term of office of the SDP/FDP Coalition from 18.2 per cent of GNP to 31.3 per cent, and inflation from 1.9 per cent to 5.1 per cent, while investment had fallen from 26.5 per cent to 23 per cent. Although net income had doubled, social expenditure had trebled, until a quarter of total income was being provided from state-paid benefits. Exploitation of such benefits by people not intended to receive them was widespread. As a result cuts of DM 18 million were agreed on for the 1982 budget but they were realized only in part.

When a year later the 1983 budget began to be discussed, even sharper differences of opinion became evident. Although international comparison

218

might have suggested that West Germany was better off than anyone else in Europe, business people were loud in assertions that the economy could not afford the welfare state. Inside the Cabinet the chief proponent of this view was the FDP Economics Minister, Otto Markgraf von Lambsdorff, the former head of a big insurance company who had entered the Bundestag in 1972 and become Minister five years later. On getting back in August from one of his regular visits to the USA (where his admiration of private industry was no doubt applauded) the *Marktgraf* presented Chancellor Schmidt with a thirty-page paper headed 'Manifesto for the Market Economy'. Genscher had during the summer being having clandestine talks with Kohl and the three of them together decided that the time had come for the FDP to turn (*wenden*) back to its old association with the CDU. They expected however some antagonism to this change among the rank-and-file and therefore proposed to wait until early October. For a Land election was to be held in Hesse on 26 September and if disaffected FDP members expressed their opposition by refraining from voting, the party might fall below the 5 per cent line. But Schmidt knew all too well what was intended and took the wind out of the plotter's sails by calling on the other FDP Ministers on 17 September to disown Lambsdorff or resign. They chose the latter.

For a few days a purely SPD Government took office while negotiations went on to see whether the necessary votes would be forthcoming for carrying a motion of 'no confidence' and nominating Kohl in Schmidt's place. There was a widespread feeling, nourished by the SPD, that such a definite change in German politics ought to be referred to the West German people in an election (even though this was not explicitly required by the Basic Law). One advocate of immediate recourse to such a procedure was Strauss, who was only too keen to see the FDP disappear from the Bundestag, since his own party could then twist the arm of the CDU and the way would be open for him to become Vice-Chancellor and Foreign Minister. But this was the very situation which Kohl wanted to avoid. He insisted that an election must be postponed but propitiated those who wanted to give the voters a look in by promising to hold one in March 1983. On 1 October 1982 a vote of no confidence in Schmidt was passed and Kohl took office with three FDP Ministers in his Cabinet (the Party lost the Interior and Agriculture Ministries which they held under Schmidt but were given that of Justice in compensation and retained Economics and Foreign Affairs). This meant that no post was left vacant of enough importance to tempt Strauss to move to Bonn from his position as Minister-President of Bavaria.

To bring about the March election Kohl had to arrange for a motion of confidence to be tabled in favour of his Government and lost. No attempt was made to nominate a successor and accordingly the President under Article 68 of the Basic Law dissolved the Bundestag. There was considerable misgiving about this method of doing things since the Chancellor could have easily got a majority vote if all his supporters had voted. But the Constitutional Court, on being asked to pronounce, connived at the procedure on the ground that an election was generally desired. The FDP had in the meantime fallen below 5 per cent in Hesse, Bavaria and Hamburg. In the Federal Election, however, recognition of its role as a moderator of extremism brought it enough second votes to win 7 per cent of the poll and thirty-four seats. Schmidt had resigned the SPD leadership during the previous autumn and been succeeded by Hans-Jochen Vogel, who took a line more conciliatory to his left wing even though he did not belong to it. The Party lost twenty-five seats whereas the CDU/CSU gained eighteen, so that the Kohl Government emerged with a majority of seventy-eight even after allowing for the twenty-seven seats won by the Greens in their first appearance in the Bundestag. The electorate thus put the seal of its approval on the manoeuvrings of the previous autumn. For the second time the constitution of the Federal Republic had demonstrated its ability to permit peaceful change. But this may have been because the changes were going to be only modest.

15

THE KOHL GOVERNMENT: 1982–1989

MUCH THE SAME THING AS BEFORE

Like so many other politicians on obtaining power, the CDU/CSU/FDP Coalition found their medicine for Germany's ills easier to prescribe than to take. They managed to make DM 5,000,000 million of savings but, as soon as they began to cut down on social services and subsidies, they ran into objections from their own followers who felt their pockets touched or feared the loss of votes. The DM 29,000 million provided by the Federal Government for social purposes in 1983 was DM 2,000 million more than the figure in the last year of the Schmidt Government. The DM 100,000 million spent on subsidies in 1981 rose to DM 121,000 million in 1985. West German society was showing itself resistant to turning. Attitudes motivated by personal advantage were reinforced institutionally. The Basic Law laid down (see p. 124) that all Bills affecting the Länder required the agreement of the Bundesrat. But since the party composition in that House is often different from that in the Bundestag, and changes with almost every Land election, Federal Governments have often to make concessions so as to safeguard their legislation from being blocked by a hostile majority in the upper house.

What would have happened to the Kohl Government if the down-turn had lasted is hard to guess. But fortunately things began to recover almost immediately it took office. Whereas in 1982 the figure for growth was −1 per cent, in 1983 it was +1.8 per cent and thereafter continued positive without a break till 1990. Whereas in 1967 and 1975 the turnabout had been achieved by expanding internal demand, this time it was achieved by exports, primarily to Europe, which rose from $3,400 million in 1981 to $29,000 million in 1986. The surplus of DM 8.5 million on visible trade in 1986 was a record. The Mark was strong and the dollar weak, while a drop in the price of oil meant that in 1986 West Germany was paying less than half what she had been in 1981. Inflation stayed on average at less than 2.5 per cent till 1987. The weakest item in the economy was unemployment which rose to a record height of 3 million in November 1983 and stuck above 2 million until 1989. Extra jobs were not being created fast enough to absorb the extra numbers seeking work. The Americans pressed the Germans to bother less about price stability and more about unemployment. The Germans, remembering how steps in that direction had pushed them into the red in 1979, urged the Americans to bother more about deficits.

The FDP had made a continuation of existing foreign policy one of their conditions for engaging in *Die Wende*. The new Government announced its intention of working on the principle of *pacta sunt servanda*, that is, undertakings given in existing treaties must be honoured. The process of installing the intermediate nuclear missiles under US control went ahead. But the Americans, who had hoped to get more help from the new Government than they had from the old, were disconcerted to be told that, at a time when German welfare payments were being held down, the public would not stand for increased spending on defence. Contacts with the Democratic Republic were maintained and a number of small steps taken to remove obstacles. In July 1983 Strauss clinched by a visit to the DDR a deal on which he had been working secretly for some time and which was designed to provide the Honecker Government with a credit of DM 1,000 million, through private channels centred round the Munich State Bank (since the economy drive ruled out an official loan). The reasons for this departure from his usual anti-Communist stance are far from clear but Kohl certainly knew about it through intermediaries. Proposed visits by Honecker to Bonn in 1983 and 1984 were abandoned on Russian orders but the economic difficulties of the East Germans were increasing and their leadership was anxious to take advantage of any project (such as improvements in inter-Republic transport) which might bring them foreign exchange. By 1989 such payments put together amounted to about DM 5,000 million a year.

In the same month of 1983 as the election, however, President Reagan announced his Strategic Defence Initiative (SDI – 'Star Wars'). For thirty years the strategy of the Atlantic nations had been centred on deterrence. The object had been to maintain sufficient relative strength to make an attack by the Warsaw Pact nations so hazardous as to be unthinkable. Indeed Reagan's overall rearmament programme had the effect of increasing the weight of the blow which the USA could deliver in reply to a Soviet strike and thus challenging the USSR to an armaments race. The SDI, however, assumed that the USA would become able to repel an attack after its launching. But if it were really possible to devise a screen which would prevent any missiles landing on their soil, why did the Americans need a counter-stroke at all? The whole basis of NATO would need rethinking.

Kohl was pressed by several of his colleagues and more of his opponents to take the Americans to task for their apparent indifference to the strategic needs of Western Europe including West Germany. But one of the ways in which he had promised to do better than Schmidt had been by improving relations with the USA and accordingly he resorted to his favourite tactic of inaction. He merely sent his Minister of Economics Bangemann to Washington in the hope of securing for German industry contracts for making some of the hardware needed for Star Wars; little of practical value resulted.

But in March 1985 Mikhail Gorbachev assumed control of Russian policy as Chief Secretary of the Communist Party. He must have come to the conclusion that the cost to the Soviet Union of keeping up with the USA was going to be prohibitive. By driving the Communist world to the verge of economic collapse, the Capitalists had won the Cold War (leaving open the question as to whether they may not have bankrupted themselves in the process). After a preliminary but sterile discussion with Reagan at Reykjavik in October 1986, Gorbachev proposed in February 1987 a separate agreement on medium-range missiles by which each side would keep only 100 such weapons, and those outside Europe. Reagan, whose desire to go down in history as a peacemaker was leading him to pursue in his second term of office a policy almost diametrically opposite to that which had characterized his first, replied that he would prefer complete abolition and this in fact was agreed (with suitable procedures for verification) in the 'Double Zero' Intermediate Nuclear Forces Treaty of December 1987.

But what was to happen to the new intermediate missiles which were being installed in West Germany under the NATO 'Two Track' policy? There were Americans, Britons and Germans who argued that, if these were withdrawn, making it impossible to reach Russian territory with missiles launched from Western Europe, conventional forces, in which the Warsaw Pact was superior, would recover an importance which the whole course of Western strategy from 1949 onwards had been designed to deprive them. If so, progress on removing intermediate missiles should depend on progress in reducing conventional forces. But Reagan remained unconcerned about this danger. Kohl did not think it worth while to engage in an argument which seemed likely only to increase bad feeling. He therefore acquiesced in the new weapons being withdrawn and those old ones which they were designed to replace being left unmodernized until they were obsolete. Some Germans welcomed this solution on the ground that it lessened the danger of atom bombs being used in Germany itself but others were bitter about the way in which their views had been disregarded. A fresh cause of friction had been added to US–German relations. In June 1988 Gorbachev put forward proposals for cutting conventional forces but the negotiations to bring this about moved haltingly.

FINANCE AND POLITICS

In January 1984 Wörner, the Minister of Defence, dismissed a general as a security risk, only to find that the allegations of homosexuality which had provided the basis for the action could not be proven. Kohl, who had not been consulted, refused to intervene and remained equally aloof in the summer of 1985 when six cases of espionage brought the Minister of the Interior under fire.

It was not, however, espionage but corruption that provided the main domestic sensations during this period. Since 1967 the Government had been legally authorized to pay DM 5.00 per voter retrospectively towards the election expenses of any party which received more than 0.5 per cent of the total second votes cast. But the income thus obtained (even after the scales were raised) was far from meeting total party expenses and private subscriptions did not make up the shortfall. The gap came to be filled by contributions from rich individuals and firms. The Basic Law, however, required parties to account for the sources of their funds. But to conceal who was paying what, non-profit-making institutions were set up to act as intermediaries. Until 1984 income tax was supposed to be paid on big gifts but this requirement was often evaded.

Six months before the Wende, news leaked out that the Justice Ministry of North Rhine-Westphalia, a Land governed by the SPD, was considering bringing an action against Lambsdorff and Friedrichs, his predecessor as Minister of Economics, on the ground that they had exempted Flick, Germany's biggest private firm, from paying tax on the profits which it had made in 1975 by selling its shares in Daimler-Benz. Sums noticeably close to the money thus saved had been passed to the two Ministers, and thence to the FDP, whose finances were in low water. It looked suspiciously as though the decision to exempt from taxation had been conditional on the proceeds being devoted to this purpose. In November 1983 the examining magistrate decided that there was enough evidence to justify going to court, and in June 1984 Lambsdorff had to resign. On 16 February 1987 he and Friedrichs (by this time the Chairman of West Germany's biggest bank) were found guilty of and fined for tax evasion but acquitted on the charge of corruption. So many payments had been made at various times to the Ministers (and indeed to many other people!) that the court found itself unable to establish that these particular payments were inherently connected with any specific transaction. Lambsdorff remained a member of the Bundestag, exercising a powerful influence on economic policies, and in October 1988 became Chairman of the FDP.

In January 1984 a law was passed which put political parties on a par with charitable institutions, thus enabling them to recover tax on payments made to them. In the following May Kohl proposed that the Bundestag should grant an amnesty to all the people, said to number about 700, who had made contributions without paying tax. The reaction of the rank-and-file, particularly among the FDP, was so hostile that the idea had to be dropped.

In October 1984 it emerged that over the previous eleven years Barzel had received DM 1.7 million indirectly from the Flick firm, partly for having given up the CDU Chairmanship in December 1973 (see p. 200) to make room for Kohl; during the latter part of those years he had been the President of the Bundestag. His tenure of the Party Chairmanship (see pp. 194–200) had been so inauspicious that there were good reasons for removing him – although hardly for putting him thereafter into what is by protocol the second top job in the state. But a suspicion was inevitably left that the post of Party leader and ultimately of Chancellor had been bought for Kohl by big business. Nor did Kohl, when called to give evidence, attempt to deny that between 1975 and 1980 he too had received over half a million Marks from Flick, which he passed on to his Party's funds. Indeed the only political group which had not until recently engaged in such practices, by no means an innovation in German politics, were the Greens. The SPD did not receive much until they came into office (C. Landfried, *Parteifinanzen und Politische Macht*). Between 60 per cent and 100 per cent of Party expenses are now paid from public funds.

THE PAST THAT WILL NOT PASS AWAY

In June 1984, on the beaches of Normandy, where their troops had landed forty years earlier to begin the liberation of Europe from German tyranny, leaders of the USA, Britain and France met to celebrate the anniversary. Kohl took offence that no German had been invited. Nor was an invitation going to be sent to a ceremony held in Paris eleven months later to commemorate the German surrender in May 1945. Accordingly when the Chancellor was in Washington in the autumn of 1984, he induced President Reagan to promise that, when he came to Europe in the following spring for a summit meeting and the commemoration, they would jointly visit a German military cemetery as a gesture of reconciliation and a concentration camp site as a gesture of sympathy. The announcement of the plan provoked considerable controversy, focused on the incongruity of paying equal attention to German bravery and to German brutality; the situation was made still more difficult by the discovery that the cemetery at Bitburg in the Ardennes, chosen as the venue for the visit, contained the graves of forty-nine SS men.

Reagan had himself hesitated about the camp visit. Voices were quickly heard from many quarters urging him to give up the whole project. Kohl, however, obstinately refrained from providing him with a pretext for doing so and Reagan felt obliged out of loyalty to stick to the whole programme. (It did not escape attention that the spectacle of Chancellor escorting President might improve the chances of the CDU in the North Rhine-Westphalia election which was due later in the month – and in which as things turned out the SPD were to win a runaway victory.) The Bitburg visit passed off without disturbance on 5 May. Many admirable sentiments were expressed in speeches, although they were put into the shade by President von Weizsäcker in addressing the Bundestag on the surrender anniversary three days later.

> For us Germans the eighth of May is not a day for festivities but for memories. It is not a matter of mastering the past. To do so is impossible. The past cannot be altered or erased retrospectively. But those who shut their eyes to the past will be blind towards the future.
>
> (R. von Weizsäcker, *Von Deutschland Aus*, p. 11)

The whole episode should have proved to those Germans who wanted to put behind them the nagging nightmare of the Holocaust that the rest of the world was unlikely to assist them by ceasing to talk about it. Far from showing how good US–German relations had become, the incident lit up the considerable resentments and suspicions which lingered (although it is only fair to say that these were mostly voiced in particular circles, and notably Jewish ones, while polls showed that average Americans had other things on their minds).

It has been well said that Bitburg was not a thinking about the unthinkable but a debate over the hitherto undebatable (C. Maier, *The Unmasterable Past*, p. 12). That debate did not take long to develop. In June 1986 Professor Nolte, a philosopher-historian of West Berlin, published an article entitled 'The Past that will not pass away'. A month later this was answered by Professor Habermas, a social philosopher of Frankfurt, who took the opportunity to attack in addition some earlier writings by Professor Hillgruber, a Cologne historian. Many others joined in what became known as 'The Historians' Dispute' (*Historiker Streit*). The underlying issue was whether the Nazi treatment of the Jews was to be regarded as something unique and characteristically German, thus making it impossible for any Germans of good-will ever again to regard their country's past with pride, or whether it was merely an exceptionally large-scale example of behaviour which could be observed elsewhere, notably in the Communist world. Should National Socialism be condemned without qualification for violating all the standards on which European civilization has been based or was it to be understood as a not unnatural product of Germany's particular history? Emphasis on Nazism's causes led easily to an interpretation of that history which came close to the one which had been propounded for so long by the conservatives (see p. 27), an interpretation which many non-German historians consider to deserve some of the blame for the two wars. On this showing Hitler's anti-Communism became intelligible and to some extent justifiable by the need to defend Europe against the red peril. In that case, the Wehrmacht in Russia had been fighting Europe's cause. The dictates of Germany's external situation could thus be reinstated in their primacy. Too extensive an internal pluralism of values and interests which some supporters of the Federal Republic sought to achieve in it was held to be dangerous, since politically destabilizing. While there had been general agreement that National Socialism had been a profound mistake, its goals were not regarded by people like Nolte as altogether misconceived. The views which Habermas was attacking in the name of Liberalism were a natural concomitant of the Cold War and correspond in the ideological world to the political reversion involved in Die Wende. As has been said (see p. 95), many Germans for some time after 1945 regarded Nazism as a 'good thing badly carried out'.

The Bitburg controversy damaged Kohl's reputation. He came under attack on the other side from Strauss and the CSU who put the blame for the débâcle in North Rhine-Westphalia (NRW) on his unwillingness to provide leadership and back them rather than the FDP in framing government plans. In May 1985 a poll showed him winning only 35 per cent of the electorate as against 48 per cent for the SPD candidate Rau, the victor in NRW. Kohl did not help himself in November by appearing to speak of Gorbachev in the same breath as Goebbels. But the SPD failed to present a convincing account of how it intended to win a majority and what it would do if it did win. The Greens were split between the 'Fundis', who put fidelity to principle above power, and the 'Realos', who were ready to compromise if it brought them office. An experiment in Hesse where the latter held three posts for a few months did not encourage its repetition elsewhere. But probably the most influential factor in the Federal Election of 25 January 1987 was the continuing prosperity. The CDU/CSU/FDP Coalition won over 50 per cent of the votes and a majority of sixty-two seats. But the CDU reckoned to have lost 800,000 of their normal supporters to the FDP and 400,000 to the SPD, while 800,000 had not bothered to vote at all.

THE INTAKE FROM OUTSIDE

The indigenous population of the Federal Republic reached a peak of 58 million in 1973, when there were in addition 4 million foreigners living within its frontiers. But the birth-rate of eleven per year per 1,000 inhabitants (1988) was relatively low. (East Germany at 12.9 was only a little more prolific.) If things were to remain unchanged the combined total would fall below 60 million by the year 2000. A fall of this dimension would bring problems, notably in keeping up the strength of the armed forces (Bundeswehr). But in other directions such as housing and schools it would bring relief. Moreover unemployment was above 2 million for almost all of the 1980s.

The demographic situation was, however, complicated by four separate groups (if one disregards the short-term visitors from the Democratic Republic, of whom 1.5 million, mostly pensioners, came in 1983. By 1987 that number had risen to 2.5 million).

First, foreigners, often euphemistically called 'guests', had been coming to work in West Germany since the 1950s. Entry began to be restricted in

1973 but in 1991 there were still 5 million of them. About one-third of these were Turks but Yugoslavs and Italians were also prominent. The theory had always been that these people would in due course return home, taking their savings with them. But many have by now been in Germany for ten years or more and show every sign of settling down for good, even when they have no steady job; 80 per cent of their children were born in Germany. In 1984 various schemes came into force for inducing them to leave but the practical effect has not been great. They are discriminated against in practice although not by law. Only 120,000 live in the new Länder, which does not prevent considerable xenophobia there.

A second category consists of non-Germans (and mostly non-Europeans) who claimed on arrival to be seeking asylum from political persecution in their own home countries. When the Basic Law was drafted, memories of how Germans had had to seek asylum were still vivid and a clause was included in its Article 16 guaranteeing entry to such people. To cancel it now would be difficult but there is justifiable suspicion prevalent that the real aim of many of the arrivals is to join in enjoying German prosperity. By 1980 the annual intake had risen to 100,000. Tribunals were set up to test whether cases were genuine and by 1983 the number allowed to stay was down to 20,000 – but by no means all those nominally turned out actually left. By 1986 the figure was back at 42,000, 60 per cent of whom had travelled in Communist transport to East Berlin. To have refused them entry into West Berlin would have been incompatible with the Western contention that the city was an indivisible whole. The East German authorities were, however, induced to make transport to their sector of the city dependent on the possession of West German visas. Any allowed to come through are given basic social security but forbidden to work for five years. Each costs the authorities DM 12,000 a year. In 1990 the arrivals numbered 98,000.

Third, 25,000 persons claiming a German origin were allowed by the Polish authorities to leave that country for West Germany in 1971 (see p. 204). Thereafter the numbers fell and persistent pressure was needed to keep the stream moving at all. By 1986, however, the total of 'ethnic' Germans entering from Eastern Europe and Communist-ruled Asia was 43,000 (including 12,500 from the USSR and 27,000 from Poland). In 1990 the figure was 397,000.

Fourth, during the 1980s the numbers arriving in the Federal Republic from the Democratic Republic began to rise again from the low figures to which they sank after the building of the Wall. In 1984 the DDR authorities took to encouraging potential trouble-makers to get out in the (mistaken) belief that those who remained would be more co-operative and in that year the total reached 30,000. In Czechoslovakia 143 took refuge in the West German Embassy (the only country East Germans could visit without a visa) and after long negotiation were allowed to leave for the West. Their example did not go unnoticed. Any DDR citizen arriving in the Federal Republic was automatically entitled to a West German passport.

If all these arrivals had been coming to a country with an expanding population of her own, the pressure would have been serious and, as it was, the short-term problems were considerable. The Mayor of Stuttgart said he 'needed four town halls to house my lot'. But as things are, the annual arrivals are only about double the annual excess of deaths over births. For a long time, however, Western voices have been calling on Communist regimes in the East to relax controls over the movement of their subjects and permit free emigration. This might result from the abandonment of Communism. If so, we may well see during the next five or ten years a horde of several millions presenting themselves at the frontier posts of freedom and demanding admission. This would be a problem for the whole of the West but Germany is the country which it may be expected to hit first.

There will be no great eagerness to let everyone in. The Germans are not unique in disliking foreigners and a vigorous nationalistic backlash would not be surprising. But it is hard to keep out indefinitely people who are determined to get in. How far moreover is a rigid policy of 'no admission' compatible with internal freedom? History suggests that countries generally benefit from a generous immigration policy and, with the indigenous population falling, shortages of personnel might be a constraint on growth. But too many strangers, admitted too fast, can be a serious obstacle to consolidation. Germany does not want her task of reintegration made more difficult than it is anyhow likely to be.

IN BRIEF

In February 1985 terrorism raised its head again. Between then and April 1991 three top businessmen and a diplomat were murdered and two officials had narrow escapes. Oskar Lafontaine, the SPD candidate for the Chancellorship in 1990, and Wolfgang Schäuble, Kohl's Minister of the Interior, were both seriously wounded. The last two were the deeds of lone wolves but perhaps the most disturbing thing about the other cases was the inability of the authorities to trace the criminals who had clearly learnt a number of precautions by watching how previous terrorists had been caught. The most serious loss was Detlev Rohwedder, the man in charge of privatizing East German industry.

In July 1987 Bonn's attention was drawn by Washington to the plant for making chemical weapons which a Baden firm had been exporting to Libya. The German authorities took no action (probably because the evidence was too flimsy) and were consequently embarrassed when the story broke in *Der Spiegel* in January 1989.

During a Land election in Schleswig-Holstein in September 1987 a journalist disclosed that he had been hired by the CDU Minister-President Barschel to engage in dirty tricks against the SPD leader Bjorn Engholm. After flatly denying the story, Barschel committed suicide. The ensuing vote left the CDU dependent on an estranged FDP for a majority of two; after eight uncomfortable months, a fresh election brought the SPD 54 per cent of the votes.

In November 1987 Honecker was at last allowed by the Soviet Union to visit West Germany and see once again his birthplace in the Saar. The number of visits in both directions which were taking place at this period included a private one by Kohl to Dresden.

In October 1988 Franz Joseph Strauss died suddenly. He left behind him no successor with an equally forceful character and the Atlantic Alliance lost a champion.

In the following November a mishandled ceremony in the Bundestag celebrating the fiftieth anniversary of the *Kristallnacht* (see p. 66) led to the resignation of the Chairman, whose speech was misinterpreted as an apologia for the Nazis – another reminder of how sensitive the subject still was.

None of these episodes did anything to help Kohl's image and speculation was growing as to whether the SPD would be able to reach a sufficiently firm relationship with the Greens to enable them to form a government after the 1990 election.

In reality of course West Germany was on the verge of a transformation which would alter many things, including the historical reputation of Helmut Kohl.

16

THE IMPOSSIBLE HAPPENS:
1989–1990

Torrents sometimes start as trickles. Early in May 1989 the Hungarians, in the process of absconding from Communism, began dismantling the barriers which separated them from Austria and allowing refugees from the DDR to pass through without the documentation which had usually been required. This was reported on West German television, watched widely in East Germany, and thus became common knowledge. In August 600 East Germans, who had been allowed to attend a Pan-European Conference at the Hungarian town of Sopron, decided to go west rather than home. The number of those waiting in Budapest refugee camps to follow their example grew so fast that early in September the Hungarian authorities decided to disregard their arrangements with the DDR regime and allow campers to leave without formality; 15,000 did so in the next three days and 50,000 before the end of October. Others sought sanctuary in the West German Embassies in Prague and Warsaw and after elaborate negotiations were taken in sealed trains across East Germany to the West. The monthly total of emigrants had reached the level at which it had been decided in 1961 that a wall was indispensable.

Ironically, plans had been made to celebrate on 7 October the fortieth anniversary of the Democratic Republic's establishment. Honecker, who had been ill, returned to work and Gorbachev came to Berlin for the occasion. Over a thousand people gathered where he was staying and shouted for him to come out. They were dispersed by the police with some brutality but the man for whom they were calling made clear to his hosts that the time had come for changes, including the removal of their chief: 'Life Punishes Those Who Arrive Late'. He also told them that Russian troops would not be allowed to take any part in repression.

For some time past the Protestant Churches in East Germany had been encouraging non-violent agitation for reform, without any mention of reunification. On several recent Mondays, crowds had gathered at a church in Leipzig to pray for peace and demonstrate for freedom. On 9 October the number grew to about 70,000. Honecker and other hard-liners wanted to take a leaf out of the Chinese book and open fire; as a preparation powerful forces had been brought into the city. There is some dispute as to who took the decision not to use them. There is a story that it was brought about by the conductor Kurt Masur, a priest and a cabaret artist. But the main responsibility almost certainly lay with Egon Krenz, a member of the Politburo who nine days later succeeded Honecker.

The younger generation who were taking over the Government in what amounted to a DDR Wende were at their wits' end. The hopes for a better future which had sustained them for a few years after the Wall was built were fading. Only the lavish payments from the BRD were saving them from economic collapse. The renewed stream of emigrants was making sound organization impossible and demonstrating that they had not won the hearts of their subjects. Unless they were prepared to be brutal their authority was lost. Little help could be expected from the Russians who were in not much better shape themselves; indeed in some directions Moscow was making things harder for them, as by denying them the benefit of lower oil prices. It was not as though they were agreed among themselves on what to do next. Could the system be reformed or must it be scrapped? Only a few people as yet realized that scrapping would remove the justification for existence as a separate state.

The Communists who still ruled in Prague were afraid that, if emigrants from the DDR went on getting out through Czechoslovakia, they would exercise a disturbing influence on that country. The DDR Government was accordingly asked to discharge them directly to the West. The question of freedom to travel abroad was as a result one of the first topics to be considered by the new Politburo under Krenz. Knowing that the ban on travel was one of the main grievances and wishing to get off to a good start, they decided to remove it. The decision was announced at a television News Conference in East Berlin at 7 p.m. on Thursday 9 November. It took a little while for the news to spread and for the implication to sink in that this meant the end of the Wall. But by 10 p.m. a considerable crowd had collected at the *Invalidenstrasse* crossing-point, demanding to be let through. The guards seem to have been without instructions and at first tried to stick to the rule that everyone must have a visa. But the crowd was growing so fast that this line could not be held for long. Over the weekend 2 million East Germans passed through, each collecting the DM 100 which it was the Federal Republic's practice to give to every arrival. The great majority then went home again but only after seeing with their own eyes what a wealthy modern metropolis was like. On 13 November Krenz was replaced on Russian initiative by Hans Modrow, a moderate Communist from Dresden.

Three factors combined to make the continued existence of a separate East German state impossible. First came Gorbachev's decision to abandon the Soviet Union's domination over Eastern Europe. It had been a fundamental assumption of 'Kremlin watchers' that 'the Soviet Union would rather go to war than let somebody take away from it the main prize of its historic victory in the Second World War – Eastern Europe' (V. Micunevic, *Moscow Diary*, 22 March 1956). Gorbachev must be presumed to have decided that the Union did not have enough resources to keep up militarily with the Americans and at the same time modernize itself. Moreover the Soviet Union badly needed German help for that modernization. Thus the impossible could happen. Second, the new men in the DDR brought to light the extent to which their predecessors had been feathering their own nests. Private citizens who had been accepting sacrifices to keep the regime going lost their willingness to continue doing so. Finally personal contact with West Germany drove home the amount of things – by no means all material – which were missing in the East.

What would have happened without Gorbachev is hard to say – probably a different crisis later. But apart from him it is to the men and women in the streets that the credit must go – 'We the people' as they described themselves in their proclamations. Many of those who might have helped to give a lead had left the country but enough stayed to prevent the upheaval from being a mere change of Communist bosses. It took some time for the Germans on the west side of the Elbe to appreciate the full significance of what was happening. In answers to opinion polls they had nearly all professed to want unification but seemed in no great hurry to bring it about: those who expected it to come quickly had fallen from 88 per cent in 1966 to 3 per cent in 1987.

Kohl had as usual been playing for time but now one of his moments of action arrived; he decided to exploit the East German movement for reform in order to secure unification. Modrow had talked in a Policy Declaration of 7 November of a 'Community based on Treaty' (*Vertragsgemeinschaft*). On 28 November Kohl propounded a ten-point programme to the Bundestag. He caused offence among the occupying Powers by failing to clear it in advance with them but considered, probably rightly, that he had no time to lose.

> We are prepared to take an even more decisive step – namely to develop a confederal structure between both states in Germany with the aim of creating a Federation, that is to say a federal order. But that calls urgently for a legitimate democratic government in the DDR. State organization almost always in our history means Confederation or Federation. We have these historical precedents to go on. What a reunited Germany will ultimately look like is something nobody knows today. But I am convinced that such a unity will come if the people of Germany want it.

Other proposals were:

1 Free elections in the Democratic Republic.
2 Changes in the constitution to allow independent parties to compete.

3 Unconditional immediate humanitarian aid.
4 An Inter-German Fund from which DDR citizens could draw Deutsch-marks for travel abroad. The DDR in return to abolish visa restrictions and compulsory payments by West Germans going east.
5 Negotiations to protect the environment and improve motorways.
6 Co-operation in science and technology.

Three weeks later Kohl met Modrow in Dresden where he confirmed his desire for a Vertragsgemeinschaft and expressed the hope that they could get a document creating such an institution not just drafted but signed by the late spring. Modrow spoke of discussing unity in a year or two's time. Most people were still thinking on such a time scale. A long process of debate would lead to the drafting of a new constitution embodying ideas from the East as well as the West. But it was not clear whether Modrow's Government carried enough weight to negotiate reunion and reform the country at the same time.

On 22 December Kohl and Modrow joined in a ceremonial re-opening of the Brandenburg Gate in Berlin; it had been postponed for over a month while Kohl ensured that he got the lion's share of the publicity. But January 1990 was a month of uncertainty. In February five decisions clarified the way forward. Gorbachev gave his blessing to Modrow's ideas. Kohl, instead of supporting Modrow, undermined his authority by saying that the Federal Government would not negotiate until a free election had shown what the people of East Germany really wanted. The date for the election was brought forward to 18 March. A '2+4' procedure was settled by which proposals agreed between the two Germanies should be approved by the four Occupying Powers and finally submited to the (Helsinki) Conference for Security and Co-operation in Europe. Preparation began for replacing the East German Mark with the Deutschmark.

At about this time the idea began to spread that the easiest route to reunification lay in Article 23 of the Basic Law which provided for that Law to be put in force in 'other parts of Germany' (over and above the original Länder). If the Democratic Republic were again divided into the five Länder of Mecklenburg, Brandenburg, Thuringia, Saxony and Saxony-Anhalt (as it had been from 1949 to 1952), each could then accede individually and there would be no need to draft a new constitution. This course had the additional advantage of committing the new entrants to the safeguards for democracy which the Basic Law contained (see p. 126) and confirming the signature by the united Republic of the Nuclear Non-Proliferation Agreement, both of which steps were calculated to reassure Germany's neighbours. On the other hand, it dashed the hopes of those, particularly in the DDR, who wanted to see a Constituent Assembly called to draft a new Constitution amending the Basic Law in a popular direction. To proceed by Article 23 meant that the Basic Law would become the permanent constitution and could be amended only by the rather exacting procedures laid down in its Article 73.

The weeks preceding 18 March were hectic. Emigrants were still streaming westwards; 145,000 left between the New Year and the election. Bonn's Interior Minister refused to discourage them by suspending the payments made on arrival. Nobody had any faith in a currency due to disappear (on terms not yet settled) within four months. There were rumours of a counter-revolution led by the Security Police (*Stasi*). The 'Potemkin' parties which had been allowed to coexist with the Socialist Unity Party in the DDR had no knowledge of how to organize a democratic election campaign and little money with which to do so. Their Western counterparts (and particularly the CDU) moved in and took over. The situation was typified by the story of the taxi-driver who, on being asked how he would vote, replied 'Kohl' and proved not to know who led the CDU in the East. The SPD, who had been unable to decide whether they wanted reunification quickly, or even at all, were left at the post. Although an opinion poll a week beforehand gave them 44 per cent of the votes, in the event they received only 22 per cent as against 48 per cent for the CDU 'Alliance for Germany'. The only other Party to get any appreciable number of votes was the Socialist Unity (SED), rechristened the Party of Democratic Socialism, with 16 per cent.

A Coalition government was set up, headed by a viola player called Lothar de Maizière. There was some resentment among the Eastern politicians about the way in which they felt they had been hustled but Kohl clearly considered that, as Bismarck once said, he had 'felt the footsteps of God sounding through history and lent forward to catch the hem of his cloak'. He could not be sure how long Gorbachev would continue to control Soviet policy.

At that stage unification was still thought to be some way ahead, perhaps coinciding with the completion of the Common Market in 1992. The next step towards it was currency conversion. The official rate of exchange was four East German Marks for one Deutschmark, the black market rate even lower. Otto Pöhl, the President of the Bundesbank, considered that the most generous rate which could be afforded was two to one. Anything higher would involve the creation of so much money as to provoke inflation. Pöhl is a man of great authority and the law establishing the Bundesbank made it free from political control. But if the two to one rate had been adopted, the average monthly wage of an East German worker, already half that obtaining in West Germany, would have been halved again (and prices were expected to rise). The flood of refugees, instead of slackening, would increase. Kohl intervened to lay down that the rate would be one to one and that it would be introduced on 1 July. Pöhl had to fall into line. Holders of savings accounts were, however, to exchange only 1,000 Marks at that rate; anything more was blocked for withdrawal at a later date.

The disappearance of its currency deprived the DDR Government of most of its economic functions so that a main reason for its existence had vanished and the case for bringing forward the date of reunification became strong. In his eagerness to lose no time, Kohl on 15 and 16 July broke in on Gorbachev's holiday in the Caucasus and settled the international aspects of the matter. The Soviet Union claimed that it was logistically impossible for them to withdraw their troops from their former Zone immediately. It was agreed that they might stay until 1994 and Germany promised to contribute towards the cost of their withdrawal. No NATO troops were to be stationed inside the area until Soviet troops had gone and no nuclear weapons even after that. The united Germany was to be free to join whichever alliances it chose. These arrangements were formalized in a 2+4 treaty signed in Berlin on 12 September. In that document the West German Government undertook that its all-German successor would in three to four years reduce its armed forces to 370,000 personnel. American, British and French troops would 'upon German request' continue to be stationed in Berlin as long as there were Soviet troops on German soil.

The issue which was left outstanding in this agreement was the western frontier of Poland. Kohl had more than once been pressed to give a binding guarantee that Germany would recognize the Oder–Neisse line but had always stopped short of saying so explicitly. In the end the Treaty contained a clause saying that the united Germany and the Republic of Poland should confirm the existing border between them in a treaty which would be binding under international law. (Such a treaty was in fact signed on 17 June 1991). One reason for delay was the German argument that such a promise could be given categorically only by an elected all-German Parliament. But the refugee lobby in the Federal Republic were protesting vigorously against any such commitment being given at all. Most of them were CDU voters and Kohl, to keep them faithful, may have wanted to demonstrate that not only the Russians but also the Western Powers were not going to sign any treaty which did not contain such a pledge.

A Federal election was due towards the end of the year and there was some argument as to whether reunification should take place before or after it; on 3 August an agreement was signed between the two Germanies by which it was to come first, on 3 October. The existing electoral arrangements, including the 5 per cent qualifying vote, were to be applied, although this was subsequently changed by a verdict of the Constitutional Court so that for this once the percentages were to be counted separately in each half of the state.

By now it was merely a question of working out the arrangements for assimilating East and West. For during the years in which the Democratic Republic had been a separate state, it had inevitably developed legal and social systems of its own. To replace these systems with Western ones immediately and completely was clearly impossible; the process will take several years. Only broad principles could be laid down which was done after strenuous negotiation in a treaty signed on 31 August. It included a commitment that Parliament would consider within two years whether any amendments should be made to the Grundgesetz. As a rule it was the Western text, unfamiliar to Eastern administrators, which got adopted. Two matters caused particular difficulty. One was abortion, where the Eastern law was more liberal than the Western; it was agreed to leave both in operation for the time being. The second concerned the custody of the personal files of the Eastern Secret Police, with all the light which they threw on how far individuals had secretly helped the Communists; it was agreed that for the time being these should stay in the East.

But what was to happen to property in the East which had been confiscated from or left behind by people or organizations who were now outside? This was something which could be settled only gradually, case by case. The one general principle established was that claims for compensation could not be considered if they dated from the years 1945–9 when the Occupying Powers rather than the Germans were in control. Former owners of property confiscated after 1933 or 1949 had a right to restitution or compensation. There was also the problem of how far the new regime would continue to employ the officials, not to mention the troops, who had served the old one. Rather than agree to some of the solutions proposed, the SPD and FDP representatives in the East German Ministry resigned towards the end of August.

Unification took place on 3 October. Weizsäcker became the First President of the new Germany and Kohl Chancellor; 144 members of the People's Chamber joined the Bundestag; the arrangements for the Bundesrat had still to be settled (but see p. 128). Five ministers from the East moved to Bonn and were given offices but nothing specific to do. These arrangements were temporary until after the first all-German election on 2 December. But on 14 October the five new eastern Länder elected their assemblies according to normal West German law. The CDU gained an absolute majority in Saxony and were the strongest party in Mecklenburg, Thuringia and Saxony-Anhalt. Only in Brandenburg did the SPD come out top.

On 9 November, the anniversary of the opening of the Wall, Gorbachev came to Bonn to sign a Treaty of Good Neighbourliness, Partnership and Co-operation, another on economic, scientific and technical co-operation and two more regulating the position of Soviet troops in Germany until 1994. This was his reward for his willingness to acquiesce in reunification.

The whole process was completed by the all-German election on 2 December. This was won comfortably by the CDU/CSU with 43.8 per cent. The SPD fell to 33.5 per cent whereas the FDP rose to 11 per cent. The most surprising result was provided by the Greens who fell to 3.9 per cent in the country as a whole; they did, however, obtain 5.9 per cent in the East and as this was in this election alone being counted separately, they got two seats. If the country had been treated as a single unit, only the three major parties would have secured representation. Overall Kohl had a majority of 134.

When it came to distributing Cabinet seats at the end of December, only three out of twenty went to people from the East. De Maizière fell under suspicion of having helped the Secret Police and retired into the background, giving up politics altogether eight months later.

17

WHAT NOW?

A main theme of this book has been the ebb and flow of integration in Germany through the centuries. The power amassed by several great Emperors between Charlemagne and Barbarossa was lost by their successors to Popes and Princes. Centrifugal forces waxed as the Middle Ages waned. They were further strengthened by the Reformation and the Thirty Years' War. Only towards the end of the eighteenth century did the tide begin to turn; only by a compromise between local and national loyalties did unification become possible. After it was achieved the process of consolidation developed steadily until in 1914 the Social Democrats voted for the war credits. But it was not long before disintegration set in and continued until 1933. The Nazis then made the creation of a single united people (*ein Volk*) top priority and, in spite of their brutalities, had gone a long way to success by June 1940. By the time of the *Stunde Null* in 1945, consensus had been lost again. Success led the citizens of the Federal Republic to take a pride in their four-fifths of a nation but the rulers of the remainder were incapable of rousing enough loyalty to make their society durable. Now the political framework of a single German nation has been re-established in a form which assigns a considerable role to the Länder Governments. Is it likely to prove more permanent than its predecessors?

I

The task which has faced the Government of Reunited Germany since the middle of 1990 is, at first sight, predominantly one of economic management. Can sufficient resources be deployed in the area of the former Democratic Republic for it to achieve reasonably soon a standard of living approximating to that of the rest of the country? In the autumn of 1990 the capital stock of the western areas was estimated at DM 62,000 per inhabitant and that of the eastern at DM 12,000. On that basis there is therefore a gap to be filled of DM 50,000 per inhabitant, that is DM 800 billion. In the summer of 1991 the West was said to be transferring funds to the East at a rate of 5 to 6 per cent of its gross national product (DM 2,260 billion in

239

1989) say, about DM 132 billion per annum. If all those funds could be directed to re-equipment, the process could be complete in about six years. But all along the trouble has been the many other calls being made on the money available. As firms closed down are no longer able to pay their taxes, the Land and local authorities have no longer been able to pay wages to those in work or give relief to those out of it and the gap has had to be subsidised. The Office of the Trustee carrying through the privatization has had to be financed. DM 15 billion is going to help Russia meet evacuation expenses, DM 11.6 billion to help meet Allied expenses in the Gulf War. It was said that, of the first DM 100 billion made available, only a quarter was actually used for its original purpose. Some of the hard cash handed out to individuals was spent on replacing shoddy domestic goods with high-class imports from the West. This gave the West its biggest growth figure for fourteen years but did little to solve the basic problem of how obsolete factories in the East were to be got going again.

No doubt it was such experiences which led one commentator to predict that even if the East were to grow at the rate of Japan in the 1960s, the job would not be completed this side of the millennium. Such pessimism overlooks the possibilities that many of these expenses will not recur and that before long the East may start contributing to its own renewal.

The collapse of Communism came so unexpectedly that the Bonn Government can hardly be criticized for not having worked out how to meet it. But one cannot help feeling that after that collapse a more thorough-going attempt should have been made to fix on a figure for overall expenses and balance it against resources. Instead Kohl rushed into assurances that nobody would be any the worse off and that taxes would not have to be raised. If his aim was to avoid frightening the public about the size of the task facing them, and thereby lose votes, he achieved the opposite of his intention.

A further mistake was made over the clause in the Treaty of Union, promising restitution or compensation to all who had lost property since 1949. The mere filing of the 1.2 million claims took several months while few could be accepted without scrutiny, which involved East German lawyers trying to understand West German law. Consequently, there are many cases where nobody can yet be certain what liabilities or obligations are attached to particular pieces of land or property. Few business people are ready to risk their money until they have some assurance as to what the final bill will be. The transfer of emphasis from restitution to compensation was made only after time had been lost. Fixing the scales of compensation has proved unexpectedly difficult, with principles being laid down by judges rather than Ministers (see p. 132). For some years the impact on the budget may be considerable.

Kohl himself does not seem to have much interest in, or understanding of, economics while Waigel, the Minister of Finance, and Möllemann, the

Minister of Economics (said to be at daggers drawn), compare badly with Erhard, Schiller and Schmidt. They may have saddled their country with a bigger burden than they had realized; the Government is overspending by DM 200 billion in 1991 and is likely to do the same in 1992. Plans to reduce this by cutting subsidies have run into obstruction. The Balance of Payments went into deficit for the first half of 1991.

To have spent any less, however, would have increased the risk of the 'Ossies' remaining poor relations with a grievance. And the Germans are as well qualified as anyone to succeed. Their capacity for organization, public spirit and determination is well known. They have the third largest economy in the world. Nearly all the capital expenditure will stay in the country. By the time the programme has been carried through, East Germany should have some of the most up-to-date production equipment in the world. The prospect of higher wages should induce workers to make the most of it.

II

Economics must be the first priority but economics are not everything. Integration means not merely establishing the institutions and procedures of Liberal democracy through the five 'new' Länder but also convincing the inhabitants that Liberal democracy is a good way of running a country. There has been a tendency to assume too easily that this will be self-evident, that the new citizens will embrace the open society with open arms. But this is not necessarily so. A number of people in the DDR had hoped to work out for themselves how they were to be governed instead of having the West German system imposed upon them. If all their ideas are persistently disparaged, if all the top jobs (in culture as well as government) go to incomers from the West, if hopes of quick economic improvement are disappointed, if state-sponsored services from which they have benefited disappear without being replaced by voluntary ones, if the price of opera tickets goes up and the amount spent on sports equipment goes down, it is not impossible that people who have not known self-government for over fifty years will start saying 'Well, at least under Ulbricht we had ...'. The Adenauer regime, for reasons which have been explained (see p. 152), showed leniency towards those who had gone along with the brown oppressors. Can its grandchildren treat those who went along with the red ones in the same spirit? A fine line needs to be drawn between criminality and collaboration. The shift of the capital to the heart of the old DDR may help to improve the victor's appreciation of the loser's point of view. And Kohl will hardly want to alienate marginal CDU voters. (What has been said about absorbing immigrants, see pp. 227–9, also applies here.)

It is important in this context to realize that the strength shown by the CDU in December 1990 was probably illusory. Prior to 1933 Saxony and Thuringia were strongholds of the left and, unpopular as Communism may have made itself, enough of the tradition might have been expected to remain for the SPD to benefit. Yet as things turned out, all the thirty-three constituencies in those two Länder returned CDU candidates, while the SPD only managed to win nine of the seventy-one seats in the East. The tarring of Socialism with a Communist brush, assiduously practised by CDU speakers, had clearly been more effective than outside observers realized, while the SPD had been made to pay throughout the DDR years for its refusal to join the SED in 1946 and had difficulty in improvising a machine to fight the election. Moreover, the SPD in West Germany had been uncertain about, and in some cases openly hostile towards, reunification. The vigorous way in which Kohl had carried through the process was much admired and his promises to bring prosperity were, for a time, accepted at face value. But this state of affairs is unlikely to last. By February 1991 opinion polls had begun to show that the two major parties were level again and this was more than confirmed by the Rhineland-Palatinate election in the following April. Even in the December Election the CDU only achieved 44 per cent of the votes so that, unless their policies are bringing indisputable benefits by 1994, they will be unlikely to win an outright majority and might even fall below the SPD.

But the SPD lack a solid core of committed members and their new leader, Engholm, has still to prove himself. They, too, are therefore unlikely to win an outright majority. Both the main parties will need to find allies before they can form a government. Attention therefore turns to the FDP which has two-thirds of its 206,000 members in the East. Reasons have already been given (see p. 218) to explain why this party has cleared the 5 per cent hurdle in recent elections and there is no obvious reason for them ceasing to apply. For a decade or more, the Party has been dominated as regards internal affairs by Count von Lambsdorff, in spite of the blots on his record. But he is due to resign the leadership in 1993, if not before. Once he has gone, the obstacles to a 'reverse turn' (*Gegenwende*) back to a coalition with the SPD will be considerably reduced and this seems the most probable course. Genscher, the elder statesman of the Party, is also likely to retire but, as a native of Saxony-Anhalt, he would hardly object to a change of alliance which brought a more conciliatory policy towards the eastern Länder. What Mölleman, the most likely successor as leader, will favour is hard to say.

Another surprise in the 1990 election was the poor showing of the Greens, who, as has been explained (see p. 237), won only two seats and those in special circumstances which will not be repeated. As the causes of their fall are not clear, the chances of it being permanent are hard to guess. The stock explanation of it is that the 'Realos' have had so many of their distinctive environmental ideas stolen by the other parties as to have no special appeal for the average voter, while the characteristics of the 'Fundis' are so outlandish as to deter such a voter. The Party now appears to have split, leaving it less attractive than ever to the SPD in its search for a coalition partner.

Another party which failed to reach 5 per cent but which was not helped by any 'once only' arrangement, was the Republicans, a neo-nationalist group which a few years ago attracted attention by winning seats in Land elections, notably in Bavaria. Only when one remembers how wrong those people proved who between 1923 and 1933 wrote off the Nazis as a spent force does one hesitate to do the same with the Republicans, especially since their leaders have been quarrelling. There are undoubtedly a certain number of unregenerate authoritarian nationalists in Germany, as there are in most societies. There is in particular an implacable refugee lobby who will go on calling for the recovery of the land lost to Poland and Russia in 1945, as well as of the Sudetenland (which was under German rule only from 1938 to 1945). They are already saying that justified German demands have been sacrificed in the Treaty which Kohl signed with Poland and seem intent on demanding further concessions. How much response they will get from the public remains to be seen but the Government is paying a surprising amount of attention to them. Such is Kohl's anxiety about refugee votes that, when it came to a Treaty with Czechoslovakia, he refused to give any assurance about renouncing claims for lost property. The chief hope for the future is that their leaders are by now very old men. What is less reassuring is that neo-Nazi youth gangs are active in the East.

Under a label of Democratic Socialism, the former DDR Communists did manage to win 2.4 per cent of the votes in December 1990 and as a result hold sixteen seats. If, however, they did the same again in 1994, the 5 per cent bar would apply to keep them out of the Bundestag; to surmount it, they would have to win more seats in the West than they have ever done since 1949. They seem to have acquired some former Communist funds and put them out of reach abroad. Much will depend on where German radical thought is going to find its inspiration now that, as it seems, both Marxism and the centrally planned economy are discredited. If all the various streams could manage to combine they might make up a force to be reckoned with; on past showing, however, they are more likely to fragment into ineffective-ness. Even so, they would complicate the political scene. The disturbing effect which any appreciable number of left-wingers, mainly based in the East, would have on social relationships would be exacerbated by lingering suspicions as to the help which individuals may have given to the Stasi.

Any great increase in votes for either the Democratic Socialists or the Republicans would involve a reversion to the political situation of 1928–33 and be a sign that the trend towards integration had halted. But while the dangers from the extremes should not be trivialized, neither should they be exaggerated. The course on which the German Government has embarked is no forlorn hope, even though if it is to succeed it will need good judgement to be displayed in allocating resources between the innumerable calls made on them. Moreover a number of Germans have learnt lessons since 1945 and had their eyes opened by defeat and by all that the name Auschwitz symbolizes. The bulk of the Western population takes a well-deserved pride in what has been achieved, especially when contrasted with the failure next door. Democracy probably now has the numbers prepared to act in its defence who were lacking in 1930. This time the radicals might be faced by a Great Coalition which did not break up.

III

Two international relationships have been established to protect the Western community against both Communism and Nationalism. There is first of all NATO, with its policy of 'Double Containment', devised primarily in North America with the aim of containing the Soviet Union by organizing the Atlantic World in a military alliance and of containing Germany by entangling her in that alliance. Western politicians are fond of expressing confidence that this will not change. But the substitution by the Russias of self-containment for self-aggrandisement is (if permanent) a major change and we must take seriously the question of how far the repercussions from it can be kept within limits. What useful purpose can NATO serve now that the threat which it was designed to counter appears to exist no longer? What are its personnel going to talk about when they meet which cannot be discussed more effectively somewhere else? Nobody is likely to court unpopularity by proposing NATO's dissolution. But might it not degenerate into what Churchill called 'innocuous desuetude'?

Moreover, there are signs that one of the assumptions underlying NATO is starting to lose validity. Hitherto the Germans have accepted without demur the ban on their freedom to manufacture atomic, bacterial and chemical weapons, on the understanding that the United States would provide them with nuclear and other cover. But the USA, aware of the need to match their commitments with their resources, are increasingly anxious to economize by withdrawing from Europe. The Germans hesitate to trust a cover provided from the other side of the Atlantic. If they do not start making their own bombs, it will not be for lack of know-how but because of the extra financial burden at a time when they have so many other calls on their resources, reinforced by the pathological nervousness of sections of their population to anything connected with nuclear power, even for peaceful uses. While it is to be hoped that nuclear weapons will be reduced in number, they are unlikely to disappear altogether.

The Americans for their part are becoming increasingly restive at the German addiction to high interest rates. Haunted by the memory of the

1930s slump they want above all else to maintain high employment and regard tight interest rates as an obstacle to doing so. The Germans, haunted by the memories of two inflations, want above all else to keep their currency stable and regard tight rates as the best way of doing so. The Americans are prepared to risk inflation to create jobs, the Germans to risk unemployment to keep prices down. The deficits which reunification is bringing will make their monetary authorities more obstinate. Kohl is said to be a fervent supporter of the Atlantic Alliance. Can he reconcile the two views?

Further discord has resulted from the second relationship established as a safeguard against German expansion – the European Community. When this was first proposed, Americans welcomed it in the belief that a United States of Europe would lead to prosperity, just as a United States of America had done, and thus be in a better position to defend themselves against Communism. They did not envisage the possibility that measures taken to make the Community prosperous would act as a barrier to American exports. The high prices, with their protective effect, which characterize the Common Agricultural Policy, originated from a German wish to safeguard their small farmers. More recently the Federal Republic, with the same interest in mind, has taken a lead in encouraging the Community to resist an American demand for a lowering of duties on food, with the result that the Uruguay Round of negotiations under the General Agreement on Tariffs and Trade came to a halt and may still end without agreement. Seeing how dependent the Federal Republic is on exports, this deference to a domestic lobby seems short-sighted.

At Maastricht the Community set itself an ambitious programme and the question naturally arises as to whether the timetable can be kept. Can the Community be widened by taking in new members and at the same time deepened by the responsibility for additional vital decisions being trans ferred from the individual governments to the centre? Can the decisions be taken and acted on speedily? Will the écu supersede the various national currencies and will uniform interest rates be fixed by a Central Bank? How immune will that Bank be from political pressure by the various member governments?

Much is clearly going to depend on the willingness of Germany to allow the écu to replace the Deutschmark. The German price for such a surrender will be high. Candidates for inclusion in an écu Zone will have to prove that they have achieved and can maintain strict standards of sound finance. If enough states qualify to justify the creation of such a Zone it will be dominated by Germany (unless the effort to absorb the eastern lands undermines her own financial standards). She will be achieving by consent the position which she so nearly imposed by force in 1940. But if too few states pass the test, or if too many decide against attempting it, the Community may gradually grind to a halt and Germany find herself free to deploy her power in other directions.

Eastern Europe is the most obvious of these. There still seems to be just a chance of governments being established in that area which are reasonably prosperous, reasonably stable and reasonably humane. Alternatively, there is an obvious danger of a descent into 'Balkanization' – small units inadequately integrated and ruled, as a result, by people unwilling to risk being tolerant either at home or abroad. Which of the two possibilities is realized will depend largely on the volume of resources (including men as well as money) which can be deployed in the area during the next few years. The indigenous ones are palpably inadequate and there must be limits to what can be spared from outside.

Here again eyes turn eagerly towards Germany. She would be the first to suffer if Eastern Europe disintegrates but Kohl has emphasized that the task of preventing this cannot be left to her alone. Nor would the rest of the world be happy if in the course of establishing order she obtained a dominating control over the area's resources. A Germany backed up by Russia has long been a statesman's nightmare. Who would be strong enough to contain the combination? Much has been heard of another Marshall Plan, in which Germany would be reinforced by American resources to modernize Eastern Europe. But will those Americans who see that the US cannot disinterest itself in Europe be able to prevail for a second time in very different circumstances over those who say that they have enough on their hands at home? Here is another possible cause of recrimination between Washington and Bonn/Berlin.

The tide of German power has a prospect of rising higher than ever before in peacetime. But for it to get and stay there, her rulers must show vision in two directions. One is to convince her newly acquired citizens (and particularly the workers) that they are getting a fair deal; failure in this could mean internal weakness, at worst civil war. The second is to convince her neighbours that she will use her strength for the benefit of others as well as herself; failure here could mean a return to 'encirclement', at worst international war. The task of the other Western nations is to convince her that, if she will give the integration of the Continent priority over empire-building, they will be ready to meet her halfway.

ANNEXE: THE CURRENT VOTING SYSTEM FOR FEDERAL ELECTIONS

Each voter has two votes. To exercise them, the voter must be over 18 and must have resided in a constituency district for at least three months prior to the election. The elector can then vote without further formality in that district. If unable to do so, he/she can apply for a voting card which enables the vote to be cast either in any other district of that constituency or by post.

Germany is divided into 328 constituencies roughly equal in population; their boundaries have to be reappraised in the year following an election by a commission of seven appointed by the President; the Commission reports to the Government which is bound to submit the report to the Bundestag.

The elector's first vote has to be given to an individual candidate in the relevant constituency. Nobody can stand in more than one constituency. Whichever candidate gets a simple majority on the first ballot is elected (as in a British election).

The second vote, which can be cast independently of the first, is for a party. Each party draws up a list of candidates for each Land; no candidate can stand on more than one Land list. This provision is designed to ensure that candidates are chosen by the Land organization, not centrally. Candidates may, however, stand both for a Land list and for a constituency. The names of candidates who are successful in the constituencies are then automatically removed from the Land list.

Until the election of 1987 a complicated system, called the d'Hondt method, was used for translating the number of second votes cast for each of the parties into the number of seats allocated to them in the Bundestag. In 1987 this was given up for the Hare-Niemeyer method, which is supposed to counter possible bias in favour of large parties in its predecessor. In the Hare-Niemeyer method, each party's total second votes are multiplied by the total number of seats in the Bundestag and the resulting figure is then divided by the total number of second votes received by all parties. The quotient gives the total number of seats to which the party is entitled. This is now divided between the Länder according to the proportion of its total second votes which the party has won in each Land. The number of seats won by each party in constituency contests in each Land is then subtracted from the total number to which it is entitled in that Land. The remaining seats are then allocated to the appropriate number of candidates in the order in which they stand on the Land list. If a party wins more constituency seats than its proportional vote justifies, it retains them, the total number of seats being raised accordingly. This happened in six cases in 1990 and as a result the total number of seats in the Bundestag rose to 662.

No party can have its Land lists taken into consideration unless it wins three constituency seats or obtains 5 per cent of the votes cast in the Federation as a whole. Votes cast for candidates of such parties are not reckoned in working out the share of seats. If Deputies die or retire, they are automatically succeeded by the first candidate left on the Land list for their party at the previous election who did not get a seat.

STATISTICAL APPENDIX

LIST OF TABLES

1 The Länder
2 Party strengths in Bundestag 1949–90 (election years)
3 Party strengths in Länder (Bundestag election, December 1990)
4 Populations in eight countries 1988
5 Growth of populations in eight countries 1871–1988
6 Gross domestic product in six countries 1899–1988 (per head in US dollars)
7 Growth rates in gross domestic product in six countries 1955–88 (averages of annual percentage increases)
8 National expenditure on consumption and investment in seven countries 1938–88 (proportion of GDP)
9 Unemployment in six countries 1970–89 (% of working population yearly average)
10 Comparative burdens of taxation in six countries 1990
11 Consumer price index in five countries 1948–89
12 Balance of payments of the Federal Republic on current account 1950–90 (DM billion)
13 Exports of the Federal Republic by destination and description 1989
14 Percentage shares of world trade in manufactures 1899–1989
15 Defence burden in eight countries 1990
16 Percentage of 16–18 age group participating in education and training in seven countries 1986

Table 1 The Länder

Land	Area in sq km	Pop. in 1989 (000)	% of total population	Pop. per sq km	Capital	Year of next election	Composition of government
Baden Württemberg	35,751	9,619	17.2	269	Stuttgart	1992	CDU
Bavaria (Bayern)	70,554	11,221	14.2	159	Munich	1993	CSU
Berlin	883	3,410	4.3	3,862	Berlin	1993	CDU/SPD
Brandenburg	29,059	2,641	3.3	91	Potsdam	1994	SPD/FDP/Bündnis 90
Bremen	404	674	0.9	1,668	Bremen	1995	SPD
Hamburg	755	1,626	2.1	2,154	Hamburg	1995	SPD
Hesse	21,114	5,661	7.2	268	Wiesbaden	1995	SPD/Green
Lower Saxony	47,344	7,238	9.2	153	Hanover	1994	SPD/Green
Mecklenburg–Vorpommern	23,838	1,964	2.3	82	Schwerin	1994	CDU/FDP
North Rhine–Westphalia	34,070	17,104	21.6	502	Düsseldorf	1994	SPD
Rhineland–Palatinate	19,849	3,702	4.7	186	Mainz	1995	SPD/FDP
Saarland	2,570	1,065	1.3	414	Saarbrücken	1994	SPD
Saxony (Sachsen)	18,337	4,901	6.2	267	Dresden	1994	CDU
Saxony–Anhalt	20,445	2,965	3.7	145	Magdeburg	1994	CDU/FDP
Schleswig–Holstein	15,729	2,595	3.3	165	Kiel	1992	SPD
Thuringia	16,251	2,684	3.4	165	Erfurt	1994	CDU/FDP
Total country	356,953	79,070	100.0	222			

Source: Statistisches Jahrbuch 1990.
Notes: West Germany population 62,636,000; East Germany population 16,434,000; in 1988 West Germany contained 26.5 million Catholics and 25.2 million Protestants.

Table 2 Party strengths in Bundestag 1949–90 (election years)

Party	1949	1953	1957	1961	1965	1969	1972	1976	1980	1983	1987	1990
CDU	115	187	215	192	195	192	176	190	174	191	174	269
CSU	24	57	55	50	50	50	49	53	52	53	49	51
SPD	131	150	169	190	202	224	229	214	218	193	186	238
FDP	52	48	41	67	49	30	42	39	53	34	34	79
KPD	15	—	—	—	—	—	—	—	—	—	—	17 (PDS)
Refugees	—	27	—	—	—	—	—	—	—	—	—	—
Greens	—	—	—	—	—	—	—	—	—	27	42	8
German	17	15	17	—	—	—	—	—	—	—	—	—
Centre	10	3	—	—	—	—	—	—	—	—	—	—
Others	38	—	—	—	—	—	—	—	—	—	—	—
Total	402	487	497	499	496	496	496	496	497	498	485	662

Table 3 Party strengths in Länder (Bundestag Election, December 1990)

Land	CDU	SPD	FDP	PDS	B90/Gr
Baden Württemberg	36 + 3	1 + 23	0 + 10	0 + 0	0
Bavaria	43 + 8 (CSU)	2 + 24	0 + 9	0 + 0	0
Berlin	8 + 4	4 + 5	0 + 3	1 + 2	1
Brandenburg	7 + 1	5 + 2	0 + 2	0 + 3	2
Bremen	0 + 2	3 + 0	0 + 1	0 + 0	0
Hamburg	2 + 5	5 + 0	0 + 2	0 + 0	0
Hesse	13 + 9	9 + 11	0 + 6	0 + 0	0
Lower Saxony	20 + 11	11 + 16	0 + 7	0 + 0	0
Mecklenburg–Vorpommern	8 + 0	1 + 3	0 + 1	0 + 2	1
North Rhine–Westphalia	33 + 30	38 + 27	0 + 17	0 + 1	0
Rhineland–Palatinate	12 + 5	4 + 9	0 + 4	0 + 0	0
Saar	0 + 4	5 + 1	0 + 1	0 + 0	0
Saxony	21 + 0	0 + 8	0 + 5	0 + 4	2
Saxony–Anhalt	12 + 0	0 + 6	1 + 4	0 + 2	1
Schleswig–Holstein	9 + 2	2 + 8	0 + 3	0 + 0	0
Thuringia	12 + 0	0 + 5	0 + 3	0 + 2	1
Totals	236 + 84	90 + 148	1 + 78	1 + 16	0 + 8
	320	238	79	17	8

Source: Handbuch des Bundestags.
Notes: The first figure in each pair gives the number of seats won by direct election, the second the number drawn from the Land list. The B90/Gr won no seats by direct election. The figures relate to the Bundestag, not to the various Landtäge.

Table 4 Populations in eight countries 1988

Country	Area (sq km)	Total population (million)	Pop. per sq km	Percentage of total population engaged in (1988)		
				Agriculture	Industry	Services
W. Germany	248,640	61.4	247	4.3	41.2	54.5
E. Germany	107,174	16.4	153	n.a.	n.a.	n.a.
France	549,000	56.2	102	6.8	30.4	62.9
Italy	301,300	57.4	190	9.9	32.6	57.5
Japan	372,030	122.7	330	7.9	34.1	58.0
UK	244,100	57.0	233	2.2	29.4	68.3
USA	9,160,453	246.3	29	2.9	26.9	70.2
USSR	22,654,730	283.7	12.5	n.a.	n.a.	n.a.

Source: EEC, *Basic Statistics of the Community 1990*, p. 17.

Table 5 Growth of populations in eight countries 1871–1988

Country	1871	1891	1913	1936	1946	1966	1988
France	36.1	38.2	39.7	41.9	45.6	49.1	56.2
Germany	41.0	49.4	66.8	68.8	65.2	76.1	77.8
W. Germany	—	—	—	(39)	46.7	59.3	61.4
Italy	n.a.	30.2	34.7	42.4	45.6	53.0	57.4
Japan	35.0	40.0	53.0	69.0	80.0	99.7	122.7
UK	27.4	34.2	45.6	47.1	46.8	54.7	57.0
Russia/USSR	76.5	118.0	175.0	193.0	n.a.	227.3	283.7
USA	38.5	63.0	97.1	128.0	143.7	197.6	246.3

Table 6 Gross domestic product in six countries 1899–1988 (per head in US dollars)

Country	1899	1913	1929	1937	1957	1960	1978	1983	1988
France	360	400	605	540	1,015	3,547	7,120	12,129	17,168
Germany	525	560	625	687	—	—	—	—	—
W. Germany	—	—	—	(775)	1,070	4,323	7,840	12,146	17,907
Italy	185	225	275	260	520	1,909	3,751	10,996	16,422
Sweden	160	475	720	705	1,225	5,384	8,484	12,698	18,675
UK	830	920	915	1,055	1,280	2,988	4,446	11,076	16,994
USA	790	1,000	1,380	1,330	2,185	5,160	8,101	16,064	24,721

Sources: 1899–1957: A. Maizels, *Industrial Growth and World Trade;* 1960–78: OECD, *National Accounts;* 1983–8: EEC, *Basic Statistics of the Community 1990.*

Table 7 Growth rates in gross domestic product in six countries 1955–88 (averages of annual percentage increases)

Country	1955–60	1960–5	1965–70	1970–5	1976–7	1979–81	1983–8
France	4.6	5.9	5.8	4.2	3.1	0.8	2.1
W. Germany	6.3	4.8	4.5	2.4	2.8	0.3	2.5
Italy	5.5	5.1	6.0	3.1	1.7	3.2	3.0
Japan	9.7	10.0	11.8	5.6	6.0	7.7	4.4
UK	2.3	3.2	2.5	2.2	1.2	−3.3	3.6
USA	2.2	4.9	3.2	2.6	4.8	2.3	4.4

Source: EEC, *Basic Statistics of the Community 1990*, p. 40.

Table 8 National expenditure on consumption and investment in seven countries 1938–88 (proportion of GDP)

Country	1938	1948	1957–9 (average)	1971	1978	1988
Private consumption						
France	n.a.	72	66	59	62	60
W. Germany	60	65	59	54	60	61
Italy	62	70	64	64	63	61
Japan	n.a.	n.a.	55	52	57	57
Sweden	71	69	61	54	53	n.a.
UK	77	72	66	62	60	63
USA	75	72	66	63	64	66.5
Public consumption						
France	n.a.	12	14	12	15	19
W. Germany	19	18	13	17	14	13
Italy	20	12	14	14	16	17
Japan	n.a.	n.a.	18	9	10	9
Sweden	11	13	18	23	29	20
UK	14	15	16	19	20	20
USA	12	11	18	21	18	18
Gross fixed capital investment home						
France	n.a.	19	21	26	21	20
W. Germany	19	20	24	27	21	20
Italy	19	21	21	20	19	20
Japan	n.a.	n.a.	22	35	32	30.5
Sweden	19	19	21	21	19	–
UK	10	13	16	18	18	19
USA	11	18	18	17	18	17

Source: EEC, *Basic Statistics of the Community 1990*, p. 43.

Table 9 Unemployment in six countries 1970–89 (% of working population yearly average)

Country	1970	1980	1985	1989
W. Germany	0.6	2.5	7.2	5.5
France	2.5	6.3	10.2	12.1
Italy	5.4	7.7	10.2	12.1
Japan	1.2	2.0	2.6	2.3
UK	2.4	6.1	11.6	6.2
USA	5.0	7.2	7.2	5.3

Source: OECD.

Table 10 Comparative burdens of taxation in six countries 1990

	Personal Income Tax (maximum rate %)	Corporate Income Tax (maximum rate %)	VAT	Petrol (US$ per hectolitre)	Cigarettes (US$ per 20)	Alcohol (US$ per hectolitre)	Total Corporate Tax burden (as % of profit)
W. Germany	53	50	14	28.79	31.95	1,287.88	66.2
France	56.8	37	18.6	43.40	49.40	1,172.22	55.9
Italy	58.1	46.4	19	57.57	56.30	380.30	46.4
Japan	65	44	3	31.78	0.70	2,309.60	59.3
UK	40	35	17.5	29.74	22.13	2,492.93	35.0
USA	36.6	45.3	—	4.51	0.70	706.00	45.3

Source: Institut der Deutschen Wirtschaft 1991, Tables 53–4.

255

Table 11 Consumer price index in five countries 1948–89

Country	1948	1953	1963	1970	1979	1983	1989
France	57	82	105	146	319.7	88	112.7
W. Germany	92	92	111	133.75	209.6	95.7	104.2
Italy	78	88	117	143	447.6	82.7	123.8
UK	64	84	112	151.5	454.6	89.8	121.8
USA	83	93	106	134.4	249.6	92.6	115.3
			1958 = 100			1985 = 100	

Source: Statistisches Jahrbuch.

Table 12 Balance of payments of the Federal Republic on current account 1950–90 (DM billion)

1950	−0.4	1970	2.7
1951	2.3	1971	2.9
1952	2.5	1972	2.6
1953	3.8	1973	12.3
1954	3.6	1974	26.6
1955	2.2	1975	1.0
1956	4.4	1976	1.0
1957	5.8	1977	0.5
1958	5.8	1978	18.4
1959	4.0	1979	−11.0
1960	4.5	1980	−29.5
1961	2.8	1981	−17.3
1962	−2.0	1982	8.2
1963	0.07	1983	13.5
1964	−0.02	1984	27.9
1965	−6.8	1985	48.3
1966	0.07	1986	85.8
1967	9.5	1987	82.5
1968	11.0	1988	88.7
1969	6.2	1989	107.6
		1990	77.4

Source: Bundesbank.
Note: The figures for the second half of 1990 include the external transactions of the former DDR.

Table 13 Exports of the Federal Republic by destination and description 1989

Destination	DM million	Description		DM million
EEC	352,961	Finished products		455,067
Other European countries	117,883	of which Machinery	179,795	
USA, Canada	51,776	Vehicles	114,451	
Developing countries	61,742	Chemicals	83,088	
State trading countries	29,314	Electrical	67,646	
Other	27,866	Clothing	10,587	
		Components		108,438
		Semi-finished goods		36,255
		Raw materials		7,476
		Foodstuffs		4,948
		Other		29,158
Total	641,342			

Table 14 Percentage shares of world trade in manufactures 1899–1989

	France	Germany/ W. Germany	Japan	UK	USA	Rest of world
1899	14.4	22.4	1.5	33.2	11.7	13.4
1913	12.1	26.6	2.3	30.2	13.0	13.4
1929	10.9	20.5	3.9	22.4	20.4	18.6
1937	5.8	16.5	6.9	20.9	19.2	23.5
1950	9.9	7.3	3.4	25.5	27.3	26.6
1958	8.6	18.5	6.0	18.1	23.3	18.5
1970	8.7	19.8	11.7	10.8	18.5	23.3
1979	10.8	20.7	13.6	9.7	15.9	21.2
1989	9.0	20.4	17.6	8.2	15.8	29.0

Sources: 1899–1958: A. Maizels, *Industrial Growth and World Trade;* 1970–89: CSO Monthly Review of External Trade Statistics.

Table 15 Defence burden in eight countries 1990

Country	Defence expenditure ($bn)	Number in active service
France	35.09	461,250
W. Germany	33.92	469,000
E. Germany	11.86 (1989)	137,700
Italy	21.68	389,600
Japan	28.12	249,000
UK	34.88	306,000
USA	300.33	2,117,900
USSR	117.48	3,988,000

Source: Institute of Strategic Studies, *The Military Balance 1990–91.*

Table 16 Percentage of 16–18 age groups participating in education and training in seven countries 1986

Country	16	17	18	16–18
France	87	78	56	74
W. Germany	100	92	80	90
Italy	69	70	56	65
Japan	96	91	51	71
Sweden	92	86	55	78
UK*	89	61	42	64
USA	94	88	59	80

Source: Department of Education and Science, *Statistical Bulletin* January 1990.
Note: * The UK figures for 1988 were 91, 75, 42 and 69 respectively.

FURTHER READING

There are so many books about Germany that it has seemed best to confine the following list (which is far from complete) to secondary works in English. No attempt has been made to cover the military history of the wars or general international history. Many of the books listed themselves contain bibliographies. No book is mentioned more than once. The first section contains books that are also of general interest.

1 FROM TRIBE TO NATIONAL STATE: THE FIRST REICH

Barraclough, G. *Factors in Modern German History* (Oxford, 1946)
Blackbourn, D. and Eley, G. *The Peculiarities of German History* (Oxford, 1984)
Carr, W. *A History of Germany 1815–1945*, 4th edn (London, 1972)
Clapham, Sir John. *The Economic Development of France and Germany*, 3rd edn (Cambridge, 1968)
Craig, G.A. *The Politics of the German Army 1660–1945* (Oxford, 1955)
Dehio, L. *Germany and World Politics in the Twentieth Century* (Eng. transl., London, 1957)
Epstein, K. *The Genesis of German Conservatism* (Princeton, NJ, 1966)
Hamerow, T. *Restoration, Revolution, Reaction: Economics and Politics in Germany 1851–1871* (Princeton, NJ, 1958)
——*The Social Foundations of German Unification* (Princeton, NJ, 1969)
Henderson, W.O. *The Rise of German Industrial Power 1834–1914* (London, 1975)
Holborn, H. *A History of Modern Germany, vol. III 1840–1945* (London, 1969)
Iggers, G.L. *The German Conception of History* (Middletown, Conn., 1968)
Krieger, L. *The German Idea of Freedom* (Boston, Mass., 1957)
Mann, G. *The History of Germany since 1789* (Eng. transl., London, 1968)
Meinecke, F. *The German Catastrophe* (Eng. transl., Cambridge, Mass., 1950)
Morgan, R.P. *The German Social Democrats 1864–1872* (Cambridge, 1965)
Pflanze, O. *Bismarck and the Development of Germany* (Princeton, NJ, vol. I 1815–71, 1963, 2nd edn 1990; vol. II 1871–80, 1990, vol. III 1880–98, 1990)
Pounds, N. *The Economic Pattern of Modern Germany* (London, 1963)
Sheehan, J.J. *German History 1770–1886* (Oxford, 1990)

2 THE SECOND REICH: 1871–1918

Balfour, M. *The Kaiser and his Times* (London, 1964; Harmondsworth, 1975)
Berghahn, V.R. *Germany and the Approach of War in 1914* (London, 1973)

Chickering, R. *We Men Who Feel Most German: A Cultural Study of the Pan-German League* (Boston, Mass., 1984)

Craig, G.A. *Germany 1866–1945* (Oxford, 1978)

Demeter, K. *The German Officer Corps* (Eng. transl., London, 1965)

Eley, G. *Reshaping the German Right* (New Haven, Conn., 1980)

Evans, R. (ed.) *Society and Politics in Wilhelmine Germany* (London, 1978)

—— *Rethinking German History* (London, 1987)

Fischer, F. *Germany's Aims in the First World War* (Eng. transl., London, 1967)

—— *War of Illusions: German Policies from 1911 to 1914* (Eng. transl., London, 1975)

Gall, L. *Bismarck, The White Revolutionary* (Eng. transl., 2 vols, London, 1986–7)

Geiss, I. (ed.) *July 1914, The Outbreak of the First World War: Selected Documents* (Eng. transl., London, 1967)

Guttsman, W. *The German Social Democratic Party 1875–1933* (London, 1981)

Jacob, H. *German Administration since Bismarck* (New Haven, Conn., 1963)

Joll, J. *The Origins of the First World War* (London, 1984)

Kennedy, P.M. *The Rise of the Anglo–German Antagonism 1860–1914* (London, 1980)

Knight, M. *The German Executive 1890–1933* (Stanford, Calif., 1953)

Mayer, J.P. *Max Weber and German Politics*, 2nd edn (London, 1956)

Mommsen, W. (ed.) *The Emergence of the Welfare State in Britain and Germany 1850–1950* (London, 1981)

Mosse, G. *The Crisis of German Ideology* (New York, 1964)

von Müller, G.A. (ed. Goerlitz) *The Kaiser and his Court* (Eng. transl., London, 1961)

Nichols, J.A. *Germany after Bismarck* (Cambridge, Mass., 1958)

Pulzer, P.J. *The Rise of Anti-Semitism in Germany and Austria* (New York, 1964)

Röhl, J. *Germany without Bismarck: The Crisis of Government in the Second Reich 1890–1900* (London, 1967)

Schorske, C. *German Social Democracy 1905–17* (Cambridge, Mass., 1955)

Steinberg, J. *Yesterday's Deterrent* (London, 1964)

Stern, F. *The Politics of Cultural Despair* (Berkeley, Calif., 1961)

—— *Gold and Iron: Bismarck, Bleichröder and the Building of the German Empire* (London, 1977)

Stolper, G. *et al. The German Economy, 1870 to the Present*, 2nd edn (Eng. transl., New York, 1967)

Taylor, A.J.P. *Bismarck* (London, 1955)

Veblen, T. *Imperial Germany and the Industrial Revolution* (New York, 1915)

Wehler, H.-U. *The German Empire 1871–1918* (Eng. transl., Leamington Spa, 1985)

Woodward, Sir Llewellyn. *Great Britain and the German Navy* (Oxford, 1935)

3 THE FIRST ATTEMPT AT DEMOCRACY: 1918–1933

Bennet, E.W. *Germany and the Diplomacy of the Financial Crisis 1931* (Cambridge, Mass., 1962)

—— *German Rearmament and the West 1932–3* (Princeton, NJ, 1980)

Carsten, F. *The Reichswehr and Politics 1919–33* (Oxford, 1966)

Childs, D. *Germany since 1918*, 2nd edn (London, 1980)

Dorpalen, A. *Hindenburg and the Weimar Republic* (Princeton, NJ, 1957)

Dyck, H.L. *Weimar Germany and Soviet Russia 1926–33* (London, 1966)

Eksteins, M. *The Limits of Reason: The German Democratic Press and the Collapse of Weimar Democracy* (Oxford, 1975)

Epstein, K. *Matthias Erzberger and the Dilemma of German Democracy* (Princeton, NJ, 1959)

Fischer, C. *Stormtroopers 1929–35* (London, 1983)
Gatzke, H. *Stresemann and the Re-armament of Germany* (Baltimore, Md, 1954)
Gay, P. *Weimar Culture: The Outsider as Insider* (London, 1969)
Gordon, H. *The Reichswehr and the German Republic 1919–26* (Princeton, NJ, 1957)
—— *Hitler and the Beer Hall Putsch* (Princeton, NJ, 1972)
Halperin, S.W. *Germany Tried Democracy 1919–33* (London, 1963)
Hardach, K. *The Political Economy of Germany in the Twentieth Century* (Berkeley, Calif., 1980)
Hiden, J. *Germany and Europe 1919–39* (London, 1977)
Hunt, R.N. *German Social Democracy 1918–33* (London, 1964)
Kunz, A. *Civil Servants and the Policy of Inflation in Germany 1914–1924* (Berlin, 1986)
Lane, B.M. *Architecture and Politics in Germany 1918–45* (Cambridge, Mass., 1968)
Maier, C. *Recasting Bourgeois Europe: Stabilisation in France, Germany and Italy in the Decade after World War I* (Princeton, NJ, 1975)
Nettl, J.P. *Rosa Luxemburg*, 2 vols (London, 1966)
Nicholls, A. *Weimar and the Rise of Hitler*, 2nd edn (London, 1980)
Noakes, J. *The Nazi Party in Lower Saxony 1921–1933* (Oxford, 1971)
Post, G. *The Civil–Military Fabric of Weimar Foreign Policy* (Princeton, NJ, 1973)
Ryder, A.J. *The German Revolution of 1919* (Cambridge, 1967)
Stachura, P.D. *The Weimar Era and Hitler, 1918–1933: A Critical Bibliography* (London, 1977)
—— (ed.) *The Shaping of the Nazi State* (London, 1978)
Turner, H.A. *Stresemann and the Politics of the German Republic* (Princeton, NJ, 1963)
Wheeler-Bennett, Sir John. *The Nemesis of Power: The German Army in Politics 1918–45*, 2nd edn (London, 1967)
Wright, J.R.C. *'Above Parties': The Political Attitudes of the German Protestant Church Leadership 1918–1933* (Oxford, 1974)

4 THE THIRD REICH: 1933–1945

Allen, W.S. *The Nazi Seizure of Power: The Experience of a Single German Town* (Chicago, Ill., 1965)
Ayçoberry, P. *The Nazi Question: An Essay on the Interpretations of National Socialism 1922–75* (Eng. transl., London, 1981)
Balfour, M. *Propaganda in War 1939–45: Organisations, Policies and Publics in Britain and Germany* (London, 1979)
—— *Withstanding Hitler* (London, 1988)
Balfour, M. and Frisby, J. *Helmuth von Moltke: A Leader against Hitler* (London, 1972)
Bethge, E. *Dietrich Bonhoeffer* (Eng. transl., London, 1970)
Beyerchen, A.O. *Scientists Against Hitler* (New Haven, Conn., 1977)
Bielenberg, C. *The Past is Myself* (London, 1968)
Boelcke, W. *The Secret Conferences of Dr Goebbels 1939–43* (Eng. transl., London, 1970)
Bracher, K. *The German Dictatorship: The Origins, Structure and Effects of National Socialism* (Eng. transl., London, 1970)
Bull, H. (ed.) *The Challenge of the Third Reich* (Oxford, 1986)
Bullock, A. *Hitler: A Study in Tyranny*, revised edn (London, 1964)
Carr, W. *Arms, Autarky and Aggression: A Study in German Foreign Policy 1933–39* (London, 1972)

Carroll, B. *Total War: Arms and Economics in the Third Reich* (The Hague, 1968)
Cecil, R. *The Myth of the Master Race: Alfred Rosenberg and Nazi Ideology* (London, 1972)
Childers, T.C. *The Nazi Voter* (Chapel Hill, NC, 1983)
Conway, J.S. *The Nazi Persecution of the Churches* (London, 1968)
Deist, W. *The Wehrmacht and German Rearmament* (London, 1981)
Deutsch, H. *The Conspiracy Against Hitler During the Twilight War* (London, 1968)
—— *Hitler and his Generals: The Hidden Crisis January–June 1938* (Minneapolis, Minn., 1974)
Dicks, H.V. *Licensed Mass Murder* (London, 1972)
Farquharson, J.L. *The Plough and the Swastika: The NSDAP and Agriculture in Germany 1928–1945* (London, 1967)
Fest, J. *Hitler* (Eng. transl., London, 1974)
Gillingham, J.R. *Industry and Politics in the Third Reich, Ruhr Coal, Hitler and Europe* (London, 1985)
Gordon, S. *Hitler, Germany and the Jewish Question* (Princeton, NJ, 1984)
Graml, H. *et al. The German Resistance to Hitler* (Eng. transl., London, 1970)
Hale, O.J. *The Captive Press in the Third Reich* (Princeton, NJ, 1964)
Hildebrandt, K. *The Foreign Policy of the Third Reich* (Eng. transl., Berkeley, Calif., 1973)
Hoffman, P. *The History of the German Resistance 1933–1945* (Eng. transl., London, 1977)
Kater, M.H. *The Nazi Party: A Social Profile* (Oxford, 1983)
Kershaw, J. *The Nazi Dictatorship: Problems and Perspectives of Interpretation* (Oxford, 1984)
Kogon, E. *The Theory and Practice of Hell* (Eng. transl., London, 1950)
Lerner, D. *The Nazi Elite* (Stanford, Calif., 1951)
Lewy, G. *The Catholic Church and Nazi Germany* (London, 1964)
MacDonough, A. *A Good German, Adam von Trott* (London, 1989)
Manvell, R. and Fraenkel, H. *Hermann Goering* (London, 1962)
—— *Heinrich Himmler* (London, 1965)
Merkl, P.H. *Political Violence under the Swastika: 581 Early Nazis* (Princeton, NJ, 1975)
Merson, A. *Communist Resistance in Nazi Germany* (London, 1987)
Milward, A. *The German Economy at War* (London, 1964)
—— *War, Economy and Society 1939–45* (London, 1977)
von Moltke, H.J. *Letters to Freya* (Eng. transl., London, 1990)
Mommsen, W.J. and Kettenacker, L. *The Fascist Challenge and the Policy of Appeasement* (London, 1983)
Nicholls, A. and Matthias, P. (eds) *German Democracy and the Triumph of Hitler* (London, 1971)
Nicosia, F. and Stokes, L. (eds) *Germans Against Nazism* (New York and Oxford, 1990)
Noakes, J. and Pridham, G. (eds) *Nazism 1919–1945: A Documentary Reader* (four vols, Exeter, 1984–91)
Orlow, D. *The History of the Nazi Party 1919–45* (two vols, Pittsburgh, Pa., 1973)
Peterson, E.N. *The Limits of Hitler's Power* (Princeton, NJ, 1964)
Reitlinger, G. *The Final Solution* (London, 1953)
—— *The SS, Alibi of a Nation* (London, 1956)
Rich, N. *Hitler's War Aims: Ideology, the Nazi State and the Course of Expansion* (two vols, London, 1973)
Schoenbaum, D. *Hitler's Social Revolution* (London, 1967)
Scholder, K. *The Churches and the Third Reich* (vol. I 1918–34, vol. II 1934, Eng. transl., 1987–8)

Schöllgen, G. *A Conservative Against Hitler: Ulrich von Hassell* (Eng. transl., London, 1991)
Schweitzer, A. *Big Business in the Third Reich* (London, 1964)
Shirer, W. *The Rise and Fall of the Third Reich* (New York, 1960)
Smelser, R.M. *The Sudeten Problem 1933–1938:* Volkstumspolitik *and the Formulation of Nazi Foreign Policy* (London, 1975)
Speer, A. *Inside the Third Reich* (Eng. transl., London, 1970)
Stachura, P.D. *The German Youth Movement 1918–45* (London, 1981)
Stein, G.H. *The* Waffen SS: *Hitler's Elite Guard at War 1939–45* (London, 1966)
Steinert, M. *Hitler's War and the Germans* (Eng. transl., Columbus, Ohio, 1977)
Stevenson, J. *Women in Nazi Germany* (London, 1975)
Trevor-Roper, H. *The Last Days of Hitler* (London, 1947)
—— (ed.) *Hitler's Table Talk* (London, 1953)
—— (ed.) *Hitler's War Directives 1939–45* (London, 1964)
Turner, H.A. *Big Business and the Rise of Hitler* (New York, 1985)
Waite, R.G. *Adolf Hitler: The Psychopathic God* (New York, 1977)
Walker, M. *German National Socialism and the Quest for Nuclear Power* (Cambridge, 1990)
Watt, D.C. *How War Came: The Immediate Origins of the Second World War* (London, 1989)
Zeman, Z.A.B. *Nazi Propaganda*, 2nd edn (London, 1973)

5–7 THE POST-WAR PERIOD 1945–1949

Balfour, M. *Four-Power Control in Germany 1945–6* (in the series Toynbee (ed.) *Survey of International Affairs 1939–46*, London, 1956)
Cairncross, Sir Alec. *The Price of War: British Policy on German Reparations* (Oxford, 1986)
Clay, L.D. *Decision in Germany* (New York, 1950)
Davison, W.P. *The Berlin Blockade* (London, 1958)
Ebsworth, R. *Restoring Democracy in Germany: The British Contribution* (London, 1960)
Farquharson, J.L. *The Western Allies and the Politics of Food* (Leamington Spa, 1985)
Feis, H. *Between War and Peace: The Potsdam Conference* (Princeton, NJ, 1960)
Gimbel, J. *The American Occupation of Germany: Politics and the Military 1945–1949* (Stanford, Calif., 1968)
Hearnden, A. (ed.) *The British in Germany: Educational Reconstruction after 1945* (London, 1978)
Heidelmeyer, W. and Hindrichs, G. *Documents on Berlin 1943–1965* (Eng. transl., Munich, 1965)
Hendry, J.D. and Wood, M.C. *The Legal Status of Berlin* (Cambridge, 1987)
Leonhard, W. *Child of the Revolution* (Eng. transl., London, 1957)
Ruhm von Oppen, B. *Documents on Germany 1945–55* (London, 1955)
Smith, B.F. *Reaching Judgement at Nuremberg* (London, 1977)
Snell, J.L. *The Origins of the East–West Dilemma over Germany* (New Orleans, La, 1959)
Wallich, H.C. *Mainsprings of the German Revival* (New Haven, Conn., 1955)
Willis, F.R. *The French in Germany 1945–1949* (Stanford, Calif., 1955)
Zink, H. *The United States in Germany* (Princeton, NJ, 1957)

8–14 THE GERMAN REPUBLICS 1949–1982

Abenheim, D. *Reforging the Iron Cross: The Search for Tradition in the West German Armed Forces* (Princeton, NJ, 1989)

Adenauer, K. *Memoirs 1945–1953* (Eng. transl., London, 1966–8; later vols not translated)

Ardagh, J. *Germany and the Germans* (Harmondsworth, 1988)

Berghahn, V. *Modern Germany* (Cambridge, 1982)

—— *The Americanisation of West German Industry 1945–73* (Leamington Spa, 1986)

Braunthal, G. *The Federation of German Industry in Politics* (Ithaca, NY, 1965)

—— *Political Loyalty and Public Service in West Germany: The 1972 Decree against Radicals* (Amherst, Mass., 1990)

Catudal, H.M. *The Diplomacy of the Quadripartite Agreement on Berlin* (Berlin, 1978)

—— *Kennedy and the Berlin Wall Crisis* (Berlin, 1981)

Cerny, K.H. (ed.) *Germany at the Polls: The Bundestag Elections of the 1980s* (Duke, NC, 1990)

Childs, D. *The G.D.R.* (London, 1983)

Childs, D. and Johnson, J. *West Germany, Politics and Society* (London, 1981)

Cullingford, E.C.M. *Trade Unions in West Germany* (London, 1976)

Dahrendorf, Sir Rolf. *Society and Democracy in Germany* (Eng. transl., London, 1968)

Dyson, K.H.F. *Party, State and Bureaucracy in West Germany* (Beverly Hills, Calif., 1977)

Edinger, L. *Kurt Schumacher* (Oxford, 1965)

Evans, R.J. *In Hitler's Shadow: West German Historians and the Attempt to Escape from the Nazi Past* (London, 1989)

Golay, F. *The Founding of the Federal Republic of Germany* (Chicago, Ill., 1958)

Grosser, A. *Germany in our Time* (Eng. transl., London, 1971)

Hallet, G. *Housing and Land Politics in West Germany and Britain* (London, 1977)

Hanrieder, W.F. *Germany, America, Europe: Forty Years of German Foreign Policy* (New Haven, Conn., 1989)

Hearnden, A. *Education in the Two Germanies* (Oxford, 1974)

Heidenheimer, A. *Adenauer and the CDU* (The Hague, 1960)

—— *The Governments of Germany* (London, 1966)

Lowenberg, G. *Parliament in the German Political System* (Ithaca, NY, 1966)

Ludlow, P. *The Making of the European Monetary System* (London, 1982)

Maier, C.S. *The Unmasterable Past* (Cambridge, Mass., 1988)

Merkl, P.H. *The Origin of the West German Republic* (New York, 1963)

Morgan, R. *The United States and West Germany 1945–1973* (London, 1974)

Preece, R.J.C. *Land Elections in the German Federal Republic* (London, 1968)

Pridham, G. *Christian Democracy in West Germany* (London, 1977)

Pritchard, R.M.O. *The End of Elitism? The Democratisation of the West German University System* (Oxford, 1990)

Prittie, T. *Konrad Adenauer* (London, 1972)

Roberts, G.K. *West German Politics* (London, 1972)

Sandford, J. *The Mass Media of the German-speaking Countries* (London, 1976)

Smith, E.O. *The West German Economy* (London, 1983)

Smith, G. *Democracy in Western Germany* (London, 1987)

Sontheimer, K. *The Government and Politics of West Germany* (Eng. transl., London, 1972)

Sowden, J.K. *The German Question 1945–1973* (Bradford, 1975)

Spiro, H.J. *The Politics of German Co-Determination* (London, 1977)

INDEX

Adenauer, Dr Konrad: attitudes
  towards: Erhard 155, 170; European
  integration 139; ex-Nazis 151–2;
  de Gaulle 167–8, 170; Kennedy 164;
  rearmament 141, 143, 160, 161, 163;
  Ruhr 137; Saar 138; Strauss 169;
  background 119–20, 122; Chairman of
  the Parliamentary Council 123;
  Chancellor 134; election successes
  153; leader of CDU 120; Presidency
  155; retires 170; *Spiegel* Affair 169–70;
  treatment of colleagues 130, 143, 169,
  170; visits Moscow 156
Air Force (*Luftwaffe*) 59, 62, 68, 70, 79
air raids 62, 64, 65, 68, 71, 77–8, 79, 84
Alliances: Anglo-Japanese (1902) 29;
  Austro-German (1879) 29; Franco-
  British Entente (1904) 29; Franco-
  Czech (1921) 65; Franco-Russian
  (1899) 23, 28; Italo-German 'Axis'
  (1936) 63, 67; Russo-British Entente
  (1907) 30; Three Emperors (1881) 21
Anglo-German relations: pre-1914 23–4,
  29, 30–2; 1914–39 33, 46, 63, 65;
  1939– 46 68, 71, 77, 79, 86; 1947–52
  120, 142; 1952–71 146, 171, 191; since
  1971 193, 195
anti-semitism 19, 47, 48, 55, 58, 66; *see
  also* Jews
Austria (1867–1918 Austria-Hungary)
  20, 21, 31, 37, 41, 48, 50, 63, 64, 162

Baden 27, 97; facts about 250; Land of
  Baden-Württemberg 97, 129, 152, 175,
  183; Prince Max of 37
banks: Bank Deutscher Länder 105, 113,
  126; Bundesbank 105, 149, 174, 177,
  178, 190, 196; Reichsbank 47

Basic Law (*Grundgesetz*): amendment in
  1969 179; Articles: (3) 126; (5) 202;
  (12) 112, 127, 202; (16) 228; (19) 126;
  (21) 153, 201, 224; (23) 127, 193, 234;
  (67) 174; (68) 129, 196, 219; (110) 174;
  (131) 151; (146) 132; drafting of
  123– 5; preamble 125; revision 237
Barzel, Dr Rainer 194–6, 200, 225
Basic Treaty (*Grundvertrag*) between
  West and East German Republics
  (1972) 196–7
Bavaria, Land 85, 97, 124; in 1870 13, 14;
  in 1923 44; Bavarian Party 133; CSU
  in 95; elections in 175, 199, 219; facts
  about 250; northern distrust of 199,
  215
Berlin: in 1848 9; in 1945 80, 81, 83, 86,
  87; air raid on (1940) 71; blockade of
  87, 106–9; Congress of 21; facts about
  250; foundation of 4; Jews in 19; Kapp
  Putsch (1920) 43; reinstated as capital
  241; rising in 1918 37; rising in East
  Berlin (1953) 147; second crisis 161–2;
  status of 98, 106, 125, 142, 171, 182,
  193; University 7; unrest in 185; Wall
  164, 166, 167, 171, 231–2
Bethmann Hollweg, Theobold von 28,
  32, 35
Bismarck, Prince Otto von: appointed
  Chancellor 11; character 11, 122;
  policies in office 11–20; quoted 11, 22,
  164, 235
blockade: Allied (1914–18) 33–5, 42;
  Hitler's precautions against 61;
  Russian, of Berlin 106–8, 124
Blomberg, Field Marshal Werner von 53,
  59, 60, 64
Bonn 123, 133; Treaty of 142–3

Brandenburg, Land 4, 235, 237
Brandt, Willy: Chancellor 197, 199, 205, 207; fall of 207; Foreign Minister 176, 182; in 1972 Election 194–7; Lord Mayor of Berlin 154; relations with Jusos 198; relations with Schiller 196; SPD leader 166, 168, 173; visit to Warsaw 192; weaknesses 205–6
Bremen, Land 97, 98, 154; facts about 250
Brezhnev, Leonid: visits Berlin 203
Britain: battle of 70–1; differences between Germany and: Building Societies 150; closed shop 127; consumption–investment ratio 113; delay in forming cabinets 138; education 5, 24, 258; growth of nation state 2; Industrial Revolution 2, 22; mediaeval integration 2; non-conformity 3; Reformation 3; regulation by law 127; size of army 2, 32, 61, 65, 257; see also Anglo-German relations
Brüning, Dr Heinrich 50, 52

cartels: pre-1914 24, 116; Cartel Office 193; decartellization 158
Centre Party: 1871–1914 15, 26, 27, 28, 35; 1919–33 40, 43, 51, 52, 95; wound up 154
Chancellor 13, 14, 15, 22, 40, 60, 129–30, 174; see also individual holders
Christian Democratic Union (CDU): composition 119; Die Wende 217, 220; form coalition government 133; foundation of 95; future 242; in Great Coalition 175, 177, 179; in Parliamentary Council 123, 124; oppose Ostpolitik 194; programmes 121; strengths 98, 251; views on Basic Law 127–8; see also Elections, individual leaders and events
Christian Social Union (CSU): fiasco over Ostpolitik 195; foundation of 95; separate identity of 188, 199, 215, 217; strengths 251; views on policy 159, 217; see also Strauss and Elections
Churchill, Winston: European defence 141, 142; forms government (1940) 69, 72; withdrawal to Elbe (1945) 86; quoted 244; unconditional surrender 75, 76; views on reparations 82
Civil Service 5, 39, 56, 151, 153, 202; see also Radical Decree
Clay, General Lucius 107, 121, 123
closed shop 111, 127
coal 94, 96, 98, 99, 100, 109, 137, 139, 178
co-determination 112, 150, 179, 189, 196, 200
Communists: in 1933 53, 54, 55; after 1919 40, 46–9, 51; after 1945 96, 97, 133, 145, 153, 185, 201; foundation of Party 39; future 243; see also German Democratic Republic
concentration camps 55, 74, 104, 204
Conference on Security and Co-operation in Europe (Helsinki CSCE) 191, 234
Conferences, Summit: Berlin 21; Casablanca 75; Geneva 156; Munich 65; Paris 163; Potsdam 87–90, 92, 95; Versailles 41; Yalta 81–2, 83, 88, 147
Constitutional Court 127, 131–2, 153, 201, 202, 214, 220, 236
Constitutional State (Rechtsstaat) 5, 7, 8, 17, 56–7
Constructive vote of no-confidence 129, 194, 219
Control Council and Commission: breakdown 101, 104; establishment of 81, 89; working of 83, 86, 87, 89, 90, 92, 98, 145
Corn and Iron Alliance 17, 26, 47
Council for the Humanities and Sciences (Wissenschaftsrat) 153
cultural fight (Kulturkampf) 15
currency reform 17, 44–5, 105–6, 109– 12, 235
Czechoslovakia 46, 64–6, 85, 100, 181, 182, 228, 231–3, 243

Defence Authority (Wehrmacht) 60, 71–3; see also Federal Defence Force and Imperial Defence Force
denazification 85, 87, 90, 102, 103, 151
Denmark 68, 74
disarmament 43, 46, 76, 92, 223

Ebert, President Friedrich, 37–40, 46
economic conditions: 1873 16; pre–1914 23–4; 1923 44; 1929 49; 1937 60–1;

1945 88, 92–4; 1948–58 105–16; 1961
149; 1966 172–4; 1967–8 177–80;
1969–71 188–90; 1973 200; 1974
209; 1978 213–14; 1981–2 218;
1982–3 221; 1990 239; statistics
252–5
Education 5, 55, 153, 184, 202–3
Ehard, Hans 134
Eisenhower, General and President
Dwight D. 75, 77, 79, 80, 84, 140, 163
Elections: 1862 11; 1877 15; 1890 22;
1912 27; 1919 40; 1928 47; 1930 50;
1932 52; 1933 54; 1949 133; 1953;
1957 153; 1961 167; 1965 173; 1969
188; 1972 197; 1976 211; 1980 216;
1983 220; 1987 227; 1990 37; Berlin
97; comrade trend 189; electoral
system 247; expenses 224–5; filling of
vacancies 174; see also individual
Länder
Emergency legislation 183, 185
Engholm, Björn 230, 242
Erhard, Ludwig: in Bizonia 109;
Chancellor 166, 168, 170, 171, 174,
189; Minister of Economics 110,
113–14, 122, 134, 155, 158, 168;
resigns 175
Erzberger, Matthias 35, 37, 43, 70, 201
Europe, Council of 138, 141
European Coal and Steel Community
(ECSC) 139–40, 148, 157
European Defence Community (EDC)
141–6
European (Economic) Community
(EEC) 110, 148, 154, 157, 188,
245
European Monetary System (EMS) 210
European Recovery Programme
(Marshall Aid) see Marshall

Federal Assembly (Bundestag): in Basic
Law 125, 128–30, 132, 247–8; Berlin
representation 125, 193; Chairman
resigns 230; composition of 251;
dissolution of 197, 219; functions in
emergency 183; mediation committee
128, 211; see also Imperial Assembly
Federal Council (Bundesrat): after 1815
8; after 1871 13; in Basic Law 124,
127–32; composition after 1990 128;
functions in emergency 183; see also
Federal Assembly, Länder

Federal Defence Force (Bundeswehr)
158–9, 164, 169, 223; see also Defence
Authority and Imperial Defence Force
Five-per-cent voting barrier 125, 198,
236–7, 242–3
Flags 40, 54, 127
Foreign Ministers Meetings: Geneva,
May 1955 156; Geneva, May 1959
159; London, December 1947 and
Spring 1948 101, 122; Messina, May
1955 157; Moscow, March 1947 99;
Paris, May 1949 124
Foreign Workers: 1940–5 74, 84; after
1961 172, 227
Fourteen Points (1918) 36, 41, 42, 75
Franco-German relations: pre–1914 6, 8,
20, 23, 29, 30, 32, 34; 1914–39 43, 44,
46, 50, 63, 68; 1939–46 70, 81;
1947– 52 98, 101, 138–42; 1952–71
145, 167, 170, 171; since 1971 193
Free Democratic Party: change in
character 186; coalition with SPD 166,
187–8, 194, 200, 206, 208; foundation
of 95; future 242; in elections 217, 220,
237; in Parliamentary Council 122–4;
in Spiegel Affair 169–70; new sources
of strength 186; relations with CDU
122, 133–4, 153, 173–5, 202, 211;
Wende 217–18, 220
Freikorps 39, 43, 59

Gaulle, General Charles de 89, 167, 172,
173, 179, 199
General Staff, German 5, 17, 31–2, 43,
64–5, 147
Genscher, Hans Dietrich 188, 206,
217–18, 242
German Democratic Republic (Deutsche
Demokratische Republik): agents in
Federal Republic 206; basic treaty
196–7; development of 141, 145, 158;
dissolution of 231–7; establishment of
108, 135; political events in 147, 161,
191, 193; wall 164–5, 171
German Party 122, 133, 153, 166
Goebbels, Dr Joseph 55, 59, 79, 148, 227
Göring, Field-Marshal Hermann, 53, 56,
59, 60, 69, 73, 90
Gorbachev, Mikhail 223, 227, 231–3,
234, 236–7
Great Coalition 44, 47, 99, 133, 166, 173,
176–87

Greens 214, 217, 220, 227, 230, 242
Gross National Product *see* economic situation
Guilt *see* responsibility
Gulf War 127

Habsburgs *see* Austria
Hallstein doctrine 156, 170, 182, 190
Hamburg, Land 77, 98, 154, 220; facts about 250
Heinemann, President Gustav 143, 170, 187, 206
Hesse, Greater Land 96, 97, 154, 175, 199, 219, 220, 227; facts about 250
Heuss, President Professor Theodor 134, 153, 155
Himmler, Heinrich 56, 59, 60, 73
Hindenburg, Field Marshal Paul von 33, 35, 36, 38, 43, 46, 50, 51, 54, 59, 60, 62
Historians Dispute (*Historiker Streit*) 74, 226, 230
Hitler, Adolf 45, 48–9, 51–2, 54–80, 89
Holocaust 74, 226, 230; *see also* concentration camps
Honecker, Erich 193, 205, 222, 230, 231
Housing 111, 149, 174
Hugenberg, Alfred 47, 51, 52, 59

Immigrants 85, 110, 161, 192, 204, 206, 211, 227–9, 231, 235
Imperial Assembly (*Reichstag*): after 1871 13, 14–15, 26, 35–6; after 1919 40, 45–6, 48, 50, 54, 68; fire 54; *see also* Federal Assembly
Imperial Defence Force (*Reichswehr*): after 1919 43–5, 51, 52; after 1933 59, 61; *see also* Defence Authority and Federal Defence Force
Independent Socialists 35, 39–40; *see also* Communists
Inflation *see* economic conditions
Insurance Schemes, Social 16, 25, 150
Investment *see* economic conditions
Italy 8, 20, 21, 46, 63, 77, 100, 228; *see also* Mussolini

Japan 28, 29, 67, 69, 72, 84, 86, 240; figures for 252–5, 257–8
Jews 12, 15, 18, 64, 74, 149, 226; *see also* Holocaust

Kaiser, the *see* William II

Kapp Putsch (1920) 43–4
Kennedy, President John F. 163, 164, 167; assassination (1963) 171
Kerensky, Alexander, 34, 38
Khrushchev, Nikita 144, 147, 162, 163, 167
Kiesinger, Dr Kurt Georg 175–7, 180–2, 185, 189, 194
Kohl, Dr Helmut: Bitburg visit 225; Chancellor 219, 220, 223, 227, 230; during reunification 233–7, 240; leader CDU 200, 211, 215, 217; payments for industry 224–5; Polish Treaty 236, 243; and Strauss 217, 219, 222; *Wende* 219–20
Korean War: effect of 113, 114, 140

Labour Front (*Arbeitsfront*) 61
Labour Service (*Arbeitsdienst*) 55
Labour supplies (in BRD) 111, 172
Lambsdorff, Markgraf Otto von 219, 224, 242
Lands (*Länder*): after 1919 40; in Basic Law 123–4, 126–32; facts about 250; relations with Bund 221
League of Nations 46, 62, 63, 138
Lenin, Vladimir Ilych 12, 34
'Levelling of burdens' (*Lastenausgleich*) 105, 151
Liberals 9–12, 14, 15, 17, 26, 27, 40, 44, 86, 95, 217
Liebknecht, Karl 40
Locarno Treaties 46
Lower Saxony, Land 98, 153, 202, 207, 214; facts about 250; Land Party 96, 112; *see also* Saxony, Saxony-Anhalt
Lübke, President Heinrich 155, 187
Ludendorff, General Erich 33, 36, 45
Luther, Martin 1, 3

Marks: Deutschmark 105, 115, 149, 171, 179, 187, 210, 234; in East Germany 106, 234–5; Reichsmark 44, 45, 84, 105, 115; Rentenmark 45
Marshall, General George C. 99, 100; Marshall Aid 101–2, 110–11, 113
Mecklenburg, Land 234, 237; facts about 250
Mediterranean War 71, 75, 77
Military Governors, Military Government 90, 123–5, 133
Ministers and Parliament 14, 36, 40, 128

Molotov, Vychslav 71, 89, 99, 100, 147
Morgenthau, Henry Jnr 82, 88, 99
Moscow 72, 86, 136; Adenauer visits 156
Munich 37, 40, 45, 200; Agreement (1938) 65
Mussolini, Benito 62–5, 67, 70, 71, 77

National Democratic Party (Neo-Nazis) 175, 181, 183, 186–7
National Liberal Party see Liberals
National Socialist German Workers Party (Nationalsozialistische Deutsche Arbeitspartei NSDAP): before 1933 45, 47, 49, 50–3; strength of 57, 94, 103, 227; treatment of victims 95, 151; see also denazification
Nationalization of industry 96, 121
Navy, German 27, 30, 33, 37, 59, 62, 68, 70
Night of the Long Knives (30 June 1934) 59, 62
North Atlantic Treaty Organization (NATO): creation of 109, 140, 142; France and 180; future of 222, 237, 244; Spiegel and 169; strength of 140, 143, 159, 163; 'Two Track' policy of 208, 209, 223
North Rhine Westphalia, Land 98, 121, 224; elections in 160, 174, 188, 216, 225, 227; facts about 250
Nuclear power: BRD and renunciation of 146, 187, 234, 244; controversies over civilian use of 214, NATO policy on 208–9, 222–3; weapons 90–1, 108–9, 140, 158–61
Nuremberg Tribunal 90

Occupation Statute 136–7, 142
Oder–Neisse Line 81–2, 85, 89, 110, 118, 167, 192, 236
Oil 61, 79, 100, 109, 213, 221, 232
Ostpolitik 180–1, 190–8, 209
Organization for European Economic Co-operation (OEEC) 101, 113, 139, 148

Papen, Franz von, 52–3, 55, 58–9
Parliamentary Council (1948–9) 123–5, 133
Payments, Balance of see economic conditions, figures 256

Pensions 150, 172, 208; for members of Bundestag 194
Peoples' Party 40, 49; see also Liberals
Planning 173, 178
Poland: after 1919 41, 42; 1939–45 46, 62, 66–8, 77, 79; 1945–70 81–2, 86, 89, 100, 145, 182; since 1970 191, 216; partitions of 5, 6; Treaty (December 1970) 192–204, 211, 228; Treaty (June 1991) 236, 243
Population: in seventeenth century 2; in 1815 8; 1939–46 110; 1973 227; comparative figures 252
President: elections 129, 182, 193; powers of 1919 40; powers of 1949 129–30; see also Heuss, Lübke, Heinemann, Weizsäcker
Primacy of external/internal policy 27, 31, 185
Progressive Party (Fortschrittliche Partei) 14, 17, 26–7, 35, 37, 40; see also Liberals
Protestants 1, 3, 4, 58, 95, 118, 231
Prussia: after 1919 45, 53, 79; after 1945 98, 118; Army 5, 7, 11, 76; early history 1, 3, 8–10; wars of unification 11 12

Radical Decree (Radikaler Beschluss) 201–2
Reagan, President Ronald 209, 222–3, 225
rearmament, German: after 1919 46, 61; after 1950 141–4, 158–62
re-education 102, 103
refugees 134, 144, 151, 152, 164, 204
Refugee Party 153, 154
reparations: 1871 20; 1940 70, 74; after 1919 42, 45, 47; after 1945 83, 89, 92–3, 99; in DDR 147
Republican Party 243; see also National Democratic Party
responsibility 42, 88, 95, 104, 185, 225–7, 230
reunification 123, 126, 141, 142, 144–5, 172, 192, 231–7
Rhine, Rhineland 8, 27, 44, 46, 63, 147, 183
Rhineland-Palatinate, Land 98; facts about 250
Rome, Treaty of (1957) 157, 172

Roosevelt, President Franklin D. 67, 71, 73, 75–6, 82
Ruhr: coal 9; internationalization of 82, 121, 137–9; occupation of (1923) 42, 44, 63; restructuring 178
Russo–German relations: 1919–33 44, 46; 1933–45 63, 67, 71, 75; 1945–70, 81–2, 92, 97, 143, 147, 156, 190, 195; pre-1919 20–3, 30, 32, 34, 36; since 1970 203, 205, 216, 231, 233, 236–7, 246

Saar, Land 98, 138–40, 142, 156, 202, 211, 216; facts about 250
St Petersburg (Leningrad, Petrograd) 21, 29, 35
Saxony, Land 1, 13, 37, 44–5, 234, 237, 240; facts about 250
Saxony-Anhalt, Land 234, 237; facts about 250; see also Lower Saxony
Schacht, Dr Hjalmar 47–8, 60–1
Scheel, Dr Walter: Foreign Minister 188, 194–5; leader FDP 187; President 206
Schiller, Professor Karl 154, 176–7, 179–81, 188, 190
Schleswig-Holstein, Land 98, 153, 183, 229; facts about 250
Schmidt, Helmut: Chancellor 166–213, 215; and left wing 217; loses vote of confidence 219–20; Minster 188, 197
Schröder, Dr Gerhard: Defence Minister 176, 181; Foreign Minister 152, 168, 170–1, 173; and Presidency 187
Schumacher, Kurt: background 119; death 143; illness 123; meets Adenauer 118; mistakes 154; and Parliamentary Council 123–4; prefers Frankfurt as capital 133; rebuffs CDU 121; stands for President 134; taunts Adenauer 137
Schuman Plan 139–41
Security Service (Schutzstaffel SS) 56, 60, 74; in DDR 213, 225
Seeckt, General Hans von 43, 45–6
Silesia 3, 5, 9, 27, 79, 81–2
Social Democratic Party (Sozialdemokratische Partei Deutschlands, SPD): after 1875 23, 25–8; 1914–19 34–7, 239; 1919–33 38–42, 44, 49–50, 53; 1933–45 54; after 1945 96, 98, 118; attitude to reunification 235, 237, 242; in Berlin

97, 171; coalition with FDP 188; elections 154, 166, 174, 197 (strongest party 217, 237); foundation of 15; Godesberg Programme 154; in Great Coalition 175, 177, 179, 186; Jusos 88, 198, 208, 209; opposed to integration with West 139, 143; views on Basic Law 123–4, 126
Social Reich Party (Sozialistische Reichspartei) 153
Social Unity Party (Sozialistische Einheitspartei) 47, 147, 235
Sovereignty, German after 1945 83, 126, 138, 147
Spiegel, Der 169–70
Speer, Albert 73, 79–80
'Stab in the back' 43, 76
Stalin, Joseph (real name Dzhugashvili) 67, 71, 79, 82, 88–9, 144, 147
Stalingrad 75
State Secretaries 13, 118; Parliamentary 130
Strauss, Franz Josef: after 1972 election 199–200; in elections (1976 and 1980) 211, 215; backs Kiesinger as Chancellor 175; and Barzel 200, 215; character 199; death 230; Finance Minister 176–7, 179, 182, 187; Foreign Policy 168; and Kohl 217, 222; leads CSU 170, 173; Minister 159, 161; Spiegel Affair 169–70; stays in Bavaria 219
Stresemann, Gustav 44–6
strikes 112, 151, 200
Storm Detachments (Sturmabteilungen, SA) 51, 54, 57, 59, 60
Sudeten Germans see Czechoslovakia

tariffs 16, 110, 149
taxation 44, 84, 131, 149, 150, 172, 174, 208, 240; comparative figures 255
terrorism 212–13, 229
Thuringia, Land 45, 234, 237, 242; facts about 250
trade unions 111, 158, 172, 187
Truman, President Harry S. 87, 109

Ulbricht, Walter 86, 97, 119, 147, 164, 181, 182, 191–2, 241
unconditional surrender 75–6, 95, 102–3, 126
unemployment see economic conditions

universities 7, 55, 153, 184, 202
U(nter see)-boats 35, 77
US–German relations: 1917–41 35–6, 41, 43, 45, 48, 71–2, 75–7, 80; 1941–6 72, 75–7, 80, 82, 86, 87–8, 90, 96; 1947–52 100, 122, 141–2, 148; 1952–71 160, 163, 193; since 1971 195, 208–9, 222–3, 225, 229, 244–6

Vatican (Papacy) 1, 15, 58, 119
Versailles Treaty (1871) 13; (1919) 41–3, 46, 51, 62
Vienna 8, 9, 31, 48, 62, 64, 86, 163–4
Vietnam 171–84, 209, 213
Volk 19, 71
voting system: after 1919 40; after 1949 247–8; Prussian 11

wages see economic situation
Wall, Berlin 164, 166, 167, 171, 231–2
war crimes see Nuremberg
war damage 37, 80, 84
war 'guilt' see responsibility
Warsaw 79, 146, 180, 192, 222, 223, 231
Wehner, Herbert 154, 176, 188, 199, 205

Weizsäcker, President Richard von 226, 237
Wende, Die 217–20, 227, 232
West European Union (WEU) 146
Widerstand (anti-Nazi activities) 57, 65, 77, 78, 189
William I, King of Prussia and German Emperor 11, 13, 21
William II, 'the Kaiser', German Emperor and King of Prussia 22, 26, 28, 30, 32, 36, 37, 63
Wilson, President Woodrow 36, 41, 42, 75
Works Council (Betriebsrat) 150, 189
Württemberg 13, 14; see also Baden-Württemberg

Yugoslavia 20, 31–2, 72, 157, 181–2, 228

Zones of occupation 81, 83, 86, 89, 90, 100–1; Bizonic 98, 101, 109, 121; British 98, 120; French 98, 101; Soviet 85, 97–8, 118, 135, 147, 169, 236; US 94, 97